EFFECTIVE SHELL

EFFECTIVE SHELL

A Practical User's Guide to Working Smarter on the Command Line

by Dave Kerr

no starch
press®

San Francisco

Printed in the United States of America

First printing

29 28 27 26 25   1 2 3 4 5

ISBN-13: 978-1-7185-0414-1 (print)
ISBN-13: 978-1-7185-0415-8 (ebook)

Published by No Starch Press®, Inc.
245 8th Street, San Francisco, CA 94103
phone: +1.415.863.9900
www.nostarch.com; info@nostarch.com

Publisher: William Pollock
Managing Editor: Jill Franklin
Production Manager: Sabrina Plomitallo-González
Production Editor: Jennifer Kepler
Developmental Editor: Rachel Monaghan
Cover Design: Gina Redman
Interior Design: Octopod Studios
Technical Reviewer: Mitch Frazier
Copyeditors: James Brook and Rachel Monaghan
Proofreader: Daniel Wolff
Indexer: BIM Creatives, LLC

Library of Congress Control Number: 2024048644

[S]

For Mum and Dad, who always got me books

About the Author

Dave Kerr is a technology consultant and software engineer who helps teams design and launch new products, scale high-performance systems, and modernize complex platforms. Passionate about automation, site reliability engineering, and developer experience, he loves coding, mentoring, publishing, contributing to open source, and writing. When he's not in the shell, he's in the mountains or rock climbing.

About the Technical Reviewer

Mitch Frazier is a programmer who works for Emerson Electric doing mostly embedded systems programming in C. He also occasionally writes code in Golang, Python, Tcl, JavaScript, and bash. He previously worked for *Linux Journal*, both as a technical editor and as a system administrator.

BRIEF CONTENTS

Acknowledgments xxi

Introduction xxiii

PART I: CORE SKILLS 1

Chapter 1: Flying on the Command Line 3

Chapter 2: Thinking in Pipelines 13

Chapter 3: Finding Files and Folders 31

PART II: MANIPULATING TEXT AND STREAMS 45

Chapter 4: Regular Expression Essentials 47

Chapter 5: Getting to Grips with grep 61

Chapter 6: Slicing and Dicing Text 71

Chapter 7: Advanced Text Manipulation with sed 83

Chapter 8: Building Commands on the Fly 99

PART III: SHELL SCRIPTING 107

Chapter 9: Shell Script Fundamentals 109

Chapter 10: Using Variables to Store, Read, and Manipulate Data 121

Chapter 11: Mastering Conditional Logic 141

Chapter 12: Using Loops with Files and Folders 155

Chapter 13: Functions, Parameters, and Error Handling 173

Chapter 14: Useful Patterns for Shell Scripts 189

PART IV: BUILDING YOUR TOOLKIT 205

Chapter 15: Configuring Your Shell 207

Chapter 16: Customizing Your Command Prompt 221

Chapter 17: Managing Your Dot Files 237

Chapter 18: Controlling Changes with Git 249

Chapter 19: Managing Remote Git Repositories and Sharing Dot Files 275

PART V: ADVANCED TECHNIQUES 295

Chapter 20: Shell Expansion 297

Chapter 21: Alternatives to Shell Scripting 313

Chapter 22: The Secure Shell 327

Chapter 23: The Power of Terminal Editors 343

Chapter 24: Mastering the Multiplexer 363

Afterword: Generative AI and the Shell 377

Appendix A: Setup 381

Appendix B: Shell Basics 393

Index 421

CONTENTS IN DETAIL

ACKNOWLEDGMENTS   **xxi**

INTRODUCTION   **xxiii**

What Is the Shell? xxiv
Who Should Read This Book xxv
What's in This Book? xxv
How to Read This Book. xxix
Bugs and Suggestions. xxx
Sample Files and Online Resources xxx

PART I: CORE SKILLS   **1**

1
FLYING ON THE COMMAND LINE   **3**

Basic Navigation Techniques. 4
     Go to the Beginning or End of a Line 4
     Move Back or Forward One Word 4
     Delete a Word 5
     Delete a Line 5
     Undo a Change 6
Search Commands. 6
Editing in Place 7
Other Useful Shortcuts 9
     Clear the Screen 9
     View Your Command History 9
     Show All Shortcuts 10
     Transpose Text 10
Summary 11

2
THINKING IN PIPELINES   **13**

The IPO Pattern 14
     Streams 15
     stdin, stdout, and stderr 15
Pipelines in Action 17
     Standard Input Applications 18
     Standard Output Applications. 21
     Standard Error Applications 23
     Redirection with Both stdout and stderr 26
The T-Pipe 27
Pipelines and the Unix Philosophy 28
Summary 29

3
FINDING FILES AND FOLDERS 31

Searching with the find Command 31
Refining a Search with find 33
    Searching for Only Files or Folders 33
    Searching by File or Folder Name. 34
    Searching by Path. 35
    Specifying More Than One Search Option. 35
    Running Case-Insensitive Searches. 36
    Grouping Parts of an Expression. 36
    Excluding Search Results with the NOT Operator 38
Acting on Search Results. 38
    Printing Paths 39
    Deleting Files 39
    Executing Commands 39
    Confirming Commands Before Execution 40
Handling Symbolic Links. 40
Going Further with find. 41
Summary 43

PART II: MANIPULATING TEXT AND STREAMS 45

4
REGULAR EXPRESSION ESSENTIALS 47

Regexes in a Nutshell 48
Building Regexes 48
    Regex Engines 50
    Quantifiers. 51
    Character Sets and Metacharacters. 52
    Anchors. 55
    Capture Groups 56
    Lazy and Greedy Expressions. 57
Advanced Regex Concepts 57
    Backtracking. 58
    Lookarounds. 58
    Atomic Groups 59
Summary 59

5
GETTING TO GRIPS WITH GREP 61

What Exactly Is grep?. 62
Searching Through Text. 63
Using grep with Regular Expressions 64
Advanced grep Features. 65
    Making a Search Case-Insensitive 66
    Getting Additional Context for Search Results. 66
    Searching Through Multiple Files. 67
    Filtering and Piping grep Output. 68
    Combining grep with other Commands 69

Alternatives to grep 69
Summary 70

6
SLICING AND DICING TEXT   **71**

Extracting Heads and Tails 71
Replacing Text 74
Cutting Text 75
Reversing Tex 78
Sorting Text and Removing Duplicate Lines 79
Paging Through Text 80
Summary 81

7
ADVANCED TEXT MANIPULATION WITH SED   **83**

Transformations with sed 84
    Replacing Text 84
    Applying Multiple Expressions 85
    Stripping Comments 89
    Appending Text 89
    Prepending Text 90
    Extracting Information 91
Advanced Applications 92
    Restructuring Text 92
    Creating Template Files 96
    Editing in Place 96
Alternatives to sed 97
Summary 97

8
BUILDING COMMANDS ON THE FLY   **99**

Introducing xargs 100
Handling Whitespace, Special Characters, and Tracing 101
Customizing How xargs Processes Input Lines 102
Organizing the Parameters for Commands 103
Running Commands Interactively 105
Running a Command for Each Input 106
Summary 106

PART III: SHELL SCRIPTING   **107**

9
SHELL SCRIPT FUNDAMENTALS   **109**

Why Shell Scripts? 110
Creating a Basic Shell Script 110
    Adding Code Comments 111
    Adding and Formatting Commands 112
    Pipelining Commands 113

Making Shell Scripts Executable 115
Specifying What Program Should Run a Script 116
Sourcing Shell Scripts 117
Installing Scripts Locally 118
Summary 120

10
USING VARIABLES TO STORE, READ, AND MANIPULATE DATA   121

Understanding Variable Scope: Environment vs. Shell Variables 122
Exporting Shell Variables as Environment Variables 123
Variable Syntax 124
Quoting Variables and Values 124
Using Braces to Reference Variables Explicitly 127
Common Variable Operations 127
Storing a Command's Output in a Variable 127
Managing Multiple Values with Arrays 128
Storing Complex Data with Associative Arrays 130
Expanding Shell Parameters 130
Reading and Storing User Input in Variables 132
Performing Arithmetic Operations 135
Enhancing the common Command with Variables 137
Summary 139

11
MASTERING CONDITIONAL LOGIC   141

The if Statement 142
The test Command 143
Using test Operators with Expressions and Files 143
Checking Multiple test Conditions Simultaneously 145
Combining Statements on a Single Line 145
The else Clause 146
The elif Clause 146
The case Statement 148
Conditional Expressions 149
Chaining Commands 151
Extending the common Command to Handle Different Shells 152
Summary 154

12
USING LOOPS WITH FILES AND FOLDERS   155

The for Loop 156
Looping Through Arrays 157
Splitting Loop Input into Words 157
Looping Through Files and Folders 150
Looping Through find Command Results 152
Iterating with C-Style Loops 153
Looping over Sequences 154
The while Loop 155
Looping Through the Lines in a File 156
Looping Forever 158

The until Loop 168
The continue and break Statements 169
Creating Compact Loops. 170
Updating the common Command to Loop Through Results. 171
Summary 172

13
FUNCTIONS, PARAMETERS, AND ERROR HANDLING   173

Creating a Function 174
    Variables in Functions 174
    Variable Scoping 175
Passing Parameters to Functions. 177
    Using Array Operators in Parameter Variables 179
    Shifting Parameters 179
Function Return Values 180
    Writing Results to Standard Output 181
    Avoiding Pitfalls with Command Output. 182
    Returning Status Codes 183
Error Handling. 185
Simplifying the common Command with Functions 187
Summary 188

14
USEFUL PATTERNS FOR SHELL SCRIPTS   189

Ensuring Exit on Failure. 190
Debugging Shell Scripts with the Trace Option. 191
Checking for Existing Variables or Functions 192
Unsetting Values. 193
Trapping Signals and Events 193
Processing Complex Script Parameters 195
Adding Syntax Highlighting 197
Checking the Operating System 199
Checking for Installed Programs 200
Showing a Menu 200
Running Commands in Subshells 201
Anti-patterns 201
    Omitting Shebangs 202
    Configuring Options in Shebangs 203
    Using Complex Logic in Shell Scripts 203
Summary 204

PART IV: BUILDING YOUR TOOLKIT   205

15
CONFIGURING YOUR SHELL   207

Interactive Shells 207
    The Default Shell Startup File 208
    Common Startup File Customizations. 209

Non-interactive Shells 214
    Understanding Shell Script Behavior 214
    Loading a Startup File with BASH_ENV 216
Login Shells 216
    Checking Whether You're in a Login Shell 217
    Loading the Shell Startup Files 217
Changing Your Shell 219
Summary 220

16
CUSTOMIZING YOUR COMMAND PROMPT   221

The Command Prompt Structure 222
    The Prompt String 223
    Escape Sequences 223
Adding Color and Text Formatting to Your Prompt 225
Adding Data to the Command Prompt 228
Additional Shell Prompt Variables 229
    PS2 229
    PS3 230
    PS4 230
    PROMPT_DIRTRIM 230
    PROMPT_COMMAND 231
Writing a Shell Script to Customize the Command Prompt 231
Summary 235

17
MANAGING YOUR DOT FILES   237

Dot Files Defined 238
The Default Shell Dot File 238
Creating Your Own Dot Files 241
    Creating the Dot Files Folder 241
    Creating shell.sh 241
    Adding Custom Configuration 242
Testing the Shell Dot File 244
Sourcing the Shell Dot File 245
Sourcing Files from a Folder 245
A Dot File Installation Script 247
Summary 248

18
CONTROLLING CHANGES WITH GIT   249

What Is Git? 250
Creating a Git Repository 250
Adding and Resetting Changes to the Index 251
Committing Changes 254
Working with Branches 257
    Creating Branches 257
    Performing Fast-Forward Merges 260
    Performing Recursive Merges and Handling Diverged Branches 261
The Git Log 262

Resolving Conflicts 264
Managing Files in Your Repository 267
    Deleting Files 267
    Restoring and Renaming Files 268
Restoring Your Working Tree 270
Git Command Quick Reference 272
Summary 273

19
MANAGING REMOTE GIT REPOSITORIES AND
SHARING DOT FILES

                                                                                       275
Getting Started with GitHub 276
    Creating a Repository 276
    Pushing Changes 280
    Fetching Changes 281
    Pulling Changes 284
Sharing Your Dot Files 285
Collaborating with Other Users 286
    Forking 286
    Making Pull Requests 287
Writing a Shell Function to Open a Pull Request 288
Showing Git Information in the Command Prompt 290
Diving Deeper into Git 291
Git at a Glance: A Recap of Key Concepts and Commands 293
Summary 294

PART V: ADVANCED TECHNIQUES   **295**

20
SHELL EXPANSION

                                                                                                297
Shell Expansion Operations 298
    Brace Expansion 298
    Tilde Expansion 299
    Parameter Expansion 299
    Command Substitution 305
    Arithmetic Expansion 306
    Word Splitting 306
    Pathname Expansion 309
Summary 311

21
ALTERNATIVES TO SHELL SCRIPTING

                                                                                              313
When to Avoid Shell Scripting 314
Choosing a Programming Language 314
Characteristics of Shell-Friendly Tools 315
Writing a Dictionary Lookup Tool in Python 316
    Defining the Tool's Basic Structure 317
    Downloading the Definition 319
    Formatting the Output 321

Installing the Lookup Tool 324
Improving the Lookup Tool 325
Summary 325

22
THE SECURE SHELL
327

What Is SSH? 327
Creating a Key Pair 328
Setting Up an AWS Account 329
Creating a Virtual Machine on AWS 331
    Choose an Amazon Machine Image 333
    Choose an Instance Type 333
    Review the Instance Launch 333
Using SSH to Connect to a Virtual Machine. 335
Dealing with Key Permission Errors. 336
Configuring SSH Hosts 337
Running SSH Commands 338
Handling Disconnections. 339
Transferring Files with scp 339
Summary 341

23
THE POWER OF TERMINAL EDITORS
343

Why Use a Terminal Editor? 344
Getting Started with Vim 345
    Building a Cheatsheet 347
    Creating a File 348
Navigating Through Text 350
Adding a Command Count 352
Inserting Text at Specific Positions. 352
Operating on a Range of Text 354
Searching for Text Patterns 355
Editing Commands. 358
Updating and Styling Your Vim Cheatsheet 359
Going Further with Vim. 360
    Vimtutor. 361
    Vimcasts 361
    Practical Vim and Modern Vim 361
Summary 361

24
MASTERING THE MULTIPLEXER
363

Benefits of Using a Multiplexer. 365
Installing tmux 365
Window Management with tmux 367
    Creating and Moving Between Panes 367
    Zooming Panes. 367
    Creating and Moving Between Windows. 367
Session Management with tmux 368
    Starting a New Session 368
    Attaching and Detaching from Sessions 368

Configuring tmux 369
    Setting the Default Shell 370
    Specifying the Working Directory 370
    Naming and Numbering Windows 370
    Splitting Windows More Intuitively 371
    Sending Commands to Nested Sessions. 371
    Enabling Mouse Support 371
    Interfacing with Vim. 372
    Setting Advanced Configuration 372
Collaboration with tmux 372
A tmux Quick Guide. 373
Next Steps with tmux 375
Summary 375

AFTERWORD
GENERATIVE AI AND THE SHELL   **377**
Installing and Running the Terminal AI Tool 378
Chatting with ChatGPT 378
Copying or Saving Results. 379
Executing AI-Generated Scripts 379
Redirecting Responses to a File 380
The Shell of the Future. 380

A
SETUP   **381**
Accessing the Shell. 381
    Microsoft Windows 381
    macOS 382
    Linux 382
Configuring the Shell 382
    Microsoft Windows 383
    macOS 390
    Linux 392

B
SHELL BASICS   **393**
Navigating Your Filesystem 393
    Identifying the Working Directory 394
    Listing the Contents of the Working Directory 394
    Changing the Directory 395
    Returning to the Home Directory 396
    Using Absolute and Relative Paths. 397
    Moving Around Efficiently 397
Managing Your Files and Folders 400
    Downloading a File. 400
    Unzipping a File 402
    Deleting a File 403
    Viewing a Directory Tree 404
    Copying a File 404
    Renaming and Moving Files 405
    Creating a Folder 407

Creating a File 408
Working with Wildcards 409
Deleting a Folder 409
Showing Text Content 410
Zipping a File 411
The Clipboard 412
Mastering Clipboard Essentials 412
Creating Custom Clipboard Commands 413
Copying and Pasting with pbcopy and pbpaste 414
Getting Help 415
Using the Manual 415
Summarizing Output with tldr 418
Accessing Online Cheat Sheets 420

INDEX   **421**

ACKNOWLEDGMENTS

Over 2024, progress on this book ground almost to a halt as I fought through an extremely challenging collapse in my health. I cannot imagine how hard it must be for people to face times like these alone, and I cannot express how grateful I am to have had the care and love of so many wonderful people.

Michelle, Mum, Dad, and James, words fail me beyond *thank you*. Whitney and Judy, your kindness and compassion never failed to lift me and give me courage. Rob, Kov, and Ellie, you were wonderful friends and brought joy into the year. Dr. Downie, Dr. Wilson, Dr. Orum, and Dr. Kumar, you have all been amazing.

I also want to thank those who made this book possible: Bill, who believed in the idea; Jill, who guided us through the journey; Rachel, who taught me how to write; Jennifer, who never stopped making it better; Mitch, from whom I learned so much; and the rest of the team—this wouldn't have happened without you.

INTRODUCTION

I've been lucky enough to spend many years working as a software engineer, and I've worked with data scientists, data engineers, site reliability engineers, and technologists of all sorts. One trait that stands out in great technologists is their ability to make their tools work for them by stitching the tools together in creative ways to suit their unique styles and needs. This book will help you do just that by using the shell.

This isn't a book on shell scripting or Linux administration. Each chapter presents a set of techniques to help you work more efficiently, understand your system in more depth, and craft your environment to suit your individual workflow. This book doesn't ask you to totally change the way you work or to drop your current tooling. Instead, it brings together a set of skills that you can add to your toolkit and incorporate as you like. But before you can do that, you need to understand what exactly the shell is and why you might want to use it.

What Is the Shell?

The shell is the simple, text-based interface used to control a computer or a program. In Windows, it looks like this:

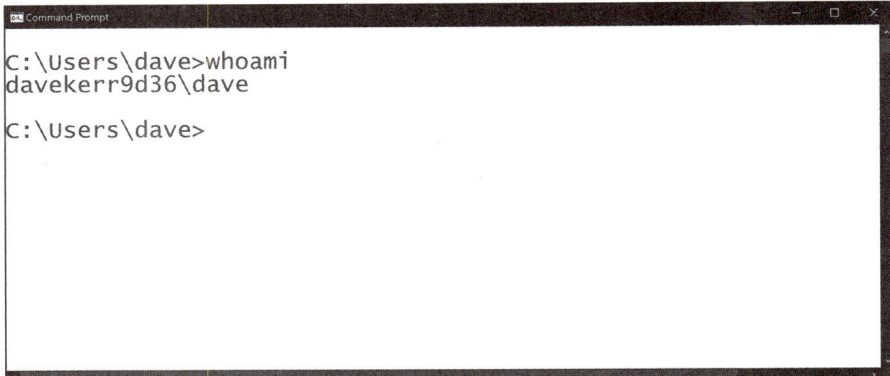

Here's what it looks like on a Mac:

And here's what it looks like on Fedora, a popular Linux distribution (this book focuses on the Linux shell):

There are several reasons why you might want to use the shell instead of a *graphical user interface (GUI)*, the visual point-and-click interface you're probably using now:

- Using the shell can help you learn more about your computer's internals. This can be really helpful if you're a technology professional or if you simply want to better understand how your computer works.

- There are some scenarios where you *have* to use a shell. Not every program or system can be operated with a GUI.

- Often, it's more efficient to use the shell. Some operations that are time-consuming or repetitive to perform using the GUI are much faster to perform in a shell. You can also write *shell scripts* to automate such operations.

- The simplicity of the shell's text-based interface makes it a distraction-free environment to work in.

Investing just a few hours in learning to use the shell for your computer can have an enormous impact on your productivity. It can also make your work more fun, allowing you to maintain a state of creative flow and work more effectively.

Who Should Read This Book

This book's primary audience will be readers who have some basic programming knowledge and familiarity with the command line on a Windows, macOS, or Linux system. If you're totally new to the shell environment, be sure to start with the book's appendixes before you dive in to Chapter 1. There, you'll learn fundamentals such as setting up the shell on your system and navigating the files and folders on your machine. Afterward, you should be better equipped to follow along with the book and get the most out of its examples.

Developers, data scientists, and engineers should find almost every chapter of this book immediately applicable in their day-to-day work. Whether you use Python, Golang, JavaScript, .NET, Java, or another language, an integrated development environment (IDE) or the terminal, the skills you'll learn here will improve your ability to quickly solve problems by using a simple, adaptable, and general-purpose toolkit.

Site reliability engineers, system administrators, and DevSecOps professionals will also find essential tips and tricks. If you regularly administer remote machines, connect to containers, or manage clusters or cloud environments, you'll find many techniques to help you work more efficiently.

What's in This Book?

Each chapter presents a stand-alone set of techniques that you should be able to apply immediately. I have focused on keeping the information to the essentials that enable you to use the skill rather than giving an exhaustive description of every possible feature. This should allow you to pick up the book, read a chapter over coffee, and try out the skills straightaway. Depending on your familiarity with and comfort in the shell, you can generally skip straight to chapters you're interested in rather than having to read the book in order. The exception is Part III of the book, where you'll progressively build and enhance a shell script as you pick up new techniques in each chapter. Numerous cross-references throughout the book will point you in the right direction if you get stuck or need a refresher on a topic.

Part I, Core Skills, introduces essential concepts and techniques that you'll use again and again in your everyday work.

Chapter 1: Flying on the Command Line This chapter introduces keyboard shortcuts and commands for entering and manipulating text on the command line quickly and easily. You'll learn navigation techniques like moving forward and backward through a line or word, as well as how to search your shell history and access your text editor from the shell.

Chapter 2: Thinking in Pipelines   This chapter explores the *pipeline*, the pattern that all command line programs follow to handle input and output. It also introduces basic *redirection*, a process that allows you to send a program's output to a file or use a file's contents as program input. These concepts will be essential in more advanced chapters.

Chapter 3: Finding Files and Folders   Using the shell to search for files and folders makes quick work of a task that can be tedious in a GUI environment. In this chapter, you'll meet the built-in find command and learn all about how this versatile tool can make your search operations more efficient.

Part II, Manipulating Text and Streams, demonstrates techniques for working with text, whether it's in code, data, or configuration files.

Chapter 4: Regular Expression Essentials   Regular expressions, or regexes, have a reputation for being complex but can hugely simplify many tasks, such as finding and altering text patterns across a file. In this chapter, you'll learn about regex fundamentals such as character sets and capture groups, and see several practical examples that will make regexes more approachable. This foundation will prepare you to use regexes with the shell tools introduced in the following chapters.

Chapter 5: Getting to Grips with grep   The grep tool is a real workhorse for shell users. Once you've learned how to use it, you'll find yourself turning to it again and again. This chapter explains how to use grep to find and filter text in files, as well as how to combine grep with regexes and pipelines for more complex search operations.

Chapter 6: Slicing and Dicing Text   Searching and filtering aren't the only text operations you can perform in the shell. This chapter walks you through several techniques for manipulating text, introducing commands such as head, tail, sort, and uniq to extract, sort, and deduplicate (remove duplicates from) text.

Chapter 7: Advanced Text Manipulation with sed   The powerful stream editor utility sed allows you to manipulate text in more sophisticated ways by specifying *expressions*, or sets of operations you want it to perform. You'll learn how to combine expressions to remove or replace parts of a line in a configuration file, among other examples. You'll also see some advanced sed applications, such as editing a file in place and combining sed with grep and regexes to restructure text.

Chapter 8: Building Commands on the Fly   This chapter introduces the xargs command, which you'll combine with techniques from earlier chapters to dynamically build complex commands by converting input into command arguments. With xargs, you can pass data to other commands you've worked with, and you can even preview the commands you construct before executing them. This chapter will lay the groundwork for the next part of the book, where you'll turn your commands into shell scripts.

Part III, Shell Scripting, is a crash course in the art of automating sequences of commands with shell scripts. You'll apply the techniques from previous chapters and add several more skills to build tools and scripts that perform complex operations efficiently.

Chapter 9: Shell Script Fundamentals In this chapter, you'll write a basic script to build a command called common that will output the shell commands you use most often. You'll learn how to add, format, and chain commands; how to make shell scripts executable; and how to install your scripts locally. In the following chapters, you'll extend the common script with additional features to make it more powerful and user-friendly.

Chapter 10: Using Variables to Store, Read, and Manipulate Data Variables in shell scripts allow you to store and reuse values instead of repeating them, which makes your scripts easier to maintain and reduces the risk of errors. In this chapter, you'll learn how to create and format variables to read user input, perform arithmetic operations, and more. You'll update your common command script with variables to configure how much of the shell history it reads and how many commands it returns.

Chapter 11: Mastering Conditional Logic By this point, you'll be a pretty solid shell scripter! In this chapter, you'll learn how adding conditional logic to your scripts, using tools like if and case statements, allows you to control how they behave in different scenarios. You'll also work with more advanced constructs like conditional expressions with regexes. To see how conditional logic works in practice, you'll update the common command so that it can determine whether you're using bash or the Z shell and, based on that condition, read the appropriate history file.

Chapter 12: Using Loops with Files and Folders This chapter demonstrates one of the most practical applications of scripts: running loop operations over sets of files and folders to efficiently execute repetitive tasks. Loops run a sequence of commands based on whether certain conditions are met, and as such are a form of conditional logic. You'll learn how to use for loops, while loops, and until loops to iterate over different parts of the filesystem, and then add loops to your common script to return more user-friendly output.

Chapter 13: Functions, Parameters, and Error Handling Functions are another invaluable tool for reducing repetition in your scripts, and in this chapter you'll learn how to create them, pass parameters to them, and work with the values they return. The chapter also covers some ways to handle errors in the event that a command or function in your script fails. Then you'll restructure the common script with error handling logic and functions to make the code more readable and maintainable.

Chapter 14: Useful Patterns for Shell Scripts To close the section on shell scripting, this chapter looks at some conventions you may find useful when working with your own or other people's scripts, including debugging with the trace option, adding syntax highlighting, and checking for the presence of a specific operating system, program, or command. You'll also see examples of anti-patterns—shell practices that are common but ill advised.

Part IV, Building Your Toolkit, delves into techniques for customizing your environment to your specific needs and preferences. You'll build and extend a personal library of customizations and configurations that you can share across your machines or with others.

Chapter 15: Configuring Your Shell In this chapter, you'll learn about the three types of shells and their startup behaviors, how their different shell configuration files work, and how to change the default shell settings in the ~/.bashrc file.

Chapter 16: Customizing Your Command Prompt This chapter shows you how to change the command prompt to display only the information you want to see. You'll learn how to use the PS1 variable, escape sequences, and ANSI formatting to control both the content and look of your command prompt. Finally, you'll create a script that allows you to set your own command prompt theme from a list that you can extend over time.

Chapter 17: Managing Your Dot Files As you customize different aspects of your shell and environment, you'll need a place to store that configuration. In this chapter, you'll learn how to create and organize these configuration files, known as *dot files*, so that you can easily track changes over time and keep them separated from system settings. You'll also learn how to use your dot files across different shells.

Chapter 18: Controlling Changes with Git In this chapter you'll use Git, a popular version control tool, to manage your personal configuration settings. You'll create a virtual storage space known as a *repository* and learn Git syntax to track and make changes, resolve conflicting changes, and remove or rename files from the command line.

Chapter 19: Managing Remote Git Repositories and Sharing Dot Files You'll use the web-based platform GitHub in this chapter to publish your local Git repository to a remote repository so that you can share your configuration across machines or with other users.

Part V, Advanced Techniques, explores how to work more effectively in the shell environment. You'll gain a deeper understanding of shell mechanics, learn when to use alternatives to shell scripts, and master powerful terminal-based tools for remote access, text editing, and workspace management.

Chapter 20: Shell Expansion   Shell syntax has oddities that can be confusing. This chapter delves a little deeper into how the shell interprets and transforms commands, showing ways to use this behavior to your advantage, such as creating multiple files with less typing and quickly selecting groups of files by their names.

Chapter 21: Alternatives to Shell Scripting   This chapter will help you identify when it's appropriate to move from a simple shell script to a more sophisticated solution. You'll explore options other than shell scripting and then use the popular Python programming language to build a tool that looks up a definition in an online dictionary—a task that would be quite complex in the shell.

Chapter 22: The Secure Shell   This chapter introduces the Secure Shell (SSH), a network protocol that allows you to securely connect to remote machines. You'll learn how to configure SSH, create a cloud-based virtual machine on Amazon Web Services, and connect to the virtual machine from your local computer.

Chapter 23: The Power of Terminal Editors   Text editors that run in the shell can take your productivity to a whole new level. In this chapter, you'll meet the Vim editor and see how it can greatly speed up many of your everyday tasks. For example, with Vim you can quickly write detailed messages for your Git commits and edit shell commands without having to leave your terminal, helping you maintain your flow.

Chapter 24: Mastering the Multiplexer   A terminal multiplexer allows you to run multiple shell sessions and programs. This chapter will focus on the tmux multiplexer, showing you how to organize your tmux workspace with windows and panes, configure tmux to match your workflow, and use tmux for remote work and real-time collaboration.

Excitement and development around generative AI have increased enormously over the past few years. In the book's **afterword**, we look at how this technology can bring us to new levels of efficiency in the shell, a tool that lets you directly interact with AI systems from the shell, and what the future might hold.

Appendixes A and B cover setup instructions and shell navigation basics, respectively. Although this content is targeted primarily to novices, more advanced users may also find some useful tips and tricks here.

How to Read This Book

Commands that you can enter into your shell, such as grep, are shown as monospaced text. Paths to files and folders, such as the *~/effective-shell* folder, are shown in *italics*.

In code examples, the dollar sign ($) command prompt indicates where you start typing. The text that you enter is shown in **monospace bold**:

```
$ echo "my shell is $SHELL"
my shell is /bin/bash
```

The output of commands, such as my shell is /bin/bash in this example, is shown in regular monospace.

In examples of navigating through text, the cursor position is indicated with gray shading:

```
This cursor is at the beginning of the line.
```

This book assumes that you are using a bash-like shell, which is installed by default on most Linux systems. Given the popularity of the Z shell (zsh), which is now the default for macOS, I'll call out Z shell–specific variations in a note like so:

NOTE *Z shell specifics are highlighted like this.*

Bugs and Suggestions

I've made every effort to keep samples bug-free and cross-platform. However, tools and operating systems change, and it's impossible to catch every issue. If you find a bug, or if you have any suggestions, please open an issue in the GitHub repository at *https://github.com/dwmkerr/effective-shell*.

Sample Files and Online Resources

Effective Shell started as a free and open source book available at *https://effective-shell.com*. Updates to this site have been infrequent while I have been working on the book; however, it is now ready for a refresh! Check the website occasionally to see updates and new chapters, or to see animated versions of many of the samples.

All code samples are available to download from *https://effective-shell.com/downloads/effective-shell.zip*. Better yet, install the samples from the shell as follows:

```
$ curl effective.sh | sh
```

Ready to master the command line and have some fun in the process? Let's get started.

PART I

CORE SKILLS

1

FLYING ON THE COMMAND LINE

Being able to rapidly move around the shell and manipulate text on the command line is critical to being an effective shell user. As you spend more time in the shell and start composing larger and more complex commands, it's especially important that you can work efficiently. In this chapter, we'll look at some techniques to help you do just that. Before long, you'll be navigating the command line at lightning speed.

To see this chapter's examples in action, go to *https://effective-shell.com*, where you'll find animated images of each technique. I encourage you to also try them out as you go along.

Basic Navigation Techniques

In this section, we'll look at a number of shortcuts you can use to maneuver the cursor. To begin, use the following command to write the quote to a text file:

```
$ echo "When you light a candle, you also cast a shadow." - Ursula Le Guin >> note.txt
```

Once you have executed this command by pressing ENTER, the quote will be written to a file called *note.txt*.

The shortcuts introduced in this chapter allow you to move around and manipulate the command line much more quickly and efficiently than if you were using only the arrow keys or delete key.

To work through the examples in this section, press the up arrow key, which will bring the command back up in your shell with the cursor at the end of the line.

Go to the Beginning or End of a Line

You can quickly jump to the beginning of the text, no matter where your cursor is currently positioned, with CTRL-A:

```
echo "When you light a candle, you also cast a shadow." - Ursula Le Guin >> note.txt
echo "When you light a candle, you also cast a shadow." - Ursula Le Guin >> note.txt
```

The shortcut CTRL-E takes you to the end of the line:

```
echo "When you light a candle, you also cast a shadow." - Ursula Le Guin >> note.txt
echo "When you light a candle, you also cast a shadow." - Ursula Le Guin >> note.txt
```

These are two of the most useful shortcuts, and I highly recommend that you incorporate them into your regular shell usage.

Move Back or Forward One Word

You can also quickly jump backward or forward one word at a time. Use ALT-B to move back one word:

```
echo "When you light a candle, you also cast a shadow." - Ursula Le Guin >> note.txt
echo "When you light a candle, you also cast a shadow." - Ursula Le Guin >> note.txt
echo "When you light a candle, you also cast a shadow." - Ursula Le Guin >> note.txt
```

In this example, using ALT-B once takes you back one word to the start of txt. Using it a second time takes you to the start of note. The shell uses the dot (.) character as a word separator; therefore, note and txt are treated as two separate words (they could also be separated by a space or some other non-alphanumeric symbol).

To go back to the beginning of the line (if you are not there already), use CTRL-A:

```
echo "When you light a candle, you also cast a shadow." - Ursula Le Guin >> note.txt
```

Now use ALT-F to go forward one word at a time:

```
echo "When you light a candle, you also cast a shadow." - Ursula Le Guin >> note.txt
echo "When you light a candle, you also cast a shadow." - Ursula Le Guin >> note.txt
echo "When you light a candle, you also cast a shadow." - Ursula Le Guin >> note.txt
```

Notice that these shortcuts not only jump over each space between the words but also differentiate between symbols and actual words. In this example, the cursor moves from the beginning of the line to the end of the word echo, which is the space that follows it. The space and the quotes that follow echo are two sequential characters that are not part of a word, so the next time ALT-F is pressed, the cursor moves to the end of the next word (the space after When).

Delete a Word

To quickly delete a word, place the cursor at the end of it and use CTRL-W. If your cursor is at the end of the line as in the following example, pressing CTRL-W would work like so:

```
echo "When you light a candle, you also cast a shadow." - Ursula Le Guin >> note.txt
echo "When you light a candle, you also cast a shadow." - Ursula Le Guin >>
echo "When you light a candle, you also cast a shadow." - Ursula Le Guin
echo "When you light a candle, you also cast a shadow." - Ursula Le
```

If the cursor is halfway through a word, CTRL-W will delete only from the beginning of the word to the cursor position:

```
echo "When you light a candle, you also cast a shadow." - Ursula Le Guin >> note.txt
echo "When you light a candle, you also cast a dow." - Ursula Le Guin >> note.txt
```

To delete the next word or character to the right, use ALT-D:

```
echo "When you light a candle, you also cast a shadow." - Ursula Le Guin >> note.txt
echo "When you light a , you also cast a shadow." - Ursula Le Guin >> note.txt
echo "When you light a  also cast a shadow." - Ursula Le Guin >> note.txt
```

Notice that CTRL-W defines a word as any nonspace character, whereas ALT-D defines a word as only alphanumeric characters. This is because under the hood different "delete word" functions are available in the shell, and the default keyboard shortcuts use different variants for deleting a word and deleting the next word.

You can look up how each shortcut works by running man bash to open the man page for bash and searching for "commands for moving."

Delete a Line

In bash, you can delete everything from the current cursor position to the beginning of the line with CTRL-U:

```
echo "When you light a candle, you also cast a shadow." - Ursula Le Guin >> note.txt
Ursula Le Guin >> note.txt
```

If you're using the Z shell, this key combination will delete the entire line regardless of where your cursor is. If you're not sure what shell you're using, look at the prompt next to your cursor. If it starts with a hash mark (#) or dollar sign ($), it's probably bash. If it starts with a percent symbol (%), it's probably the Z shell. On most Linux machines, your shell will be bash by default. On macOS systems from 2019 onward, it will be the Z shell. To see exactly what shell you have, run echo $SHELL.

To delete everything from the cursor to the end of the line, use CTRL-K:

```
echo "When you light a candle, you also cast a shadow." - Ursula Le Guin >> note.txt
echo "When you light a candle, you also cast a shadow."
```

This should work the same way in bash and the Z shell.

Undo a Change

Bash also has an undo shortcut: CTRL-_ (underscore) will undo the most recent change.

If you find yourself repeatedly using the arrow or delete keys, refer back to this section to remind yourself of the shortcuts. They'll save you a lot of time in the long run!

Search Commands

Once you have the basic navigation commands down, the next essential shortcuts are search commands. Starting with the current line, you can search backward or forward in your command history with CTRL-R and CTRL-S, respectively.

Let's look at an example. Run these commands on three separate lines to create nine empty files:

```
$ touch file1 file2 file3
$ touch file4 file5 file6
$ touch file7 file8 file9
```

Now press CTRL-R to start searching, and you'll see a search prompt in your shell. Because you're searching backward, the prompt tells you that you're doing a reverse search. At the prompt, enter **file** and press CTRL-R repeatedly:

```
(reverse-i-search)`file': touch file7 file8 file9
(reverse-i-search)`file': touch file7 file8 file9
(reverse-i-search)`file': touch file7 file8 file9
(reverse-i-search)`file': touch file4 file5 file6
```

The shell will search the previous commands for the term file, jumping farther back each time you press CTRL-R. This is quite hard to visualize in printed text, so be sure to try it out in your shell. When the shell reaches the end of the search and can't find any more file entries, the prompt will change to something like:

```
(failed reverse-i-search)
```

Press ENTER to get back to the regular prompt. Searching forward with CTRL-S works in much the same way.

If your code lines are long, these two shortcuts are often the fastest ways to move to the desired location in the current line. You can also use them to quickly search through your entire command history. For example, to find your last mkdir ("make directory") command, press CTRL-R, enter mkdir, and then press CTRL-R again to search backward through all mkdir commands stored in your history.

A quick way to test this is also to search for echo. If you've been using the echo command to enter the quote as in the earlier examples, it should be the first result that the reverse search finds.

When you find the command you want, just press ENTER to execute it. If you want to edit the command first, use the left or right arrow keys to go back into normal editing mode. This would be useful if, say, you want to rerun a long *commandname* command but on a different file. You can search for *commandname* and then change the filename.

If you want to cancel the search completely, press CTRL-G. The search prompt will disappear, and whatever you had in the command prompt before you started searching will be returned.

Editing in Place

When working with a long or complex command, you might find it easier to use a text editor instead of the shell. You could just copy the command, paste it into your favorite editor, edit it, and then paste it back into the shell. However, in most cases you can open your text editor right inside the shell.

The default editor for the shell is often set to Vim, which you'll see in detail in Chapter 23. Before going any further, set your editor to nano, which is more user-friendly, like so:

```
$ export EDITOR=nano
```

If this command doesn't make sense at the moment, don't worry—it will soon. You'll also learn more about customizing shell features such as the default editor in Chapter 15.

Now that you've set the default editor to nano, you need to enter two shortcut combinations to open it: first, press CTRL-X to signal to the shell that you're about to enter a command, and then press CTRL-E to edit in place. If you don't have any unexecuted code on your command line, the text editor will be empty when it opens; otherwise, it will show your current command.

Let's see this in action. Begin entering a command to write the list of programs in your */usr/bin* folder to a file:

```
$ ls -al /usr/bin >> binaries.txt
```

But instead of pressing ENTER to execute this code, press CTRL-X, CTRL-E to edit it in place (see Figure 1-1).

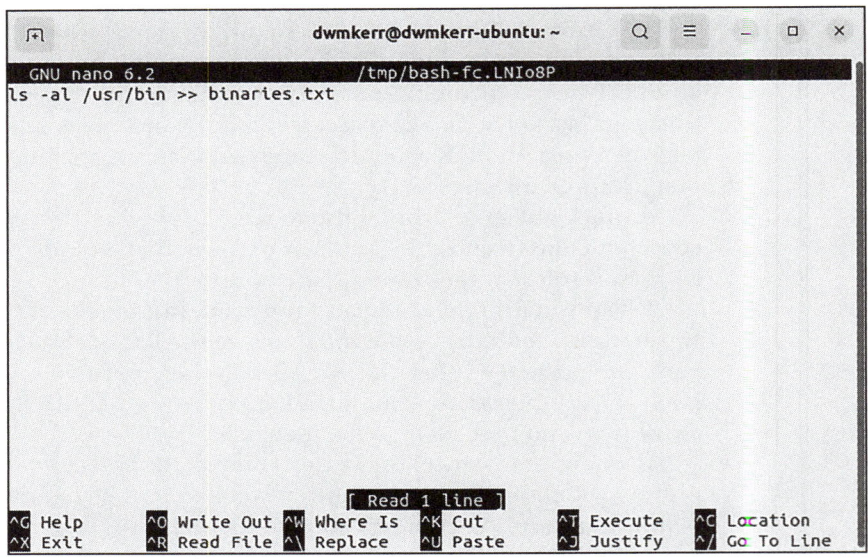

Figure 1-1: The "edit in place" functionality in nano

The nano editor uses keyboard shortcuts to save, close, cut, copy, paste, and so on. These shortcuts are shown at the bottom of the screen. You won't be able to click any buttons or menus.

Now you can edit the command text by deleting characters and typing new ones. Save your changes with CTRL-S, and exit the editor with CTRL-X. The shell will then run the edited command. You can see the most recent command by pressing the up arrow. If you want to discard your changes without running the command, close the editor without saving.

NOTE   *If the editor does not look like the screenshot in Figure 1-1, you may have opened Vim by mistake. If so, type* **:q!** *and press ENTER to exit Vim, then enter* **export EDITOR=nano** *to change the default editor for your shell.*

Keep in mind that the CTRL-X, CTRL-E shortcut opens the shell's *default* editor, which might not be the one you expect. For example, your shell is unlikely to use Visual Studio Code for editing commands unless you configure it to do so, even if you have set it as your editor for shell scripts. The default editor will be one that works *inside* a shell, because the shell doesn't assume that you have a windowing system running that can open a full-featured editor like Visual Studio Code, Notepad++, or other popular editors.

As you saw at the beginning of this section, you can override the shell's default editor by setting the EDITOR environment variable (see Chapter 10 for more on variables). On my personal machine, I use Vim as my command line editor. To check which editor you're using, enter the following:

```
$ echo $EDITOR
vim
```

For now, I wouldn't recommend changing your editor to a graphical one like Visual Studio Code for a couple of reasons. First, some interfaces, like a virtual machine or Raspberry Pi, won't have a desktop system to run a graphical editor, so you'll need to be familiar with a shell-based editor. Second, an external graphical editor runs in a separate window, meaning you've moved out of the shell and away from where you're working. Effective shell users want as few interruptions as possible between coming up with an idea, entering the text, and running a command.

We'll look at some more advanced editors in Chapter 23.

Other Useful Shortcuts

There are a few other shortcuts that, while they don't fit into the categories we've looked at so far, are just as handy.

Clear the Screen

The shortcut CTRL-L clears the screen but doesn't affect anything unexecuted in your current line. This is very helpful if you have a lot of "noisy" output on the screen and want to clean it up.

View Your Command History

Running the history command prints the recent history of commands you've entered:

```
$ history
    1  pwd
    2  ls
    3  git status
    4  clear
    5  curl effective.sh | sh
  ...
```

You'll get a numbered list of your command history, with the latest at the bottom. By default, the shell saves about 10,000 lines of history.

NOTE *This command works even if you've used CTRL-L to clear the screen.*

If you want to rerun any of the commands in your history, enter an exclamation mark (!) and the command's number like so:

```
$ !5
effective-shell: preparing to install the 'effective-shell.com' samples...
```

The 5 corresponds to the command curl effective.sh | sh, which installs the *effective-shell* samples. Most shells maintain your command history in a history file, and this number is just the line number from that file. You can find the history file's location by running:

```
$ echo $HISTFILE
/home/dwmkerr/.bash_history
```

Where the history file is kept depends on your shell, configuration, and operating system, but in most cases the HISTFILE variable will find it for you.

Show All Shortcuts

The bindkey command returns a list of all keyboard shortcuts:

```
$ bindkey
"^@" set-mark-command
"^A" beginning-of-line
"^B" backward-char
"^D" delete-char-or-list
"^E" end-of-line
"^F" forward-char
"^G" send-break
"^H" backward-delete-char
"^I" expand-or-complete
"^J" accept-line
"^K" kill-line
"^L" clear-screen
...
```

This is an extremely useful command if you forget a specific keyboard shortcut or even if you just want to see the shortcuts available to you. If bindkey doesn't work for you, try using the alternative form bind -p.

Transpose Text

Transposing text just means swapping it with some other text. Using the ALT-T shortcut transposes the two words before the cursor:

```
$ cp destination source
$ cp source destination
```

Using the CTRL-T shortcut will transpose the two *letters* before the cursor.

Summary

In this chapter, you learned shortcuts for maneuvering your cursor in the shell, which allows you to edit your code quickly and easily. You also saw how to list and search your command history, edit in place with the shell's default text editor, and take advantage of other techniques to work more efficiently on the command line.

In the next chapter, we'll look at how to find files and folders on your system, a process that is often complex and time-consuming even in a GUI environment but is a snap with the shell.

2

THINKING IN PIPELINES

Understanding pipelines and how input and output work for command line programs is critical to using the shell effectively. In this chapter, we'll look at how programs handle input and output, and then you'll learn how to chain multiple commands together with pipelines. I'll also share some tips and tricks for using pipelines that I hope will make your life easier. Finally, I'll briefly touch on the "Unix philosophy," an approach to building programs that enables you to efficiently perform highly complex tasks. Learning these concepts will open up a new world in terms of what you can do with the shell.

NOTE *If you're new to the command line or just need a refresher, make sure to read the appendixes before you start this chapter.*

The IPO Pattern

Most programs that are designed to be used in the shell or a Linux-like system use a pattern known as *input-process-output (IPO)*, which means "take input, process it in some way, and then produce output" (see Figure 2-1). In fact, many programs outside of the shell and Linux can be said to use this pattern.

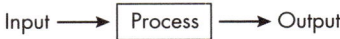

Figure 2-1: The IPO pattern

In the shell, when we use the output of one program as the input of another, we are using a pattern known as a *pipeline*. Figure 2-2 shows a more concrete example of a pipeline using the sort ("sort lines alphabetically") command, which sorts the input in alphabetical order. You can see this in action by running sort in a shell.

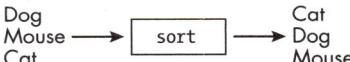

Figure 2-2: The sort program takes the input, sorts it, and outputs the result.

Start the sort program, enter some text, and then press CTRL-D (which appears in the shell as ^D) like so:

```
$ sort
dogs
chase
cats
and
cats
chase
mice
^D
```

The ^D command signifies the end of transmission (EOT), telling the program that you've finished entering your input. The shell then sorts that input and returns the alphabetically ordered output:

```
and
cats
cats
chase
```

```
chase
dogs
mice
```

Behind the scenes, sort is using two special channels of data called *stdin* and *stdout*. These channels, known as *streams*, are critical to how programs and the shell work.

Streams

A *stream* is nothing more than a flow of data. A YouTube video is a stream. Your browser doesn't download the entire video and start playing from beginning to end; instead, it streams the data, downloading only what it needs to play the current frame and the next few seconds. If you skip to a later part of a video, you don't download all the frames in between—you just start streaming the video from the later location.

Streams in Linux and the shell work the same way. Say I write a program that reads text from a large file and searches for a certain word. In general, it won't read the entire file and then search through it for the word; rather, it will stream the file into the program, reading a line or two at a time and searching in just those lines before moving on to the next couple of lines. This is far more efficient, as reading the entire file into the program's memory would take unnecessary time and resources. For example, you could read a file that is larger than the computer's total available memory and still search through it, even though the entire file is never loaded at once, just a chunk of it at a time.

Streams allow you to easily process input and output. You can read from files, network locations, special devices, or keyboards as input streams, and you can write to files, screens, network locations, or a printer as output streams. These are just examples; you can use many other different types of inputs and outputs.

Streams are an incredibly powerful abstraction that means programs don't need to know anything about the internet, the printer, the network, or even how files are stored—they just need to know how to read from or write to a stream. The device's operating system and drivers will handle turning the stream into files, print output, or whatever is needed.

stdin, stdout, and stderr

Every program has access to the three special streams—stdin, stdout, and stderr—shown in Figure 2-3.

Figure 2-3: Programs have access to three special streams: stdin, stdout, and stderr.

The *stdin (standard input)* stream is where programs read their input from; by default, in most cases this will be the input from the keyboard. The *stdout (standard output)* stream is where programs write their output to; the default in most cases will be the screen. Finally, the *stderr (standard error)* stream is where programs write error messages to, which is typically the screen (just like stdout). You might sometimes see these streams referred to as files, which is partly accurate. The system can treat them just like files—opening them, reading them, writing to them, and so on.

NOTE *Many programs don't require you to make any configuration to use these three special streams, as they're used by default. You're free to choose how a program will read input and write output, and some programs might not follow these conventions. Chapter 21 will cover how to write tools that follow these conventions and how to customize the storage of input and output.*

When you run programs in a shell, the shell attaches your keyboard to the program's stdin and attaches the terminal's display to stdout and stderr, as shown in Figure 2-4. Thus, by default, your key presses are taken as input, and any output or errors are delivered to the screen.

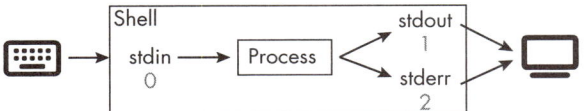

Figure 2-4: A shell program generally attaches your keyboard to stdin and sends stdout and stderr to the screen.

Here you can see the beauty of streams. Your program doesn't need to know that it's getting its input from the keyboard; it just receives information via stdin. You use the keyboard to type text, which is streamed into the program's input. The program writes its output to the stdout and stderr streams, and the shell streams this output as text on the screen. But you could just as easily pass other types of input to the program, such as files, and it will work; you'll see how to do this in the next section.

Each stream has a special number, shown in gray in Figures 2-3 and 2-4, known as the *file descriptor.* Whenever you open a file, the operating system allocates it a new file descriptor to keep track of any files in use. The descriptors 0, 1, and 2 are reserved for stdin, stdout, and stderr, respectively. To check this, run the following command:

```
$ ls -al /dev/std*
lrwxrwxrwx 1 root root 15 Apr  2 19:01 /dev/stderr -> /proc/self/fd/2
lrwxrwxrwx 1 root root 15 Apr  2 19:01 /dev/stdin -> /proc/self/fd/0
lrwxrwxrwx 1 root root 15 Apr  2 19:01 /dev/stdout -> /proc/self/fd/1
```

Here you list the contents of the */dev* directory and filter the output to just files that start with *std* by using the wildcard asterisk (*). Each stream's special file descriptor appears at the end of its line.

Pipelines in Action

A pipeline is a way to connect streams by chaining simple commands together to perform more complex tasks. Let's look at an example from the book's resources: *simpsons-characters.txt* is a simple file containing a few lines of text you can use to practice commands.

NOTE *If you haven't done so already, download the book's sample files from* https://effective-shell.com/downloads/effective-shell.zip. *To install this chapter's samples to the ~/*effective-shell *folder, run this command:*

```
$ curl effective.sh | sh
```

First, use the cat ("concatenate") command to write the contents of *simpsons-characters.txt* to the screen:

```
$ cat ~/effective-shell/text/simpsons-characters.txt
Artie Ziff
Kirk Van Houten
Timothy Lovejoy
Artie Ziff
Nick Riviera
Seymore Skinner
Hank Scorpio
Timothy Lovejoy
John Frink
Cletus Spuckler
Ruth Powers
Artie Ziff
Agnes Skinner
Helen Lovejoy
```

Next, you'll clean this data up by sorting it and removing duplicates. To do so, you *pipe* the output of the cat command into the sort command to alphabetize it and then pipe that output into the uniq ("omit duplicate lines") command to remove duplicates:

```
$ cat ~/effective-shell/text/simpsons-characters.txt | sort | uniq
Agnes Skinner
Artie Ziff
Cletus Spuckler
Hank Scorpio
Helen Lovejoy
John Frink
Kirk Van Houten
Nick Riviera
Ruth Powers
Seymore Skinner
Timothy Lovejoy
```

You'll see more of sort and uniq in Chapter 6. Note that when you used sort in the previous example, you were providing keyboard input. In this case, the sort command has used the output of the cat program (and you didn't have to tell the sort command to do so). It just reads from the input stream, no matter where that comes from.

The *pipe operator* (|) has a very specific meaning in the shell: it attaches the stdout of the first command (in this case, cat) to the stdin of the second (sort). In other words, the shell is connecting one stream to another, so this is a pipeline, as shown in Figure 2-5.

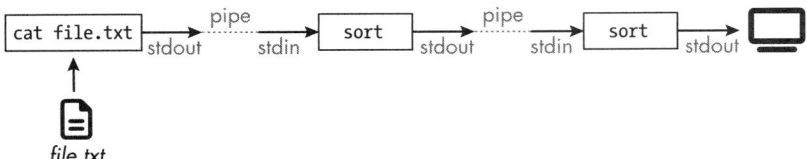

Figure 2-5: The pipeline is used to sort and deduplicate text.

As you can see, a pipeline is just a set of programs connected with pipes—easy! You can pipe as many programs together as you like.

Pipelines let you create complex sequences of operations that work quickly, even on very large files, because programs can read and process one chunk at a time. This kind of efficiency was particularly critical in the early days of Unix, when memory and resources were limited, and it's still essential today when you're working with large files or streams that might be slow to read, such as files you are downloading from the internet.

Next, we'll look at each stream in a little more detail by exploring some of their common uses in pipelines for practical, day-to-day work.

Standard Input Applications

Figure 2-6 shows some of the common sources of standard input for various programs.

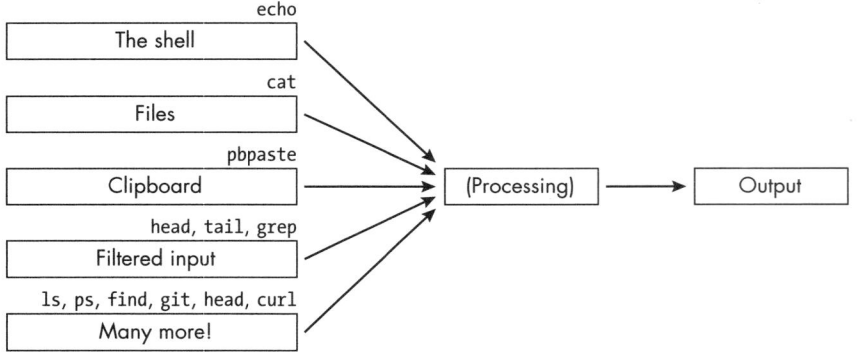

Figure 2-6: Common sources for standard input for pipelines

This list is by no means exhaustive; in fact, with a bit of tinkering, you can make almost anything work as the input to almost anything else. Let's review each of these sources one by one.

Using Output from Shell Code as Input

Anything that is written as output from one command can be used as input to another program. Try this example:

```
$ echo "Hello everyone!" | sed 's/Hello/Goodbye/'
Goodbye everyone!
```

Here you use echo program to write a message to stdout. This is piped to the sed ("stream editor") command. The parameters for sed are s/Hello/Goodbye, which instruct it to substitute (s) the text Hello with the text Goodbye. Chapter 7 discusses the sed command in detail.

Using Files as Input

As you've seen, you can use files as input to a pipeline. Earlier you used cat to write the *simpsons-characters.txt* file to stdout. In many cases, however, you don't need to use cat; lots of programs accept the filepath as a parameter, so you can just tell the program to open the file directly. Let's look at an example.

First, use cat as usual to read the file, and then pipe the output to the wc ("word count") command to count the number of lines:

```
$ cat ~/effective-shell/text/simpsons-characters.txt | wc -l
    14
```

Even though the wc program stands for "word count," it can count words, lines, characters, and bytes. Passing it the -l option indicates you want to count lines. Note that, unlike most shell programs, the wc program indents its output.

Now try the simpler version. Pass the filepath directly to the wc program like so:

```
$ wc -l ~/effective-shell/text/simpsons-characters.txt
    14 /Users/dwmkerr/playground/text/simpsons-characters.txt
```

Passing a filepath as an argument to wc eliminates the need to use cat or piping to provide input. But keep in mind that not all programs use the same conventions or parameter names for providing file input.

You might have noticed that the output in the two examples is different. The second command returns both the line count and the path of the provided file as output. In the first command, since you just provided a stream of text to stdin, the wc program doesn't know where it came from; the input might have been a file, the keyboard, or a web address, for all it knows.

As a shorter form of the first command, you can also provide files as stdin with the left angle bracket (<):

```
$ wc -l < ~/effective-shell/text/simpsons-characters.txt
    14
```

The < operator redirects the standard input of a program to come from the given file. This is a *stream redirection* operator, and we'll see some others in this chapter.

For readability, I tend to use cat when building pipelines so that it's immediately clear where the data comes from, as the pipeline reads from left to right. This is just a personal preference, so feel free to use whichever option suits you best.

Now here's a cool trick to get the word count information of whatever text you enter after the wc command:

```
$ wc /dev/stdin
one two three
^D        1         3        14 /dev/stdin
```

First, you run wc and tell it that the file to read from is the special */dev/stdin* file (that is, the stdin stream). Next, you enter some text (one two three) and press CTRL-D to let the program know you're done (remember, CTRL-D means "end of transmission"). Since you didn't specify an option such as -l to tell wc what you'd like to count, the program returns everything it can count—the number of lines, words, and bytes it read from its input—followed by where it read the input from.

If a program offers the option to specify a filepath but not to read from standard input, you can often trick it into doing the latter by providing the filepath of stdin.

Using Clipboard Content as Input

You can use clipboard content in pipelines too. In your text editor, type **this is not a palindrome** and copy that text to your clipboard. Then run the following:

```
$ xclip -o | rev | xclip
```

This pipeline uses the xclip ("clipboard") command with the -o ("output") flag to paste the contents of the clipboard to stdout, pipes it to rev ("reverse text"), and then pipes the output to xclip, which, when run without the -o flag, copies the reversed text to the clipboard. When you run xclip -o again, you should see this output:

```
emordnilap a ton si siht
```

NOTE *The* xclip *command should be installed on most Linux distributions that use a windowing system. For instructions on how to access the clipboard on a macOS or Windows machine, see Appendix B.*

Processing the text on your clipboard in the shell can be very useful for building more complex commands or formatting data you have copied.

Filtering Input

You can use a pipeline to filter input. For example, say you're a data scientist and you have a huge data file called *100GBFile.csv* in your current directory. You can use pipes to show just the first part of that file:

```
$ head -n 100 100GBFile.csv > 100linefile.csv
```

The head command displays the number of lines you specify with the -n parameter. In this case, it grabs the first 100 lines of your file and puts them into a smaller, more manageable file whose name you designate after the right angle bracket (>), which is another stream redirection symbol.

There are lots of other ways to filter input, as you'll see in Part II.

Standard Output Applications

Figure 2-7 shows some of the ways you can work with standard output.

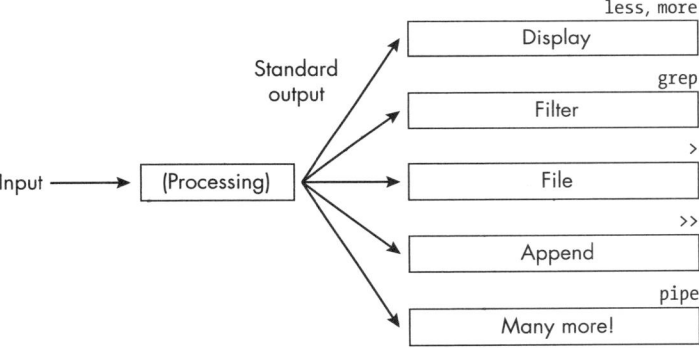

Figure 2-7: Common uses for standard output in pipelines

You've seen some of these outputs before, but here I'll go into a bit more detail.

Displaying Onscreen

Displaying output simply means the results are shown on the screen, like much of what you've seen so far. When you're working with the shell interactively, keying in commands, it's helpful to see the program's output onscreen. For, say, scheduled tasks that run overnight, however, writing to the screen is less useful. It's unlikely that you would be watching the screen then, so it would be better to write the output to a file you can read later, as described shortly.

Sometimes you'll get a lot of output that's inconvenient to scroll through in the terminal. In these cases, you can use the pager program less as follows:

```
$ ls /usr/bin /usr/local/bin /usr/sbin | less
```

This command lists the contents of two commonly used folders that store commands and then pipes the results to the less pager. The resulting list of commands is long, so it would be hard to search through the list if it were printed directly to the terminal. By passing it to the pager tool, you'll see only enough of the output that can fit on the screen. You can press the D and U keys to move through the output one "page" at a time, and the / and ? keys to search forward and backward through the output, respectively.

Piping into your pager is a useful trick. Read more about pagers in "Getting Help" on page 415.

Redirecting to a File

When you want to store some output, perhaps to review it later or because it's too big even for the pager, you'll likely want to pipe it to a file. As noted earlier, this is also a good method when you have jobs running in the background or on a timer, such as backup jobs that run nightly, as you probably won't have a terminal attached to the program to see the output when the overnight job is running.

To pipe the standard output of a program and write it to a file, use the shell's built-in redirection operator, >, as follows:

```
$ echo "Here's some data" > some_file.txt
```

It's that easy! This command will create the file *some_file.tx* if it doesn't exist but will overwrite the file's contents if it does. Now when you open *some_file.txt*, it will contain the text Here's some data.

Appending to a File

If you want to add new content to a file instead of overwriting it, you use double right angle brackets (>>), known as the *append redirection* operator, like so:

```
$ echo "Tuesday was good" >> diary.txt
$ echo "Wednesday was better!" >> diary.txt
$ echo "Thursday suuucks" >> diary.txt
$ cat diary.txt
Tuesday was good
Wednesday was better!
Thursday suuucks
```

In the first line, you use echo to write some text to the file *diary.txt*. The append redirection operator will append to the file if it exists and create it otherwise. Then, in the two subsequent echo commands, you add more text to that file.

Appending to a file is extremely useful in many scenarios—for example, when you might want to build or update a log of events over time.

Standard Error Applications

It's good practice for programs to write error messages to the stderr stream rather than to the stdout stream. This allows you to differentiate between normal messages and messages indicating problems.

Let's see the stderr stream in action. Enter these two commands, one of which will cause an error:

```
$ mkdir ~/effective-shell/new-folder
$ mkdir ~/effective-shell/new-folder
mkdir: /home/dwmkerr/effective-shell/new-folder: File Exists
```

In the first call to mkdir, the folder is created successfully. The second call, however, returns an error because the folder already exists. There's no real difference in how stdout and stderr behave in this case; stderr is just a particular channel for error messages. However, when working with these two streams, it's important to know that, by default, the pipe operator acts on stdout, not stderr. If you want to use stderr in pipelines, you have to tell the shell this explicitly.

Let's look at an example of the default behavior in action. Say you want to make your error message more obvious by making all the text uppercase with the tr ("translate characters") program. First, here's an example of how tr works on some regular stdout content:

```
$ echo 'Be quiet, this is a library!' | tr '[:lower:]' '[:upper:]'
BE QUIET, THIS IS A LIBRARY!
```

This command successfully translates all the lowercase characters to uppercase.

NOTE   *You'll see how* tr *works in a lot more detail in Part II.*

Now try using tr to set the mkdir error message in all caps:

```
$ mkdir ~/playground/new-folder | tr '[:lower:]' '[:upper:]'
mkdir: /Users/dwmkerr/playground/new-folder: File exists
```

You can see that this doesn't work. That's because the shell's pipe operator explicitly pipes to stdout, not stderr. That means your error output isn't being piped through the tr program; the mkdir command is writing the error message to stderr, and the shell writes the content of stderr to the screen, totally bypassing tr (see Figure 2-8).

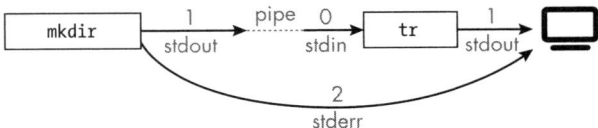

Figure 2-8: How the shell manages the mkdir *command's stderr output*

To get different output behavior from stderr, you must explicitly redirect its content. Figure 2-9 shows some common options for where you might send stderr.

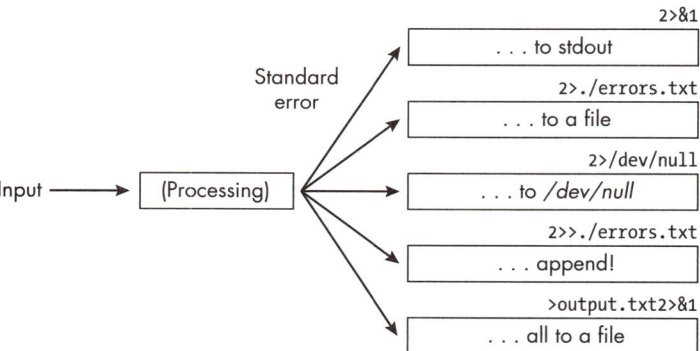

Figure 2-9: Common options for dealing with stderr

If you've done some shell scripting before, this might be an "aha" moment. Some of the obscure sequences shown in Figure 2-9, like 2>&1, might look familiar to you. We're about to go over exactly what they mean if you haven't guessed yet.

Redirecting to Standard Output

To pipe the error output to another command, you first redirect stderr to stdout, and then you can use a pipeline as usual, because the other command will be reading its stdin from the first program's stdout, not stderr. This redirection requires some more complicated-looking syntax: the 2>&1 sequence. Let's break it down:

- The 2 is the stderr file descriptor.
- The redirect symbol (>) tells the shell that you want to redirect the file with descriptor 2, which is stderr.
- The ampersand (&) tells the shell that the character that follows will be a file descriptor.
- The 1 is the stdout file descriptor.

In summary, this command says, "Take the standard error stream and pipe it to standard output." You don't need the ampersand before the first descriptor, because the shell supports output redirection only for file descriptors, so an additional ampersand would be superfluous and would cause unintended side effects).

To make the error message go through the tr command, redirect stderr to stdout like so:

```
$ mkdir ~/effective-shell/new-folder 2>&1 | tr '[:lower:]' '[:upper:]'
MKDIR: /USERS/DWMKERR/PLAYGROUND/NEW-FOLDER: FILE EXISTS
```

The error message will go to stdout and then be piped to tr, as shown in Figure 2-10.

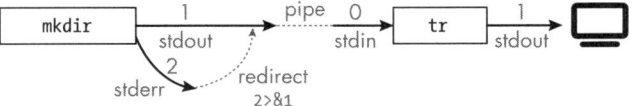

Figure 2-10: Redirecting stderr to stdout

To make sure you remember the slightly obscure & that references a file descriptor, see what happens when you don't include it:

```
$ cat some-file-that-might-not-exist 2>1
```

The shell writes stderr to a new file named *1* rather than the file that has the 1 descriptor.

Redirecting to a File

You can also redirect the standard error stream to a file with the > operator:

```
$ mkdir ~/effective-shell/new-folder 2>./errors.txt
```

This command redirects all content from stderr to a file called *./errors.txt*. You'll often use this approach when running programs and logging any error output to a logfile for later review.

NOTE *You might notice I often put the special dot folder and a slash before filenames. This has become a habit over years of working with the shell; the dot-slash makes it very clear and unambiguous to anyone reading your code that they are seeing a filepath rather than a command or some other resource. You can omit the dot and slash in this and other commands, and they will still work.*

Writing to a File

If you want to keep error messages but not see them on the screen straightaway, you can write the error output to a file with the > operator:

```
$ mkdir ~/effective-shell/new-folder 2>./errors.log
```

This is the same approach you used for stdout, except that you're explicitly saying you want to redirect file descriptor 2 (stderr) to a file. Like that operation, this one will create the file if it doesn't exist and overwrite it if it does.

Redirecting to null

Sometimes you just don't want to see the errors at all. For example, earlier you created a *new-folder* directory with mkdir and the command failed because the directory already existed. Say you don't care about that error, because it just means your task is already done.

The special file */dev/null* is used for just this purpose. When you write to this file, the operating system discards the input. To see this in action, run the mkdir command and redirect the stderr stream with file descriptor 2 to the *null* file:

```
$ mkdir ~/effective-shell/new-folder 2>/dev/null
```

This redirects all errors to a black hole named */dev/null* so that you won't see them on the screen or anywhere else. You can also use the *null* file to discard the stdout from programs.

Keep in mind that you should use this trick with caution. Make sure you really do want that output to disappear, because once it's gone, it's gone forever.

Appending to a File

You can also use standard error redirection to append to files:

```
$ mkdir ~/effective-shell/new-folder 2>>./all-errors.log
```

This can be useful if you're maintaining a file of all errors that have occurred when running a program or even a sequence of operations. As you saw earlier, you use >> to append rather than overwrite. This operation creates the file if it doesn't exist and writes the content to the end of the file if it does exist.

Redirection with Both stdout and stderr

There is an important subtlety you should be aware of when redirecting stdout and stderr together. For example, if you want to write both stdout and stderr to a file, you might try this:

```
$ ls /usr/bin /nothing 2>&1 > all-output.txt
cannot access  '/nothing'
```

This command writes stdout to *all-output.txt*, but stderr is still written to the screen, not the file. The reason is that bash (and most bash-like shells) processes redirections from left to right, and when you redirect you *duplicate* the source. This is complex, so let's break it down:

- The sequence 2>&1 ensures that the file descriptor 2 (stderr is also written to 1 (stdout), which is currently the terminal.

- The sequence > all-output.txt *duplicates* the file with descriptor 1 (stdout) and writes it to a file called *all-output.txt*. The > character is a convenient shorthand for 1> (that is, redirecting the standard output).

As you can see, at the time of the first redirection, you're redirecting to the screen, not to a file. The redirection to a file is the subsequent statement since the redirection is processed from left to right.

To write everything to the file, try this:

```
$ ls /usr/bin /nothing > all-output.txt 2>&1
```

This command will work in a way that is more sensible in most cases. Notice the difference?

- The > operator redirects stdout to the file *all-output.txt*.
- The 2>&1 sequence redirects stderr to stdout, which has already been redirected to a file.

This behavior can be tough to remember, so it's worth experimenting with it. Brian Storti's blog post "Understanding Shell Script's idiom: 2>&1" at *https://www.brianstorti.com/understanding-shell-script-idiom-redirect/* gives a very detailed description of this behavior. There are many variations you can play with, and you'll see more as you go through the book.

The T-Pipe

I can't talk about pipelines without briefly mentioning the *T-pipe*, which splits the stream in two so it can easily be sent to two different directions. For example, you can stream content to the display as well as to a file like so:

```
$ cat ~/effective-shell/text/simpsons-characters.txt | sort | tee sorted.txt
```

This command alphabetically sorts the *simpsons-character.txt* file and saves it to *sorted.txt* but also shows it onscreen. This way, you can quickly confirm the results without opening the file.

The T-pipe can be used for more complicated work too. Try this:

```
$ cat ~/effective-shell/text/simpsons-characters.txt | sort | tee sorted.txt | uniq | grep '^A'
```

Here you create a command to sort the list of *Simpsons* characters, remove duplicates with the uniq command, and then use grep to filter the results to names that start with *A*. (The grep tool allows you to search through and match patterns in text; Chapter 5 covers it in detail.) The tee command in the middle creates a T-pipe, which pipes the results of the sort command to the *sorted.txt* file before they go to the rest of the pipeline. In other words, the *sorted.txt* file contains the content after the sorting operation but before the deduplicate and filter operations; the rest of the output will continue through the pipeline as normal, as Figure 2-11 illustrates.

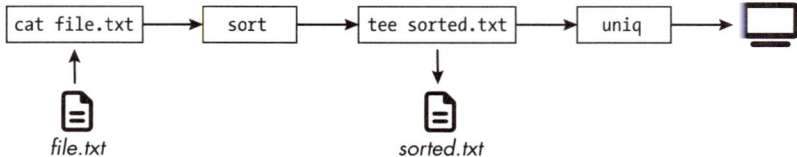

Figure 2-11: How the tee command splits a stream

You can see that tee splits off the output at a certain point and saves it in a separate file.

If you can visualize a T-pipe, it's easy to remember this useful command. You can use it in any number of more complex pipelines or scenarios to write content to a file that would otherwise go straight to another program or to the display.

Pipelines and the Unix Philosophy

Getting comfortable with pipelines opens a whole world of possibilities. As you've seen, pipelines let you manipulate the flow of data in streams, chaining programs together to handle complex operations.

The day before I wrote this chapter, I was working with a data file called *data.dat* that included empty lines and comments. I needed to find out how many unique data points the file contained; it took less than a minute to put together this working command:

```
$ cat data.dat | sort | uniq | grep -v '^#' | wc -1
```

I didn't have to install some special program to do exactly what I needed; I just incrementally built a pipeline, adding each section one by one and writing to the screen each time, until I got the results I was looking for.

NOTE *With the correct options, sed could likely do this in a single operation, but I'd probably spend a lot longer googling the right options for it!*

My thought process went as follows:

1. First, I use cat data.dat to write the content of the file to stdout. In many cases, this isn't necessary—you could simply pass the *data.dat* file as a parameter to the first command—but I find it easier to break up each step into the smallest possible chunks.

2. I use sort to put all the blank and duplicate lines together.

3. I pipe to uniq to remove duplicate lines.

4. I use grep -v '^#' to get rid of all the comments by finding lines that start with a hash mark (#). I'm counting unique data points, not comments. The -v ("invert") flag for grep inverts the results of the expression—so in this case, it will show lines that *don't* start with a hash mark (that is, lines that aren't comments).

5. Finally, wc -l counts the number of remaining lines, all of which should now be unique.

There may well be better ways to handle this task, as this one's not perfect: if there are blank lines in the file, this method will remove all but one of them rather than all of them. However, piping gave me a quick-and-dirty solution in less than a minute.

Of course, as your needs grow, you might want to build scripts (see Chapter 9) or use a programming language, but this approach illustrates a core tenet of the *Unix philosophy*: chaining together lots of small, simple programs that each do one thing well in order to accomplish a more complex task.

NOTE *While the Unix philosophy might seem intuitive or obvious today, it was ground-breaking when introduced in 1978. It vastly simplified how programmers wrote code, making programs far more flexible to work with and yielding powerful results from existing tools. The fact that it is still relevant, with very few differences from how it was conceived in the 1970s, is a testament to what a remarkable design philosophy it is. See* https://en.wikipedia.org/wiki/Unix_philosophy *for more details.*

Summary

This chapter introduced standard streams, redirection, pipelines, and other concepts that are fundamental not only to using the shell effectively but also to really understanding how computer programs work.

Don't worry if this feels like a lot to take in: you'll see more examples throughout the book that will reinforce these concepts. You can also revisit this chapter to review various topics as you progress. Many of the programs you've seen here, such as sed, tr, and grep, are workhorses you'll encounter again and again, particularly in Part II.

In the next chapter, you'll learn how to use the shell to efficiently locate folders and files on your system and then work with those search results.

3

FINDING FILES AND FOLDERS

Searching through a system to find files or folders can be a complex and time-consuming process, even with a graphical user interface. In this chapter, we'll make such searches a snap by using the shell instead. You'll also learn how to perform actions on the search results, such as deleting them or running commands on them.

Searching with the find Command

The find ("find files and folders") command is used both to search for files and folders and to perform operations on the search results. Let's see it in action by searching through the *~/effective-shell* samples folder. First, if you haven't done so already, run the following command to install the samples:

```
$ curl effective.sh | sh
```

To use find, your commands should have the following structure:

```
find options starting-point expression
```

The *options* are parameters you can set to change how find works. The *starting-point* is the folder or set of folders that find should search in, and the *expression* allows you to build more complex search patterns (you'll see these patterns in detail shortly).

The *starting-point* is the only part of the find command that's required, which means the simplest use of find looks like this:

```
$ find ~/effective-shell
.
./text
./text/simpsons-characters.txt
./scripts
./scripts/show-info.sh
./websites
./websites/simple
./websites/simple/index.html
./websites/simple/styles.css
./websites/simple/code.js
...
```

The find command lists the full hierarchy of files and folders contained in the given directory—in this case, *~/effective-shell*.

You can specify multiple directories with find, and it will display all the folders, subfolders, and files for all of those directories. Here's how you could use find to show some of the tools installed on a system:

```
$ find /usr/bin /usr/sbin
/usr/bin
/usr/bin/fwupdtool
/usr/bin/gnome-keyring
...
/usr/sbin
/usr/sbin/cupsd
/usr/sbin/pppdump
...
```

This command returns all of the files and folders in both the */usr/bin* and */usr/sbin* directories.

Now that you've seen the most basic use of find, let's look at what else it can do.

Refining a Search with find

You can use a search expression with the find command to narrow down the results it returns. For example, you can search for only files or folders, or for files with a certain name. In this section, you'll continue working with the *~/effective-shell* folder to explore some common ways to refine your searches, so move there now:

```
$ cd ~/effective-shell
```

From this point on, you can pass find the dot (.) folder as the directory to search through. The *dot folder* is the current working directory. If the dot folder is unfamiliar to you, see "Navigating with the Dot and Double-Dot Folders" in Appendix B for more information.

Searching for Only Files or Folders

You can add -type to your find command to filter your search only to files (f), like so:

```
$ find . -type f
./text/simpsons-characters.txt
./scripts/show-info.sh
./websites/simple/index.html
./websites/simple/styles.css
./websites/simple/code.js
...
```

When you specify -type, you're providing a *search expression*. The -type parameter is called a *test* and is used to filter the search results to those that match a specific format.

To return only folders, use the following command (d is for directory):

```
$ find . -type d
.
./text
./scripts
./websites
./websites/simple
...
```

By default, the find command displays folders that are normally hidden, such as the dot folder.

Searching by File or Folder Name

Use the -name test as follows to search for files or folders by name:

```
$ find . -name "simpsons-characters.txt"
./text/simpsons-characters.txt
```

You can also use wildcards to search for any file or folder name containing a particular series of characters:

```
$ find . -name "*log*"
./logs
./logs/web-server-logs.txt
./logs/apm-logs
./logs/apm-logs/apm05.logs
./logs/apm-logs/apm02.logs
./logs/apm-logs/apm03.logs
./logs/apm-logs/apm00.logs
./logs/apm-logs/apm01.logs
./logs/apm-logs/apm04.logs
```

Including the asterisk (*) wildcard before and after log finds files and folders with *log* anywhere in their name. Using wildcards like this is known as supplying a *pattern*. You can read this pattern as "find any characters (including none) followed by the characters log, followed by any other characters (including none)."

Try running the command without the wildcards:

```
$ find . -name "log"
```

This time, find doesn't return any of the *.logs* files and folders, because none of them match the exact pattern log.

The -name test is very specific; it will match only files or folders with the name provided. Try finding the *apm00.logs* file like so:

```
$ find . -name "apm00.logs"
./logs/apm-logs/apm00.logs
```

Now try searching for apm-logs instead:

```
$ find . -name "apm-logs"
./logs/apm-logs
```

The find command displays the folder named *apm-logs* but not the files in that folder.

Even if you use a wildcard pattern, you get the same results:

```
$ find . -name "*apm-logs*"
./logs/apm-logs
```

Since none of the files in the *apm-logs* folder have *apm-logs* in their name, find doesn't show them even though *apm-logs* appears in their path.

Not only is it important to be precise with the name you provide, but you also must be sure to use quotes when building your patterns. For example, this command

```
$ find . -name "*log*"
```

will give different output from this command:

```
$ find . -name *log*
```

In the first case, the quotation marks explicitly tell the shell to pass the text *log* to the find command, and find then interprets the wildcards.

In the second case without the quotes, the shell *itself* interprets the wildcards and then passes those results to find, which is quite different. This is how the shell expands the wildcard code:

```
$ parameter=(*log*)
$ echo $parameter
logs
```

Without quotes, the shell changes *log* to the only file or folder in the current folder (*effective-shell*) that matches the name, which is *logs*. Wrapping the parameter in quotes tells the shell not to interfere with the text. Chapter 20 describes shell expansion behavior in more detail. The takeaway for now is simply don't forget the quotes.

Searching by Path

By using the -path test with wildcards, you can search for patterns in a file-path and display all the files with any matching path:

```
$ find . -path "*apm-logs*"
./logs/apm-logs
./logs/apm-logs/apm05.logs
./logs/apm-logs/apm02.logs
./logs/apm-logs/apm03.logs
./logs/apm-logs/apm00.logs
./logs/apm-logs/apm01.logs
./logs/apm-logs/apm04.logs
```

Again, you must be very specific: without the wildcards, find wouldn't return anything, because none of the results have the exact path *apm-logs*.

Specifying More Than One Search Option

You can define multiple search options by using AND or OR expressions to combine parameters.

AND Expressions

Combining the -type and -name parameters allows you to run a more specific search, where find must match the given -type test *and* the given -name test. For example, you can search for only files that end in *.logs* as follows:

```
$ find . -type f -name "*.logs"
./logs/apm-logs/apm05.logs
./logs/apm-logs/apm02.logs
./logs/apm-logs/apm03.logs
./logs/apm-logs/apm00.logs
./logs/apm-logs/apm01.logs
./logs/apm-logs/apm04.logs
```

This AND-style search returns only the items that match both criteria. You can explicitly create an AND expression by using the -and operator between the tests, but it's not necessary as tests are AND expressions by default.

OR Expressions

To perform an OR search, returning items that match either pattern you specify, use the -or operator like so:

```
$ find . -name "*.js" -or -name "*.html"
./websites/simple/index.html
./websites/simple/code.js
./programs/web-server/web-server.js
```

In this case, find displays results that match either of the name expressions, returning all files that end in either an *.html* or a *.js* extension.

Running Case-Insensitive Searches

The searches you've run so far have been case sensitive, which can unintentionally restrict your results. To run a case-insensitive search instead, use the -iname test:

```
$ find . -name "*.js" -or -name "*.Js" -or -name "*.jS" -or name "*.JS"
$ find . -iname "*.js"
```

These two commands are identical, but I know which one I'd rather type.

In addition to using -iname for case-insensitive name searches, you can use the -ipath test to run case-insensitive path searches.

Grouping Parts of an Expression

You can group parts of an expression using parentheses to run a more complex search:

```
$ find . \( -name "*.js" -or -name "*.html" \) -a -path "*programs*"
./programs/web-server/web-server.js
```

The backslashes (\) before the parentheses are needed because parentheses have a special meaning in the shell. The backslash *escapes* the parentheses; that is, it tells the shell to treat these characters literally and pass them directly to the find command.

ESCAPING SPECIAL CHARACTERS

In the shell, some characters, like $, *, and (, have special meanings. Escaping tells the shell to ignore those meanings and instead treat the characters as plaintext. To escape, use a backslash before the special character, as in \$, *, and \(.

Escape special characters whenever you want the shell to treat them literally rather than interpreting them itself. For example

```
echo "\$HOME"
```

prints the literal text $HOME, not the value of the variable HOME, whereas

```
echo "$HOME"
```

prints the value of the variable HOME, which in my case would be /home/dwmkerr.

In the previous example, the parentheses group the first two expressions, which means find interprets the command as "find files with names that match *.js *or* *.html." The rest of the expression reads as "*and* their path must include the text programs."

Leaving out the parentheses changes the meaning:

```
$ find . -name "*.js" -or -name "*.html" -and -path "*programs*"
./programs/web-server/web-server.js
./websites/simple/code.js
```

This expression now reads as "find files with names that match *.js, *or* find files with names that match *.html *and* are in a directory with programs in the name." Think of the order of operations in mathematics, where operations within parentheses are evaluated before the rest of the expression, which means moving the parentheses will affect the result. If you're unsure what will be evaluated first, add the parentheses to set the order to be on the safe side.

The distinction in these two cases is subtle. Grouping expressions with parentheses not only ensures an operation runs as expected but also makes your intent clearer for anyone reading your code.

Excluding Search Results with the NOT Operator

You can use the -not operator to build expressions that exclude certain results:

```
$ find . -name "*.js" -and -not -path "*programs*"
./websites/simple/code.js
```

This expression finds files that match the pattern *.js* but excludes results that have *programs* in the path.

WHY DOES FIND HAVE WEIRD PARAMETERS?

The find command frustrated me for years because its parameters don't follow the standard patterns that we shell users have come to expect. For example, why does it use -name instead of -n or --name? This convention for parameters is based on the Portable Operating System Interface (POSIX) syntax standards, which you can read more about at *https://www.gnu.org/software/libc/manual/html_node/Argument-Syntax.html*.

The reason is that the -name, -and, -or, -ipath, and similar constructs aren't parameters, per se, but parts of a mini search language that's used to build a search expression. An expression can contain options, tests, and actions that are far more complex than what you'd normally put into a function's parameters—which is why a search expression operates more like a distinct language. As mentioned, the parameters in the example expressions in this chapter so far are actually tests that let you specify how to find files and folders, but as you'll see shortly, you can also use *actions* in expressions to operate on your search results. For further details, run **man find** to access the man page for this command.

Acting on Search Results

Expressions using the find command can also specify an action—that is, they tell find what it should do with the results. You might use find not only to search for a file or folder but also to *do* something with it, such as delete, copy, edit, or move it.

I won't go into as much detail on these actions as I did for search expressions (in Chapter 8, you'll learn about the xargs command, which has much more flexible capabilities for performing actions on files) but we'll look at the basics. You'll likely encounter these operations elsewhere, so it's good to be familiar with them.

Printing Paths

If you don't specify an action when running find, it displays or prints the results onscreen. If the command is part of a pipeline, it outputs to the next stage. You can explicitly specify the -print action as follows:

```
$ find ~ -name "*.tmp" -print
/home/dwmkerr/commands1.tmp
/home/dwmkerr/commands2.tmp
/home/dwmkerr/commands3.tmp
```

This is equivalent to running find ~ -name "*.tmp" (in other words, leaving off -print, since that's the default behavior), so it's unlikely that you'd need to use this expression in practice.

Deleting Files

You can use the -delete action to delete the files and folders returned from find:

```
$ find ~ -name "*.tmp" -delete
```

While this can be a convenient way to delete files, use this action with extreme caution. This command does not ask for confirmation or show what has been deleted, so it's easy to delete something accidentally.

The -delete action also deletes the children of a folder before the folder itself, which can cause unexpected behavior. Chapter 17 will provide a safer and more convenient solution.

Executing Commands

The -exec action allows you to execute a command on each search result, such as counting the number of words in the files returned from a find operation:

```
$ find ~/effective-shell -name "*.txt" -exec wc -w {} \;
29 /home/dwmkerr/effective-shell/text/simpsons-characters.txt
20 /home/dwmkerr/effective-shell/quotes/iain-banks.txt
16 /home/dwmkerr/effective-shell/quotes/ursula-le-guin.txt
10373 /home/dwmkerr/effective-shell/logs/web-server-logs.txt
```

First, find searches for files with the *.txt pattern in their names in the *effective-shell* folder. Then the -exec action tells find to execute a command on each result. The wc -w {} command calls the wc ("word count") command using the -w ("show word count") flag. The find command replaces the braces ({}) with the paths of the file(s) or folder(s) it finds. The semicolon signifies the end of the -exec command. Because the semicolon has a special meaning in the shell, it's escaped with a backslash.

The wc command works only on files, not folders. To avoid getting an error in the unlikely event there is a folder that has *.txt* in its name, add -type f to the pattern to return only files. The final expression looks like this:

```
$ find ~/effective-shell -type f -name "*.txt" -exec wc -w {} \;
```

This command displays the number of words in the *.txt* files it finds and skips over any folders it encounters.

Confirming Commands Before Execution

The -ok action works just like -exec but asks for confirmation before executing each command. To find and then confirm you want to delete *.txt* files, run the following:

```
$ find ~/effective-shell -name "*.txt" -ok rm {} \;
< rm ... /home/dwmkerr/effective-shell/text/simpsons-characters.txt > ? n
< rm ... /home/dwmkerr/effective-shell/quotes/iain-banks.txt > ? n
< rm ... /home/dwmkerr/effective-shell/quotes/ursula-le-guin.txt > ? n
< rm ... /home/dwmkerr/effective-shell/logs/web-server-logs.txt > ? n
```

This command prints each search result to the screen alongside a request asking whether you want to proceed. Entering n means that the rm ("remove file") command won't be executed for the given file; entering y runs the command on that file.

The -ok parameter is flexible with its input: pressing ENTER without typing anything is equivalent to saying "okay"; you can also enter yes, no, or even 0 (for no) and 1 (for yes).

If there's only one find action you learn, -ok should be it. Being able to search for files, run an action, and confirm that you're okay with the action proceeding can save you from making careless mistakes.

Handling Symbolic Links

Symbolic links, or *symlinks*, are like shortcuts to files or folders. They're worth mentioning here because of how find handles them.

Compare the output of these two commands:

```
$ find /usr/bin
/usr/bin
/usr/bin/uux
/usr/bin/cpan
/usr/bin/BuildStrings
/usr/bin/loads.d
/usr/bin/write
...
$ find /bin
/bin
```

It appears that */usr/bin* contains files that */bin* does not. However, if you run ls /bin, you'll see that it does indeed contain the same files as */usr/bin*.

NOTE *If you're using macOS, run* **find /tmp** *rather than* find /bin *to see the same behavior.*

The reason for this result is that */bin* is a symlink (a link to another folder) and */usr/bin* is not. To prove this, run the following command:

```
$ ls -l / /usr | grep bin
lrwxrwxrwx  1 root root         7 Aug  7 18:06 bin -> usr/bin
lrwxrwxrwx  1 root root         8 Aug  7 18:06 sbin -> usr/sbin
drwxr-xr-x  2 root root 40960 Jan 25 17:17 bin
drwxr-xr-x  2 root root 20480 Jan 25 16:42 sbin
```

The output on the far right shows that the root *bin* and *sbin* folders are actually just symlinks to *usr/bin* and *usr/sbin*, respectively. (The -> symbols indicate that folders are links to another location.)

By default, the find command won't return the location that the symlink points to; it displays only the symlink itself as the result. If you want to return what the symlinks are linked to, add the -L ("follow links") option:

```
$ find -L /bin
/bin
/bin/fwupdtool
/bin/gnome-keyring
/bin/dpkg-gencontrol
/bin/prltoolsd
...
```

It's important to understand these alternative ways of treating symlinks. For example, you might want to find all the symlinks in a folder and delete them, in which case you'd want find to return the symlinks themselves (otherwise, you'd delete what they point to). Or you might want to check the size of a set of files, including any files that are linked to. In that case, you'd want find to return the files the symlinks point to.

To read more about the actions you can perform with the find command, open its man page with man find.

Going Further with find

The find command is incredibly powerful. Going into detail on all of the options or potential ways to combine them could fill another book, but here are a few handy commands that show how versatile find can be:

Find large files

Use the -size test to search by file size:

```
$ find / -size +1G -500G
```

The + and - options allow you to set minimum and maximum sizes.

Find recently modified files

Use the -mtime test with a number of days to find recently modified files:

```
$ find . -not -path "*/\.*" -mtime -2
```

This example returns only files that have been modified in the last two days. The -not -path test skips dot files and folders that are normally hidden.

Find files that have had permissions changed

Use the -ctime test to find files with recently changed attributes, such as permissions:

```
$ find ~/.ssh -ctime -30
```

This example returns files whose permissions have been changed in the past 30 days.

Find executable scripts and make them non-executable

You can also search by permissions. Here's how to find and modify executable files:

```
$ find ~ -perm /a=x -exec chmod -x {} +
```

The -perm test with the /a=x pattern searches for files where all users (individual users, file owners, and group owners) have executable permissions—that is, users for whom the x ("executable") bit is set. Combining this with chmod -x removes the x bit, making the files non-executable. (The chmod command means "change permissions.")

Ending the command with + rather than ; means that find will pass all the files to chmod at the same time and execute it only once on the entire set, rather than once for each file. This approach is slightly faster and highlights that there are options for running the command specified by the -exec action.

Sometimes, running a command once with all of the find results as a single set of parameters is not just faster but essential. For example, suppose you wanted to create a single ZIP file containing three files found by find. If you used +, the find command would build the following zip command: zip archive.zip file1 file2 file3. If you instead used ;, the find command would build the following zip commands: zip archive.zip file1, zip archive.zip file2, and zip archive.zip file3.

Find empty folders and remove them after confirmation

The -empty test finds empty folders like so:

```
$ find ~ -maxdepth 3 -type d -empty -ok rmdir {} \;
```

The -maxdepth parameter allows you to limit the search to only three folders deep. By adding -ok, you'll be able to confirm whether rmdir should delete the folders.

Summary

The examples in this chapter have just scratched the surface of what find can do, but they've equipped you with the essentials. When you're comfortable with the techniques covered here, you can continue to build on your knowledge of find and discover just how powerful and versatile it can be.

The next chapter marks the start of Part II, where you'll learn how to manipulate text and streams from the command line. We'll begin by expanding on this chapter's discussion of using patterns to match text: it's time to meet regular expressions.

PART II

MANIPULATING TEXT AND STREAMS

4

REGULAR EXPRESSION ESSENTIALS

Many of the tools I'll introduce in this part of the book support *regular expressions,* or *regexes*: special patterns for identifying and matching text, such as phone numbers or parameters from a command. But before you can start using regexes in the shell, it's important to understand the basics of how they work. Regexes have a reputation for complexity that can be intimidating, but this chapter will offer tips and techniques to make them manageable. You'll learn all about regex syntax, including quantifiers, metacharacters, and capture groups, and see examples of regexes in action. With this foundation, you'll be well equipped to put regexes into practice in the chapters that follow.

Regexes in a Nutshell

Regexes allow you to specify extremely precise descriptions for the structure of text. You might use regexes to find all text that matches a particular format, such as an email address, a credit card number, or a ZIP code. This means that when you become familiar with them, you can define very specific patterns for text and then search for, replace, or alter this text.

Regexes are notorious for being complex, and it's true that their syntax can be initially overwhelming. For many years I avoided them for that very reason, but over time I discovered that, used carefully, they can be incredibly powerful and useful.

To see why they have a reputation for complexity, let's look at a particularly complicated regex. Say you want to see whether an arbitrary string matches the structure of a valid email address. A quick search on the internet returns this regex:

```
(?:[a-z0-9!#$%&'*+/=?^_`{|}~-]+(?:\.[a-z0-9!#$%&'*+/=?^_`{|}~-]+)*|"
(?:[\x01-\x08\x0b\x0c\x0e-\x1f\x21\x23-\x5b\x5d-\x7f]|\\[\x01-\x09\x0
b\x0c\x0e-\x7f])*")@(?:(?:[a-z0-9](?:[a-z0-9-]*[a-z0-9])?\.)+[a-z0-9]
(?:[a-z0-9-]*[a-z0-9])?|\[(?:(?:(2(5[0-5]|[0-4][0-9])|1[0-9][0-9]|[1-9]
?[0-9]))\.){3}(?:(2(5[0-5]|[0-4][0-9])|1[0-9][0-9]|[1-9]?[0-9])|[a-z0-9-]
*[a-z0-9]:(?:[\x01-\x08\x0b\x0c\x0e-\x1f\x21-\x5a\x53-\x7f]|\\[\x01-\x09
\x0b\x0c\x0e-\x7f])+)\])
```

This is horrendously complex—and I've already split the expression into multiple lines so that it fits on the page! This regex is so long that it's almost impossible for even an experienced user to parse, and attempting to change or modify it would risk breaking the whole expression.

Many people see examples like this and understandably decide that regexes are something they simply can't or won't learn. However, and as you'll see in this chapter, you have ways to use and manage regexes without getting overwhelmed.

Building Regexes

Regexes do not have to be—and, in most cases, shouldn't be—as complex as the previous example. My general advice for regexes is *start simple* and add complexity only if you need it.

You can build regexes by using an iterative process, starting with basic expressions, then adding more features as needed. For example, here's how you might build up a regex to validate an email address with some test data:

1. Create a short list of valid email addresses.
2. Add some items to the list that look valid at a glance but aren't quite right—for example, *@effective-shell.com* (which is missing content before the at sign).

3. Build a regex that matches a correct email address.

4. Refine the expression to eliminate the invalid addresses.

5. Repeat the previous step until most invalid addresses are eliminated.

In most cases, this process will be sufficient. Let's try it out, starting with the test data in Listing 4-1.

```
$ cat ~/effective-shell/data/email-addresses.txt
dave@effective-shell.com
dave@effective-shell
to: dave@effective-shell.com
dave@effective-shell.com <Dave Kerr>
test123.effective-shell.com
@yahoo.com
whatever123@😀.com
dave@kerr@effective.shell.com
```

Listing 4-1: Test data for email validation regex

Some of the addresses shown in Listing 4-1 are valid (but may be preceded or followed by other text), some are not, and some you might not be sure about, such as the address that includes an emoji. This address is valid if the mail server can handle Unicode characters such as emoji, but it's probably not a good address to use, as some mail programs or servers will reject it.

Now let's look at how to accurately match the address format. First, break down the email address into the following very rough structure:

1. Any set of characters

2. An at sign (@)

3. Any set of characters

That regex would look like this:

```
.*@.*
```

The dot (.) matches any character, and the asterisk (*) means "any number of times." This means that the .* part matches any number of characters up until the next pattern in the expression is matched. The next pattern here is the @, so this expression will match any characters until the first @ is found.

The final .* section is the same as the first, so it matches any characters any number of times. All in all, this regex matches any number of characters, up to an at sign, then any number of other characters.

You'll test this regex and others in this chapter using the invaluable website Regular Expressions 101 (*https://regex101.com*). This website not only lets you test regexes but also breaks down what each part of the expression does. Paste the test data from Listing 4-1 into the Test String section, and paste the regex into the Regular Expression box. My results are shown in Figure 4-1.

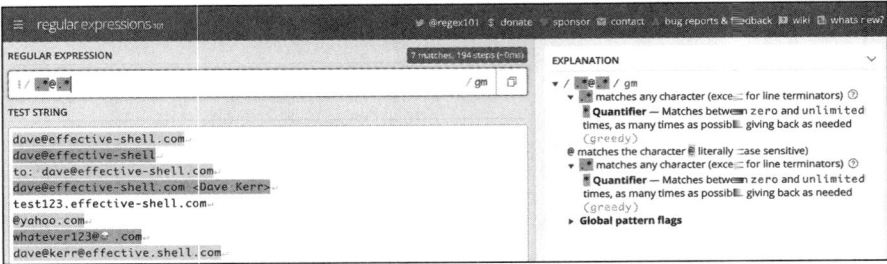

Figure 4-1: Testing the email validation regex with the data from Listing 4-1 at Regular Expressions 101

The site will highlight in blue the lines that match the pattern in the regex. Some of the matches are valid email addresses, but some are not, so this regex is not yet discriminating enough when validating email addresses. The results here give you clues about how to refine your regex. The site also shows which part of each line corresponds to which part of the expression. But perhaps the most useful feature is the Explanation section on the right, which describes exactly what each character does.

Note that the website alternates shades of blue as a helpful indicator that separate lines are *separate* matches versus one multiline chunk of text. You *can* match for multiple lines of text, but you're not doing that in this example.

NOTE *From this point onward, rather than showing screenshots of the results, I'll highlight the matched part of the text in bold. Be sure to continue running the examples in Regular Expressions 101 as you follow along so you can see a breakdown of how each part of the text is matched and what each character in the regex means.*

Now that you have a basic pattern that matches the valid addresses, you can refine it to eliminate invalid addresses.

Regex Engines

To complicate the world of regexes even further, different implementations of regex engines process regexes in slightly different ways. In Regular Expressions 101, you'll notice a list of "flavors" on the left, each representing a slightly different dialect. In general, you don't need to worry about this since you're not using highly complex expressions that will vary from engine to engine. The expressions you'll use are known as *extended regular expressions* and are Perl-compatible. In later chapters, you'll see how to specify the flavor of regexes you use in commands.

For now, just be aware if you go deeper that some shortcuts and special functions may not be available in every engine or every regex flavor. If you'd like to learn more, run `man re pattern`.

Quantifiers

The regex you're using is very simple. The complexity of regexes tends to come in when you need to accommodate *edge cases*: inputs that are unusual but possible and thus need to be accounted for. You have to be very explicit about what you can and cannot allow. You saw this with the email address example: it's not enough to just look for something before and after an at sign—you need to check for dots and invalid characters as well.

Next, you'll refine this expression to eliminate some of the invalid addresses. You'll start with the text *@yahoo.com*, which isn't a valid email address since it doesn't have anything before the at sign. The current regex matches this invalid text because it allows any characters before and after the at sign *any* number of times—which includes zero times!

You need to change the number of characters allowed before and after the at sign to be at least one. To do this, you'll use a different *quantifier*, the regex element that specifies how many characters are allowed for that part of the pattern. Table 4-1 offers a quick reference guide for regex quantifiers.

Table 4-1: Regex Quantifiers

Quantifier	Meaning
*	Any number of characters
+	At least one character
?	Between zero and one character
{n}	Exactly *n* occurrences of the character
{n,}	*n* or more occurrences of the character
{n,m}	Between *n* and *m* occurrences of the character

Currently, you're using the * quantifier to allow any number of characters. Replacing the asterisk with the plus sign (+) specifies that at least one character is required before and after the at sign:

```
.+@.+
```

Enter this new regex in Regular Expressions 101. You should get the following matches:

```
dave@effective-shell.com
dave@effective-shell
to: dave@effective-shell.com
dave@effective-shell.com <Dave Kerr>
test123.effective-shell.com
```

```
@yahoo.com
dave@
whatever123@😊.com
dave@kerr@effective.shell.com
```

As you can see, your new and improved regex has eliminated some
invalid addresses: *test123.effective-shell.com*, *@yahoo.com*, and *dave@*.

Character Sets and Metacharacters

To make your regex more accurate, you need to be more specific in what
you match—for example, you shouldn't accept a dot before the at sign. To
refine what you match, you can use a *character set*, a group of allowed characters that you build yourself, or a *metacharacter*, a predefined character set
that represents a particular range of characters.

Take the address *dave@kerr@effective.shell.com* as an example. This is
clearly invalid, as it has two at symbols. The reason that it matches the current regex is because you're using the . metacharacter before and after the
at sign. The . metacharacter means "any character except a newline," which
includes the at sign.

You have a few ways to make your regex more explicit with character
sets or metacharacters. Let's go over the options.

Specifying Ranges

One option is to create a character set by specifying the acceptable *ranges* of
characters the text can match. You start and end a character set with square
brackets, then use letters or numbers separated by hyphens to denote a
range of characters, like so:

```
[A-Z]
```

This character set includes the full uppercase alphabet, *A* to *Z*.

A character set can contain multiple ranges, in which case any characters within any of the ranges are valid:

```
[A-Za-z0-9]
```

This character set matches any uppercase letter *A* to *Z*, any lowercase letter *a* to *z*, and the digits 0 to 9. Notice that you don't put spaces between
the ranges. Replace the dot metacharacters in your current regex with this
range like so:

```
[A-Za-z0-9]+@[A-Za-z0-9]+
```

Plug this in, and you should get the following matches:

```
dave@effective-shell.com
dave@effective-shell
to: dave@effective-shell.com
```

```
dave@effective-shell.com <Dave Kerr>
test123.effective-shell.com
@yahoo.com
dave@
whatever123@🌀.com
dave@kerr@effective.shell.com
```

You can see the difference. You're getting closer, but the expression is starting to get a bit unwieldy. A cleaner option is to use a metacharacter to represent this range of characters. For example, the metacharacter \w represents all uppercase and lowercase letters and all digits 0 to 9 (the *w* is short for *word*). Therefore, you can shorten your current expression like this:

```
\w+@\w+
```

This shorter regex will return the same matches as the longer version did. Table 4-2 lists other common metacharacters that will come in handy for creating character sets. You can find many other metacharacters in the man re_pattern man page.

Table 4-2: Regex Metacharacters

Metacharacter	Meaning
.	Any character except for a line break
\w	Any word (alphanumeric) character, including the underscore; shorthand for [a-zA-Z0-9_]
\W	Any non-word character, which is anything *not* in the \w set above
\s	Any whitespace character (such as a space or tab)
\S	Any non-whitespace character
\d	Any digit character [0-9]
\D	Any non-digit character

Still, the current expression fails to match the valid email address *dave@effective-shell.com* and other valid addresses because your character set doesn't allow for special characters like the hyphen. You'll tackle that next.

Adding Special Characters

To include more characters in the match, you can add them directly to your character set—for example, the following pattern adds the +. Even though characters like + and * are metacharacters with a special meaning, as long as they are between square brackets, they are treated as their literal equivalents. There's one exception to this case: the hyphen (-), which can be used to form ranges (such as [a-z]):

```
[\w\-.]+@[\w\-.]+
```

Now your character set includes both the dot and the hyphen. Plug this in, and you should see more accurate matches:

```
dave@effective-shell.com
dave@effective-shell
to: dave@effective-shell.com
dave@effective-shell.com <Dave Kerr>
test123.effective-shell.com
@yahoo.com
dave@
whatever123@😂.com
dave@kerr@effective.shell.com
```

However, the final address has been incorrectly matched at the beginning because there's a second at sign in the second half of the address.

Negating Characters

You can use the circumflex (^) to *negate* a character set when you want to build a character set that *doesn't* match a pattern. Try building your email validation regex with negated characters like so:

```
[^\s@]+@[^\s@]+
```

The character set [^\s@] excludes whitespace and at signs; the \s metacharacter means "any non-whitespace character."

This expression returns the following matches:

```
dave@effective-shell.com
dave@effective-shell
to: dave@effective-shell.com
dave@effective-shell.com <Dave Kerr>
test123.effective-shell.com
@yahoo.com
dave@
whatever123@😂.com
dave@kerr@effective.shell.com
```

Notice that this pattern matches more addresses than the previous one. This is because the character set you're using is larger than the \w set, as it covers any characters that aren't explicitly excluded, including the emoji and the second @ in the final line.

Anchors

You might have noticed that the expression [^\s@]+@[^\s@]+ returns two matches that include text before and after the email address:

```
to: dave@effective-shell.com
dave@effective-shell.com <Dave Kerr>
```

To match text only in lines that *don't* include any extra characters before or after the email address, you can use *anchors*: regex syntax characters that represent particular parts of a string, such as the start or end of a line.

To match lines that contain only a complete email address, use the circumflex (^) start-of-line anchor and the dollar sign ($) end-of-line anchor. Remember that in a character set (anything between square brackets), the circumflex negates the characters. Outside of a character set, it indicates the start of a line:

```
^[^\s@]+@[^\s@]+$
```

You should get these matches now:

```
dave@effective-shell.com
dave@effective-shell
to: dave@effective-shell.com
dave@effective-shell.com <Dave Kerr>
test123.effective-shell.com
@yahoo.com
dave@
whatever123@😀.com
dave@kerr@effective.shell.com
```

This expression says that the text you're matching must start at the beginning of the line and must finish at the end of the line. In other words, do not match an address if it has any text before or after it on the line. Anchors allow you to create expressions that match patterns of text at certain points on a line.

As another example, to match any line that starts with the letters *to:* you could use this expression:

```
^to:
```

Here's the result:

```
dave@effective-shell.com
dave@effective-shell
to: dave@effective-shell.com
dave@effective-shell.com <Dave Kerr>
test123.effective-shell.com
@yahoo.com
dave@
whatever123@😊.com
dave@kerr@effective.shell.com
```

You'll see the start-of-line and end-of-line anchors used quite often, as they are extremely helpful for making a regex more specific.

Capture Groups

You can break up your expression into smaller parts with *capture groups*. Then you will have the option of performing operations on either the entire match or only the part specified in a capture group. This can be useful if you want to not just match text but also extract or change certain parts of it.

Consider this example:

```
(.+)@(.+)
```

Each capture group is surrounded by parentheses, so this example shows one full expression holding two capture groups. If you run this against just one line of the sample text, dave@effective-shell.com, it returns the following match:

```
dave@effective-shell.com
```

The full expression matches the whole line, but there are actually *three* matches here:

dave@effective-shell.com   The first match in an expression is always the complete match.

dave   The first capture group (.+) matches everything before the at sign.

effective-shell.com   The second capture group (.+) matches everything after the at sign.

You'll see how to use capture groups directly in the shell in Chapter 7, so I won't go into further detail now.

Lazy and Greedy Expressions

Regexes can be *lazy* (the regex stops searching as soon as it finds a match) or *greedy* (the regex continues until it finds no further matches).

Regexes are greedy by default; if you are matching a pattern, the regex will capture as much as it possibly can, all the way to the last match. As an example, let's look at how you might capture the contents of an HTML tag:

```
<.+>
```

This text is **bold**.

The regex `<.+>` matches against a left angle bracket, then at least one character, and then a right angle bracket. Because regexes are greedy by default, this expression continues beyond the first match (the opening `<strong>` tag) and matches the text all the way until the last angle bracket on the line (in the closing `</strong>` tag).

To create a lazy expression, you can use the question mark (?) after the + quantifier. This means that the expression will capture as few characters as possible until it finds the end of the pattern:

```
<.+?>
```

This text is ****bold****.

In this example, the regex has actually captured *two* results: the contents of the two sets of opening and closing angle brackets. Because the expression `<.+?>` is lazy, it matches until the first closing bracket it finds, yielding quite different results than the greedy version.

Lazy quantifiers are a shortcut. To get the same results without using the lazy quantifier, you'd use an expression like this:

```
<[^>]+>
```

This text is ****bold****.

In this case, you're using the ^ for negation to specify "any character that is not a closing brace."

Advanced Regex Concepts

Understanding the basics of quantifiers, character sets, metacharacters, and capture groups is sufficient for you to follow the regex-related examples in this book. However, you might encounter some more advanced topics or terms in the wild. I'll give a brief overview of some of those here, but if you've had your fill of regexes for now, you can safely skip to the next chapter.

Backtracking

Backtracking refers to how a regex engine tries to identify a greedy match. In the simplest terms, if a regex finds a potential match only to subsequently realize it's not a full match, it will back up and re-evaluate the text from the beginning. It's possible to inadvertently write a regex that looks simple but causes so much backtracking that it requires exponential processing to evaluate the input string. In the worst-case scenario, known as *catastrophic backtracking*, the processing power involved in trying to match a deceptively complex pattern can cause system failures or even lead to exploits.

> **NOTE** *There's a fascinating write-up by John Graham-Cumming about how catastrophic backtracking led to a severe Cloudflare outage in 2019; search for "details of the Cloudflare outage on July 2, 2019" at* https://blog.cloudflare.com.

Very broad and greedy expressions such as .+ (match *anything* at least once) can be susceptible to catastrophic backtracking. For example, the expression <.+> is greedy and would need to backtrack at the end of the test string <abc>hello</ab> and start again, whereas the expression < +?> is lazy and wouldn't need to. With highly complex and long strings, this can have a huge performance impact.

Be sure to test your expressions with short and long strings to see if there's a noticeable performance difference. Regular Expressions 101 and other tools can show you if your expression is consuming too many resources. To avoid unnecessary consumption, match more explicit characters and make expressions lazy when you can.

Lookarounds

Lookarounds are special constructs that match a pattern only if it comes before (a *lookahead*) or after (a *lookbehind*) another specified pattern. There are also *negative* lookaheads and lookbehinds, which essentially say, "Find me a pattern that's *not* preceded or followed by another specific pattern."

As an example, the expression \d+(?=€) matches one or more digits as long as they precede a euro symbol: the \d metacharacter indicates digits, the + quantifier specifies at least one, and the (?=€) part is a positive lookahead that says to return a match only if the pattern comes before the euro symbol.

I have yet to find a situation where I've really needed a lookaround. For example, I would write the expression \d+(?=€) more simply as:

```
\d+€
```

This regex uses a capture group to match one or more digits that precede a euro symbol.

Atomic Groups

Atomic groups are an advanced construct used to avoid backtracking. Lookarounds are atomic groups. Essentially, when an atomic group is matched, the regex stops trying to match and all backtracking ceases. This provides a "get out" clause to avoid catastrophic backtracking.

Atomic groups are a somewhat polarizing topic, but, as with lookarounds, I've yet to find a situation in my years of engineering that was genuinely simplified by the use of atomic groups. My advice is this: if you find you need to use a highly complex expression, break up the input first and then process it in multiple steps. That will likely make your code easier for others to read and understand.

USING REGEXES IN DIFFERENT LANGUAGES

Most of the features you've seen in this chapter will work the same regardless of whether you're using bash, JavaScript, Perl, Python, Golang, or another language, but as you move into more sophisticated features, you may find that some tools use slightly different syntaxes. These differences generally affect only advanced features such as named capture groups (a special syntax that allows you to give capture groups a descriptive name). Wherever you might encounter these differences in this book, I've tried to call it out. You can also quickly check how a regex works with different tools by using a website like Regular Expressions 101.

I recommend keeping your expressions as simple as possible. If they're getting too complex, break up your input or break up the processing into smaller chunks. This will help ensure they work as you expect, no matter what tool you're using.

Remember, too, that a regex isn't the only way to validate input. For example, you might use a regex to quickly confirm that an email address on a web form at least has the correct *structure* but then use a more sophisticated check later (such as sending the user an activation email) to confirm that the address is legitimate.

Summary

This chapter has given you a basic grounding in regular expressions. Knowing only a few core concepts—like character sets, quantifiers, and capture groups—is plenty for most people. The Regular Expressions 101 website is a superb way to learn and check your regexes to get more comfortable with the basics.

Now that you've learned the theory, you're ready to put it into practice. In the upcoming chapters, you'll see how you can work with text in the shell by using both regexes and a variety of other tools.

5

GETTING TO GRIPS WITH GREP

The grep command is an essential tool for shell users that enables you to search through and filter text. Once you know how to use it, you'll find yourself turning to it again and again. In this chapter, you'll see how to use grep to search for simple sequences of characters, how to combine it with regexes for more targeted text searches, and how to determine when it's the right tool for the job—and when it's not.

What Exactly Is grep?

While a tool that searches through text sounds pretty basic, a quick check of the grep man page suggests that it might actually be quite complex:

```
$ man grep

GREP(1)                         User Commands                        GREP(1)

NAME
       grep, egrep, fgrep, rgrep - print lines that match patterns

SYNOPSIS
       grep [OPTION...] PATTERNS [FILE...]
       grep [OPTION...] -e PATTERNS ... [FILE...]
       grep [OPTION...] -f PATTERN_FILE ... [FILE...]

DESCRIPTION
       grep searches for PATTERNS in each FILE. PATTERNS is one or more
       patterns separated by newline characters, and grep prints each line
       that matches a pattern. Typically PATTERNS should be quoted when grep
       is used in a shell command.

       A FILE of "-" stands for standard input. If no FILE is given,
       recursive searches examine the working directory, and nonrecursive
       searches read standard input.

       In addition, the variant programs egrep, fgrep and rgrep are the same
       as grep -E, grep -F, and grep -r, respectively. These variants are
       deprecated, but are provided for backward compatibility.
```

This command has many options and alternative forms (egrep, zgrep, and so on). It's a great deal to absorb, so you might want to try the tldr tool for the concise version (if you're not familiar with tldr, see "Summarizing Output with tldr" on page 418):

```
$ tldr grep

grep

Matches patterns in input text.
Supports simple patterns and regular expressions.
```

Much better—this summary explains that grep is used to match patterns in files. An even simpler description is that grep lets you search through or filter text. And you're not limited to searching in files: you can search through any text content. You can search for literal text, such as the word *error*, or for patterns of text by using regular expressions (covered in Chapter 4).

The grep command is such a commonly used tool that it has become a verb in tech circles. You might be asked to "grep" for something, meaning to search for it. The name comes from a command used in the original ed text editor to search for text, g/re/p, where the g indicated that the command would run globally (that is, on all lines), the re referred to searching with a regular expression, and the p specified that the results should be printed.

Now, let's put grep to work and search through your shell command history.

Searching Through Text

Most shells keep a history of the commands you enter in a special file. When you use the up and down arrow keys (or the CTRL-R shortcut, described in Chapter 1) in the shell to look through commands you entered earlier, your shell is looking through this history file under the hood.

The file storing the history can vary from shell to shell. For example, on my system, my bash history is in the *~/.bash_history* file. Most bash-like shells provide a built-in environment variable called HISTFILE that you can use to find your history file like so:

```
$ echo $HISTFILE
/home/dwmkerr/.bash_history
```

The location of your history file will vary from distribution to distribution. As mentioned, this file contains a list of the commands you've executed in your shell. You can check it like so:

```
$ cat $HISTFILE
...
cat ~/.ssh/config
ssh bastion.cloudops
help echo
help cd
exit
```

The history file is typically many lines long, and it shows some of the commands I ran recently, but I've shortened it here for the sake of brevity.

Now try using grep to search through this file for lines containing the text man as follows:

```
$ grep man $HISTFILE
```

This command returns all of the commands in the shell history that include the matching text (shown in bold):

```
...
man socket
k describe services eventstoredb-http-management
man cal
gcb refactor/performance/standardize-eventstore
vi src/tests/handlers/test_comman>d_handlers.py
gco src/handlers/command_handlers.py
gcb feat/performance/use-eventstore-writer
nvim performance.md
man grep
```

What if you use a different shell or forget where the history file lives? In that case, you can use the history ("show history") command, which prints out each line of the history file, along with the line number. This approach might be a little more intuitive than trying to remember where the history file is stored or the name of the HISTFILE variable.

The history command writes to stdout. If you don't give grep a source file, it will search through stdin. This means you can use a pipeline and just grep the output of the history command. (For more on pipelines, stdin, and stdout, see Chapter 2.) Here's how you could search the history for the text man:

```
$ history | grep man
...
 9125  man socket
 9188  k describe services eventstoredb-http-management
 9211  man cal
 9341  gcb refactor/performance/standardize-eventstore
 9344  vi src/tests/handlers/test_command_handlers.py
 9347  gco src/handlers/command_handlers.py
 9352  gcb feat/performance/use-eventstore-writer
 9355  nvim performance.md
10002  man grep
```

This demonstrates an important feature of grep: you can search through any text you pipe to it.

The number before each command is the line number of the command in the history file. These numbers are useful because you can rerun any command from the history file by entering an exclamation point followed by the line number. For example, entering

```
$ !9355
```

reruns line 9355 of the history. In my case, this is the nvim performance.md command, which opens a Markdown file I was working on in my text editor.

Using grep with Regular Expressions

The preceding output shows that searching through my history didn't just find times I executed the man command; it also found *any* line containing man.

What if you want to find only the lines that *start* with man? To search for a pattern like this, you can use a regular expression:

```
$ history | grep "[0-9]\+  man"

...
 9125  man socket
 9211  man cal
10002  man grep
```

This regex is made up of the following components:

[0-9]\+   At least one number in the range 0 to 9

man   Two spaces and the letters *man*

NOTE   *Chapter 4 covers the basics of regexes that you'll need to understand for the rest of the chapter.*

You might wonder why there's a slash before the plus sign (+). By default, grep uses *basic regular expressions,* which have a slightly different syntax from the *extended regular expressions* that are explained and used in Chapter 4. In addition to the plus sign, the ?, {, |, (, and) characters must be escaped with a backslash in basic regexes.

If you prefer to work with extended regexes, you can use the -E ("extended") flag as follows:

```
$ history | grep -E "[0-9]+  man"
```

Or you can use the egrep tool, which uses extended regexes by default:

```
$ history | egrep "[0-9]+  man"
```

I recommend always using extended regexes (egrep or grep -E) because they are widely supported and the most commonly used syntax in regex resources and examples online. To learn more about the difference between the slightly old-fashioned basic regexes and the more modern extended regexes, run man re_format to check out the regexes man page.

You may notice people using the -P ("Perl") option to enable Perl-compatible regexes. Perl regexes offer advanced features and are often considered the most versatile and powerful flavor of regex, widely adopted in modern programming tools and libraries. However, not all versions of grep and egrep offer this option. In general, the expressions shown here are also Perl-compatible.

Advanced grep Features

To illustrate some of the more advanced features of grep, we'll use files from the *~/effective-shell* sample folder. If you haven't done so already, install the book's samples like so:

```
$ curl effective.sh | sh
```

Then move into the *~/effective-shell* folder:

```
$ cd ~/effective-shell
```

All of the following examples will assume you're in this folder.

Making a Search Case-Insensitive

One of the most common parameters I use with grep is the `-i` ("case-insensitive") parameter shown in this example:

```
grep -i err somefile
```

The `-i` parameter makes the search case insensitive, so it's a very quick way to scan through a file for text matching the letters *err*—in other words, to find error messages in logfiles, regardless of whether they're uppercase or lowercase.

You can try this out with some of the logfiles in the *logs* folder:

```
$ grep -i err ./logs/web-server-logs.txt

...
2025-07-01T12:50:30.594Z: info - ...-stderr-redirect.png'...
2025-07-01T12:50:31.827Z: error - Unhandled Error EACCES trying to read
2025-07-01T12:50:31.827Z: error - Unhandled Error EACCES trying to read
2025-07-01T12:50:31.827Z: error - Unhandled Error EACCES trying to read
2025-07-01T12:50:31.848Z: error - Unhandled Error EACCES trying to read
2025-07-01T12:50:31.849Z: error - Unhandled Error EACCES trying to read
```

This trick is very useful. You could even adapt it to search for warnings or other types of messages in a logfile. (The lines in this logfile have been shortened for brevity.)

Getting Additional Context for Search Results

There are three really useful parameters for grep, which you can easily remember with the letters *ABC*. The first, the `-A` ("after") parameter, prints a given number of lines *after* each line matching the search:

```
$ grep host -A 3 ./programs/web-server/web-server.js

  host: process.env.HOST || 'localhost',
  port: process.env.PORT || getOptionalEnvInt('PORT', 8080),
  root: process.env.ROOT || process.cwd(),
  defaultPage: 'index.html',
--
  httpServer.listen({ host: config.host, port: config.port });
  log.info(`Server running on: ${config.host}:${config.port}`);
}
main();
```

This example returns the three lines after each occurrence of the word *host* in the *web-server.js* script. It quickly shows how something you search for might be used, because you can see the lines after each match.

Similarly, the `-B` ("before") parameter prints a specified number of lines that come *before* a match, which is useful if you're searching through error messages and want to see the code that caused an error, as shown here:

```
$ grep throw -B 5 ./programs/web-server/web-server.js

//  Helper to return an optional numeric environment variable or the default.
function getOptionalEnvInt(name, defaultValue) {
  const val = process.env[name];
  if (!val) return defaultValue;
  const intVal = parseInt(val, 10);
  if (isNaN(intVal)) throw new Error(`...`);
```

This example shows any line containing the word *throw* as well as the five lines that came before it.

Finally, the -C ("context") parameter is the most useful, as it provides a specified number of lines before *and* after each match. In this example, I search through my history to see what commands I ran before and after I used the git init command to create a new repository (note that because git init is more than one word, you need to surround it with single quotation marks to search for the entire command, including the space between the words):

```
$ history | grep -C 5 'git init'

5802  git push --follow-tags && git push origin
5803  cd ../java-maven-standard-version-sample
5804  rm -rg .git
5805  rm -rf git
5806  rm -rf .idea
5807  git init -h
5808  git remote add origin git@github.com:dwmkerr/java-maven-standard-version-sample.git
5809  git push origin -u
5810  git push -u origin
5811  git push --set-upstream origin master
5812  git rm --cached tpm
```

The matching command is in line 5807, with git init in bold. Now I can easily see the lines around the matching text, or the *context* of the match, to remind myself what I was doing the last time I ran this command. (See Chapter 18 for more details on the git init command.)

Finally, don't forget to capitalize the ABC flags. Knowing how to use them to find the context for a match can be a lifesaver when you're quickly searching through text.

Searching Through Multiple Files

Everything you've searched through so far has been a single file, but say you want to search a bunch of files at once. How can you identify where the matches come from?

There's a useful pair of flags for just this purpose. The -H ("header") parameter shows the filename before each match. If you provide grep with a single file, the header isn't shown. If you provide multiple files, however, the header is enabled by default. You can ensure the header is not shown by using the -h ("hide header") parameter. The -n ("line number") parameter displays the line number for the match. Here's how you might combine these parameters to search through several files at once:

```
$ grep -H -n ERROR ./logs/apm-logs/*.logs
```

The -H parameter makes showing a header explicit. If the *apm-logs* folder had only one logfile, the header wouldn't be shown. Including the flag (or the opposite flag, -h) ensures you'll get the behavior you want.

Each line of output (shortened for brevity) now shows the filename and line number (bolded) for the matching text:

```
...
./logs/apm-logs/apm02.logs:34893:2020-11-27T12:24:37.429Z      ERROR  [request]      401...
./logs/apm-logs/apm02.logs:34906:2020-11-27T12:25:11.415Z      ERROR  [request]      401...
```

You can take this even further with the -r ("recursive") flag:

```
$ grep -r -H -n -i error ./logs
```

This tells grep to search recursively and case insensitively, looking in every child folder of the *logs* folder.

You also may see commands like this written with the parameters combined like so:

```
$ grep -rHni error ./logs
```

All four parameters are combined into a single -rHni. This form is more concise and fairly common in practice; however, not all commands support it, and keeping each parameter separate improves clarity, so I prefer that approach.

Filtering and Piping grep Output

The -v ("invert") parameter tells grep to *exclude* lines that match the pattern; essentially, it makes the search work like a filter. For example, you could enter the following command to search your logfiles and exclude any messages that contain the term *debug*:

```
$ grep -v debug ./logs/web-server.logs
```

Remember, you can always pipe a series of grep commands together. Rather than trying to work out the perfect pattern to search for exactly what you want, you can compose a pipeline of grep commands:

```
$ grep -i error -r ./logs | grep -i -v memory | grep -i -v 'not found'
```

This set of small, simple commands is chained together to execute a sophisticated operation:

1. Recursively search for the text *error* in the *./logs* folder.
2. Exclude any result that matches *memory*.
3. Exclude any result that matches *not found*.

This is the essence of the Unix philosophy: chaining together a few simple tools that each do one thing well to compose a more complex workflow. Let's look at a few more examples of grep pipelines.

Combining grep with other Commands

The grep command, just like most of the tools in this section, works on stdin by default, which means you can easily grep anything that gets written to the screen. This section demonstrates a few simple examples to show you how easy it is to use grep pipelines to perform more complex tasks by combining it with other commands. I don't explain each command in detail. Instead, I highlight some parameters you haven't seen yet to reinforce the idea that as you become more familiar with grep, you'll use it more often to handle all kinds of tasks.

- Show all processes, then filter the list to only *vim* processes:

```
ps -a | grep vim
```

- Search through all of the *yaml* files in the *k8s* folder for the text *password*; show three lines of context, the filename, and the line number; and print the output in the pager so that it's easy to search through:

```
grep -H -C 3 -R password ./k8s/**/*.yaml | less
```

- Search through all of the installed programs for programs with *zip* in the name:

```
ls -al /usr/bin /bin /usr/local/bin | grep zip
```

- Show the last 10 grep commands entered in the shell:

```
history | grep grep | tail -n 10
```

You'll see a lot more examples of grep in action throughout the book.

Alternatives to grep

The grep command has been around for a long time, and over the years a number of alternatives have been developed. Most of these alternatives are designed either to be faster so that you can search through files more quickly or to be easier so that you don't have to remember too many flags.

In general, I'd avoid alternatives unless you encounter a situation where using grep genuinely limits what you can do or hampers performance. Alternatives can have a steep learning curve, may not be present or consistent across platforms, and are less likely to be available if you're writing scripts or instructions for others.

If you decide you want to add some more text-searching tools to your toolkit, three potential options are ripgrep, ag, and ack, each of which enhances performance and adds functionality. Before you install them, however, it's best to master the core grep functionality first.

Summary

If you need to find or filter text, grep should be your go-to tool. In this chapter, you used grep to search for simple sequences of characters and then combined it with regexes to search for patterns in text. You also learned how using grep with parameters and pipelines can help you accomplish more complex tasks.

In the next chapter, you'll move beyond simply searching for text by learning how to manipulate it directly from the shell.

6

SLICING AND DICING TEXT

In Chapter 5 you learned how to use the grep command to search through and filter text. In this chapter, we'll look at some of the many commands you can use to *manipulate* text. We'll start with the basics, such as cutting and replacing text, and move on to some of the more sophisticated commands in the next chapter.

Extracting Heads and Tails

The commands head and tail are very simple but incredibly useful. As their names imply, the head command outputs the first part of a file, and the tail command outputs the last part of a file. Once you start using these commands, you'll wonder how you lived without them!

To install this chapter's samples to the *~/effective-shell* folder, run this command:

```
$ curl effective.sh | sh
```

Let's start with head. Imagine you've been sent a large data file and you don't know exactly what's in it. To take a quick look at the first part of its contents, run the head command as follows:

```
$ head ~/effective-shell/data/top100.csv
"Rank","Rating","Title","Reviews"
"1","97","Black Panther (2018)","515"
"2","94","Avengers: Endgame (2019)","531"
"3","93","Us (2019)","536"
"4","97","Toy Story 4 (2019)","445"
"5","99","Lady Bird (2017)","393"
"6","100","Citizen Kane (1941)","94"
"7","97","Mission: Impossible - Fallout (2018)","430"
"8","98","The Wizard of Oz (1939)","120"
"9","96","The Irishman (2019)","441"
```

The head command shows only the first 10 lines of a file. In this case, the first few lines tell you that this is a comma-separated values (CSV) file that contains a list of movies. This list consists of the top 100 films on Rotten Tomatoes at the time of writing, with the score, tomato meter, name, and number of votes. You'll use this sample file a lot in this chapter to learn about text manipulation.

To specify the number of lines you want to see, use the -n ("number") flag with the number of your choice:

```
$ head -n 3 ~/effective-shell/data/top100.csv
"Rank","Rating","Title","Reviews"
"1","97","Black Panther (2018)","515"
"2","94","Avengers: Endgame (2019)","531"
```

This command returns only the first three lines.

The tail command works in the same way but for the end of a file. This command is more useful when you're looking at content that changes over time, like logfiles where you probably want to see only the most recent entries.

To view the 10 most recent commands you've entered in your shell, use tail with HISTFILE like so:

```
$ tail $HISTFILE
ls
ln -s $(pwd) ~/effective-shell
cat ~/effective-shell/data/top100.csv
head -n 3 ~/effective-shell/data/top100.csv
head ~/effective-shell/data/top100.csv
gcd
git stash
gcd
git stash pop
tail $HISTFILE
```

The HISTFILE variable locates your history file, and tail returns the last 10 commands from that file.

Just like with head, you can limit the number of lines tail returns by specifying a number with the -n flag:

```
$ tail -n 3 $HISTFILE
gcd
git stash pop
tail $HISTFILE
```

Now you see only the last three commands from the history file.

You can also use the tail command to show the changes to a file in real time. Add the -f ("follow") flag to follow the contents of the history file and see when a new line is added to the file:

```
$ tail -f $HISTFILE
```

Then, in another terminal window, start entering commands. You'll see that the tail command in the first window writes the updates to the terminal as you enter them. (Note that on Linux systems the history file is updated only when the shell updates.) Press CTRL-C to close the tail program.

Though it's unlikely you'll use tail to follow your shell history file in practice, it works as an example. A more common use case is to run tail on a logfile that is being written while some kind of process is running. This lets you see the log entries as they are added to the file in real time.

Another trick I use a lot with tail is to strip the first line, or header, from a file with the -n +2 parameter. The plus sign (+) indicates that you want to return everything from the line number specified (2, in this case) onward. Here's how you might use it:

```
$ head ~/effective-shell/data/top100.csv | tail -n +2
"1","97","Black Panther (2018)","515"
"2","94","Avengers: Endgame (2019)","531"
"3","93","Us (2019)","536"
"4","97","Toy Story 4 (2019)","445"
"5","99","Lady Bird (2017)","393"
"6","100","Citizen Kane (1941)","94"
"7","97","Mission: Impossible - Fallout (2018)","430"
"8","98","The Wizard of Oz (1939)","120"
"9","96","The Irishman (2019)","441"
```

This command pipes the results of the head command into tail -n +2 to grab everything from the second line onward, removing the heading line so that you see only the films, not the column names Rank, Rating, Title, and Reviews.

You'll use head and tail quite a lot when working with text. These two crucial tools can really help you be efficient, especially when you combine them with other commands or run them in pipelines (which are described in detail in Chapter 2).

Replacing Text

Next up is the tr ("translate characters") command, which you saw in Chapter 2. This program is very simple, and I use it most often to perform a simple substitution of characters.

To see how tr works, you can create a list of each of the column names in the Rotten Tomatoes CSV file like so:

```
$ head -n 1 ~/effective-shell/data/top100.csv | tr ',' '\n'
"Rank"
"Rating"
"Title"
"Reviews"
```

The head -n 1 command extracts the first line of the file: the column names. The results are then piped to the tr command, which *replaces* the first specified character, a comma (,), with the second, a newline (\n). In the output, the column titles are now separated by line breaks instead of by commas.

Now say you want to remove the quotes from the column names:

```
$ head -n 1 ~/effective-shell/data/top100.csv | tr ',' '\n' | tr -d '"'
Rank
Rating
Title
Reviews
```

Here the tr command, along with the -d ("delete") flag, *removes* the specified character (quotation marks, in this example) from each column name. Again, you're piping commands together. (For more on pipelines, see Chapter 2.) You'll see this technique—chaining together lots of simple commands in a pipeline to perform more complex operations—again and again throughout the book.

Remember that the tr command works on *characters*. For example, the following command might not work as you expect:

```
$ echo "Welcome to the shell" | tr 'shell' 'machine'
Wcicomc to tac macii
```

The reason for this output is that you're specifying character replacements, so the shell interprets this command as follows:

```
s -> m
h -> a
e -> c
l -> h
l -> i
```

In other words, it thinks you want to replace the first letter of shell with the first letter in machine, the second letter of shell with the second letter of machine, and so on.

There are several ways to replace entire words or perform more complex operations, such as using the sed or awk commands. I'll cover them in more detail in the following chapter.

You can also use tr with *character classes*, which define a set of characters to match on within square brackets ([ ]). This is easiest to explain with an example:

```
$ echo "Use your inside voice..." | tr '[[:lower:]]' '[[:upper:]]'
USE YOUR INSIDE VOICE...
```

In this case, tr transforms characters in the lower character class (lower-case characters) to the upper character class (uppercase characters).

Another way to translate characters is to specify ranges:

```
$ echo "Use your inside voice..." | tr 'a-z' 'A-Z'
USE YOUR INSIDE VOICE...
```

This example also changes characters from lowercase to uppercase but by using the ranges a-z and A-Z instead of the character classes.

I won't go further into character classes here, but you can find out more about them with man 7 regex.

Cutting Text

The cut ("remove section from line") command splits a line of text around every instance of a given delimiter. This is one way to use it:

```
$ cut -d ',' -f 3 ~/effective-shell/data/top100.csv | head
"Title"
"Black Panther (2018)"
"Avengers: Endgame (2019)"
"Us (2019)"
"Toy Story 4 (2019)"
"Lady Bird (2017)"
"Citizen Kane (1941)"
"Mission: Impossible - Fallout (2018)"
"The Wizard of Oz (1939)"
"The Irishman (2019)"
```

With the -d ("delimiter") flag, you choose a delimiter to cut the text with, then use the -f ("field") flag to choose which field you want to see. In this case, you're splitting on the comma character and showing the third field: the Title column. Notice that the short versions of a flag are often just the first letter of the long option, so in this case -d is short for --delimiter, whereas in the earlier tr example it was short for --delete. Each command knows how to process its own particular parameters correctly. You can always run man *command_name* for an explanation of each parameter.

This application of the cut command can be extraordinarily useful. For example, you could use it to work with Kubernetes pods you have running on a cluster. To do so, first you need to run the `kubectl` command to return the pod information (don't worry if you don't recognize this command; it's just an example of a command that produces some complex output for you to slice and dice):

```
$ kubectl get pods
NAME                                      READY   STATUS    RESTARTS   AGE
elastic-operator-0                        1/1     Running   0          35d
elk-apm-server-65b698fb8c-rzncz           1/1     Running   0          13d
elk-es-default-0                          1/1     Running   0          35d
elk-kb-6f8bb6457b-bbbnn                   1/1     Running   0          35d
filebeat-beat-filebeat-ccgl7              1/1     Running   1          13d
filebeat-beat-filebeat-dvf2l              1/1     Running   2          13d
filebeat-beat-filebeat-mnpms              1/1     Running   329        13d
kube-state-metrics-5cb57bdc45-mqv9d       1/1     Running   0          35d
metricbeat-beat-metricbeat-2xm7t          1/1     Running   6103       35d
metricbeat-beat-metricbeat-96dkt          1/1     Running   6097       35d
metricbeat-beat-metricbeat-n7kxm          1/1     Running   6109       35d
```

Now, to get just the pod names, you can cut the lines on the space character. Note that the cut command "cuts" on each delimiter character, not on a sequence of them. In this case, you can grab the first field like so:

```
$ kubectl get pods | cut -d' ' -f 1
NAME
elastic-operator-0
elk-apm-server-65b698fb8c-rzncz
elk-es-default-0
elk-kb-6f8bb6457b-bbbnn
filebeat-beat-filebeat-ccgl7
filebeat-beat-filebeat-dvf2l
filebeat-beat-filebeat-mnpms
kube-state-metrics-5cb57bdc45-mqv9d
metricbeat-beat-metricbeat-2xm7t
metricbeat-beat-metricbeat-96dkt
metricbeat-beat-metricbeat-n7kxm
```

Then, to strip the first line, you specify the `tail -n +2` command to show everything from the second line onward:

```
$ kubectl get pods | cut -d' ' -f 1 | tail -n +2
elastic-operator-0
elk-apm-server-65b698fb8c-rzncz
elk-es-default-0
elk-kb-6f8bb6457b-bbbnn
filebeat-beat-filebeat-ccgl7
filebeat-beat-filebeat-dvf2l
filebeat-beat-filebeat-mnpms
kube-state-metrics-5cb57bdc45-mqv9d
metricbeat-beat-metricbeat-2xm7t
metricbeat-beat-metricbeat-96dkt
metricbeat-beat-metricbeat-n7kxm
```

Bingo: you've removed the heading line. If you followed along with the examples in the previous chapter, you might have spotted that you could also just filter the content with grep to get the same result:

```
$ kubectl get pods | cut -d' ' -f 1 | grep -v NAME
elastic-operator-0
elk-apm-server-65b698fb8c-rzncz
elk-es-default-0
elk-kb-6f8bb6457b-bbbnn
filebeat-beat-filebeat-ccgl7
filebeat-beat-filebeat-dvf2l
filebeat-beat-filebeat-mnpms
kube-state-metrics-5cb57bdc45-mqv9d
metricbeat-beat-metricbeat-2xm7t
metricbeat-beat-metricbeat-96dkt
metricbeat-beat-metricbeat-n7kxm
```

Using grep with the -v flag returns all lines except the ones that match—the NAME line in this case. With just a few simple shell commands, you often have many ways to accomplish the same goal.

Another way to use cut is by slicing a number of characters from each line. Take a look at this sample web logfile:

```
$ tail ~/effective-shell/logs/web-server-logs.txt
2025-07-01T12 50:52.721Z: info - Request: GET /en.search.min.1f83b222e24a227c0f5763727cb9e4f...
2025-07-01T12 50:52.722Z: info - Serving file '../../../website/public/en.search.min.1f83b22...
2025-07-01T12 50:52.762Z: info - Request: GET /svg/menu.svg
2025-07-01T12:50:52.763Z: info - Serving file '../../../website/public/svg/menu.svg'...
2025-07-01T12:50:52.763Z: info - Request: GET /svg/calendar.svg
2025-07-01T12:50:52.764Z: info - Serving file '../../../website/public/svg/calendar.svg'...
2025-07-01T12:50:52.765Z: info - Request: GET /svg/edit.svg
2025-07-01T12:50:52.766Z: info - Serving file '../../../website/public/svg/edit.svg'...
2025-07-01T12:50:52.784Z: info - Request: GET /fonts/roboto-v19-latin-300italic.woff2
2025-07-01T12:50:52.785Z: info - Serving file '../../../website/public/fonts/roboto-v19-lati...
```

With the -c ("characters") flag, you can specify the characters in the line you want to see. To extract only the characters 12 to 19, which is the time part of each line, run the following command:

```
$ tail -n 3 ~/effective-shell/logs/web-server-logs.txt | cut -c 12-19
12:50:52
12:50:52
12:50:52
```

You can also use -c to extract everything from a specific point onward:

```
$ tail -n 3 ~/effective-shell/logs/web-server-logs.txt | cut -c 27-
info - Serving file '../../../website/public/svg/edit.svg'...
info - Request: GET /fonts/roboto-v19-latin-300italic.woff2
info - Serving file '../../../website/public/fonts/roboto-v19-latin-300italic.woff2'...
```

Cutting from the 27th character onward (-c 27-) removes the time-stamp and leaves just the log message.

As a nice trick, you can use the same syntax to split by fields, as in this example from the Rotten Tomatoes CSV file:

```
$ tail -n 3 ~/effective-shell/data/top100.csv | cut -d',' -f 3-
"Pinocchio (1940)","55"
"Chinatown (1974)","75"
"The Dark Knight (2008)","342"
```

This returns the third field, Title, onward. To output just the second and third fields, specify them like so:

```
$ tail -n 3 ~/effective-shell/data/top100.csv | cut -d',' -f 2,3
"100","Pinocchio (1940)"
"99","Chinatown (1974)"
"94","The Dark Knight (2008)"
```

You can do a surprising amount with the cut tool. As I introduce more complex tools later on, like sed and awk, you'll see other ways to accomplish the same goals. But I often find that by filtering down the content with grep first, I can cut my way to what I need without using the more complex tools.

Reversing Text

The rev ("reverse") command simply reverses the given input:

```
$ echo "A nut for a jar of tuna" | rev
anut fo raj a rof tun A
```

At first glance this doesn't seem very useful, but now try this:

```
$ pwd | rev | cut -d/ -f 1 | rev
effective-shell
```

This command reverses the current working directory, cuts the first folder, and then reverses it again. Here is what's happening at each stage:

pwd	/Users/dwmkerr/effective-shell
rev	llehs-evitceffe/rrekmwd/sresU/
cut -d'/' -f 1	llehs-evitceffe
rev	effective-shell

This neat trick extracts all of the text from the first character to the first forward slash (/). This action would be much harder to do without reversing the text first, because you don't know how many levels are in the directory. This way, you can simply extract the *last* folder without knowing how many precede it.

You probably won't use this technique very often in real-world scenarios, but it's a good reminder that you can often do more than you think by piping together simple commands.

Sorting Text and Removing Duplicate Lines

Two other commands that can be really helpful are sort ("sort lines alphabetically") and uniq ("omit duplicate lines"), both of which were introduced in Chapter 2. You can combine sort with the other commands and flags you've been working with:

```
$ cut -d',' -f 3 ~/effective-shell/data/top100.csv | sort | head
"12 Years a Slave (2013)"
"A Hard Day's Night (1964)"
"A Night at the Opera (1935)"
"A Quiet Place (2018)"
"A Star Is Born (2018)"
"Alien (1979)"
"All About Eve (1950)"
"Argo (2012)"
"Arrival (2016)"
"Avengers: Endgame (2019)"
```

Here you've grabbed the third field in the CSV file (Title), sorted its contents alphabetically, and then displayed the first 10 values.

You can reverse the direction of sort with the -r ("reverse") flag:

```
$ cut -d',' -f 3 ~/effective-shell/data/top100.csv | sort -r | head
"Zootopia (2016)"
"Wonder Woman (2017)"
"Won't You Be My Neighbor? (2018)"
"Widows (2018)"
"War for the Planet of the Apes (2017)"
"Us (2019)"
"Up (2009)"
"Toy Story 4 (2019)"
"Toy Story 3 (2010)"
"Toy Story 2 (1999)"
```

There are quite a few other options for sort; to see them, run man sort.

The uniq command removes duplicate lines from a stream of text—but only when they are next to each other, so you'll often have to sort first. You can use uniq to get all unique error messages in a logfile like so:

```
$ cut -c 27- ~/effective-shell/logs/web-server-logs.txt | grep error | sort | uniq
error - Unhandled error EACCES trying to read '../../../website/public/docs/part-1-transiti...
error - Unhandled error EACCES trying to read '../../../website/public/svg/calendar.svg', r...
error - Unhandled error EACCES trying to read '../../../website/public/svg/edit.svg', retur...
info - Request: GET /docs/1-getting-started/images/ls-applications-windows-error.png
info - Request: GET /docs/part-1-transitioning-to-the-shell/3-managing-your-files/images/rm...
info - Serving file '../../../website/public/docs/1-getting-started/images/ls-applications-...
info - Serving file '../../../website/public/docs/part-1-transitioning-to-the-shell/3-manag...
```

Let's break this command down:

cut -c 27- ~/effective-shell/logs/web-server-logs.txt   Extracts log messages from a logfile, skipping the timestamp (the date and time that starts each line)

grep error   Filters down to lines containing the word *error*

sort   Alphabetically sorts the output

uniq   Shows only unique values, removing any adjacent duplicates

If you had thousands of errors in the file, this powerful technique would ensure that you see only *distinct* errors, not all of them.

Paging Through Text

The *pager* is a shell program that lets you interactively read a file by moving backward and forward one page at a time. (A *page* in this context is a section of the output that fits on the screen rather than overflowing it.) If you want to see a little bit of a large file, or if you're trying to build a pipeline and want to see intermediate results (perhaps before you use head or tail), you can use the pager to see and move through output without filling your screen and terminal with too much text.

NOTE   *For more information about the pager, see "Getting Help" on page 415.*

One common pager program is less ("open a file for interactive reading"). When viewing the sorted list of films, for example, you might run the following:

```
$ cut -d',' -f 3 ~/effective-shell/data/top100.csv | sort | less
```

Here's a sample page of the resulting output:

```
"Jaws (1975)"
"King Kong (1933)"
"La Grande Illusion (Grand Illusion) (1938)"
"La La Land (2016)"
"Lady Bird (2017)"
"Laura (1944)"
:
```

You've cut out the film names from the data file, sorted them, and then piped the results into less so that you can page through the data to ensure it is correct.

The less prompt (:) at the bottom of the screen indicates that you can use the keyboard to enter commands. You can press the spacebar to move to the next page. You can type u to move up or d to move down; or you can use the up and down arrow keys. To exit the pager, you type q. You can find all of these commands (and others) by running man less.

Summary

This chapter explored several tools and techniques for working with text. You saw how to extract only the first or final parts of a text file; translate characters; cut, sort, and reverse text; remove duplicate adjacent lines of output; and page through the results of a large file. You'll return to these basics again and again as you work with data in the shell.

In the next chapter, you'll learn how to perform more advanced text manipulation with the sed command.

7

ADVANCED TEXT MANIPULATION WITH SED

Chapter 6 introduced some simple commands for working with text. Now we'll look at a more sophisticated and powerful command: sed. You can use sed to quickly solve problems and perform advanced manipulation of text, such as removing or replacing specific lines in a file. You'll see several common ways to use it, work through some practical examples, and learn when you might want to consider using tools like awk or a programming language instead.

The sed ("stream editor") command, as briefly defined in Chapter 2, takes input from a text stream (which in many cases is simply a file or the output of another command), performs operations on the text, and then writes the output to stdout. It's an extremely effective tool for making complex transformations. That said, operations with sed can look a little intimidating at first, so we'll start with the basics. You'll soon see just how valuable this tool can be.

Transformations with sed

Rather than dissecting every nuance of sed, I'm going to show some real-world examples of how you can use the program. This approach not only allows you to see its functionality in easier-to-digest chunks but also keeps the exercises practical and relevant.

Replacing Text

First, install this chapter's samples to the *~/effective-shell* folder:

```
$ curl effective.sh | sh
```

The *effective-shell/scripts* folder includes an example script called *backup -config.sh* that copies a set of commonly used configuration files for various cloud providers to a backup folder. To view it, run the following:

```
$ cd ~/effective-shell/scripts
$ cat backup-config.sh
#!/usr/bin/env bash

# Make sure you have a backup directory.
mkdir ~/backup

# Copy over alicloud, aws, azure, gcp, and ssh config and credentials.
cp ~/.aliyun/config.json ~/backup/settings/aliyun/
cp ~/.aws/config ~/backup/settings/aws/
cp ~/.aws/credentials ~/backup/settings/aws/
cp ~/.azure/config ~/backup/settings/azure/
cp ~/.config/gcloud/credentials.db ~/backup/settings/gcloud/
cp ~/.ssh/config ~/backup/settings/ssh/
cp ~/.ssh/id_rsa ~/backup/settings/ssh/
cp ~/.ssh/id_rsa.pub ~/backup/settings/ssh/
```

To change the backup folder (which is *~/backup/settings*), you could open the configuration file and edit each line, but that process would be time-consuming and error-prone. Instead, you can use sed to change the name of the backup folder across the file. Note that in this example you're not actually changing the file, just outputting to the console what the changes would look like.

To change part of the path of the backup folder from *settings* to *configuration*, run the following command:

```
$ sed 's/settings/configuration/' backup-config.sh
#!/usr/bin/env bash

# Copy over alicloud, aws, azure, gcp, and ssh config and credentials.
cp ~/.aliyun/config.json ~/backup/configuration/aliyun/
cp ~/.aws/config ~/backup/configuration/aws/
cp ~/.aws/credentials ~/backup/configuration/aws/
cp ~/.azure/config ~/backup/configuration/azure/
```

```
cp ~/.config/gcloud/credentials.db ~/backup/configuration/gcloud/
cp ~/.ssh/config ~/backup/configuration/ssh/
cp ~/.ssh/id_rsa ~/backup/configuration/ssh/
cp ~/.ssh/id_rsa.pub ~/backup/configuration/ssh/
```

This example shows the basics of how sed works. You give sed an *expression*, which describes a set of operations you want to perform, and it applies that expression to the file you specify. As with most commands we've covered, it can apply the expression to input from stdin or from a specific file.

Let's look at the expression s/settings/configuration/ in detail:

s   Indicates that you want to run the *substitute* function, which replaces text

/   Denotes the start of the term or pattern you are searching for

settings   Represents the pattern itself, which in this case is just the literal text *settings*

/   Denotes the start of the text to replace the pattern with

configuration   Indicates the text to replace the search pattern with

/   Denotes the end of the replacement (note that you can also add flags after this slash; we'll look at some flags shortly)

You can provide a regular expression (described in detail in Chapter 4) as the search pattern. By default, sed uses basic regular expressions. To use extended regexes, add the -E ("use extended regular expressions") flag as follows:

```
$ sed -E 's/settings/configuration/' backup-config.sh
```

For an overview of the differences between basic and extended regexes, run man re_pattern to access the man pages describing them.

Applying Multiple Expressions

You can use the -e ("expression") parameter to supply multiple expressions to sed. For example, to delete your backup folders, you could run two substitutions as follows:

1. Replace the cp command with the rmdir command.
2. Remove the first parameter, the source file for cp, since rmdir doesn't need it. With this expression, you're removing everything up to the second tilde (~).

WARNING   *If you use rm -r instead of rmdir, which is very common, you run the risk of making a big mistake: passing the source file for the cp command as the first parameter to remove. In other words, running rm -r would delete both the source files for the backup and the backup folder itself! This is one place where using rmdir over rm makes more sense: it won't delete the source files if you make a mistake.*

Let's break down these steps to see what each one does in detail.

Replacing Text on Specific Lines

You'll start with the first expression, changing cp to rmdir:

```
$ sed -e 's/cp/rmdir/' backup-config.sh
#!/usr/bin/env bash

# Make sure you have a backup directory.
mkdir ~/backup

# Copy over alicloud, aws, azure, grmdir, and ssh config and credentials.
rmdir ~/.aliyun/config.json ~/backup/settings/aliyun/
rmdir ~/.aws/config ~/backup/settings/aws/
rmdir ~/.aws/credentials ~/backup/settings/aws/
rmdir ~/.azure/config ~/backup/settings/azure/
rmdir ~/.config/gcloud/credentials.db ~/backup/settings/gcloud/
rmdir ~/.ssh/config ~/backup/settings/ssh/
rmdir ~/.ssh/id_rsa ~/backup/settings/ssh/
rmdir ~/.ssh/id_rsa.pub ~/backup/settings/ssh/
```

Here you've provided a single expression with the -e parameter. In this case, the -e parameter is superfluous because you have only one expression, but you'll be adding the second expression shortly.

This code has changed all the cp commands to rmdir. But did you notice the bug? It has also changed the letters cp in the comment from this

```
# Copy over alicloud, aws, azure, gcp, and ssh config and credentials.
```

to this (bolded for emphasis):

```
# Copy over alicloud, aws, azure, grmdir, and ssh config and credentials.
```

It isn't the worst bug in the world, but you can avoid it by changing the expression to run only on lines that *start* with the letters cp like so:

```
$ sed -e '/^cp/s/cp/rmdir/' backup-config.sh
#!/usr/bin/env bash

# Make sure you have a backup directory.
mkdir ~/backup

# Copy over alicloud, aws, azure, gcp, and ssh config and credentials.
rmdir ~/.aliyun/config.json ~/backup/settings/aliyun/
rmdir ~/.aws/config ~/backup/settings/aws/
rmdir ~/.aws/credentials ~/backup/settings/aws/
rmdir ~/.azure/config ~/backup/settings/azure/
rmdir ~/.config/gcloud/credentials.db ~/backup/settings/gcloud/
rmdir ~/.ssh/config ~/backup/settings/ssh/
rmdir ~/.ssh/id_rsa ~/backup/settings/ssh/
rmdir ~/.ssh/id_rsa.pub ~/backup/settings/ssh/
```

Before the s indicating your substitution, you've now included an *address* that tells sed which lines it should apply the expression to. The address here is /^cp, a regular expression meaning "any line starting with cp."

Let's break down the /^cp/s/cp/rmdir/ expression:

/^cp An address to find lines starting with cp

/s The substitution function for replacing text

/cp The pattern—in this case, the literal text *cp*

/rmdir The text that should replace each occurrence of cp at the beginning of a line

/ The end of the replacement

To summarize, this expression operates on lines starting with the text cp and replaces cp with the text rmdir. The forward slash (/) tells sed where the address—that is, what the search and replace expression will work on—starts and ends. Some people use a hash mark (#) or pipe (|) rather than a forward slash to delimit expressions, typically because they want to use the forward slash as part of a pattern.

Because sed uses regular expressions by default, you could also write the preceding command as follows:

```
$ sed -E -e 's/^cp/rmdir/' backup-config.sh
```

This command doesn't specify an address, but the pattern to match in the substitution, ^cp, means the same thing as the address you just used: "any line starting with the text cp." I find the previous version clearer, as the address is the first thing you see in the expression.

USING SED ADDRESSES

Addresses can be used in many sed functions and are quite sophisticated. Here are a few examples:

/test Any line matching the pattern test

/test/! Any line *not* matching test

/6 Line six

/$ The last line

/1,10 Lines 1 to 10

/1,10! Lines *except* 1 to 10

Run **man sed** to learn more about addresses.

Removing Parts of a Line

The next step is to remove the first parameter (the source file) that you used for the original cp command because you don't want rmdir to delete the source file, only the destination folder (the second parameter). Essentially, you want to change the structure of the line from c) <file to back up> <backup folder> to rmdir <backup folder>. To do so, apply a new expression:

```
$ sed -E -e '/^cp/s/cp/rmdir/' -e '/^rmdir/s/~[^ ]+ //' backup-config.sh
#!/usr/bin/env bash

# Make sure you have a backup directory.
mkdir ~/backup

# Copy over alicloud, aws, azure, gcp, and ssh config and credentials.
rmdir ~/backup/settings/aliyun/
rmdir ~/backup/settings/aws/
rmdir ~/backup/settings/aws/
rmdir ~/backup/settings/azure/
rmdir ~/backup/settings/gcloud/
rmdir ~/backup/settings/ssh/
rmdir ~/backup/settings/ssh/
rmdir ~/backup/settings/ssh/
```

Here's the breakdown of the /^rmdir/s/~[^]+ // expression:

/^rmdir Use an address that matches lines starting with rmdir.

/s Use the substitution function to replace text.

/~[^]+ Search for the tilde and any sequence of one or more non-space characters up until the first space character.

/ Replace with no content.

/ End the replacement.

In this example, you don't include a replacement. The replacement part of the expression is empty, as indicated by the two forward slashes with nothing between them at the end of the expression. This command means you search for a tilde, match everything up until the next space, and then replace it with nothing—in other words, remove it!

Note the use of the -E flag to tell sed to use extended regexes. This way, you can use the plus sign (+) without escaping it with a backslash (\) first. In general, I recommend always using extended regular expressions; they're more commonly used and will be more familiar than basic regexes, especially if you work with programming languages as well as the shell (most programming languages that support regexes use extended regexes).

Let's look at a few other ways to use sed for some common tasks.

Stripping Comments

The script you've used so far includes comments (the text that follows the hash mark). To remove comments, as well as any whitespace that precedes them, use sed as follows:

```
$ sed -E 's/\s*#.*$//' backup-config.sh
mkdir ~/backup
cp ~/.aliyun/config.json ~/backup/settings/aliyun/
cp ~/.aws/config ~/backup/settings/aws/
cp ~/.aws/credentials ~/backup/settings/aws/
cp ~/.azure/config ~/backup/settings/azure/
cp ~/.config/gcloud/credentials.db ~/backup/settings/gcloud/
cp ~/.ssh/config ~/backup/settings/ssh/
cp ~/.ssh/id_rsa ~/backup/settings/ssh/
cp ~/.ssh/id_rsa.pub ~/backup/settings/ssh/
```

This command removes the comments at the beginning of the file, as well as the comment after the cp ~/.ssh/id_rsa line. The regex matches any hash mark and strips everything following it as well as the whitespace before it.

To delete the lines that used to contain comments and are now empty, use the d function:

```
$ sed -E -e 's/#.*$//' -e '/^\s*$/d' backup-config.sh
mkdir ~/backup
cp ~/.aliyun/config.json ~/backup/settings/aliyun/
cp ~/.aws/config ~/backup/settings/aws/
cp ~/.aws/credentials ~/backup/settings/aws/
cp ~/.azure/config ~/backup/settings/azure/
cp ~/.config/gcloud/credentials.db ~/backup/settings/gcloud/
cp ~/.ssh/config ~/backup/settings/ssh/
cp ~/.ssh/id_rsa ~/backup/settings/ssh/
cp ~/.ssh/id_rsa.pub ~/backup/settings/ssh/
```

This function is applied to all lines matching the line pattern, which in this case is a regular expression (^ *$) that matches any line made up only of space characters, including zero space characters (that is, empty lines).

Appending Text

In a regular expression, the dollar sign ($) represents the end of a line. If you want to add content to the end of lines, simply search for $ and replace it with whatever you want to end the line with. For example, to add a semicolon to the end of every line, simply enter **sed s/$/;/**. To do that only on certain lines, use a line pattern to limit where to apply the expression.

You could use this technique to make sure the script doesn't fail if one of the cp commands fails by adding || true at the end of the command (you'll understand why this works after running the example).

The following command strips comments, deletes empty lines, and then adds the text || true to the end of each line:

```
$ sed -E -e 's/#.*$//' -e '/^ *$/d' -e '/^cp/s/$/ || true/' backup-config.sh
#!/usr/bin/env bash

# Make sure you have a backup directory.
mkdir ~/backup

# Copy over alicloud, aws, azure, gcp, and ssh config and credentials.
cp ~/.aliyun/config.json ~/backup/settings/aliyun/ || true
cp ~/.aws/config ~/backup/settings/aws/ || true
cp ~/.aws/credentials ~/backup/settings/aws/ || true
cp ~/.azure/config ~/backup/settings/azure/ || true
cp ~/.config/gcloud/credentials.db ~/backup/settings/gcloud/ || true
cp ~/.ssh/config ~/backup/settings/ssh/ || true
cp ~/.ssh/id_rsa ~/backup/settings/ssh/ || true
cp ~/.ssh/id_rsa.pub ~/backup/settings/ssh/ || true
```

If a cp command fails, the shell sees || true, which tells it to "pass this step whether or not the command fails." This little trick ensures that the entire script won't fail if one of the cp commands fails. (You'll see more of it in Chapter 11.)

Prepending Text

In a regular expression, the caret (^) represents the start of a line. You can apply the same trick as with the dollar sign to add two more hash marks to the start of any comment line (that is, any line already beginning with a hash mark):

```
$ sed -E -e '/#/s/^/##/' backup-config.sh
###!/usr/bin/env bash

### Make sure you have a backup directory.
mkdir ~/backup

### Copy over alicloud, aws, azure, gcp, and ssh config and credentials.
cp ~/.aliyun/config.json ~/backup/settings/aliyun/
cp ~/.aws/config ~/backup/settings/aws/
cp ~/.aws/credentials ~/backup/settings/aws/
cp ~/.azure/config ~/backup/settings/azure/
cp ~/.config/gcloud/credentials.db ~/backup/settings/gcloud/
cp ~/.ssh/config ~/backup/settings/ssh/
cp ~/.ssh/id_rsa ~/backup/settings/ssh/
cp ~/.ssh/id_rsa.pub ~/backup/settings/ssh/
```

Now you'll use echo or write the cp command to the screen. Replace the start of the line with an echo command and the end of the line with a quote, like so:

```
$ sed -E -e '/^cp/s/$/"/' -e '/"$/s/^/echo "/' backup-config.sh
#!/usr/bin/env bash
```

```
# Make sure you have a backup directory.
mkdir ~/backup

# Copy over alicloud, aws, azure, gcp and ssh config and credentials.
echo "cp ~/.aliyun/config.json ~/backup/settings/aliyun/"
echo "cp ~/.aws/config ~/backup/settings/aws/"
echo "cp ~/.aws/credentials ~/backup/settings/aws/"
echo "cp ~/.azure/config ~/backup/settings/azure/"
echo "cp ~/.config/gcloud/credentials.db ~/backup/settings/gcloud/"
echo "cp ~/.ssh/config ~/backup/settings/ssh/"
echo "cp ~/.ssh/id_rsa ~/backup/settings/ssh/"
echo "cp ~/.ssh/id_rsa.pub ~/backup/settings/ssh/"
```

You've now tweaked the script so that it doesn't actually copy the files; it just prints out the commands to the screen. The sed command you've written also demonstrates the importance of the order of the expressions: the second expression is applied after the first. If you're using multiple expressions, make sure that an earlier expression doesn't alter the line such that it breaks the next expression.

Extracting Information

What if you want to extract some information from lines in a file? Move into the *data* folder, which contains a file about movies called *top100.csv* that you may have seen in the previous chapter:

```
$ cd ~/effective-shell/data
$ head -n 3 top100.csv
"Rank","Rating","Title","Reviews"
"1","97","Black Panther (2018)","515"
"2","94","Avengers: Endgame (2019)","531"
```

To create a regular expression that finds the year for each movie, match all numeric values between parentheses like so:

```
$ head -n 3 data/top100.csv | sed -E 's/.*\(([0-9]+)\).*/\1/'
"Rank","Rating","Title","Reviews"
2018
2019
```

This command matches any text, captures any digits enclosed in parentheses (which in each case is the year the movie came out), and then prints the year to the screen with the \1 construct, which means "the first match." (See Chapter 4 for more about capture groups.)

You can also easily exclude the first line (the column heading) as follows:

```
$ sed -E -e '1d' -e 's/.*\(([0-9]+)\).*/\1/' data/top100.csv
2018
2019
```

Adding the 1d expression will delete the first line.

Advanced Applications

You've seen the basics of what sed can do, so now we'll explore some of the more sophisticated applications of the stream editor.

Restructuring Text

For this example, you'll use the *~/effective-shell/docs/chapter7.md* file, which starts with the following text:

```
$ cd ~/effective-shell/docs
$ head chapter7.md
---
title: "Advanced Text Manipulation"
slug: "advanced-text-manipulation"
weight: 14
---

# Chapter 7 - Advanced Text Manipulation

Chapter 6 introduced some simple commands to work with text...
...
```

This file has quite a complex structure—one that would be hard to manipulate without a sophisticated tool like sed.

This file starts with some YAML (Yet Another Markup Language) text in a key-value format. The key is specified first, and the value follows after the colon (:). Values can be surrounded by single or double quotes or not at all. If you're not familiar with key-value format, that's okay; this example is being used primarily to demonstrate more advanced sed techniques.

Let's say the goal is to write a sed command that shows each of the key-value pairs and adds quotes around any value that doesn't already have them. You'll use grep (covered in Chapter 5) to quickly build a regex to find the key-value pairs, and once you've verified that the regex works, you'll use it in your sed command.

First, you need to extract the keys. As you build the expression required, you're going to pipe the results to head to show only the first 10 lines (a preview of the results); otherwise, the command would show more output than fits on the screen (I've bolded the matches throughout this section for clarity):

```
$ grep -E '[^:]+:' chapter7.md | head
title: "Advanced Text Manipulation"
slug: advanced-text-manipulation
weight: 14
Let's say we have a script that is used to back up some local files
to an Amazon S3 bucket. We can see a script like this here:
...
```

Well, this kind of worked. The first three matches are correct. The command found the keys, but it also found any line that includes a colon.

The pattern [^:]+: means "find at least one character that is not the : character but is followed by the : character." This simple expression finds *everything* before the first colon, including any text in the rest of the file that contains a colon. The text beginning on the fourth line is just a sentence from the chapter.

To improve on it, you could tell the shell not to include lines that have space characters before the colon and be explicit that the pattern you're searching for must appear at the *start* of the line:

```
$ grep -E '^[^: ]+:' chapter7.md | head
title: "Advanced Text Manipulation"
slug: advanced-text-manipulation
weight: 14
"2","94","Avengers: Endgame (2019)","531"
```

Much better. The pattern now starts with the caret (^), which means "start of line," followed by [^:] to search for "anything that is not a colon or space." But notice this command also found a film title from the text, because just like the YAML, this line doesn't have any space characters before the colon.

To improve the pattern further, you could eliminate lines that have quotation marks before the colon, as quotes are not valid in YAML key names. The updated pattern looks like this:

```
$ grep -E '^[^: "]+:' chapter7.md | head
title: "Advanced Text Manipulation"
slug: advanced-text-manipulation
weight: 14
```

By refining the regex, you've ensured that now grep will find only the YAML keys. Using grep is a quick way to iteratively build your regex until it does what you need it to. Now you can take this regex and use it in sed.

BUILDING REGULAR EXPRESSIONS

I was a holdout for years, but now I readily acknowledge that regexes are incredibly useful if you take the time to learn them. Exercises like these are a great way to do so. Start simple and add the elements you need bit by bit to learn exactly what each one does.

Avoid just searching online for the perfect expression; the ones you find will often be very long (because they are bulletproof, hopefully, and cover every possible edge case). If you're building an expression that is critical to get right, then by all means search online for help if you need it, but for day-to-day tasks, practice makes perfect. See Chapter 4, which goes into regexes in detail.

To start using this regex in sed, first print all lines that match the pattern:

```
$ sed -E -n '/^[^: "]+:/p' chapter7.md
title: "Advanced Text Manipulation"
slug: advanced-text-manipulation
weight: 14
```

You've made two critical additions to sed here. The first is the -n ("no automatic printing") flag, which means sed won't show output unless you explicitly tell it to. The second is the p ("print") function, which will print any lines that match the pattern.

Without these additions, sed will output the whole file to the screen. Adding these options make sed behave like grep: it will show only the lines that match, which is useful when you're still building the command and just want to see the lines you're going to change.

Now, to put the result in quotes, you need to find lines where the value is not already quoted:

```
$ sed -E -n '/^[^: "]+: +[^"]+$/p' chapter7.md
slug: advanced-text-manipulation
weight: 14
```

Let's break down the /^[^: "]+: +[^"]+$/p expression:

/^[^ :"]+:   Match the start of a line and then any characters that are not a space, a colon, or a quote but are followed by a colon and a space.

+[^"]+$ Match at least one space and then any set of characters that don't contain a quote, all the way to the end of the line.

The pattern is working: it found the two unquoted keys. Now you'll get it to print the substitution.

First, you'll surround the key and value parts in parentheses to make them *capture groups*, or chunks of text you can use in the substitution. Here's an example that shows how to output the first capture group:

```
$ sed -E -n 's/(^[^: "]+:)( +[^"]+$)/Key is "\1"/p' chapter7.md
Key is "slug:"
Key is "weight:"
```

Remember, you're not just searching for a pattern; you're using the s function to substitute all the matched text with Key is "\1". The \1 means "the first match," or what you found in the first capture group.

You could just as easily show the second capture group, or the value, like so:

```
$ sed -E -n 's/(^[^: "]+:)( +[^"]+$)/Value is "\2"/p' chapter7.md
Value is " advanced-text-manipulation"
Value is " 14"
```

These examples don't quite split up the expression properly. The first capture group contains the colon, and the second contains the space that follows the colon. The colon and space are the separators for the key-value pair, so rather than capture them as part of the key or value, you'll make a third capture group to capture the separator:

```
$ sed -E -n 's/(^[^: "]+)(: +)([^"]+$)/Key "\1", Value "\3", Separator "\2"/p' chapter7.md
Key "slug", Value "advanced-text-manipulation", Separator ": "
Key "weight", Value "14", Separator ": "
```

At this point, the sed and p expression has been able to exactly capture the key, separator, and value.

Now, to tie it together, you can add quotes around the unquoted values:

```
$ sed -E -n 's/(^[^: "]+)(: +)([^"]+$)/\1\2"\3"/p' chapter7.md
slug: "advanced-text-manipulation"
weight: "14"
```

Awesome! Now you can take the lines that were missing quotes; break them up into keys, values, and separators; and then rewrite them in the correct format with the quotes added.

If you wanted to change the file, you could remove the -n flag in order to write out everything, which means you'd no longer need the p option at the end of the substitution. Now, run the substitution and write the results to a file called *updated.md* as follows:

```
$ sed -E 's/(^[^: "]+)(: +)([^"]+$)/\1\2"\3"/' chapter7.md > updated.md
```

Then you can use head to check the top of the file you've created to confirm that it looks right:

```
$ head -n 10 updated.md
---
title: "Advanced Text Manipulation"
slug: "advanced-text-manipulation"
weight: "15"
---
```

All the values in the YAML at the top of the file are now surrounded with quotes. You've found a very specific pattern in a large file, substituted text to match what you need, and then saved the results.

This example has just scratched the surface of what you can do with sed, but you've seen that you can accomplish an incredible amount even with the basic tools. For example, if you didn't want to quote values that are only numbers, just change the pattern like so:

```
$ sed -E -n '/(^[^: "]+:)( +[^"0-9]+$)/p' chapter7.md
slug: advanced-text-manipulation
```

All you've done is change the value pattern from [^"] ("anything except quotes") to [^0-9] ("anything except quotes and digits").

Creating Template Files

Another technique I've found useful again and again is to use sed's text replacement capabilities to create a basic templating system. For this example, you'll use the *~/effective-shell/templates/credentials.sh* file, which contains a username and password:

```
$ cd ~/effective-shell/templates
$ cat credentials.sh
USERNAME=admin
PASSWORD=ThisIsVerySensitive!
```

Say you don't want to store the password in the file itself since it might be sensitive. You could define an easy-to-find pattern as a placeholder in the file, then replace it with sed.

In the *templates* folder, you'll also find a template version of the file, which includes a placeholder for the password text:

```
$ cat credentials.template.sh
USERNAME=admin
PASSWORD=%PASSWORD%
```

Apply the substitution as follows:

```
$ sed -e 's/%PASSWORD%/secret/' credentials.template.sh
USERNAME=admin
PASSWORD=secret
```

This command has searched for the pattern and replaced it with the provided value. Note that if you find yourself creating template files like this, you might find the envsubst ("substitute environment variables") command useful to explore.

Editing in Place

The sed command includes an "in place" feature that allows you to directly change the file you pass it:

```
$ sed -i '.bak' 's/staging/production/' test.txt
```

This command performs the substitutions and puts them in a new file with a *.bak* extension. To overwrite the existing file instead, do the following:

```
$ sed -i 's/staging/production/' test.txt
```

In this case, you're not appending anything to the name of the overwritten file; instead, you're replacing the original file.

The -i ("in place") flag works differently on some systems (such as macOS), so I generally prefer to output the result of sed to a new file and then replace the old one. However, it's useful to know what this flag is and how it is used, as you'll see it often in scripts and online examples.

Alternatives to sed

The stream editor is very powerful, but it's not the right solution for every scenario. Here are a couple of common alternatives:

awk

If you're researching how to perform more complex text-based operations, you'll often see awk in the mix as a potential solution.

The awk tool is very sophisticated and has its own language to support complex text manipulation. My advice is to first master sed and then turn to awk if you regularly find that you need more than sed can offer.

Programming languages

If I have tasks that are too complex for me to solve with my fairly basic knowledge of sed, I will generally write a small program in Python, Node.js, or another high-level and expressive language to do the work, and call that instead. This code will often be easier to maintain and understand than an extremely complex sed expression, but you'll have to decide on a case-by-case basis when to move from a shell command to a programming language. (See Chapter 21 for an example of a complex operation that uses a Python script rather than the shell.)

Summary

In this chapter, you learned all about sed, the stream editor tool, and how to write expressions for it to transform or otherwise manipulate text. You got a closer look at regular expressions, saw how to apply line patterns to control which lines of text sed operates on, and explored using patterns and capture groups to extract information.

In the next chapter, you'll meet xargs, a tool that enables you to manipulate text and then execute it as a shell command.

8

BUILDING COMMANDS
ON THE FLY

This chapter will introduce you to the xargs command, a powerful tool that enables you to build and modify commands dynamically. If you've been following along with the previous chapters on text manipulation, some of these techniques will be familiar. Instead of simply manipulating existing text, however, now you'll be leveling up your skills by actually creating and executing new commands to perform complex operations.

Introducing xargs

The xargs ("build and execute commands") command takes input, uses that input to create commands, and then executes those commands. I tend to remember it as "execute with arguments," as xargs sounds a little odd! Some people pronounce the command "x-args," and others pronounce it "zargs."

It's probably easiest to understand how xargs works with some examples. To start, you'll use it to build a set of commands that will remove any empty files from a folder. First, install this chapter's samples to the ~/*effective-shell* folder:

```
$ curl effective.sh | sh
```

You'll use touch ("create files and set access times") to create some empty files that you'll be cleaning up later:

```
$ mkdir -p ~/effective-shell/tmp
$ cd ~/effective-shell/tmp
$ touch file{1..100}.txt
```

If the file you specify doesn't exist, touch creates it; otherwise, touch updates the file's last modified or last accessed time. This code uses a nice shell trick called *brace expansion*, in which the shell expands *file{1..100}.txt* to *file1.txt*, *file2.txt*, and so on, all the way to *file100.txt*. Brace expansion is just one feature of a rich set of capabilities called *shell expansion*, which Chapter 20 describes in detail.

Now you can search for empty files with the find ("find files and folders") command like so (see Chapter 3 for more on the find command):

```
$ find . -empty
file1.txt
file2.txt
file3.txt
file4.txt
file5.txt
...
```

To delete each empty file that find returned, pipe the list of files to the rm ("remove file") command:

```
$ find . -empty | rm
rm: missing operand
Try 'rm --help' for more information.
```

Uh-oh, what's going on here? The issue is that rm doesn't actually read the list of files from stdin, so you have to pass it that list as a parameter. This is where xargs can help. See what happens when you pass the list to xargs:

```
$ find . -empty | xargs
./file40.txt ./file8.txt ./file35.txt ./file81.txt ...
```

By default, xargs takes the input, separates each line with a space, and passes the list of files to the echo command. The echo command then writes the list out to the screen.

You can change the command that xargs passes the arguments to as follows:

```
$ find . -empty | xargs echo rm
rm ./file40.txt ./file8.txt ./file35.txt ./file81.txt ...
```

This tells xargs to pass the output to the echo command with rm as its first argument, which writes out rm followed by the list of files. Putting echo before whatever command you want to run is a useful way to check the command before committing to running it.

Enter the following to finish the job and delete each file:

```
$ find . -empty | xargs rm
```

Finally, run **ls** to confirm that the files have been deleted.

As you've seen, xargs constructs and executes a command with arguments from standard input. This is a great way to build complex commands dynamically. Let's see how you can take it further.

Handling Whitespace, Special Characters, and Tracing

One common challenge with xargs is how to deal with whitespace. To see what I mean, create three files with spaces in their names like so:

```
$ touch "chapter "{1,2,3}.md
$ find . -type f
./chapter 1.md
./chapter 2.md
./chapter 3.md
```

Then try deleting these files with rm:

```
$ find . -type f | xargs rm
rm: cannot remove './chapter': No such file or directory
rm: cannot remove '1.md': No such file or directory
...
```

What went wrong here? Use the -t ("trace") option to show the command that xargs actually tried to run:

```
$ find . -type f | xargs -t rm
rm ./chapter 1.md ./chapter 2.md ./chapter 3.md
```

Hopefully you can spot the error: the filenames include a space, and since you haven't enclosed them in quotes, rm thinks you're providing six files to delete rather than three.

Fortunately, find works well with xargs since they're part of the same package of tools (called findutils), and there's a special pair of options that can deal with this problem. For find, you'll use the -print0 action, and for xargs, you'll use the -0 option:

```
$ find . -type f -print0 | xargs -0 -t rm
rm './chapter 1.md' './chapter 2.md' './chapter 3.md'
```

The find command's default action is -print ("print to stdout"), which writes out the path of each item found, followed by a newline. The -print0 ("print to stdout followed by NUL") action is very similar but instead writes out each item followed by a special "null" character (normally represented as \0 or NUL). This null character is a bit like a line ending or whitespace character. Using it to separate the filenames and telling xargs to delimit its input with null fixes the issue of having spaces in the filenames.

After telling find to end each result with a special null character, you use the -0 ("use NUL as separators") option to tell xargs that this character is what separates each line of input.

NOTE   *The NUL character is the ASCII character 0 and is often used in programming to represent null or "nothing at all," as opposed to the digit zero used when printing to the screen, which is represented by decimal number 30 (or hexadecimal 48). To see the ASCII table, run* **man ascii.**

Don't worry if you don't really understand these internals. If you're a computer programmer, they might make sense since this is how strings in programming languages like C work, but otherwise all you need to know is that they prevent the xargs program from getting confused when it sees spaces, tabs, quotes, newlines, and the like in a filename.

I recommend always pairing up the -print0 action with the -0 option so you won't get caught out by odd filenames. And remember that you can always use the -t option to trace what xargs is doing!

Customizing How xargs Processes Input Lines

In the examples you've seen so far, every input to xargs has come in on its own line or separated by NULs. For instance, after creating five files, this call to find writes five lines of output, one for each file found:

```
$ touch "file"{1..5}
$ find . -type f
./file1
./file2
./file3
./file4
./file5
```

However, when this output is piped to xargs as input, xargs combines all five lines and passes them as a *set* of arguments to a single command execution:

```
$ find . -type f | xargs echo
./file1 ./file2 ./file3 ./file4 ./file5
```

You don't need to provide echo to xargs since that's the default behavior, but I've added it here for clarity. What's important to note is that echo is called just once with all five files as arguments.

You can modify this behavior by using the -L ("max lines") parameter to specify how many input lines xargs processes per command execution. The following command, for example, ensures that the echo command executes for *each* line of input rather than *all* lines:

```
$ find . -type f | xargs -L 1 echo
./file1
./file2
./file3
./file4
./file5
```

Now echo is called five times rather than just once.

Processing all arguments in a single command execution is typically faster, but there are limits to how many arguments a command can handle at once. The -L flag helps you work around this limitation by breaking the input into smaller chunks.

Let's look at another example. This command processes three lines at a time:

```
$ find . -type f | xargs -L 3 echo
./file1 ./file2 ./file3
./file4 ./file5
```

Specifying L -3 means echo will run twice, processing three files the first time and the remaining two files the second time. If there were seven input files, it would run three times: twice with three files and once with one file.

You might not use the -L parameter very often, but it's important to understand what it does because many of the other options you'll use *imply* -L 1. You'll see these options in the next set of examples.

Organizing the Parameters for Commands

You've probably noticed by now that xargs puts the arguments it is given at the end of the command you write. For example, if the command you provide is rm, the parameters *follow* the rm command that is written.

But what if you need the arguments to go somewhere other than the end of the command? For example, what if you wanted to copy every text file in a folder to another location? In that case, you need the *first* parameter of copy to be the source file and the *last* parameter to be the destination folder.

Here's how you might start building this command:

```
$ find . -name "*.txt" -print0 | xargs -0 -t cp ~/backups
cp /home/dwmkerr/backups ./file2.txt ./file3.txt ./file1.txt
cp: target './file1.txt' is not a directory
```

Obviously, this went wrong. The problem is that the destination location for the files has to be the *last* parameter, but xargs has made it the *first* parameter and put the list of files at the end of the command.

To fix this issue, you can tell xargs where to put the list of arguments with the -I ("replace string") parameter:

```
$ find . -name "*.txt" -print0 | xargs -0 -t -I {} cp {} ~/backups
cp ./file2.txt /home/dwmkerr/backups
cp ./file3.txt /home/dwmkerr/backups
cp ./file1.txt /home/dwmkerr/backups
```

This code sets the replacement string to a pair of braces ({}), which tells xargs "every time you see {} in the command string, replace it with your output." The {} is the first parameter for cp, which xargs expands to the list of files, ensuring that the cp command is constructed properly.

Using the -I parameter automatically implies -L 1, which means the resulting command is run once for each individual input line. This is helpful because xargs can perform the replacement multiple times. To see why this only makes sense with -L 1, look at this command:

```
$ find . -name "*.txt" -print0 | xargs -0 -t -I {} cp {} {}.backup
cp ./file2.txt ./file2.txt.backup
cp ./file3.txt ./file3.txt.backup
cp ./file1.txt ./file1.txt.backup
```

This uses the replacement string {} twice: once for the source file and once to create a new destination file with the same name but ending with .backup. Note that {} includes the full path, so files in subdirectories would be expanded like this:

```
bash
cp ./tmp/file1.txt ./tmp/file1.txt.backup
```

This may not be what you want if you're trying to put all backups in the current directory.

Processing all files at once with a single cp command wouldn't work because cp can have only one destination argument. By automatically using -L 1, xargs ensures that *each* input file gets its own separate cp command.

As you can see, the -I flag's ability to insert arguments anywhere in a command makes xargs much more versatile, enabling file operations and custom command structures that wouldn't be possible with the default argument placement.

Running Commands Interactively

The -p ("prompt") option tells xargs to ask you to confirm each command before running it. To test this, enter the following command to create a new *pics* folder in your home directory:

```
$ mkdir -p ~/pics
```

Now move to the *pictures* folder and interactively copy its contents to the new *pics* folder. For each picture, you'll be asked to enter y ("yes") to confirm and run the command or n ("no") to skip the command:

```
$ cd  ~/effective-shell/pictures
$ ls | xargs -t -I {} -p cp {} ~/pics/{}
cp .notes /home/dwmkerr/pics.notes?...n
cp laos-gch.JPG /home/dwmkerr/pics/laos-gch.JPG?...y
cp nepal-mardi-himal.jpeg /home/dwmkerr/pics/nepal-mardi-himal.jpeg?...y
```

This example shows how easily you can sort through a collection of photos or other files and interactively decide whether to copy each one. As a bonus, xargs tells you exactly what command it's planning to run, making it much easier to spot mistakes in commands before they're executed.

Running a Command for Each Input

If you want to run a command for each value in a string that's separated by a specific character, you can use the -d ("delimiter") parameter to specify how xargs should break up the input. As an example, say you want to run a command for each path in the PATH variable (the set of folders the shell will use to search for commands). Here's how this variable is structured:

```
$ echo $PATH
/usr/local/sbin:/usr/local/bin:/usr/sbin:/usr/bin:/sbin...
```

A single line of text shows each path separated by a colon (:). To pass each path to xargs, you'd have to split this string up into multiple lines. Instead, you can use the -d parameter to tell xargs that each input is separated by a colon:

```
$ echo $PATH | xargs -d ':' -p -L 1 ls
ls /usr/local/sbin ?...n
ls /usr/local/bin ?...n
```

The -L 1 and -p parameters ensure one command will be run for each input folder and display both a preview of the command and a prompt for confirmation before showing each folder's contents.

Summary

This chapter introduced xargs, a powerful utility that allows you to dynamically build complex commands. You can use it to preview how the resulting command will look, prompt for confirmation before executing a command, control how many commands are run, and more.

With the examples you've seen in this chapter, you'll be well equipped to use xargs in your day-to-day work. If you're interested in reading about more options for the xargs command, run man xargs.

This concludes Part II of the book, which introduced essential skills to manipulate text, search through and operate on files, and dynamically create commands that you can run interactively.

In the next part of the book, you'll learn how to write and run your own programs to automate tasks and tackle complex operations from the command line: it's time to meet *shell scripting*.

PART III

SHELL SCRIPTING

9

SHELL SCRIPT FUNDAMENTALS

In this chapter, you'll learn how to build *shell scripts*, text files made up of commands that run in sequence, allowing you to automate tasks and perform complex workflows. In addition, you'll explore different ways to run scripts, how to structure shell script files, and how to install scripts locally.

Even if you're already familiar with shell scripts, I suggest you skim this chapter to make sure you understand the core concepts, particularly the section "Specifying What Program Should Run a Script" on page 116, which describes how to make your scripts more portable. Also, you'll be iterating and improving on the basic shell script you create in this chapter later in Chapters 10 through 14, so you should familiarize yourself with it before skipping ahead.

Why Shell Scripts?

As soon as you find yourself repeating the same sequence of commands in a shell, it's time to consider saving those commands to a file and running the file instead.

Saving commands as a shell script has a number of benefits. It saves time since you don't have to type the commands whenever you want to run them. You can use your favorite editor to build the script file, and you can add comments to describe what you're trying to achieve (which will make it far easier for you or others to update the script over time). You can also easily share these script files, meaning you can copy them to other machines and run them in different locations or share them with people who might find them useful.

Creating a Basic Shell Script

To learn how to build and structure a shell script, you'll create a script that shows your "common" commands—that is, those you run most often in your shell. You'll enhance this basic script throughout the following chapters as you learn new techniques.

If you've been reading this book sequentially, many of the commands and techniques you'll use will already be familiar to you. You're just piecing them together in one place, which is the essence of the script-building process.

The script will do the following:

1. Read the commands from the shell history.
2. Sort the commands and count the number of duplicates to get an accurate total of how many times each command was run.
3. Sort this list to show the most commonly run commands.
4. Print the results to the screen.

If you haven't done so already, install this chapter's samples to the *~/effective-shell* folder:

```
$ curl effective.sh | sh
```

First, you'll create a place to hold your scripts and a file for the script itself. Enter the following commands to create a folder called *scripts* in your home directory, and add a new empty file to it called *common.v1.sh*:

```
$ mkdir -p ~/scripts
$ touch ~/scripts/common.v1.sh
```

The mkdir command creates a directory. The -p ("create parent directories if needed") flag stops the command from returning an error if the directory already exists. The touch command creates an empty file with the given name.

Adding Code Comments

Now that you've created your script file, you'll add some helpful comments to explain what the code does. *Comments* are notes you add to a script or program to help the reader (or your future self) understand what is going on. Any text that follows a hash mark (#) is a comment. The shell ignores comments whether you type them in a script or directly on the command line.

Here are a few examples of how comments can be used:

```
# This is a comment - use this to describe what you're trying to do.

echo "Hello Shell" # Comments can also go at the end of a line.

# You can also "comment out" a line of code so the shell ignores it:
# echo "Goodbye Shell"
```

The first comment takes up a whole line, the second comment is a briefer explanation at the end of a line, and the third comment demonstrates "commenting out" code—that is, putting a hash mark in front of a command so that it won't be executed.

Open your *common.v1.sh* file. Shell scripts are plaintext only, so you'll need to use a basic text editor like Gedit on Linux, Notepad on Windows, TextEdit on macOS, or a code editor like Visual Studio Code, Sublime Text, or Notepad++ to work with them. You can also edit files directly in the shell by using a terminal editor or Vim (see Chapter 23).

Add the following text to the beginning of the file:

```
# Inform the user of the output they can expect.
echo "common commands:"
```

The first line is a comment explaining your intention (namely, informing the user of the output they should expect from this script). Then echo prints the text common commands: to the screen. Once the script is finished, the commonly used commands will follow this title line.

Comments are most useful when they describe *why* you're doing something rather than *what* you're doing. After all, the "what" should be clear from the commands themselves, but your intent might not always be. That's why Inform the user of the output they can expect is a stronger comment than, say, Print "common commands:" to the screen would be.

If you don't come from a programming background, many of these comments might seem a little obvious. But as you write more and more code, you'll realize that something that seemed obvious to you when you wrote it can look surprisingly baffling even just a few days later.

From this point on, I'll use comments to explain what you're trying to accomplish with each section of your script.

Adding and Formatting Commands

Next, you'll add some commands to the *common.v1.sh* file. If you've installed the book's examples, copy and paste the commands from the *~/effective-shell/ scripts/common.v1.sh* file (be sure to add the backslashes and line breaks, which I'll discuss in a moment) or just directly edit your file so that it looks like this:

```
# Inform the user of the output they can expect.
echo "common commands:"

# Show the most commonly used commands.
tail ~/.bash_history -n 1000 \
    | sort \
    | uniq -c \
    | sed 's/^ *//' \
    | sort -n -r \
    | head -n 10
```

This short script takes the last 1,000 lines of the *~/.bash_history* file and performs various operations joined into a pipeline to show the most commonly used commands.

Rather than having one long line for the pipeline, you're breaking it into multiple lines using the backslash (\) as a *continuation character*, which tells the shell that the command continues across more than one line.

You can break commands up into as many lines as you like. However, the continuation character must be the last character on the line. If you add something after it (such as a comment), the command will fail.

Next, we'll take a closer look at each component of the script so far. Before proceeding, make sure to read the box about how to follow along.

FOLLOWING ALONG WITH THIS CHAPTER'S EXAMPLES

For the shell script you're writing in this chapter, you can either use your own history file, in which case your output will differ from what's shown here, or you can use the simplified history file at *~/effective-shell/data/history.txt*, which will make it a little easier to understand what's happening at each step. Here's how to do the latter:

```
$ cp ~/.bash_history ~/.bash_history.backup
$ cp ~/effective-shell/data/history.txt ~/.bash_history
$ history -c
$ history -r
```

First, you make a copy of your history file (so that you can restore it later) and then replace it with the book's sample history file. Using the history command with the -c ("clear") and -r ("reload") parameters tells the shell to reload the history file so that your bash history will match the one shown here.

> When you're ready to restore your original history, run the following commands:

```
$ mv ~/.bash_history.backup ~/.bash_history
$ history -c
$ history -r
```

Let's begin with the `tail` command and then look in turn at each command in the pipeline acting on its output.

Pipelining Commands

First, the `tail` command reads up to 1,000 of the most recent commands in your history file:

```
$ tail -n 1000 ~/.bash_history
vi README.md
git status
git checkout main
git status
restart-shell
git status
open .
vi README.md
open .
```

Next, the `sort` command puts duplicate lines next to each other so that you can easily count them later:

```
$ tail ~/.bash_history -n 1000 \
> | sort
git checkout main
git status
git status
git status
open .
open .
restart-shell
vi README.md
vi README.md
```

Notice that when you enter the backslash continuation character and press ENTER, the shell starts a new line with the right angle bracket (>). Anything you add after this symbol is "joined" to the previous line, as with the sort command here.

Next, `uniq` removes duplicate adjacent lines. Combining it with the -c ("show count") flag precedes each remaining line with some whitespace and the number of times the command occurred in the input (that is, the count of each command):

```
$ tail ~/.bash_history -n 1000 \
> | sort history.txt \
> | uniq -c
  1 git checkout main
  3 git status
  2 open .
  1 restart-shell
  2 vi README.md
```

The sed command removes the whitespace just added by the uniq -c command (for more on sed, see Chapter 7):

```
$ tail ~/.bash_history -n 1000 \
> | sort history.txt \
> | uniq -c
> | sed 's/^ *//'
1 git checkout main
3 git status
2 open .
1 restart-shell
2 vi README.md
```

Now you have a list of the commands from the history along with a count of how many times they've each been used. Using the sort command with the -n ("numerical sort") flag and the -r ("reverse") flag sorts the list in descending order to make it more readable:

```
$ tail ~/.bash_history -n 1000 \
> | sort history.txt \
> | uniq -c
> | sed 's/^ *//'
> | sort -n -r
3 git status
2 vi README.md
2 open .
1 restart-shell
1 git checkout main
```

The list of commands is now displayed with the most commonly used first, then the next, and so on.

NOTE *The -n flag tells sort to treat numbers as numerical values instead of as text, which ensures that larger numbers (such as 100) are correctly ordered before smaller ones (like 10), which wouldn't happen in the default text-based sort.*

Finally, `head -n 10` limits the results to the first 10 items, or the 10 most commonly used commands:

```
$ tail ~/.bash_history -n 1000 \
> | sort history.txt \
> | uniq -c
> | sed 's/^ *//'
> | sort -n -r
> | head -n 10
3 git status
2 vi README.md
2 open .
1 restart-shell
1 git checkout main
```

Now, rather than entering each command in the pipeline, you can run the following shell command to execute the script:

```
$ sh ~/scripts/common.v1.sh
```

The `sh` command starts a new shell. When you pass the path of a shell script as a parameter, `sh` runs that script and then exits.

This isn't the only way to run a shell script, however. You can also make it executable.

Making Shell Scripts Executable

To make a shell script executable, you must change its permissions with the `chmod` ("change permissions") command:

```
$ chmod +x ~/scripts/common.v1.sh
```

The `+x` option tells `chmod` to add the executable permission to the script (under the hood, this changes the file *mode*, hence the name `chmod`). Now you can simply enter its path into the shell and run it like any other command:

```
$ ~/scripts/common.v1.sh
```

In this example, the shell used to execute the script will depend on your system configuration. For example, bash will run the script in a new bash instance, whereas the Z shell typically runs scripts in `sh` (which may in turn be linked to *another* shell on your system).

Fortunately, there's a way to avoid this type of ambiguity and explicitly state what program should run your script.

Specifying What Program Should Run a Script

A *shebang* is a special construct that tells the system what program it should use to run a script. The shebang is composed of the hash mark (#) and the exclamation point (!) and is placed at the beginning of the file.

Here's how the *common.v1.sh* file would look with the shebang (although not required, it's common practice to add a blank line following the shebang line):

```
#!/usr/bin/sh

# Inform the user of the output they can expect.
echo "common commands:"

...
```

Immediately after the shebang, you write the full path to the program that should be used to open the file—in this case, that's the sh program.

To write a script that should run in Python, you could use the shebang as follows:

```
#!/usr/bin/python3

print('Hello from Python')
```

Or to explicitly use bash to run a script, you might write:

```
#!/usr/bin/bash

echo "Hello from bash"
```

There's one catch. This technique works only if the user running the script has the program installed in the location specified after the shebang. If they don't, the script will fail to run.

If you don't know where a program is installed, you can use the env ("set or print environment and execute command") command. While env is often used to display environment variables, you can also use it to find and run programs when you don't know their exact location on your system. It searches through the directories listed in your PATH variable to find the path of the command to execute.

For example, here's how you can use env to run the Python program:

```
$ env python3
Python 3.13.0 (main, Oct  7 2024, 05:02:14)

[GCC 9.3.0] on linux
Type "help", "copyright", "credits" or "license" for more information.
>>>
```

In this case, env works out the path for the python3 command on your system.

To use env in a shebang, specify the full path to env (which should be the same on all Unix-like systems) and then provide the program name like so:

```
#!/usr/bin/env bash

echo "Hello from bash"
```

Here's another example:

```
#!/usr/bin/env ruby

puts 'Hello from Ruby'
```

Combining a shebang with the env command like this is generally the safest and most portable way to specify how a shell script should run.

Sourcing Shell Scripts

Sourcing a shell script—that is, loading its contents into your current shell session and running commands there—is quite different from executing it. Executing a shell script creates a new shell as a child process of the current session. This means that if you change something in the environment, such as a variable, it won't affect the original shell environment (the one that ran the script). If your script crashes or exits the shell, it will only crash or exit the shell it is running in; your original shell will remain active.

When you source a script, however, you can change the current shell session directly and—if you're not careful—even end the shell process.

Let's look at an example. Create a script called *set_editor.sh* that sets the EDITOR environment variable to the nano text editor as follows (this script is also available at *~/effective-shell/scripts/set_editor.sh*):

```
EDITOR=nano
echo "Editor changed to: $EDITOR"
```

Check what your current editor is and then use the source ("execute commands from a file") command to load the *set_editor.sh* file:

```
$ echo $EDITOR
vim
$ source ~/effective-shell/scripts/set_editor.sh
Editor changed to: nano
$ echo $EDITOR
nano
```

Running echo $EDITOR a second time confirms that your editor has been changed from Vim to nano in the current shell rather than in a new one.

NOTE *You can use a slightly more concise syntax to source a script:* dot notation. *When the shell sees a dot (.) character, it will source the file that follows the dot just as if you'd spelled out the word* source. *In other words,* . ~/effective-shell/scripts/show -info.sh *is equivalent to* source ~/effective-shell/scripts/show-info.sh.

Now make the script executable and execute it to see the difference between sourcing and executing:

```
$ echo $EDITOR
vim
$ chmod +x ~/effective-shell/scripts/set_editor.sh
$ ~/effective-shell/scripts/set_editor.sh
Editor changed to: nano
$ echo $EDITOR
vim
```

Notice that although you changed the EDITOR environment variable in your script, the change has not persisted in the current shell; you're still using the Vim editor, not nano. This is because each shell (and in fact, each process) gets its own *copy* of the environment.

To demonstrate this even more clearly, try it using the *show-info.sh* script from the *scripts* folder. This script contains the pstree ("show process tree") command, which shows the current process and its parent process.

First, source the script:

```
$ source ~/effective-shell/scripts/show-info.sh
bash
  └─pstree -l -a -s 2169
```

This output is simple: your shell (the bash process) has run the pstree command.

Now see what happens when you execute the script:

```
$ ~/effective-shell/scripts/show-info.sh
bash
  └─sh /home/ubuntu/effective-shell/scripts/showpstree.sh
      └─pstree -l -a -s 2240
```

This time the pstree command was run as a child sh process. In other words, bash has run the *show-info.sh* script in a child shell.

In most cases, you'll want to execute a script in its own shell so that if the script changes the environment, exits, or crashes, your original shell is unaffected. You'll typically only source a shell script when you want to change the current shell—for example, to configure certain shell behaviors.

Installing Scripts Locally

Before we wrap up this discussion of shell script fundamentals, you'll install your script locally to make it even more convenient and easy to run. Your *common.v1.sh* script (with the added shebang) should currently look like this:

```
#!/usr/bin/env sh

# Inform the user of the output they can expect.
echo "common commands:"

# Show the most commonly used commands.
tail -n 1000 ~/.bash_history \
    | sort \
    | uniq -c \
    | sed 's/^ *//' \
    | sort -n -r \
    | head -n 10
```

If you didn't run `chmod` earlier to make your script executable, do so now:

```
$ chmod +x ~/scripts/common.v1.sh
```

To install this script as a local command that you can run easily, you can create a symbolic link to it in the */usr/local/bin* folder:

```
$ sudo ln -s ~/scripts/common.v1.sh /usr/local/bin/common
```

A *symbolic link* is like a shortcut in Windows and other operating systems. In this example, the `ln` ("create link") command creates a symbolic link called *common* in your */usr/local/bin* folder, pointing to your script. The sudo ("run command as superuser") command will ask for your password; this command is needed on most systems to grant permission to change the contents of this folder.

NOTE *Using the* /usr/local/bin *folder rather than the* /usr/bin *folder is just a convention. In general, the* /usr/bin *folder is for commands installed with package manager tools like* apt *on Debian-based distributions or Homebrew on macOS. The* /usr/local/bin *folder is typically used for commands you create and manage yourself on your local machine.*

Now you can run the `common` command from any folder without having to specify its path:

```
$ common
common commands:
3 git status
2 vi README.md
...
```

When the shell sees a command, it searches through the folders in the PATH environment variable to find the command. Because */usr/local/bin* is one of the folders in PATH, and that's where you put your symbolic link, the shell finds and runs your script when you type the `common` command.

Summary

In this chapter, you've learned how to create and run a shell script, how comments work, how to handle multiline commands, how shebangs and the env command work, how to make a shell script executable, and how to install scripts locally. Several topics we've touched on here—using dot notation, customizing the shell by sourcing scripts, and installing custom commands on your system—are covered in more depth in Chapter 15.

In the next chapter, you'll level up your shell scripting skills by learning how to add logic to your scripts. You'll then apply that new knowledge to enhance the basic *common.v1.sh* script you've built here.

10

USING VARIABLES TO STORE, READ, AND MANIPULATE DATA

A *variable* is a named container that stores data such as text, numbers, or command output. If you're reading this book in order, you've already seen variables a few times; for example, you may have used EDITOR and HISTFILE to specify your text editor and get your recent shell history, respectively. In this chapter, you'll learn all about how to use variables in your shell scripts to configure system settings, prompt for and read user input, calculate arithmetic values, and more. I'll walk you through the different types of variables, syntax conventions, and operations commonly performed with variables. Finally, you'll apply this knowledge to update your basic script from Chapter 9.

Let's begin by looking at the two main categories of variables: environment and shell variables.

Understanding Variable Scope: Environment vs. Shell Variables

Variables can be broadly categorized by their *scope*, or where they can be accessed. An *environment variable* is shared across your shell session and any commands you run. By convention, environment variables appear in all uppercase letters, and they often contain useful values that describe your system and how it is configured, like those listed in Table 10-1.

Table 10-1: Commonly Used Environment Variables

Variable	Description
SHELL	The current shell, such as bash
USER	The current user (on my machine, this is *dwmkerr*)
HOME	The current user's home directory (on my machine, this is */home/dwmkerr*)

To use the value of a variable in the shell, you start with the dollar sign ($) to specify the variable name:

```
$ echo "Your pager is: $PAGER"
Your pager is: less
```

The PAGER variable specifies what pager program the shell should use—in this case, the less program.

To see a list of the environment variables currently set in your system, use the env ("set or print environment and execute command") command:

```
$ env
SHELL=/bin/zsh
LSCOLORS=ExFxBxDxCxegedabagacad
COLORTERM=truecolor
PYENV_SHELL=bash
...
```

This list will vary depending on the operating system you are using and its configuration, but it will often be quite long.

Unlike environment variables, *shell variables* aren't shared across programs but exist only within your current shell session. These variables let you store temporary values for use in scripts or at the command line. To create or set a shell variable, enter the name you want to use followed by an equal sign (=) and the value to assign within double quotes:

```
$ name="Dave"
$ location="Singapore"
$ echo "Hello $name in $location"
Hello Dave in Singapore
```

This command creates two variables: one called name with the value Dave, and one called location with the value Singapore. As with environment variables, when you want to use the value of a shell variable in a command, you put a dollar sign before it.

It's best practice to use lowercase for shell variables to distinguish them from environment variables. This convention also helps reduce the risk of overwriting the value of an environment variable, which can have unexpected results.

For example, in this snippet I accidentally overwrite the USER variable:

```
USER="Dave Kerr"
```

Now, if I try to go to my home directory with cd /home/$USER, this command will fail because my system expects USER to be my username, dwmkerr, but I've set it to something else. Instead of */home/dwmkerr*, my system is looking for a directory named */home/Dave Kerr*, which doesn't exist.

Fortunately, if you overwrite an environment variable like this, the impact is limited to the script you're running or your current shell session; other running programs won't be affected.

Exporting Shell Variables as Environment Variables

By default, shell variables are isolated to the current process. That means if you run another process from your shell, such as another shell script or program, by design your shell variables won't be inherited by that child process. But what if you want them to be?

In that case, you can use the export ("set export attribute") built-in keyword to tell the shell to export the variable as an environment variable. Environment variables are always inherited by child processes, so if you need to pass along certain values or settings to a child process, you'll likely want to export your shell variable.

As an example, say you want to be able to have programs run in a "debug mode" where they display more diagnostic information to the user. You could set the following variable to activate this option:

```
$ export DEBUG_MODE=1
```

The export keyword promotes the DEBUG_MODE shell variable to an environment variable so that it's accessible to any child processes. (Notice the all-caps convention here since you're using an environment variable.) Now, any new program you create can just check the value of DEBUG_MODE to determine whether to output the extra diagnostic information. You can test it out by running a new shell with the sh command:

```
$ sh -c 'echo "Debug Mode is: ${DEBUG_MODE}"'
```

The -c ("command") parameter tells the sh program you're providing a *literal command* that will run in its own process (often called a *subshell*). Don't worry if the echo command doesn't totally make sense to you right now; we'll unpack it in the next section. The takeaway for now is that the subshell can access the value of the DEBUG_MODE variable to run in debug mode. Without the export keyword, `DEBUG_MODE` would remain a shell variable, invisible to any child processes.

Variable Syntax

You might have noticed that the echo command in the preceding example appears within single quotation marks and the `DEBUG_MODE` variable appears within braces ({}). These are two of the syntactical conventions you should be aware of when writing and referencing variables in your shell scripts. This section will cover these and other types of variable syntax.

Quoting Variables and Values

One topic often causes a lot of confusion for new shell users: When should you surround a variable with quotes? While it might sound like a purely stylistic question, quotes (or the lack thereof) can dramatically change how your script works.

Single Quotes

There are two main scenarios in which you use single quotes. The first is when you want to use special characters in a variable declaration without the shell trying to interpret them:

```
$ message='   ~~ Save $$$ on with ** "this deal" ** ! ~~   '
$ echo "$message"
   ~~ Save $$$ on with ** "this deal" ** ! ~~
```

When special characters or variables appear within single quotes, the shell treats them literally. In this example, the shell hasn't tried to interpret the tilde (~) as */home/dwmkerr* or the asterisks (*) as a wildcard pattern, and it hasn't tried to use the dollar sign to reference a variable.

Let's revisit the export example from the previous section:

```
$ sh -c 'echo "Debug Mode is: ${DEBUG_MODE}"'
```

The single quotes around `'echo "Debug Mode is: ${DEBUG_MODE-"'` prevent the current shell from expanding the `DEBUG_MODE` variable (that is, replacing it with its value, 1) so that it will pass the variable to the child process literally. When the child process inherits the current shell's environment, it effectively receives this command:

```
echo "Debug Mode is: ${DEBUG_MODE}"
```

Because the child process's input is *not* surrounded with single quotes, the child process expands and uses the `DEBUG_MODE` value to run in debug mode.

The second primary way to use single quotes is for *ANSI C quoting*, which allows you to include special characters that are used in the C programming language. To use ANSI C quoting, you put a dollar sign before the open quote:

```
$ message1='Hello\nWorld'
$ echo "Message 1: $message1"
Message 1: Hello\nWorld
$ message2=$'Hello\nWorld'
$ echo "Message 2: $message2"
Message 2: Hello
World
```

In the `message1` value, the newline escape sequence \n is interpreted incorrectly as literal text. But the `message2` value, where you use ANSI C quoting instead, displays correctly.

Double Quotes

Double quotes allow you to combine literal text and variable values in one declaration:

```
$ deal="Buy one get one free"
$ message="Deal is '$deal' - save \$"
$ echo "$message"
Deal is 'Buy one get one free' - save $
```

When you set the `message` variable, the shell doesn't treat the single quotes around `$deal` as special characters, because the whole value has been enclosed in double quotes. Instead of using `$deal` literally, the shell performs *parameter expansion*, replacing the `deal` variable with its value in the output. The backslash before the last dollar sign is an *escape character*: it tells the shell you want to use a literal dollar sign at the end of the message. In the output, the backslash is omitted.

Although expansion is the shell's default behavior, the double quotes are required here to ensure the shell expands only what you intend and ignores the rest.

No Quotes

If you leave out quotes altogether when declaring a variable, the shell will try to expand it by default:

```
$ home=~
$ echo "My home is: $home"
My home is: /home/dwmkerr
```

Here, the shell has expanded the tilde (~) to the home directory. See what happens when you add quotes around the tilde:

```
$ tilde="~"
$ echo "A tilde is: $tilde"
A tilde is: ~
```

Now the shell uses the literal value: the tilde character.

In addition to the tilde expansion shown here, the shell can perform these types of expansion:

Brace expansion   Expands values between braces, such as `touch file{1,2,3}` into `touch file1 file2 file3`

Parameter and variable expansion   Expands terms that start with a dollar sign into parameter values, such as `echo $SHELL` into `echo /usr/bin/sh` (as you've seen, using double quotes as in `echo "$SHELL"` also works for parameter expansion)

Command substitution   Evaluates the contents of `$(command)` sequences to run commands in a subshell, as in `echo $(date)` to echo the results of the date command (using double quotes as in `echo "$(date)"` also works for command substitution)

Arithmetic expansion   Evaluates the contents of `$((expression))` sequences to perform basic mathematical operations, such as `4 * 4` in `square=$((4 * 4))`

Word splitting   Splits up text and input into "words," or sequences of text that you can run operations such as loops over (a more complex topic covered in Chapter 12)

Pathname expansion   Expands wildcards and special characters in pathnames, such as `ls *.txt` to return all filenames that include *.txt*

Later in this chapter, I'll talk more about parameter expansion in the section "Expanding Shell Parameters" on page 130, and more about arithmetic expansion in "Performing Arithmetic Operations" on page 135. Brace expansion and other types of shell expansion are covered in more detail in Chapter 20.

QUOTING RULES OF THUMB

Quoting can seem confusing, but remember these tips and you'll generally be on the right path:

- Use **double quotes** most of the time: they handle variables and subshells for you and don't do complex operations like word splitting.
- Use **single quotes** for literal values.
- Use **no quotes** if you want to use all shell expansion features.

Hopefully you're a little clearer now on when to use each type of quoting, but if you ever need a reminder, run `man bash` and search for the text `QUOTING`.

Using Braces to Reference Variables Explicitly

When you append text directly to a variable name, the shell can't tell where the variable name ends and the additional text begins. For example:

```
$ echo "Creating backup folder at: '$USER_backup'"
$ mkdir $USER_backup
Creating backup folder at: ''
usage: mkdir [-pv] [-m mode] directory ...
```

Rather than creating a folder called *dwmkerr_backup* (which is my USER variable followed by the text *_backup*), this script fails because it's looking for a variable named USER_backup, which does not exist.

To avoid such errors, you can surround the variable name with braces to refer to a variable more explicitly:

```
$ echo "Creating backup folder at: '${USER}_backup'"
$ mkdir "${USER}_backup"
Creating backup folder at: 'dwmkerr_backup'
```

Now the script correctly interprets the command and creates the *dwmkerr _backup* folder.

If there's ever any potential ambiguity with a variable name, enclose it with braces to be on the safe side. This is exactly why DEBUG_MODE was enclosed in braces when you launched the shell earlier to run a child process in debug mode. Some people *always* use braces to be as explicit as possible about the variable name and reduce the risk of mistakes if someone comes along later to edit or change the code.

To improve this script further, you could create a new variable that holds the backup directory:

```
$ backupdir="${USER}_backup"
$ echo "Creating backup folder at: '${backupdir}'"
$ mkdir "${backupdir}"
```

Creating the backupdir variable saves you from having to repeat the ${USER}_backup text each time you want to use it.

Common Variable Operations

Now that you've got the syntax down, you're ready to see how you can put variables to use in your shell scripts. This section will walk you through some of the most common operations you'll perform with variables.

Storing a Command's Output in a Variable

You can use a subshell to store a command's output in a variable using the following format:

```
variable=$(command)
```

Say you're creating a variable to hold a user's password but you want to mask the password onscreen by replacing the characters with asterisks:

```
$ password="somethingsecret"
$ masked_password=$(echo "$password" | sed 's/./*/g')
$ echo "Setting password '${masked_password}'..."
Setting password '***************'...
```

First, you define a variable called `password` with the value `somethingsecret`. Then you use `sed` (covered in Chapter 7) to replace each letter with an asterisk for privacy, storing that output in another variable called `masked_password`. Finally, you print a message to the screen that displays the masked password.

Managing Multiple Values with Arrays

Arrays are variables that can store multiple values, which make them useful for working with sequences of values such as numbers, sets of files, or collections of user input. To create an array, give it a descriptive name followed by the equal sign, and then enclose the array values in parentheses:

```
$ days=("Monday" "Tuesday" "Wednesday" "Thursday" "Friday" "Saturday" "Sunday")
```

Once you've defined your array, you can retrieve an element at a given *index* (position) by putting the index between square brackets and surrounding the entire expression in braces:

```
$ echo "The first day is: ${days[0]}"
The first day is: Monday
$ echo "The last day is: ${days[6]}"
The last day is: Sunday
```

In the first example, you specify an index of 0 to print the value of the first element of the array. In the second example, specifying an index of 6 prints the value of the last element of the array.

NOTE *Arrays in bash start at index 0, whereas arrays in the Z shell start at index 1. Therefore, the first item in a Z shell array is in position 1, the second is in position 2, and so on. Keep this distinction in mind; otherwise, you may read the wrong element of an array by mistake.*

Braces are required when you're using array expressions to read values but not when you're *setting* array values (as with the days array at the start of the section). This is consistent with what you've seen so far with other types of variables: you read values using the dollar sign and braces and set values with just the variable name.

There are many different ways to access an array's elements or to perform operations on an array. Table 10-2 lists some of the most common array operations. You'll find even more in Chapter 11.

Table 10-2: Common Array Operations

Operation	Syntax	Example
Create array	array=()	`$ days=("Monday" "Tuesday" "Wednesday" "Thursday" "Friday" "Saturday" "Sunday")`
Get array element	${array[index]}	`$ echo ${days[2]}` `Wednesday`
Get all elements	${array[@]}	`$ echo ${days[@]}` `Monday Tuesday Wednesday Thursday Friday Saturday Sunday`
Set array element	${array[index]}=value	`$ days[0]="Mon"`
Get a subset of elements	${array[@]:start:number}	`$ echo ${days[@]:5:2}` `Saturday Sunday`
Get array indexes	${!array[@]}	`$ echo ${!days[@]}` `0 1 2 3 4 5 6`
Get array length	${#array[@]}	`$ echo ${#days[@]}` `7`
Append to array	array+=(val1 val2 valN)	`$ days+=("Birthday "); echo ${days[@]}` `Monday Tuesday Wednesday Thursday Friday Saturday Sunday Birthday`

Arrays in bash can be *sparse*, meaning you can have "gaps" in your array. As an example, here's how you could create and show a leaderboard that contains only a few scores:

```
$ leaderboard=()
$ leaderboard[0]="First Place: Alice"
$ leaderboard[4]="Fifth Place: Bob"
$ leaderboard[8]="Ninth Place: Eve"
$ echo ${leaderboard[0]}
First Place: Alice
$ echo ${!leaderboard[@]}
0 4 8
```

You begin by creating an empty array named leaderboard. Then, you use "set array element" syntax to assign values to a few indexes (remember that bash array indexes start from 0!), use the "get array element" syntax to show the person in the lead, and finally use the "get array indexes" syntax to show which positions in the leaderboard have been filled.

Storing Complex Data with Associative Arrays

More recent versions of bash support *associative arrays*, in which you associate a string (known as a *key*) with each element, rather than a numeric index. This creates a key-value structure similar to the dictionaries you might have seen in other languages.

To create an associative array, use the declare ("set variable") command with the -A ("associative array") flag followed by the array name you want to use:

```
$ declare -A book
```

Now you can use the "set array element" syntax to specify some details about the book array:

```
$ book[title]="Effective Shell"
$ book[author]="Dave Kerr"
```

Here you're setting title and author as keys and assigning them the string values Effective Shell and Dave Kerr, respectively. Now you can refer to these elements of the array by name, rather than number, which can be far more convenient:

```
$ echo "Book details: ${book[title]} - ${book[author]}"
Book details: Effective Shell - Dave Kerr
```

If you find yourself regularly using associative arrays, however, there's a good chance you're trying to do something more complex than is suitable for a shell script. See Chapter 21 for some alternative options.

Expanding Shell Parameters

In most examples thus far, you've seen simple shell parameter expansion where the variable is expanded into its value like so:

```
$ echo "My shell is ${SHELL}"
My shell is: /usr/bin/sh
```

But shell parameter expansion isn't just about replacing variables with their values. You can also use it to transform or manipulate variables in various ways. Let's look at some of the most common ones.

Returning the Variable Length

The ${#*var*} operator returns the length of a variable:

```
$ var="The quick brown fox jumps over the lazy dog"
$ length=${#var}
$ echo "Length: $length"
Length: 43
```

You begin by defining a var variable with the value The quick brown fox jumps over the lazy dog. Next, you use parameter expansion to count the characters in var (including the spaces) and store that number in length, whose value then gets printed to the screen.

Returning a Default Value

The ${*var*:-*default*} operator returns the value of the *var* variable or the text *default* if *var* isn't found:

```
$ read -p "Enter your username: " user
Enter your username: dave
$ username=${user:-$USER}
$ echo "Username: $username"
Username: dave
```

First, the read command (which you'll learn about shortly) prompts the user for their username and stores that input in the user variable. The next line uses parameter expansion to set username with a default value, essentially saying, "If user has a value, use that; otherwise, use the USER value." Because I entered dave, that value is stored in username and printed to the screen.

Let's see what happens if I press ENTER without providing a username:

```
$ read -p "Enter your username: " user
Enter your username:
$ username=${user:-$USER}
$ echo "Username: $username"
Username: dwmkerr
```

Now the value of USER (which on my system is dwmkerr) is printed instead.

Returning a Substring

The ${*var*:*start*:*count*} operator returns a subset of the string the *var* variable contains, starting at position *start* and extracting up to *count* characters:

```
$ path="~/effective-shell"
$ echo "First part of the path: ${path:0:2}"
First part of the path: ~/
$ echo "Last part of the path: ${path:2}"
Last part of the path: effective-shell
```

The first line creates a path variable with the value ~/effective-shell, and the second line uses parameter expansion to extract a substring: :0 starts at the first character and :2 extracts two characters, so ${path:0:2} returns ~/. In the third line, :2 starts at the third character (position 2) but no *count* is specified, so the shell returns everything from *start* to the end, printing effective-shell.

Transforming to Uppercase

The ${*var*^^} operator returns the value of *var* in all uppercase:

```
$ message="don't shout"
$ echo ${message^^}
DON'T SHOUT
```

This one's fairly self-explanatory: ${message^^} tells the shell to put the value of the message variable, don't shout, in all caps.

Transforming to Lowercase

The ${*var*,,} operator returns the value of var in all lowercase:

```
$ message="DON'T SHOUT"
$ echo ${message,,}
don't shout
```

Again, this operation is intuitive: it takes the all-caps value of message and sets it to lowercase.

Using Variable Indirection

The ${!*var_name*} operator returns the value of the variable with the name specified in the *var_name* variable:

```
$ read -p "Enter a variable name: " var_name
Enter a variable name: SHELL
$ echo "The value of '${var_name}' is: ${!var_name}"
The value of 'SHELL' is /bin/bash
```

First, you use read to prompt the user, storing their input—in this case, SHELL—in the var_name variable. Then, ${!var_name} tells the shell to look at what's in var_name (SHELL) and get the value of the variable by that name—that is, the value of SHELL, which is /bin/bash.

This technique, called *indirection*, lets you access variables dynamically when their names are stored in other variables. This operation s useful if you want to get the value of a variable but don't know the variable's name.

There are several other options for shell parameter expansion. If you're interested in seeing the full list, run man bash and search for the text expansion.

Reading and Storing User Input in Variables

The read ("read from standard input") command reads a line of text from stdin and stores that value in a variable called REPLY. Here it is in action:

```
$ echo "What is your name?"
$ read
```

When you run read, the shell will wait for you to key in some input. Enter a name, and then press ENTER.

```
What is your name?
$ Dave
```

If you don't press ENTER, read will keep reading until it reaches the end of a line. You could also press CTRL-D to signal the end of transmission.

You can then use REPLY to display the stored text:

```
$ echo "Hello, ${REPLY}"
Hello, Dave
```

While REPLY is the default variable for storing input, you can also specify your own variable name.

Reading into a Custom Variable

To tell the read command to store the input it reads into a variable other than REPLY, specify your preferred variable name after the command, like so:

```
$ echo "What is your name?"
$ read name
```

Remember, the dollar sign applies only when you want to *use* the variable, not when you want to *set* the variable, so it's not used for name here.

In general, you should provide a variable name for read as it will make your script a little easier to understand. Not every user will know that the REPLY variable is the default location, so they might find it confusing if you don't explicitly specify a variable name.

Providing a variable name also demonstrates good coding practices. Variable names should be descriptive, indicating what the variables are likely to be used for, which makes your scripts easier to follow and maintain over time.

Prompting for Input

Before you run the read command, you can prompt for input with the echo command, as shown earlier, or with the -p ("prompt") parameter:

```
$ read -p "Please enter your name: " name
Please enter your name: Dave
$ echo "$name"
Dave
```

NOTE *If you're using the Z shell, this command will fail, as zsh doesn't use the -p parameter for a prompt. Instead, insert a question mark before the line of text prompting the user:*

```
% read "?Please enter your name: " name
% Please enter your name: Dave
$ echo "$name"
Dave
```

The command prompts the user for their name, stores that value in the name variable, and then prints it to the screen.

Hiding Input

You can use the -s ("silent") flag to hide input as it's being entered, which is useful in cases such as keeping a password private:

```
$ read -s -p "Enter a new password: " password
Enter a new password:
$ masked_password=$(echo "$password" | sed 's/./*/g')
$ echo ""
$ echo "Your password is: $masked_password"
Your password is: ********
```

When you run this read command, you'll be prompted for input just as in the previous examples, and the shell will store that input in the password variable; however, because you've used the -s flag, the shell won't print what you type or add a newline when you press ENTER. The empty echo command writes a newline before the output so that it doesn't appear on the same line as your password; otherwise, it would appear as follows:

```
Enter a new password: Your password is: ********.
```

As you saw in the section "Storing a Command's Output in a Variable" on page 127, in the second echo command you're using sed to replace each character in the password with an asterisk, creating a masked version of the password that you can print to the screen.

Limiting Input

There may be times when you don't want to require the user to press ENTER to indicate that they've finished entering input, such as having them enter y for "yes" or n for "no." You can handle this case in a couple of ways. The first is to use the -n ("number of characters") parameter to limit the number of characters that are read:

```
$ read -n 1 -p "Continue? (y/n): " yesorno
Continue? (y/n): n
```

Using the -n flag with the value 1 tells read to accept only a single character. You can see what the user entered by running the following commands:

```
$ echo ""
$ echo "You typed: ${yesorno}"
You typed: n
```

Like the -s flag for hiding input, the -n flag does not add a newline automatically, so you need to write an empty echo command to insert one. Otherwise, the output would look very confusing, like this:

```
Continue? (y/n): nYou typed: n
```

The same issue would occur if you used read -n 2 to have the user type no: read would read two characters, but it would not add the newline it automatically inserts when the user presses ENTER.

Any time you use the -n or -s flag for read operations, you should write an empty newline to separate the output from the input.

The second way to limit input is to use the -d ("delimiter") flag to specify a character that indicates when read should stop reading input:

```
$ read -d 'X' -p "Enter your favorite word (then X): " word
Enter your favorite word (then X): shellX
$ echo ""
$ echo "Your favorite word is: ${word}"
Your favorite word is: shell
```

The -d 'X' parameter tells read to read up until it finds an X. Keep in mind that this can be confusing for users: if they press ENTER, expecting to end the input, read will read it as a newline and continue waiting for an X. Be explicit in your prompt so the user knows to finish their input with the delimiter you've set. Better yet, avoid potential confusion altogether by sticking with the default newline delimiter and having the user press ENTER, or use sed to extract everything from their input up to the point you want.

To view other options for the read command, type help read.

Performing Arithmetic Operations

Variables are frequently used for arithmetic operations, and fortunately the shell has some built-in features to help you perform them.

You might assume that you can use symbols like the plus sign (+) directly in your math-based scripts, but they don't always perform as expected. For example, here's what happens if you try to add two numbers together with the plus sign:

```
$ read -p "Enter a number: " number1
Enter a number: 23
$ read -p "Enter another number: " number2
Enter another number: 34
$ sum=$number1+$number2
$ echo "The sum of $number1 and $number2 is $sum"
The sum of 23 and 34 is 23 + 34
```

This result is obviously not the sum of 23 and 34 and likely not what you were looking for. Instead of adding the values together, the shell uses the + to *concatenate*—that is, join together—the two strings.

To tell the shell that you want to perform an arithmetic operation, use the double parentheses syntax as follows:

```
$ read -p "Enter a number: " number1
Enter a number: 23
$ read -p "Enter another number: " number2
Enter another number: 34
$ sum=$(($number1+$number2))
$ echo "The sum of $number1 and $number2 is $sum"
The sum of 23 and 34 is 57
```

Surrounding the addition operation in two sets of parentheses returns the result you were looking for. This syntax, known as *arithmetic expansion*, is part of the set of shell expansion features mentioned earlier in this chapter.

NOTE   *Dollar signs are optional before variable names within double parentheses, as are spaces around the plus sign and other arithmetic operators. However, if you intentionally want to perform a concatenation operation like the first example, you must omit the spaces around the plus sign.*

You can also use the `let` keyword as follows to tell the shell you want to perform an arithmetic operation:

```
$ let sum="$number1+$number2"
```

While I've included the `let` keyword here for completeness, I recommend using the double parentheses syntax since it is more common.

The plus sign is just one arithmetic operator you can use with variables in the shell. Table 10-3 lists several other arithmetic operators and how they're used.

Table 10-3: Arithmetic Operators

Operator	Description	Example
+	Addition	echo $((3+4)) # prints 7
-	Subtraction	echo $((4-2)) # prints 2
*	Multiplication	echo $((4*2)) # prints 8
/	Division	echo $((4/2)) # prints 2
**	Exponent	echo $((4**3)) # prints 64

Operator	Description	Example
%	Modulus	echo $((7%3)) # prints 1
++i	Prefix increment	i=1; echo $((++i)) # prints 1, i is set to 2
i++	Postfix increment	i=1; echo $((i++)) # prints 2, i is set to 2
--i	Prefix decrement	i=3; echo $((--i)) # prints 3, i is set to 2
i--	Postfix decrement	i=3; echo $((i--)) # prints 2, i is set to 2
i+=n	Increment	i=3; echo $((i+=3)) # prints 6, i is set to 6
i-=n	Decrement	i=3; echo $((i-=2)) # prints 1, i is set to 1

Let's look at another example. You can combine mathematical operators to convert a value in degrees Celsius to Fahrenheit as follows:

```
$ read -p "Enter a value in Celsius: " celsius
Enter a value in Celsius: 12
$ fahrenheit=$(( (celsius * 9/5) + 32 ))
$ echo "${celsius} degrees Celsius is ${fahrenheit} degrees Fahrenheit"
12 degrees Celsius is 53 degrees Fahrenheit
```

First, read stores the input temperature in the celsius variable. Next, arithmetic expansion tells the shell to multiply celsius by 9, divide that result by 5, add 32, and then store the result in the fahrenheit variable. Finally, the echo command prints the result to the screen.

Note that the shell's arithmetic uses only integers (whole numbers), so 12°C shows as 53°F rather than 53.6°F. If you need to be able to use decimals, consider a more full-featured programming language, as discussed in Chapter 21.

Also notice the use of parentheses in (celsius * 9/5) to specify the order in which the calculations should be performed (that is, the order of operations). Using parentheses this way is a good habit to get into as it makes your scripts clearer to the reader. The default order of operations is detailed in the man page; to access it, enter man bash and search for the text ^ARITHMETIC\ EVALUATION (be sure to include the backslash to escape the space between the words). This page also lists the complete set of available arithmetic operators.

Enhancing the common Command with Variables

With your new understanding of variables, you can improve the common command from Chapter 9 by extracting certain values into variables so that you can more easily change them. If you've forgotten the example or haven't read that chapter yet, it's located at *~/effective-shell/scripts/common.v1.sh*. To install the sample files to the *~/effective-shell* folder, run this command:

```
$ curl effective.sh | sh
```

The *common.v1.sh* script currently looks like this:

common.v1.sh
```
# Inform the user of the output they can expect.
echo "common commands:"

# Show the most commonly used commands.
tail ~/.bash_history -n 1000 \
    | sort \
    | uniq -c \
    | sed 's/^ *//' \
    | sort -n -r \
    | head -n 10
```

To improve on this script, you'll create variables for the number of lines of history to search and for the number of commands to show. Create a copy of the *common.v1.sh* script, save it as *common.v2.sh*, and update it as follows:

common.v2.sh
```
# Inform the user of the output they can expect.
echo "common commands:"

# The following variables control how the command runs.
history_lines=1000 # The number of lines of history to search through
command_count=10   # The number of common commands to show

# Show the most commonly used commands.
tail ~/.bash_history -n ${history_lines} \
    | sort \
    | uniq -c \
    | sed 's/^ *//' \
    | sort -n -r \
    | head -n ${command_count}
```

By replacing the static values 1000 and 10 with the shell variables history_lines and command_count, respectively, you've made the script easier to understand and maintain. The variables have descriptive names, and if you need to update these values later, you'll only need to change the script in one place rather than hunting through the code for every instance.

To replace the installed common command with this new one, update the symlink in your */usr/local/bin* folder as follows:

```
$ sudo ln -sf $HOME/effective-shell/scripts/common.v2.sh /usr/local/bin/common
```

Note the use of the -f ("force") flag to ln to force the creation of the symlink even though one already exists at this location.

Summary

In this chapter, you learned all about variables—what they are, why they're useful, how to create and format them properly, and how to use them in your shell scripts to perform common operations like storing and reading user input.

A few new constructs from this chapter will appear again and again throughout the book. I've summarized them here so you'll recognize them more easily:

${variable}   Gets the value of *variable*. The braces surround the variable name.

$(echo "$VARIABLE")   Runs the echo command in a subshell. The parentheses indicate that you're running a subshell.

$(($number1 + $number2))   Adds the values in the variables *number1* and *number2*. The double parentheses indicate that you're performing an arithmetic operation.

The next chapter discusses adding *conditional logic* to scripts (that is, running commands only when certain conditions are met). With this incredibly powerful technique, you'll be able to create much more sophisticated scripts.

11

MASTERING CONDITIONAL LOGIC

A shell script normally executes commands in sequence, but what if you wanted it to act differently under certain circumstances? Enter *conditional logic*, which lets you control how your scripts behave based on specific conditions, such as how a user responds to a query or whether certain files exist. In this chapter, you'll learn how to use tools like `if` statements and `case` statements to have your scripts check conditions and run different commands based on the results. We'll also cover more advanced constructs such as using conditional expressions with regular expressions and chaining commands to make your scripts more flexible and responsive.

The if Statement

You can use an if statement to perform operations in shell scripts only when certain conditions are met. The if statement has the following structure:

```
if test-commands
then
    conditional-command 1
    conditional-command 2
    conditional-command n
fi
```

The statement begins with the if command and then specifies one or many conditions to test. Following that is the then keyword and the commands to be run if the conditions are met. If the results of the test-commands are all 0 (indicating success), each conditional-command in the then block will be run. The fi keyword (if written backward) closes the if statement.

To get a better idea of how the if statement is used, let's look at a simple example:

```
if mkdir ~/backups
then
    echo "Successfully created the 'backups' folder"
fi
```

First, the mkdir command tries to create a folder. As long as you don't already have a folder called *backups* in your home directory, mkdir will return 0 and the conditional echo command will execute, returning the following output:

```
Successfully created the 'backups' folder
```

If you run the script again, though, the mkdir command will fail because the directory already exists. In that case, it returns 1 (indicating failure) and the echo command won't be executed. You'll also see an error message from the mkdir command:

```
mkdir: /home/dwmkerr/backups: File exists
```

You might be surprised that the result of the test command has to be 0 for the conditional commands to run. This is the opposite of how most programming languages work, where 0 normally would be considered false (meaning the test command failed and the conditional commands would not run). In computer programs that run in the shell, however, 0 generally means success, and any nonzero value typically indicates an error code. The error code indicates the type of error; for example, code 1 means "general error," but code 127 means "command not found." Different programs can also specify their own error codes.

The test Command

The test ("evaluate expression") command checks whether a certain condition is true before the shell attempts to run the commands in the then block. As long as the condition is true, test returns 0 to indicate success and the shell will run the conditional commands.

You could improve the preceding if statement with test to create the *backups* folder only if it doesn't already exist. Whereas in the previous example mkdir failed with an error if the *backups* folder was already present, test will simply skip the mkdir command altogether if the condition returns false. Here's how the if statement looks with the test command:

```
if ! test -d ~/backups
then
    echo "Creating backups folder"
    mkdir ~/backups
fi
```

The test command evaluates the expression -d ~/backups, where -d ("file exists and is a directory") checks to see whether the provided path is a directory. Since you want to create the directory only if it *does not* exist, you use the not operator (!) to "invert" the result of test.

Instead of entering test explicitly, you can surround an expression with square brackets:

```
if ! [ -d ~/backups ]
then
    echo "Creating backups folder"
    mkdir ~/backups
fi
```

The shell will evaluate this expression exactly the same way as the previous one. This square bracket syntax is frequently used as a shorthand for test and can make your scripts far more compact. Be sure to include a space before and after the opening and closing square brackets.

Using test Operators with Expressions and Files

You can use many operators in a test expression. Table 11-1 lists some of the most common ones.

Table 11-1: Common Operators for test Expressions

Expression part	Meaning
-n	True if the length of a string is nonzero
-z	True if the length of a string is 0
"$var"	True if the variable var is set and is not empty
s1 = s2	True if the strings s1 and s2 are identical
s1 != s2	True if the strings s1 and s2 are not identical

(continued)

Table 11-1: Common Operators for test Expressions *(continued)*

Expression part	Meaning
n1 -eq n2	True if the numbers n1 and n2 are equal
n1 -ne n2	True if the numbers n1 and n2 are not equal
n1 -lt n2	True if the number n1 is less than n2
n1 -le n2	True if the number n1 is less than or equal to n2
n1 -gt n2	True if the number n1 is greater than n2
n1 -ge n2	True if the number n1 is greater than or equal to n2

The test command also provides a number of operators that specifically work with the filesystem, which are very handy when building shell scripts. You've already seen the -d operator. Table 11-2 lists some other useful options.

Table 11-2: Common test Operators for Files

Expression part	Meaning
-d	True if the file exists and is a folder
-e	True if the file exists, regardless of the file type
-f	True if the file exists and is a regular file
-L	True if the file exists and is a symlink
-r	True if the file exists and is readable
-s	True if the file exists and has a size greater than zero
-w	True if the file exists and is writable
-x	True if the file exists and is executable; if it is a directory, checks if it can be searched
file1 -nt *file2*	True if *file1* exists and is newer than *file2*
file1 -ot *file2*	True if *file1* exists and is older than *file2*
file1 -ef *file2*	True if *file1* and *file2* exist and are the same file

Earlier you saw the ! operator in action to invert the test result. You can place the operator either before or after the test command, so

```
if ! test -d ~/backups
```

is equivalent to:

```
if test ! -d ~/backups
```

To see all of the many operators available for the test command, run man test.

Checking Multiple test Conditions Simultaneously

You'll often want to check more than one test condition at a time. To do so, you can use the *and* (&&) and *or* (||) operators:

```
if [ $year -ge 1980 ] && [ $year -lt 1990 ]; then
    echo "$year is in the 1980s"
fi
```

This script checks to see whether the value of the variable year is greater than or equal to (-ge) 1980 *and* less than (-lt) 1990, effectively searching within a range of years.

Alternatively, you could use the -a ("and") and -o ("or") operators. Here's how the previous script looks using the -a operator:

```
if [ $year -ge 1980 -a $year -lt 1990 ]; then
    echo "$year is in the 1980s"
fi
```

This form of the *and* and *or* operators can lead to some subtle problems, so I don't recommend using them. However, it's important to be able to recognize them, since you might see them in someone else's script.

You will also likely see the following syntax, which uses double square brackets to indicate a conditional expression:

```
if [[ $year -ge 1980 && $year -lt 1990 ]]; then
    echo "$year is in the 1980s"
fi
```

You'll learn all about this format in "Conditional Expressions" on page 149.

Combining Statements on a Single Line

You might have noticed the use of the semicolon in the previous examples where you checked multiple test conditions. By default, the shell assumes that each individual line is a single statement, so if you want to put more than one statement on a line, you need to let it know where one statement ends and another starts. That's where the semicolon comes in. The shell interprets the semicolon as a "command separator" symbol.

You'll often see if and then statements on the same line like this:

```
if ! [ -d ~/backups ]; then
    mkdir ~/backups
fi
```

In this example, then doesn't require a semicolon because it is a keyword rather than a command.

If you hadn't included a semicolon after the `if` command, the shell would have assumed that the entire line was a single statement, giving you the following error:

```
bash: syntax error near unexpected token `fi'
```

You can put as many statements on a single line as you like. You could even write the script like so:

```
if ! test -d ~/backups; then mkdir ~/backups; fi
```

However, I suggest you start by writing `if` statements with `if` and `then` on separate lines. Once you're more familiar with the syntax, you can combine the lines if you prefer, but generally speaking, keeping commands on separate lines makes your scripts more readable for other users.

The else Clause

The `else` clause defines a series of statements that should be executed if the condition in the `if` statement is not true. For example, the following script tells the user whether they've installed the `common` command:

```
if [ -e /usr/local/bin/common ]
then
    echo "The 'common' command has been installed in the local bin folder."
else
    echo "The 'common' command has not been installed in the local bin folder."
fi
```

The `-e` ("file or folder exists") operator checks whether a file or folder exists in the location */usr/local/bin/common* (see Chapter 9 for a full discussion of the `common` command).

If you run the script and you haven't installed the `common` command, you'll see the following output:

```
The 'common' command has not been installed in the local bin folder.
```

Note that you still need to use the `fi` keyword to close an `if` statement with a nested `else` statement.

The elif Clause

The `elif` (short for "else if") clause creates additional checks and defines statements that should run if *other* conditions are true.

This example updates the preceding script to check whether the `common` command is executable, using the `-x` ("is executable") operator:

```
if [ -x /usr/local/bin/common ]; then
    echo "The 'common' command has been installed and is executable."
elif [ -e /usr/local/bin/common ]; then
    echo "The 'common' command has been installed and is not executable."
else
    echo "The 'common' command has not been installed."
fi
```

The message you see will depend on whether you have installed the common command in your local binaries folder and whether the script is executable. If you want to see all of the various messages this snippet can output, experiment with the following code to add or remove common or to change its executable permissions. These statements allow you to test each condition in the previous example:

```
# Create a link to the "common" command in the local binaries folder.
sudo ln -s $HOME/effective-shell/scripts/common.v1.sh /usr/local/bin/common

# Remove the "executable" flag from the "common" command.
chmod -x $HOME/effective-shell/scripts/common.v1.sh

# Add the "executable" flag to the "common" command.
chmod +x $HOME/effective-shell/scripts/common.v1.sh

# Remove the link to the "common" command from the local binaries folder.
sudo rm /usr/local/bin/common
```

The elif statement looks very similar to the if statement. The statement takes a set of commands, which could be normal shell commands or test commands.

It's very important to consider the order in which the if and elif statements will be executed. If the previous script were written like this, it wouldn't have worked:

```
if [ -e /usr/local/bin/common ]; then
    echo "The 'common' command has been installed and is executable."
elif [ -x /usr/local/bin/common ]; then
    echo "The 'common' command has been installed and is not executable."
else
    echo "The 'common' command has not been installed."
fi
```

This script first checks whether the file exists. If it does, the -e operator returns true and the check in the elif statement does *not* run. This means you'll *never* successfully evaluate the statements in the elif block, because for the file to be executable, it must exist, so the first condition in the if statement will always take precedence.

The case Statement

If you find yourself writing overly complex if statements, a case statement might simplify your code. A case statement works by matching an expression against different patterns. Here's the general structure:

```
case expression in
    pattern1)
        pattern1-commands
        ;;
    *)
        default-commands
        ;;
esac
```

The *expression* is the value you want to test against *pattern1*. If *pattern1* matches, its associated commands run. The *) pattern uses the asterisk (*) wildcard to match anything not matched by previous patterns causing the default commands to run. The double semicolon (;;) tells the shell when the commands for a specific case end. The indentation shown here is optional but is considered best practice as it makes it easier to quickly see the patterns and their associated commands. As with if and fi, to close the case statement you use esac (case reversed).

Of course, this is a basic example that you could probably handle with an if statement, so let's look at a more likely scenario. Here's how you'd structure a case statement that checks an expression against multiple patterns:

```
case expression in
    pattern1)
        pattern1-commands
        ;;
    pattern2 | pattern3)
        pattern2and3-commands
        ;;
    *)
        default-commands
        ;;
esac
```

The pipe (|) lets you test more than one pattern at a time: if *expression* matches either *pattern2* or *pattern3*, the corresponding commands will run.

Typically, you'll provide the case statement with a variable to check against a number of values. For example, you could use case to check whether a variable contains a yes or no response:

```
read -p "Yes or no: " response
case "${response}" in
    y | Y | yes | ok)
        echo "You said yes "
        ;;
```

```
    n | N | no)
        echo "You said no "
        ;;
    *)
        echo "'${response}' is not a valid response"
        ;;
esac
```

Note that this also handles case *), where the user types something other than the acceptable input, and runs the default command to tell them they've entered an invalid response.

The preceding example uses very simple text patterns, but you can make them more sophisticated:

```
read -p "Yes or no: " response
case "${response}" in
    [yY]*)
        echo "You have (probably!) confirmed"
        ;;
    [nN]*)
        echo "You have (probably!) denied"
        ;;
    *)
        echo "'${response}' is not a valid response"
    ;;
esac
```

The [yY]* pattern means either the y or the Y character followed by zero or more characters, so this statement will match replies like yes, YES, and yay. There's a similar pattern for the negative response. These patterns look a bit like regular expressions, but they actually are shell *globs* (patterns that include wildcards, as I'll discuss in Chapter 12).

Even if they take more lines to write than the equivalent if statements, case statements can make your code more readable, so they're often worth the bit of added complexity.

Conditional Expressions

Conditional expressions are a feature of bash and bash-like shells that offer a more sophisticated way of performing conditional checks. Conditional expressions use two square brackets rather than one, as in this example from earlier in the chapter:

```
if [[ $year -ge 1980 && $year -lt 1990 ]]; then
    echo "$year is in the 1980s"
fi
```

The conditional expression in this if statement allows you to test multiple conditions simultaneously in a more concise format than plain test commands. Conditional expressions have a number of other advantages over test commands:

- You can use the && and || operators without the potential problems that using them with test can cause.

- If you use an || expression and the left-hand side of the expression is true, the right-hand side won't be evaluated. This isn't always the case with older versions of test when you use the -o operator, which is a subtle difference but one that can help avoid incorrect behavior.

- If you use a && expression and the left-hand side of the expression is false, the right-hand side won't be evaluated. As with the || operator, this is useful to know in case you're expecting the right-hand side to always be evaluated.

- Numbers are correctly compared even if they're in different formats (for example, you can compare hexadecimal and octal numbers, which does not work in the standard test expression).

- You can use the incredibly useful =~ operator to include a regular expression (regex) in your condition. We'll look at this shortly.

Some people prefer to use single square brackets so that their script is more portable, as the double square brackets are specific to bash and bash-like shells. Others prefer the double-bracket syntax so that they can take advantage of the additional features it provides.

The following example determines whether the user's shell is the Z shell by checking whether the shell's path ends with *zsh*:

```
zsh_regex="zsh$"
if [[ $SHELL =~ $zsh_regex ]]; then
    echo "It looks like your shell '$SHELL' is Z shell"
fi
```

First, this conditional expression defines a variable called zsh_regex to store the zsh$ regex pattern, where zsh matches the literal text *zsh* and $ matches the end of the line.

NOTE *It's a good practice to declare the regex in a variable rather than include it directly in the expression; otherwise, you'd have to escape special characters like the dollar sign.*

The =~ operator is then used to compare the value in SHELL against the value in the zsh_regex variable. If the result is true (the user's shell path ends with *zsh*), the shell prints the following confirmation message:

```
It looks like your shell '/bin/zsh' is Z shell
```

Any time you use the =~ operator, matches are automatically stored in the BASH_REMATCH array. The item at index 0 is always the full matched text (so, in the previous example, BASH_REMATCH[0] would contain zsh). But if you use capture groups in your regex to help extract text, additional items will be added to the BASH_REMATCH array. A *capture group* is a part of a regex that "captures" or remembers the matched text so you can reference it later (see Chapter 4 for more on capture groups and regexes in general).

Let's look at an example. You can get the name of the current shell binary as follows:

```
shell_regex=".*\/(.+)$"
if [[ $SHELL =~ $shell_regex ]]; then
    echo "Your shell binary is: ${BASH_REMATCH[1]}"
    echo "BASH_REMATCH is: ${BASH_REMATCH[*]}"
else
    echo "Unable to extract your shell binary"
fi
```

In this example, the regular expression .*\/(.+)$ has a single capture group denoted with parentheses, which captures everything from the final forward slash to the end of the line. Therefore, if SHELL is /bin/bash, then /bin/bash (the full match) is stored at index 0 in the BASH_REMATCH array, and bash (the capture group match) is stored at index 1. Then the shell prints the BASH_REMATCH array to illustrate what was captured. If there's no match on the regex pattern, the else clause prints an alternative message.

I get the following output on my machine:

```
Your shell binary is: bash
BASH_REMATCH is: /bin/bash bash
```

For more details on conditional expressions, enter man bash and search for \[\[(two square brackets, each escaped with a backslash). For more about how arrays work and how to print all of an array's elements, see Chapter 10.

Chaining Commands

One final conditional logic technique is *chaining* commands together in the shell (that is, running a command based on the result of a previous one). Here's one way it works:

```
mkdir -p ~/backups && cd ~/backups
```

In this case, two commands are being chained together with the && operator. The shell runs the cd command only if the mkdir command succeeds; that is, it *evaluates* the result of mkdir, and if mkdir is successful, the shell runs the cd command. Both commands must succeed for the overall result to be true. In pseudocode, it looks like this:

```
if command1; then
  command2
fi
```

If command1 fails, the shell doesn't need to evaluate command2. The overall result *must* be false because the first command has already failed.

Contrast this to the || operator:

```
[ -d ~/backups ] || mkdir ~/backups
```

In this case, mkdir is evaluated *only* if the first command fails. Here's the pseudocode:

```
if ! command1; then
  command2
fi
```

If *command1* succeeds, the shell doesn't need to evaluate *command2* because the result is already true. However, if *command1* fails, the shell must evaluate *command2* to see if it succeeds.

In summary, here's how command chaining works:

```
# Run command1; if it succeeds, run command2.
command1 && command2

# Run command1; if it fails, run command2.
command1 || command2
```

This syntax is common in shell scripts because it's very succinct. It's also very useful when you're using the shell interactively. For example, this command is almost second nature to me:

```
make build && make deploy
```

Here I'm using the make ("build programs") command. If the build step for a project succeeds, I want to run the deploy step. But obviously I *don't* want to run the deploy step if the build step fails!

Compare this example to the following command:

```
make build; make deploy
```

In this case, the two commands are separated by a semicolon, and the second command will always run, regardless of whether the first succeeds.

Extending the common Command to Handle Different Shells

With your new knowledge of conditional logic, you can continue updating the common command from Chapters 9 and 10. This time, you'll update it to check whether the user is using bash or the Z shell and then, based on that result, search appropriately through the history for the most commonly used commands.

If you haven't done so yet, install the sample files to the *~/effective-shell* folder like so:

```
$ curl effective.sh | sh
```

Here's the *common.v2.sh* command from the previous chapter:

```
# Inform the user of the output they can expect.
echo "common commands:"

# The following variables control how the command runs.
history_lines=1000 # The number of lines of history to search through
command_count=10   # The number of common commands to show

# Show the most commonly used commands.
tail ~/.bash_history -n ${history_lines} \
    | sort \
    | uniq -c \
    | sed 's/^ *//' \
    | sort -n \
    | tail -n ${command_count}
```

And here's a new version of the script called *common.v3.sh* that checks what the currently running shell is and then reads from the appropriate command history file:

```
# The following variables control how the command runs.
shell_binary=""     # You'll work out what shell you're in later.
history_file=""     # You'll work out the history file later.
history_lines=1000 # The number of lines of history to search through
command_count=10    # The number of common commands to show

# Check whether you can determine the name of the shell binary.
shell_regex="[^/]+$)"
if [[ $SHELL =~ $shell_regex ]]; then
    # Depending on the name of the shell binary, set the history filepath.
    shell_binary=${BASH_REMATCH[1]}
    if [[ $shell_binary == "bash" ]]; then
        history_file=~/.bash_history
    elif [[ $shell_binary == "zsh" ]]; then
        history_file=~/.zsh_history
    fi
fi
# If you are searching through the bash history, you can look at the history file
# to get the most common commands.
if [[ $shell_binary == "bash" ]]; then
    # Show the most commonly used commands.
    tail "${history_file}" -n ${history_lines} \
        | sort \
        | uniq -c \
        | sec 's/^ *//' \
        | sort -n -r \
        | head -n ${command_count}
elif [[ $shell_binary == "zsh" ]]; then
    # Z shell history lines look like this:
    # : 1621_35004:0;uname -a
    # Run the same command as above, and extract everything _after_ the
    # semicolon, which is the command text.
```

```
    tail "${history_file}" -n ${history_lines} \
        | cut -d';' -f2 \
        | sort \
        | uniq -c \
        | sed 's/^ *//' \
        | sort -n -r \
        | head -n ${command_count}
else
    # Show a warning to the user that you don't know where the history file
    # is for their shell.
    echo "Sorry, I don't know where to find the history for '${SHELL}'"
fi
```

This script first sets up two new variables: `shell_binary` to store which shell you're using, and `history_file` to store the path to your history file. Then it checks whether it can extract the name of the shell binary from the shell path. If it can, it stores its name and its associated history in the `SHELL` and `HISTFILE` variables, respectively.

Then, when the script searches through the history, it checks the shell binary using the same conditional expression with the regex and capture group that you saw earlier in the chapter. If the shell is bash, the script runs the usual `tail` command. If the shell is zsh, it runs a similar command that accounts for the fact that the Z shell history file has some extra content that needs to be removed. If the shell is neither bash nor zsh, an error message is shown to the user.

This example demonstrates several good shell script practices: using more variables and if statements, *nesting* if statements (putting one if statement inside another), including conditional expressions, and making comments very descriptive. Each comment gives clear information on what you're trying to accomplish, which should make the script easier to maintain.

If you want to replace the `common` command you have installed with this new one, update the symlink in your */usr/local/bin* folder:

```
$ sudo ln -sf $HOME/effective-shell/scripts/common.v3.sh /usr/local/bin/common
```

The `-f` ("force") flag forces the creation of the symlink even though one already exists at this location.

Summary

In this chapter, you learned about if statements, the test command, and operators that allow you to perform conditional logic. You also saw examples of more advanced constructs like case statements, conditional expressions with regexes, and chained commands. You can find the documentation for conditional logic on the bash man page; run `man bash` and search for `GRAMMAR`.

In the next chapter, we'll explore another crucial logical feature of the shell: loops.

12

USING LOOPS WITH FILES AND FOLDERS

A *loop* is a fundamental programming construct that performs a sequence of operations based on whether certain conditions are met. You can run loops over multiple items, such as files, folders, variables, or the results of a command, and then perform actions on these items. Loops allow you to efficiently execute repetitive tasks, saving time and reducing the risk of errors in your scripts.

In this chapter, you'll learn all about for, while, and until loops and how to use them to work with files and folders. You'll then revisit the common command you created in Chapter 9 by adding some loops to make your script more efficient.

To follow along with the chapter's examples, you'll need to install the book's sample files to the *~/effective-shell* folder:

```
$ curl effective.sh | sh
```

Let's get started.

The for Loop

A for loop executes a sequence of commands for every item in a list and has the following structure:

```
for name in words
do
    conditional-command 1
    conditional-command 2
    conditional-command n
done
```

The for loop defines a variable called *name*, and that variable will take on each value from the list of items during each iteration of the loop. The list name *words* comes from the for loop documentation. There's a technical (and complex) reason for this name, as I'll explain shortly. The do keyword begins the block of commands to execute for each item. Finally, the done keyword closes the for loop. This is inconsistent with the shell syntax for the if statement, which is closed with if backward (fi), and the case statement, which is closed with case backward (esac). The shell is an old platform, so it has some oddities like this.

Here's a simple example of how the for loop works:

```
for item in ~/effective-shell/*
do
    echo "Found: $item"
done
```

This code loops through every item in the *effective-shell* folder, one at a time, storing its filepath in the item variable and then printing the item's name to the screen at each iteration.

You should see output like the following when you run this oop:

```
Found: /home/dwmkerr/effective-shell/data
Found: /home/dwmkerr/effective-shell/docs
Found: /home/dwmkerr/effective-shell/logs
Found: /home/dwmkerr/effective-shell/pictures
Found: /home/dwmkerr/effective-shell/programs
Found: /home/dwmkerr/effective-shell/quotes
Found: /home/dwmkerr/effective-shell/scripts
Found: /home/dwmkerr/effective-shell/templates
Found: /home/dwmkerr/effective-shell/text
Found: /home/dwmkerr/effective-shell/websites
```

Notice how the shell is smart enough to expand the wildcard expression in the for loop (the asterisk in ~/effective-shell/*). Just as you can use wildcards in commands such as ls, cp, or mv, you can use them in for loops—in fact, you can use them in any statement.

Also notice how the loop implicitly creates the item variable from the name provided (remember, you omit the dollar sign when you're setting a variable). There's no need to explicitly assign a variable value since the variable declaration is built in to the for loop syntax.

Looping Through Arrays

You can easily loop through the items in an array with a for loop as well:

```
days=("Monday" "Tuesday" "Wednesday" "Thursday" "Friday" "Saturday" "Sunday")
for day in ${days[@]}
do
    echo -n "$day, "
done
echo "happy days!"
```

To loop through every item in the array, you use the ${days[@]} syntax to specify "all elements." The -n ("don't output a trailing newline") flag tells the echo command not to write each day on its own line.

If you run these commands, you'll get the following output:

```
Monday, Tuesday, Wednesday, Thursday, Friday, Saturday, Sunday, happy days!
```

See Chapter 10 to review the syntax for the most common array operations.

Splitting Loop Input into Words

Type the following in your shell to see the for loop documentation:

```
$ help for
for: for NAME [in WORDS ... ] ; do COMMANDS; done
    Execute commands for each member in a list.
...
```

The term WORDS refers to the list of items that the loop processes one by one. The shell automatically splits the input into separate items (or words) based on whitespace or other delimiters, and the loop iterates over each one. The following example illustrates this behavior:

```
sentence="What can the harvest hope for, if not for the care of the Reaper Man?"
for word in $sentence
do
    echo "$word"
done
```

The sentence variable is set explicitly since it's outside the for loop. Then, in the for loop, the shell splits the value of sentence into separate words based on the spaces between them, storing each in the word variable.

Here's the resulting output:

```
What
can
the
harvest
hope
for,
if
not
for
the
care
of
the
Reaper
Man?
```

The reason the shell splits up loop input into words is that it's a *text-based environment*, and its designers have taken that into account when building its functionality. Most of the time when you're running shell commands in a terminal, those commands simply output text. Thus, if you want to be able to use their output in constructs like loops, the shell has to decide how to split up that output.

For example, see how the ls command writes its output:

```
$ ls ~/effective-shell
data   docs   logs   pictures   programs   quotes   scripts   templates   text   websites
```

The output from the ls program is plaintext. It's not an array; it's just a set of filenames separated by spaces. What would you expect the shell to do if you ran the following command?

```
files=$(ls ~/effective-shell)
for file in $files
do
    echo "Found: $file"
done
```

Here's the output:

```
Found: data
Found: docs
Found: logs
Found: pictures
Found: programs
Found: quotes
Found: scripts
Found: templates
Found: text
Found: websites
```

You can see why the shell splits up words in a sentence: it assumes that you want to loop over each word and is splitting the output into sensible "chunks."

NOTE *If you're using the Z shell, the sentence will not be split up into words. To see the same results in zsh, you'd define the set of words as an array.*

When you operate in a shell for day-to-day work, you don't have to use the more specific syntax that you'd use in a programming language. The main advantage of the shell is that it lets you write short statements and work with files quickly. It's not designed as a general-purpose programming tool, which is why it makes assumptions like this.

WORD SPLITTING AND EXPANSION BEHAVIOR

As you've seen, the shell will split the words in a loop by default, as shown here:

```
$ sentence="Here are some words"
$ for word in $sentence; do echo "$word"; done
Here
are
some
words
```

However, wrapping the sentence variable in quotes will prevent the word splitting:

```
$ sentence="Here are some words"
$ for word in "$sentence"; do echo "$word"; done
Here are some words
```

In the first example, because the sentence variable is *not* quoted, it follows the standard rules for shell expansion. In the second example, the sentence variable *is* quoted, which typically means that it is treated literally—but parameter expansion is an exception. In this case, quoting the sentence variable allows parameter expansion to take place without word splitting.

Let's look at another example demonstrating some expansion behavior you might not expect. This for loop uses a wildcard to list files:

```
$ touch file\ with\ spaces.test
$ for file in *.test; do echo "Found: $file"; done
Found: file with spaces.test
```

In this case, *.test isn't quoted, so why doesn't word splitting happen? The reason is that the shell applies expansions in a certain order:

1. Brace expansion
2. Tilde expansion

(continued)

3. Parameter and variable expansion

4. Command substitution

5. Arithmetic expansion

6. Word splitting

7. Pathname expansion (wildcard expansion)

Word splitting happens *before* pathname expansion, and pathname expansion is what replaces the asterisk with the list of files. At the point that pathname expansion happens, word splitting has already been applied, so it won't be applied again.

In most circumstances, you'll probably want to quote your variables so that the shell won't perform word splitting on them. But if you *do* want expansion and splitting to occur, *don't* quote the text. For more on quoting syntax, see Chapter 10.

Looping Through Files and Folders

One of the most common scenarios for using a for loop is to run operations on a set of files or folders. As you saw earlier in this chapter, using a wildcard pattern in the for loop statement is a simple way to do this:

```
for script in ~/effective-shell/scripts/*.sh
do
    echo "Found script: $script"
done
```

The output looks something like this:

```
Found script: /home/dwmkerr/effective-shell/scripts/common.mac.sh
Found script: /home/dwmkerr/effective-shell/scripts/common.sh
Found script: /home/dwmkerr/effective-shell/scripts/common.v1.sh
Found script: /home/dwmkerr/effective-shell/scripts/common.v2.sh
Found script: /home/dwmkerr/effective-shell/scripts/common.v3.sh
Found script: /home/dwmkerr/effective-shell/scripts/show-info.sh
```

You must be careful when using a wildcard, however. By default, if the shell doesn't find anything matching a wildcard pattern, *it does not expand it.* Consider this example:

```
for script in ~/bad-shell/scripts/*.sh
do
    echo "Found script: $script"
done
```

You might think the logical result is that nothing is printed. There's no *bad-shell* folder, so the pattern shouldn't find any files. But instead, it returns the following output:

```
Found script: ~/bad-shell/scripts/*.sh
```

By default, if a shell *glob* (a pattern that includes a wildcard) doesn't match any files, the shell simply leaves the pattern as is. That's why, instead of finding no files, the loop actually runs once, storing the literal string ~/bad-shell/scripts/*.sh in the script variable and then printing that value to the screen.

There are two ways to deal with this problem. The first is to enable the nullglob ("return null for unmatched globs") command:

```
shopt -s nullglob
for script in ~/bad-shell/scripts/*.sh
do
        echo "Found script: $script"
done
```

The shopt ("set and unset shell option") command allows you to configure shell options like nullglob, which changes the shell behavior so that if a wildcard pattern doesn't match any results, its value is set to a null string.

NOTE *There's a good reason that the shell does not return null by default for an unmatched glob. As an example,* ls *.nothing-here *shows a warning that* *.nothing-here *doesn't exist. If the glob automatically expanded to an empty string, it would be equivalent to running* ls *with no arguments, so* ls *would list the current directory (its default behavior when no path is specified). See the StackExchange discussion at* https://unix.stackexchange.com/questions/204803/why-is-nullglob-not -default *for more on this topic.*

The second way to deal with the unmatched glob problem is to just use a test command, which is more readable than the shopt solution. Here's how it would look using the square bracket notation for the test command:

```
for script in ~/bad-shell/scripts/*.sh
do
        # If the file or folder doesn't exist, skip it.
        if ! [ -e "$script" ]; then continue; fi
        echo "Found script: $script"
done
```

The -e ("exists") operator in a test command checks whether the file exists. If it does *not* exist, as denoted by the ! operator, the continue ("resume loop") statement executes, skipping the current item in the loop and moving to the next one.

Looping Through find Command Results

If the files you're trying to loop through are too complex to match with a shell pattern, you can use the find command to narrow them down, then loop through the results. (See Chapter 3 for more on the find command.)

The following example uses the find command to run a loop that prints every symlink in the user's home directory. But before running the loop, it creates a symlink with a space, which causes some interesting output:

```
# Create a symlink (with a space) to "effective-shell".
ln -s ~/effective-shell ~/effective\ shell
# Find all symlinks and print each one.
links=$(find ~ -type l -maxdepth 1)
for link in $links
do
    echo "Found Link: $link"
done
```

If you run this script, the specific links you see will depend on how your system is set up, but you'll also see results like these:

```
...
Found Link: /home/dwmkerr/effective
Found Link: shell
...
```

The problem is that the shell has performed word splitting at the space in the path */home/dwmkerr/effective shell*. As a result, it looks like two links have been found: */home/dwmkerr/effective* and *shell*. This is a persistent headache for anyone who needs to build shell scripts.

You can solve the problem in a number of ways, but the most common solution is to temporarily change the delimiter the shell uses to split text into words, using a special variable called IFS ("internal field separator"). The IFS variable tells the shell what characters to use as delimiters when splitting text into words. By default, IFS uses whitespace, which includes spaces, tabs, and newlines. Telling it to split *only* on newlines solves the issue of files with spaces in their paths:

```
# Save the current value of IFS, so you can restore it later. Split on newlines.
old_ifs=$IFS
IFS=$'\n'
# Find all symlinks and print each one.
links=$(find ~ -type l -maxdepth 1)
for link in $links
do
    echo "Found Link: $link"
done
# Restore the original value of IFS.
IFS=$old_ifs
```

Now the `find` command will put each file it finds on its own line and will *not* split up files with spaces or other whitespace in their names. If you run this command, you should see this output:

```
...
Found Link: /home/dwmkerr/effective shell
...
```

The symlink correctly appears with a space in its name.

NOTE   *Be careful when changing the IFS variable as it could cause subsequent commands to behave in unexpected ways. This is why you first copy the current value into a variable (old_ifs), then change it, and then set it back after you have run your commands. In general, if you are changing the IFS variable, it's a good sign you might be doing something that would be better done with a programming language.*

This solution will cover you in most cases, but it's not ideal for several reasons:

- It's verbose. You must store the current value of the IFS variable and then reset it later.
- It's not quite foolproof. On some systems, filenames can have a newline character, so this script would fail for those files.
- You must use the ANSI C quoting syntax—surrounding the variable with single quotes—to set IFS to a newline (see "Quoting Variables and Values" on page 124 for more about quoting syntax).
- If someone reading the code doesn't know what IFS is, the entire script will be difficult for them to follow.

For these reasons, it's probably best not to use a shell script in this case. No solution is particularly clean or simple, so you might be better off with a programming language. See Chapter 21 for more details on alternatives to shell scripting.

Iterating with C-Style Loops

If you've used programming languages like C, C++, Python, or Java, you may be familiar with this "C-style" loop structure (note the spaces between the expressions and the parentheses):

```
for (( expression1 ; expression2 ; expression3 ))
do
    command 1
    command 2
    command n
done
```

This loop structure runs with three arithmetic expressions: an *initialize* expression, which typically sets up the loop's initial state; the *conditional* expression, which checks whether the loop is complete; and the *iterate* expression, which is evaluated after the loop commands are completed.

The following C-style for loop iterates through five numbers:

```
for (( i = 1; i <= 5; i++ ))
do
    echo "Loop ${i}"
done
```

First, this code sets a counter, an iterator variable named _, to 1 (the initialize expression). On each iteration through the loop, it checks whether i is less than or equal to 5 (the conditional expression), and if so, prints the loop number. Finally, at the end of the iteration, it adds 1 to i (the iterate expression).

Let's break it down step-by-step:

First iteration

1. Set i to 1.
2. Check if 1 <= 5. Yes, so enter the loop.
3. Execute echo "Loop 1" to print Loop 1.
4. Increment i to 2.

Second iteration

1. Check if 2 <= 5. Yes, so continue.
2. Execute echo "Loop 2" to print Loop 2.
3. Increment i to 3.

And so on until:

Sixth iteration

1. Check if 6 <= 5. No, so exit the loop.

The output of this script is as follows:

```
Loop 1
Loop 2
Loop 3
Loop 4
Loop 5
```

C-style loops can be a convenient way to run more complex loops than ones that iterate over a simple set of words.

Looping over Sequences

It's also common to use a for loop with brace expansion, which you may remember from Chapter 10. As a quick refresher on how it works, this example uses brace expansion and touch to create three files:

```
touch {coffee,tea,milkshake}-menu.txt
```

Running `ls -1 *-menu.txt` returns the following output:

```
coffee-menu.txt
milkshake-menu.txt
tea-menu.txt
```

Now let's see brace expansion in a for loop:

```
for i in {1..10}
do
    echo "Loop ${i}"
done
```

This code loops through the numbers 1 to 10 and then prints a list of loop numbers.

You can also use brace expansion to loop through a sequence of values or a range of numbers. You can even specify the increment used in a sequence like so:

```
for i in {0..25..5}
do
    echo "Loop ${i}"
done
```

The first value, 0, is the starting value of the sequence; the second, 25, is the ending value of the sequence; and the third, 5, is the increment (step) between values. Here's the output of this loop:

```
Loop 0
Loop 5
Loop 10
Loop 15
Loop 20
Loop 25
```

Next, we'll turn to another kind of loop that builds on the discussion of conditional logic in Chapter 11.

The while Loop

The `while` loop executes commands until a certain condition is met. It has the following structure:

```
while test-commands
do
    conditional-command 1
    conditional-command 2
    conditional-command n
done
```

As long as the test commands return 0, indicating success the loop will run the conditional commands. After the conditional commands have been run, the loop returns to the beginning and evaluates the test commands again.

The following example uses a while loop to generate a list of random numbers:

```
# Create an empty array of random numbers.
random_numbers=()
# As long as the length of the array is less than 5, continue to loop.
while [ ${#random_numbers[@]} -lt 5 ]
do
    # Get a random number; ask the user if they want to add it to the array.
    random_number=$RANDOM
    read -p "Add $random_number to the list? (y/n): " choice

    # If the user chose "y", add the random number to the array.
    if [ "$choice" = "y" ]; then random_numbers+=($random_number); fi
done

# Show the contents of the array.
echo "Random Numbers: ${random_numbers[@]}"
```

This script begins by initializing an empty array called random_numbers. Inside the while loop, the script generates a random number using the shell's built-in RANDOM variable, which produces a pseudorandom integer between 0 and 32,767. The user is then prompted to decide whether to add this random number to the array by entering a y or n response If they enter y, the += operator appends the number to the array.

The while loop continues until the array contains exactly five elements. At that point, the loop terminates, and the echo command prints the values in the array:

```
Add 14718 to the list? (y/n): y
Add 2646 to the list? (y/n): n
Add 11898 to the list? (y/n): y
Add 31506 to the list? (y/n): y
Add 32436 to the list? (y/n): y
Add 6803 to the list? (y/n): n
Add 25811 to the list? (y/n): y
Random Numbers: 14718 11898 31506 32436 25811
```

You typically use a while loop when you don't know how many iterations will be needed (as in this case, where you don't know how many times the user will enter y), and you need to reevaluate at each iteration whether you should continue to loop.

Looping Through the Lines in a File

You can use a while loop to iterate through each line in a file, without having to load the entire file into memory:

```
while read line; do
    echo "Read: $line"
done < ~/effective-shell/data/top100.csv
```

This example uses shell redirection to redirect the contents of the *~/effective-shell/data/top100.csv* file into the read command in the while loop. The read command will read the file, line by line, until it finds the final line.

The output will look like this:

```
Read: "Rank","Rating","Title","Reviews"
Read: "1","97","Black Panther (2018)","515"
Read: "2","94","Avengers: Endgame (2019)","531"
...
```

This script has some issues, however:

- If the last line of the file doesn't end with a newline, it is not read.

- Backslashes will be treated as escape sequences, leading to broken output.

- Leading whitespace will be removed.

It's possible to work around these challenges, but the resulting script is a lot harder to read:

```
while IFS="" read -r line || [ -n "$line" ]; do
    echo "Read: $line"
done < ~/effective-shell/data/top100.csv
```

This approach requires some complex tricks to avoid each issue:

- The || [-n "$line"] test checks that the line being read isn't zero length. As long as it's not, the loop continues iterating, ensuring that the read command reads the last line of the file even if it doesn't have a newline.

- The -r ("do not escape") option for read ensures that backlashes are not interpreted as escape sequences.

- IFS="" temporarily disables any word splitting in the loop, preserving any leading whitespace.

However, this code *still* has potential issues. For example, if commands in the loop read from stdin, the loop will have errors. Check out Chapter 21 for some better ways to read files.

I've included this example only because it's something you're likely to come across in scripts written by others. It also might be useful for simple scenarios where you're fairly sure of the structure of the file you are reading. But generally speaking, this is a case where you should consider using a programming language to create a more maintainable solution.

Looping Forever

Sometimes you might want a while loop to loop forever, which is known as an *infinite loop*. For instance, you could be writing a script that reads an option from the user, processes it, and then starts again.

This example demonstrates an infinite loop for a simple text-based game menu. The loop uses the true command, which always returns a successful status, ensuring the loop continues indefinitely:

```
while true
do
    echo "1) Move forward"
    echo "2) Move backward"
    echo "3) Turn left"
    echo "4) Turn right"
    echo "5) Explore"
    echo "0) Quit"

    read -p "What will you do: " choice
    if [ "$choice" -eq 0 ]; then
        exit
    fi
    # The rest of the game logic would go here.
    # ...
done
```

Inside the loop, the script displays a menu of options for the user. If the user selects option 0 to quit, the exit command terminates the entire script. Otherwise, the loop repeats, allowing the user to continue interacting with the menu.

This example shows a common pattern for an infinite loop: offering a menu of options that the user can call repeatedly until they decide to quit.

The until Loop

The until loop operates similarly to the while loop, except that it runs *until* the test commands return success. The structure of the until loop is just like the while loop:

```
until test-commands
do
    conditional-command 1
    conditional-command 2
    conditional-command n
done
```

As long as the test commands do *not* return success, the loop will run the conditional commands. After the conditional commands have been run, the loop returns to the beginning and evaluates the test commands again.

Here's an example of an `until` loop that builds a random number at least 15 characters long:

```
# Create an empty random number string; you'll build it up in the loop.
random_number=""
# Keep looping until the random number is at least 15 characters long.
until [ "${#random_number}" -ge 15 ]
do
    random_number+=$RANDOM
done
echo "Random Number: ${random_number}"
```

The script initializes the variable `random_number` as an empty string. Then, in each loop iteration, `${#random_number}` (the parameter expansion syntax you saw in Chapter 11) checks the string length, and `random_number+=$RANDOM` appends a new random number to the string. When the string's length is greater than or equal to 15 characters, the loop stops.

When you run this script, you should see something like this:

```
Random Number: 364272371462227929
```

In general, I recommend using `while` loops rather than `until` loops. Programming languages commonly feature `while` loops, so anyone reading the code will likely be familiar with them, whereas `until` loops are a bit rarer.

You can easily turn any `until` loop into a `while` loop simply by inverting your test commands. For example, you could rewrite the previous `until` loop like so:

```
random_number=""
while [ "${#random_number}" -lt 15 ]
do
    random_number+=$RANDOM
done
echo "Random Number: ${random_number}"
```

This changes the condition from `-ge 15` (greater than or equal to 15) to `-lt 15` (less than 15). The `while` loop version of the script will probably be a little easier for most readers to parse.

The continue and break Statements

As mentioned earlier in the chapter, the `continue` statement can be used to skip an iteration in a loop. The `break` ("exit loop") statement can be used to stop running the loop altogether.

When you use the `continue` statement, you're telling the shell that you want to stop processing the current iteration of the loop and move on to the next iteration. You can use as many `continue` statements as you like in a loop.

Here's an example of a script that lets users show the contents of a directory:

```
echo "For each folder, choose y/n to show contents, or c to cancel."
for entry in ~/*
do
    # If the file is not a directory, or it cannot be searched, skip it.
    if ! [ -d "$entry" ] || ! [ -x "$entry" ]; then continue; fi
    # Ask the user if they want to see the contents.
    read -p "Show: $entry? [y/n/c]: " choice
    # If the user chose "c" for cancel, break.
    if [ "$choice" = "c" ]; then break; fi
    # If the user chose "y" to show contents, list them.
    if [ "$choice" = "y" ]; then ls "$entry "; fi
done
```

If the directory is empty, the continue statement skips to the next directory. If the directory is not empty, the user is able to choose whether to show its contents, not show its contents, or cancel the operation. If the user cancels the operation, the break statement stops the loop from iterating.

Using break and continue statements can simplify your loops; without them, it would be much harder to write loops like this one.

Creating Compact Loops

In this chapter's examples, I've split the loop constructs so that there's only one statement per line. But just as with the if statement, you can combine any of these lines, as long as you use a semicolon to let the shell know where each statement ends.

You'll often see the do keyword on the same line as the for or while statement:

```
for script in *.sh; do
    touch "$script"
done
```

If you're simply typing in a terminal rather than writing a script, you might write the loop on a single line like so:

```
for script in *.sh; do touch "$script"; done
```

This one-liner updates the last accessed time and last modified time of all files that end with *.sh* in the current folder.

NOTE   *As with the if statement, I recommend keeping each statement on its own line until you are 100 percent familiar with its syntax. When writing a loop is second nature, you can use the more compact syntax where appropriate.*

When you're running the shell interactively (that is, typing in the shell rather than writing a shell script), you can still use multiple lines. If you type for `script in *.sh` and press ENTER, the shell will let you enter the next line. You can keep adding lines (you'll see the prompt > to indicate that you can enter more input) until you type done and press ENTER:

```
$ for script in *.sh
> do touch "$script"
> done
```

Now it's time to apply what you've learned so far in this chapter to the common command script described in previous chapters.

Updating the common Command to Loop Through Results

Chapter 11 ended with the *common.v3.sh* script, which shows common commands from the user's shell history. If you need a refresher on what's in the script, view it in your pager as follows:

```
$ less ~/effective-shell/scripts/common.v3.sh
```

Now you'll add a loop to the script to iterate through each command found and display its position in the list of results. The file is a little larger now, so I'll show only the key changes you'll make.

First, you'll use shell parameter expansion to run a subshell and store the common commands in a variable:

```
# Store the most recently used commands in the "commands" variable.
commands=$(tail ~/.bash_history -n ${history_lines} \
    | sort \
    | uniq -c \
    | sed 's/^ *//' \
    | sort -n -r \
    | head -n ${command_count})
```

Now you can loop through this new commands variable at the end of the script and show a number before each command:

```
# Print each command, showing its order in the list.
# Commands are separated by newlines, so temporarily change IFS to loop over
# each line of the commands.
counter=1
old_ifs=$IFS
IFS=$'\n'
for command in $commands
do
    echo "$counter: $command"
    counter=$((counter + 1))
done
IFS=$old_ifs
```

You've initialized a counter variable to 1 and set it to increment by 1 at each iteration of the loop. You're also applying what you learned earlier about the IFS variable to temporarily change the delimiter to a newline so that each command appears on its own line and word splitting won't be applied. After closing the for loop, you restore IFS to its original value.

Now when you run this command, each of the common commands is printed with both its order in the list and its count:

```
$ common
1: 135 gst
2: 73 vi
3: 47 gc
4: 40 ls
5: 37 ga .
6: 27 gpo
7: 25 gl
8: 24 gpr
9: 21 gcm
10: 17 make dev
```

This addition could be useful if you wanted to extend the script further to allow the user to enter a number to execute the command at that position.

The updated script is at *~/effective-shell/scripts/common.v4.sh* To update your symlink to point to this version, run the ln command with the -s flag as follows:

```
$ sudo ln -sf ~/effective-shell/scripts/common.v4.sh /usr/local/bin/common
```

As in previous chapters, you're using the -f ("force") flag to ln to force the creation of the symlink, overwriting the one that already exists at this location.

Summary

In this chapter, you learned how to use different types of loops in the shell to iterate over values in an array, words in a sentence, files and folders, and even the results of commands. You also learned how word splitting works, as well as the role of the IFS variable. Loops are a crucial part of the effective shell user's toolkit, and you'll likely find yourself using them often to streamline your tasks.

In the next chapter, we'll look at functions and parameters—two other programming must-haves that add structure and functionality to your shell scripts.

13

FUNCTIONS, PARAMETERS, AND ERROR HANDLING

Functions let you structure commands into logical blocks, reducing repetition, thus making your scripts more efficient and easier to read and manage. In this chapter, you'll learn exactly what functions are, how to create them and pass parameters to them, and what to do with the values returned from the functions you write. We'll also cover how to handle errors that can result when a command in your functions or elsewhere in your script fails. The tools and techniques you pick up in this chapter will help you build even more powerful scripts.

Creating a Function

A *function* is a set of commands that you define once and then can call at any time within your script. A function definition has the following structure:

```
function-name() {
    function-command 1
    function-command 2
    function-command n
}
```

First, you specify the name of the function followed by empty parentheses, and then, between a pair of braces ({}), you list the commands to execute when you call the function.

Here's a very simple function in action:

```
title() {
    echo "My Script version 1.0"
}
```

This script defines a function called title that prints out a message.

You call this function the same way you call any command in the shell, by entering its name and pressing ENTER:

```
$ title
My Script version 1.0"
```

In some scripts, you might see functions defined with the function keyword:

```
function title() {
    echo "My Script version 1.0"
}
```

This is somewhat less standard, however, so I don't recommend it. If you do use the function keyword, adding parentheses after the function name is optional.

Variables in Functions

A function can read and write to any variables in the current shell session:

```
# Set some variables.
title="My Cool Script"
version="1.2"
succeeded=0

# Create a function that writes a message and changes a variable.
write_title() {
  # You can create and read variables within a function...
❶ title_message="${title} - version ${version}"
❷ echo "${title_message}"
```

```
      # ...and set them as well.
❸   succeeded=1
    }

    # Show the value of "succeeded" before and after the function call.
❹   echo "Succeeded: ${succeeded}"
    write_title
❺   echo "Succeeded: ${succeeded}"
    echo "Title Message: ${title_message}"
```

This script assigns three variables and then creates a function called
write_title, which reads the title and version variables and stores their values in a new title_message variable ❶.

The next part of the script prints the initial value of succeeded, which is
0 ❹, and calls the write_title function to print title_message to the screen ❷
and set the value of succeeded to 1 ❸. Finally, the script prints the new value
of succeeded followed by the title_message again ❺.

Here's the output of this script:

```
Succeeded: 0
My Cool Script - version 1.2
Succeeded: 1
Title Message: My Cool Script - version 1.2
```

As this script shows, functions can work with variables in multiple ways:
they can define new variables, use the variables available in the shell, and
overwrite variable values.

Variable Scoping

In the preceding script, the shell was able to read the value of the title
_message variable even though that variable was set in the write_title function. If you come from a programming background, you might find this
behavior odd. The reason for it is that shell scripting uses *dynamic scoping*,
where variables are visible to any code that runs after they were created,
regardless of their scope (that is, where they were defined in the code).
Many common programming languages, such as Python, JavaScript, C,
and Java, use an alternative mechanism called *lexical scoping*, where a variable's visibility is determined by where it's defined, preventing you from
using it outside its scope. Lexical scoping can reduce errors by ensuring
that if you define a variable in a function, you won't accidentally overwrite
a variable of the same name that's being used elsewhere.

By default, all variables in shell scripting are *globally scoped*, meaning
they can be used anywhere. However, you can use the local keyword to
define a *locally scoped* variable, meaning one that is available to the current
function (and, thanks to dynamic scoping, to any functions it calls directly
or indirectly):

```
run_loop() {
    local count=0
```

```
    for i in {1..10}; do
        # Update the counter.
        count=$((count + 1))
    done
    echo "Count is: ${count}"
}
```

This code defines a run_loop function that creates a locally scoped count variable. The counter starts at 0 and increments by 1 at each iteration of the for loop. After 10 iterations, the loop ends and the value of count is printed.

Here's what happens when you run this function:

```
$ run_loop
Count is: 10
$ echo "Count: ${count}"
Count:
```

Because you declared the count variable with the local keyword, it's available to the run_loop function and any functions run_loop calls. If you try to access count outside of those contexts, however, it is undefined.

In general, you should use local variables inside functions, which can help you avoid problems where calling a function can have unintended side effects. Consider this example, where you set a count variable and then call the previous run_loop function:

```
# Set a count variable somewhere in the script.
count=3

# Call the "run_loop" function.
run_loop

# Write out the value of "count".
echo "The 'count' variable is: ${count}"
```

The output of this script is:

```
Count is: 10
The 'count' variable is: 3
```

Even though you've defined a variable named count in the run_loop function, it doesn't overwrite the count value you set outside of the function (3 in this case) since it is locally scoped. If you had defined the count variable *without* the local keyword when you created the run_loop function, however, running this script would give you the following output:

```
Count is: 10
The 'count' variable is: 10
```

Without the local keyword, calling run_loop overwrites the count variable defined outside of the function. Others reading your script might not expect this behavior and will be unpleasantly surprised when calling your function overwrites the variables they're using.

Passing Parameters to Functions

Parameters are input values that can make your shell functions more flexible. Instead of having to write separate functions for each value you need, you can reuse the function with different parameters. You can pass any number of parameters to a shell function. This simple sum function takes two parameters and adds them together:

```
sum() {
    local value1=$1
    local value2=$2
    local result=$((value1 + value2))
    echo "The sum of ${value1} and ${value2} is ${result}"
}
```

You can pass parameters to the sum function as follows:

```
$ sum 3 6
The sum of 3 and 6 is 9
$ sum 10 33
The sum of 10 and 33 is 43
```

When you pass parameters into a shell function, they're automatically stored in special built-in variables known as *parameter variables*. In this script, the parameter variables 1 and 2 contain the first and second parameters, respectively. At the beginning of the function, putting 1 and 2 into local variables with slightly more descriptive names (value1 and value2) makes the script more readable. The function could also have been written like so:

```
# Create a function that calculates the sum of two numbers.
sum() {
    echo "The sum of $1 and $2 is $(($1 + $2))"
}
```

For a short and simple function, you might just use the parameter variables directly like this. However, for anything more complex than a one-line script, I recommend creating a local variable with a more descriptive name for the sake of readability.

The shell provides several other parameter variables in addition to 1 and 2. Table 13-1 lists some of the most common ones.

Table 13-1: Common Parameter Variables

Parameter variable	Description
0	The name of the shell script, which the shell provides automatically.
-	The options that have been set in the shell.
1	The first parameter.
2	The second parameter.

(continued)

Table 13-1: Common Parameter Variables *(continued)*

Parameter variable	Description
n	The *n*th parameter (this starts from position 1, because position 0 is always reserved for the name of the shell script itself).
{11}	The 11th parameter; if the parameter is more than one digit, you must surround it with braces.
#	The number of parameters.
@	The full set of parameters expanded as a list and then split into words. When @ is used inside double quotes ("$@"), each parameter becomes a separate word in the list but no further word splitting is applied.
*	The full set of parameters expanded and then split into words. When * is used inside double quotes ("$*"), the result is a single word, with each parameter separated by the first character of IFS (or a space if IFS is not set).
{@:*start*:*count*}	A subset of *count* parameters starting at parameter number *start*.

The behavior of the @ and * parameter variables is essentially identical unless they are surrounded by double quotes. As an example, given three parameters

```
beagle
greyhound
german shepherd
```

both * and @ would result in four words:

```
beagle
greyhound
german
shepherd
```

However, "$@" would result in three words (the same as the original parameters):

```
beagle
greyhound
german shepherd
```

And "$*" would result in one word, with the first character of IFC (usually a space, as shown here) separating the parameters in that word:

```
beagle greyhound german shepherd
```

Let's look at the @ parameter in action. Here's how you could update the preceding sum function with the @ and # parameter variables:

```
# Create a function that sums a set of numbers.
sum() {
```

```
        local total=0
        for value in $@; do
            total=$((total + value))
        done

        # Write out the result.
        echo "Summed $# values for a total of: ${total}"
}
```

You can call this updated function with any number of parameters:

```
$ sum 1 2 3 4 5
Summed 5 values for a total of: 15
```

The @ variable expands into the full list of parameters, allowing you to process them all in a single loop. Without @, you'd have to explicitly reference each parameter with 1, 2, and so on, as in the previous example. The # variable contains the number of parameters provided to the function.

Because the @ variable isn't in double quotes, you could just as easily have used * since, without double quotes, @ and * behave the same way.

Using Array Operators in Parameter Variables

If you've read Chapter 10, you might notice that parameter variables are similar to the array operators used to get the members or the length of an array. This function combines the "get a subset of elements" array operator (known as an *array slice*) and the @ parameter variable:

```
# Show the top "n" values of a set.
show_top() {
    local n=$1
    local values=${@:2:n}
    echo "Top ${n} values: ${values}"
}
```

As with the sum function, you can call show_top with any number of parameters:

```
$ show_top 3 10 20 30 40 50
Top 3 values: 10 20 30
```

Using the array slice on the @ variable returns a subset of the full array of parameters. This script is a little odd to read in that when you set the values variable, you need to "skip" past the first positional parameter because that parameter indicates the number of values to show (3, in this case), so the subset starts at the second parameter (10).

Shifting Parameters

You can use the shift ("shift positional parameters") command to remove some parameters from the beginning of the positional parameters array and move the remaining parameters to take their place.

The following example uses `shift` with the `show_top` function:

```
# Show the top "n" values of a set.
show_top() {
    # Grab the number of values to show, then shift.
    local n=$1
    shift

    # Get the set of values to show.

    local values=${@:1:n}
    echo "Top ${n} values: ${values}"
}
```

Notice that you're starting in position 1 now. Arrays normally start at 0, but @ indexing starts at 1 because the shell always sets 0 to the name of the script. After getting the value of the first parameter, you shift, removing it from the list of positional parameters so that you can deal with the remaining parameters.

This approach has the same effect as specifying `${@:2:n}` from the previous example: skipping the first parameter and starting at the second. As you can see, the output of the function is the same as before:

```
$ show_top 3 10 20 30 40 50
Top 3 values: 10 20 30
```

In a scenario where you have multiple parameters that precede a list, using `shift` can make your code more readable. If you find you're having to write a lot of complex code to shift parameters around, however, you might be better off using a programming language rather than the shell. See Chapter 21 for alternatives.

Function Return Values

A return value is what a function "gives back" when it finishes running, such as the result of a calculation or a success or failure status. You can return a value from a shell function in two ways. The first is simply to set the value of a variable like so:

```
is_even() {
    local number=$1

    # A number is even when you divide it by 2 and there is no remainder.
    # Set "result" to 1 if the parameter is even and to 0 otherwise.
    if [ $((number % 2)) -eq 0 ]; then
        result=1
    else
        result=0
    fi
}
```

This function returns a value by setting a variable called result to 1 if the parameter provided to the function is even, and 0 if it is odd.

Here's how you could use the is_even function to check whether the number 33 is even:

```
$ is_even 33
$ echo "Result is: $result"
Result is: 0
```

You could set any number of variables within your function definition to return values. In general, though, you should avoid this method of returning values. Because result is a global variable, it would overwrite the value of another variable of the same name in your script when you call this function. Declaring result with local would avoid that problem, but then you'd have no way to retrieve its value elsewhere in your script, making it fairly useless.

A safer and more common way to return a value from a function is to write its result to stdout.

Writing Results to Standard Output

If you write the result of a function to stdout (that is, print it to the screen), you can access that return value in a far more readable way:

```
lowercase() {
    local all_parameters="$@"
    # Translate all uppercase characters in the input to lowercase.
    echo "$all_parameters " | tr '[:upper:]' '[:lower:]'
}
```

This example defines a function named lowercase. It then creates a local variable called all_parameters, which is set to @, the parameter variable that contains all the parameters provided to the function. Next, lowercase writes these parameters to the tr ("translate characters") command and tells it to translate uppercase letters to lowercase letters. The final output is then written to stdout.

If you *source* the preceding script (that is, load it into your current shell session, as described in Chapter 9), you can call lowercase and capture its output into a variable simply by executing the function like so:

```
$ result=$(lowercase "Don't SHOUT!")
$ echo "$result"
don't shout!
```

This captures the output of the lowercase function into the result variable. The $(*function*) syntax means "execute this function in a subshell" (covered in Chapter 10).

If you have a programming background, it might seem strange to return the result of a function by writing to stdout. Remember, however, that the shell is a text-based interface to the computer system. The majority of shell commands that provide output (ls, find, cat, and so on) write it to the screen. When you echo a result from a function, you're really just following the Unix standard of writing the results of a program to the screen.

Running the `lowercase` function directly in a shell prints the output to the screen:

```
$ lowercase "PLEASE don't SHOUT!"
please don't shout!
```

Shell functions are designed to behave in a similar way as shell commands: they write their output to stdout. It's up to the person calling the function to decide whether to display that output, capture it into a variable, or pass it to another command (see the discussion of pipelines in Chapter 2).

Avoiding Pitfalls with Command Output

Writing the results of a function to stdout is a tried-and-tested method of returning values. However, you need to be careful, as this example demonstrates:

```
# This function creates a temporary folder for today and returns its path.
temp_today() {
    # Get today's date in the format YYYY-MM-DD.
    local today=$(date +"%Y-%m-%d")

    # Create a temporary directory for today and return it.
    tmpdir_today="/tmp/${today}"
    echo "Creating folder '${tmpdir_today}'..."
    mkdir -p "${tmpdir_today}"
    echo "${tmpdir_today}"
}
```

The `temp_today` function creates a temporary folder whose name is based on the current date, but if you try to grab the result of the function and change to that folder

```
# Go to today's temporary folder.
folder=$(temp_today)
cd "${folder}"
```

the script fails, with the following output:

```
'Creating folder \'/tmp/2025-05-28\'...\n/tmp/2025-05-28': No such file or directory
```

What's going on here?

The problem is that the `temp_today` is outputting two results: the status message and the folder path. When you capture the folder's output with `folder=$(temp_today)`, you're capturing *all* of that output, not just the folder path. As a result, when you run `cd "${folder}"`, the shell sees the entire string, including the status message, and the `cd` command fails because it's trying to change into a directory that doesn't exist.

Remember, any command you call in a function that might write to stdout could cause problems by writing text to your output. Take a look at another example, a function called `command_exists` that uses type ("display information about command") to check whether a given command is available on the system:

```
command_exists() {
    if type "$1"; then
        echo "1"
    else
        echo "0"
    fi
}
```

Here's what happens when you try to store the result of the `command_exists` function in a variable:

```
$ result=$(command_exists "touch")
$ echo "Result is: ${result}"
Result is: touch is hashed (/usr/bin/touch)
1
```

The result variable should have been set to 1 or 0. However, type does two separate things—writes a message to stdout *and* returns the success/failure status—so result=$(command_exists "touch") captures all of that output. That's why the result variable ends up containing the text touch is hashed (/usr/bin/touch) in addition to the status code 1 you expected.

Chapter 2 explains that you can discard a command's output by redirecting it to the *null* file. You can use this trick within your functions to stop commands from "polluting" your function's output:

```
command_exists() {
    if type "$1" >> /dev/null; then
        echo "1"
    else
        echo "0"
    fi
}
```

This command discards the text output from type instead of capturing it, so now if you run the `command_exists` function, you'll see only the status code in the result.

Returning Status Codes

The return ("return from shell function") command causes a function to exit with a given status code. You might remember from Chapter 11 that when a command runs successfully, it should return a status code of 0, whereas any nonzero status code is an *error code*.

Here's how you might rewrite the `command_exists` function from the previous example to set a status code:

```
command_exists() {
    if type "$1" >> /dev/null; then
        return 0
```

```
        else
            return 1
        fi
}
```

Now you can use `command_exists` in an `if` statement like so:

```
if command_exists "common"; then
    echo "The 'common' command is installed on your system"
else
    echo "The 'common' command is not installed on your system"
fi
```

If the `type` command succeeds (meaning the `common` command exists), `command_exists` returns 0 and prints the first message; otherwise, it returns 1 and prints the second message.

Many shells will allow you to set values only from 0 to 255, and, again, most users will expect a command to return 0 for success and a nonzero value for a failure. If you need to provide output for a command beyond a status code, you should write it to stdout or, if you must, set the value of a global variable.

The status code of the most recently executed command is always available in the ? variable. Here's how you could use it:

```
$ type "test"
test is a shell builtin
$ echo "Result: $?"
Result: 0
```

The test command returns 0 to indicate that it executed successfully and also writes a message to stdout.

PARAMETERS AND STATUS CODES FOR SCRIPTS

Everything you've learned about parameters applies to scripts themselves. You can pass parameters to scripts and read them with special variables such as 1 and 2. The only difference is that instead of using the return command, you use the exit ("exit the shell") command to exit a script with a status code.

Be careful with the exit command, however. If you're running a script (that is, working in a non-interactive shell), exit will simply close the subshell the script is running in. But if you type exit in an interactive shell, it will end your session or close your terminal window.

You've learned a lot about what you can do with functions and how they can make your scripts more efficient and manageable. But even the most well-crafted script can sometimes cause unexpected errors, so let's look at some ways to handle those next.

Error Handling

If a command in your function or elsewhere in your script fails, the script will still continue to run, which can easily lead to issues. Let's look at an example and then see how to avoid this kind of problem.

Create a script called *today.sh* that makes a new temporary folder for the current date and puts a symlink to that folder in your home directory:

```
#!/usr/bin/env sh

# Get today's date in the format YYYY-MM-DD.
today=$(date +"%Y-%m-%d")

# Create a path to today's temp folder and then make sure the folder exists.
temp_path="/tmp/${today}"
mkdir -p "${temp_path}"

# Now make a symlink to the folder in your homedir.
ln -sf "${temp_path}" "${HOME}/today"

# Write out the path you created.
echo "${temp_path}"
```

Now make the script executable and then run it as follows:

```
$ chmod +x ./today.sh
$ ./today.sh
/tmp/2025-05-28
```

You've successfully created a new folder in */tmp* with the current date as its name, created a symlink called */today* in your home directory to point to that temp folder, and then printed out the folder's path.

Let's see what happens if one of the commands in the script fails. First, delete both the symlink and the temp folder you just created:

```
$ rm -rf ~/today
$ rm "/tmp/$(date +"%Y-%m-%d")"
```

Now use the touch command to create a file in the same location where the today command will try to create its *today* folder:

```
$ touch "/tmp/$(date +'%Y-%m-%d')"
```

If you run the script now, you'll see a problem:

```
$ ./today.sh
mkdir: /tmp/2025-05-28: Not a directory
/tmp/2025-05-28
$ cd ~/today
bash: cd: /home/dwmkerr/today: Not a directory
```

The mkdir command fails because there's a file already in the location where you're trying to create the *today* folder. But the script keeps running and creates a symlink to this file rather than to the *today* folder as expected. Then, when you try to move to the *today* folder, you get another error because it's a link to a file, not a folder.

In general, if a command fails in your shell script, you probably want the entire script to stop executing. Otherwise, you can get this cascading effect as commands continue to return even after the failure, which can cause all sorts of unexpected behavior.

To tell the shell to exit when a command fails, use the set ("set option") command, which turns shell options on and off, with the -e ("exit if any command exits with a nonzero status") option:

```
#!/usr/bin/env sh

# Exit if any command fails.
set -e

# ...
```

Now clean up your folder again:

```
$ rm -rf ~/today
```

And finally, create the same file that caused the failure and rerun the script:

```
$ touch "/tmp/$(date +"%Y-%m-%d")"
$ ./today.sh
mkdir: /tmp/2025-05-28: Not a directory
```

In this case, the script stops running as soon as the mkdir command fails, so the symlink is never created.

When you call set to set a shell option, the special $- ("shell options") parameter is updated to include the option you've added. Calling set -e will prepend the letter *e* to the value of $-. You can run echo $- to see which options have been set.

The set -e option affects only the final command of a pipeline. This means that if you have a pipeline like this one

```
grep '[:space:]*#' ~/effective-shell/scripts/common.sh | tr 'a-z' 'A-Z'
```

the script will still run if the grep command fails. To ensure that the shell terminates if a command in a pipeline fails, you must set the pipefail option:

```
set -o pipefail
```

Chapter 14 covers set -e and set -o pipefail in more detail.

If you set up your scripts to fail on errors (which is always a good idea), make sure to properly handle commands that you suspect *might* fail. For example, if you want to delete a file in a script but don't want to stop if the deletion fails for some reason, you could use an if block to "catch" the error and show a warning:

```
if ! rm ~/my-file.text; then
    echo "warning: unable to delete file"
fi
```

Another option is to use a conditional expression:

```
rm ~/my-file.txt || true
```

This expression always evaluates to true so it will not stop the script if the rm command throws an error.

For more on if statements and conditional expressions, see Chapter 11.

Simplifying the common Command with Functions

Now let's turn back to the common command script (introduced in Chapter 9), which shows the most commonly used commands from your shell history. Chapter 12 left off with the *common.v4.sh* file, the latest version of the script.

If you haven't yet looked at the past few chapters or need a refresher on what's in the script, install the sample files to your *effective-shell* folder like so:

```
$ curl effective.sh | sh
```

Then open the *common.v4.sh* file in your editor.

Let's make a couple more changes based on what you've learned in this chapter. First, make sure to exit the script if one of the commands fails by putting this line at the top of your script:

```
# Exit if any command fails.
set -e
```

Next, update the script on line 7 to store the first parameter provided to the script in a variable called command_count:

```
...
command_count=${1:-10} # The number of common commands to show
...
```

The 1 variable indicates the first parameter, but you're also using shell parameter expansion (described in Chapter 10) to provide a default value to use if the first parameter is not set. In this case, the default is set to 10 commands.

Currently, the script shows the count (that is, the number of times the command appears in the history) before the command's name. Change this behavior by defining a function that writes each command as a numbered line of text with the count *after* the command name:

```
write_command_then_count() {
    # Get the command and count, which currently looks like:
    #    '43 git commit'
    # Then write the command with the count afterward.
    local line="$1"
    local count=$(echo "${line}" | cut -d' ' -f1)
    local command=$(echo "${line}" | cut -d' ' -f2-)
    echo "${command} (${count})"
}
```

You can then rewrite the for loop to make it a little cleaner

```
counter=0
for command in $commands
do
    echo "$counter: $(write_command_then_count "$command")"
    counter=$((counter + 1))
done
```

Now when you run the common command, you can optionally provide the number of commands to show as a parameter:

```
$ common 5
common commands:
1: gst (139)
2: vi (74)
3: gc (42)
4: ga . (36)
5: gl (31)
```

Notice that the count comes after the command name in the output.

This revised script is in *~/effective-shell/scripts/common.v5.sh*. To update your link to point to that version, run the ln command with the -s and -f flags:

```
$ sudo ln -sf ~/effective-shell/scripts/common.v5.sh /usr/local/bin/common
```

Summary

In this chapter, you've learned all about how to use functions to provide more structure to your shell scripts, as well as how to use parameters, work with return values from functions, interpret status codes, and handle some common errors that you might encounter in your scripts.

In the next and final chapter of Part III, we'll look at some more advanced techniques that you'll find useful when writing shell scripts.

14

USEFUL PATTERNS
FOR SHELL SCRIPTS

To close this part of the book, we're going to look at some common patterns you'll encounter in shell scripts. You'll find these standard practices useful when building your own scripts, and you'll likely come across them in scripts others have written as well. You'll also learn about anti-patterns, or approaches that you might see in the wild but should generally avoid.

Although this chapter focuses on patterns that are useful in scripts, keep in mind that you can also apply them interactively when you are working in the shell. Even if you don't expect to write scripts yourself, you'll find it helpful to understand these techniques as you operate in the shell.

Ensuring Exit on Failure

Chapter 13 explained that, by default, shell scripts will continue to execute if a command fails. This behavior makes sense for an interactive shell, where you wouldn't want the shell to close if a command fails. For a shell script, however, continuing to run after an error has occurred will most likely cause unexpected behavior.

Two options override this default behavior:

set -e   Ensures that the shell script will exit if a command fails

set -o pipefail   Ensures that the shell script will exit if any command in a pipeline fails

In a pipeline, the set -e option causes the script to exit only if the *final* command in the pipeline fails. Thus, for most pipelines, you'll want to use the pipefail option instead to ensure that the script exits if *any* command fails.

Here's an example showing why these options are useful:

```
# Create the effective-shell folder.
mkdir -p ~/effective-shell

# Download and untar the effective-shell samples.
samples_uri='https://https://effective-shell.com/downloads/effective-shell-samples.tar.gz'
$ wget -c "${samples_uri}" -O - | tar -xz -C ~/effective-shell
```

Without the set -e option, if the mkdir -p command fails, the script will continue to run. Specifically, it will attempt to download and untar a file into a nonexistent folder. Why might mkdir -p fail? Although mkdir -p succeeds even if the folder exists, it still fails if there's a file in the location specified, if you don't have the right permissions to create the folder, and so on. You must be careful even with commands you assume will run successfully.

The second part of this snippet uses the wget ("web get") command to download the samples and pipe the results to tar to extract them. In this case, if you've *only* set set -e and wget fails (for example, if the address is wrong or you're offline), the shell will continue trying to run the script's subsequent commands and call tar, which won't work as expected.

If you have a command that you suspect might fail, but you want to continue execution even if it does fail, use the OR operator (||):

```
# Remove the shell configuration.
rm "$HOME/.shell.sh" || true
```

As described in Chapter 11, the OR conditional operator ensures that even if the rm command fails for some reason, the statement's overall result will be true and the script won't exit.

Debugging Shell Scripts with the Trace Option

Tracing is an incredibly useful debugging technique in which the shell writes each statement to stdout before evaluating it, letting you see the commands that will be run. To enable tracing, use the set ("set option") command with the -x ("trace") option.

The following example shows the technique applied in the *today.sh* script, which creates a temporary folder for the current date:

```
# today.sh creates a "today" symlink in the home directory folder to a fresh
# temporary folder each day.

# Enable tracing in the script.
set -x

# Get today's date in the format YYYY-MM-DD.
today=$(date +"%Y-%m-%d")

# Create a path to today's temp folder and then make sure the folder exists.
temp_path="/tmp/${today}"
mkdir -p "${temp_path}"

# Now make a symlink to the folder in your homedir.
ln -sf "${temp_path}" "${HOME}/today"

# Disable tracing now that you are done with the work.
set +x

# Write out the path you created.
echo "${temp_path}"
```

The set -x command enables tracing early on in the script, and set +x disables it toward the end. You generally don't want to leave tracing on once you've finished debugging as it can slow down execution, clutter your script, and potentially expose sensitive information.

Running this script should return the following output:

```
$ ~/effective-shell/scripts/today.sh
++ date +%Y-%m-%d
+ today=2025-05-29
+ temp_path=/tmp/2025-05-29
+ mkdir -p /tmp/2025-05-29
+ ln -sf /tmp/2025-05-29 /home/dwmkerr/today
+ set +x
/tmp/2025-05-29
```

The shell writes each command to stdout before executing it. The parameters are expanded, making it far easier to see what's going on and to troubleshoot issues.

The plus signs (+) differentiate the trace lines from the script's normal output. The final line of output in this example doesn't begin with a plus sign, because it's actual output from the echo command, rather than a trace line.

The number of plus signs on each line indicates the *level of indirection*, which is how many subshells are running. Each subshell is traced on its own line. This makes tracing complex commands that execute subshells far easier:

```
$ set -x
$ echo "Name of home folder is $(basename $(echo ~) )"
+++ echo /home/dwmkerr
++ basename /home/dwmkerr
+ echo 'Name of home folder is dwmkerr'
Name of home folder is dwmkerr
```

Tracing shows each command in the order in which it runs, with each additional plus sign indicating another nesting level. This example has three levels of indirection: the main shell (+) runs the final echo command, the first subshell (++) runs the basename command, and the second subshell (+++) runs the innermost echo command.

I often start my shell scripts with a snippet like this:

```
# Fail on errors in commands or in pipelines.
set -e
set -o pipefail

# Uncomment the next line to enable tracing to debug the script.
# set -x
```

This combines the first two patterns you've seen: failing on errors and tracing a script.

Checking for Existing Variables or Functions

You can optionally use the declare ("set variable values and attributes") command to explicitly declare that you're creating a variable. Sometimes this command is required—for example, when you want to create an associative array (as discussed in Chapter 10).

The declare command has a number of options, but a particularly useful one is -p ("display attributes and value"), which shows all variables of a certain type. For example, you can show all of the associative arrays that have been created like so:

```
$ declare -p -A
declare -A BASH_ALIASES=()
declare -A BASH_CMDS=()
...
```

You can also use `declare` within an `if...else` statement to check whether a variable has been set:

```
if declare -p -A my_options 2>1 /dev/null; then
    echo "'my_options' exists"
else
    echo "'my_options' does not exist"
fi
```

Unless you want `declare` to print a message if the variable doesn't exist, you need to silence its error output by sending the output to *\/dev\/null* as shown here.

You can also use these `declare` tricks to show all declared functions, to show the value of a function, or to check whether a function exists.

Unsetting Values

Use the `unset` ("unset variables or functions") command to clean up variables and functions you no longer need:

```
# Remove the "is_even" function from the shell session.
unset -f is_even
```

Unsetting shell variables and functions is important, especially in *.bashrc* or *.bash_profile* files. These files are sourced at shell startup to apply customizations, so leaving unnecessary values can inadvertently clash with other configurations or scripts. Chapter 15 covers the *.bashrc* and *.bash_profile* shell initialization files and many other details about configuring your shell.

Note that if a user simply runs the script in a subshell, no variables will be retained unless they were set with `EXPORT`.

Trapping Signals and Events

The `trap` ("trap signals and events") command specifies commands to run when the shell receives certain signals or when a particular condition occurs, such as the script exiting or a function returning.

One very common use for traps is to create a cleanup function that runs when the script is interrupted—for example, when the user cancels the script's execution by pressing CTRL-C (which sends the INT, or "interrupt," signal):

```
# Create a temporary folder for the effective-shell download.
source="https://effective-shell.com/downloads/effective-shell-samples.tar.gz"
tmp_dir=$(mktemp -d 2>/dev/null || mktemp -d -t 'effective-shell')
tmp_tar="${tmp_dir}/effective-shell.tar.gz"

# Define a cleanup function to call when the script exits or is canceled.
cleanup() {
    if [ -e "${tmp_tar}" ]; then rm "${tmp_tar}"; fi
    if [ -d "${tmp_dir}" ]; then rm -rf "${tmp_dir}"; fi
```

```
}

# Clean up on interrupt or terminate signals and on exit.
trap "cleanup" INT TERM EXIT

# Download the samples.
curl --fail --compressed -q -s "${source}" -o "${tmp_tar}"

# Extract the samples.
tar -xzf "${tmp_tar}" -C "${tmp_dir}"
```

This script sets a trap to clean up a temporary folder when a script exits or is interrupted. It begins by defining a function called cleanup and then uses the trap command to ensure that cleanup will be called if the INT or TERM signal is sent, or the script exits.

Using trap can be very useful in scripts that take a while to execute. For example, this script downloads the *effective-shell* samples from the internet, so if the user is having connectivity issues, they may end up canceling the script because the download is taking too long. The trap command ensures that the temporary folder is cleaned up.

You may see INT written as SIGINT in some cases. The SIG at the beginning of a signal name is optional but not supported in all shells, and a signal number can be used instead. Thus, SIGINT, INT, and 2 are all equivalent options for the trap command. INT is the most portable and easiest to read, so that's what I recommend using. Run man signal to look up all signals and their signal numbers.

You can also use traps to discourage a user from interrupting your script, as in this example:

```
interrupt_count=0
on_interrupt() {
    if [ $interrupt_count -lt 1 ]; then
        echo "Canceling this operation can cause errors."
        echo "Press Ctrl-C again if you are sure you want to cancel."
        interrupt_count=$((interrupt_count + 1))
    else
        # Convention is to use the status code 130 for interrupted scripts.
        echo "Canceling long operation"
        exit 130
    fi
}

trap on_interrupt INT

total_time=0
while true; do
    echo "Long operation: ${total_time} seconds elapsed"
    sleep 3
    total_time=$((total_time + 3))
done
```

When running this script, the user must press CTRL-C *twice* to cancel the operation:

```
$ ~/effective-shell/scripts/long-operation.sh
Long operation: 0 seconds elapsed
Long operation: 3 seconds elapsed
Long operation: 6 seconds elapsed
^CCanceling this operation can cause errors.
Press Ctrl-C again if you are sure you want to cancel.
Long operation: 9 seconds elapsed
Long operation: 12 seconds elapsed
^CCanceling long operation
```

Asking the user to confirm cancellation can help them avoid stopping the operation by accident. The warning message also tells them what might happen if they cancel the script before it finishes executing.

The following list describes some other specifics about the trap command you should be aware of:

- You can use trap -l or kill -l to list the signals available, but special conditions such as EXIT and RETURN won't be listed. To find those, enter help trap in your shell.

- To stop a signal from being processed, use trap "" *SIGNAL*, which means that the shell won't execute any commands when it receives the signal specified.

- To reset a trap, run trap - *SIGNAL*, which will remove any trap handler.

- Test your traps by sending a signal explicitly to your script with kill -s *SIGNAL*.

Processing Complex Script Parameters

The getopts ("parse option arguments") command makes it much easier to handle the options that users set when calling your scripts. It takes two parameters. The first is an *option string*, which defines what options are allowed. This string starts with a colon followed by one or more letters, where any letter followed by a colon expects you to provide a value. The second parameter is the name of the variable that will store each option as getopts processes it.

You typically use getopts in a while loop with a case statement to iterate through each option and determine what it should do.

Say you want to update the common command from the previous chapters to support the -h ("help") and -e ("execute") parameters. The processing could look like this:

```
# Helper function to show how the command should be invoked
show_help() {
    echo "usage:"
    echo "  common [-h] [-e <command_number>] count"
}
```

```
    # Process the options.
❶ while getopts ":he:" option; do
    case ${option} in

        # Handle the "help" option.
        h )
            show_help
            exit 0
            ;;

        # Handle the "execute command" option by storing the value provided
        # for the option.
        e )
            execute_command=${OPTARG}
            ;;

        # If you have an invalid argument, warn and fail.
      ❷ \? )
            echo "The value '${OPTARG}' is not a valid option"
            exit 1
            ;;

        # If you are missing a required argument, warn and exit.
      ❸ : )
            echo "The option '${OPTARG}' requires an argument"
            ;;
    esac
done
```

First you call the getopts command with an option string and iterate through the results in a while loop ❶. Notice in the option string :he: that e is followed by a colon, meaning it expects an argument.

If you set an invalid option letter, the value of the option variable is set to \? ❷, and you can handle this in your case statement.

If you provide a letter that expects an argument but fail to specify that argument, the value of the option variable is set to : ❸, and you can also handle this in your case statement.

In more complex scenarios, you might see scripts that use multiple loops to process sets of options. It's common to end complex option processing with the following line:

```
shift $((OPTIND - 1))
```

The ${OPTIND} variable stores the index of the last option processed. Shifting this value by one removes the processed options from the $@ ("all parameters") array so that getopts won't try to process them again.

The ~/effective-shell/scripts/common.sh script processes parameters with the getopts command. You can use this script as a template to help you write your own scripts. If you haven't already, install this script and the sample files with:

```
$ curl effective.sh | sh
```

Adding Syntax Highlighting

You can use certain escape sequences (character combinations that tell the shell how to format output) to color the text displayed in the shell. This technique is sometimes called *syntax highlighting*:

```
green='\e[0;32m'
reset='\e[0m'
echo -e "Do you like ${green}apples${reset}?"
```

On most terminals, you'll see the following output with the word apples rendered in green:

```
Do you like apples?
```

The sequence \e[0;32m means "set the text color to green." The sequence \e[0m means "reset the text color." These codes are ANSI escape sequences that have been defined to control how content in a terminal is formatted. There are a number of formatting options, such as foreground and background colors, bold, and underline. Search online for "ANSI color codes" to find all of the possible codes.

It's important to provide the -e flag to the echo command so that it correctly processes the color code escape sequences. In fact, a better option is to use the printf ("format and print arguments") command, as it behaves more consistently across different versions of Unix and Linux:

```
printf "Do you like ${green}apples${reset}?"
```

Syntax highlighting can be helpful for a user in an interactive shell, but there are certain circumstances where you wouldn't want to use color codes. Let's walk through an example that shows why.

This rainbow function writes out a message in several colors:

```
rainbow() {
    local message="$1"
    local reset='\e[0m'
    for ((color=31; color<=37; color++))
    do
        color_code="\\e[0;${color}m"
        printf "${color} - ${color_code}${message}${reset}\n"
    done
}
```

In most terminals, running this function displays the color code followed by the word *hello* in the corresponding color:

```
$ rainbow hello
31 - hello
32 - hello
33 - hello
34 - hello
35 - hello
```

```
36 - hello
37 - hello
```

Here's what you get when you write the rainbow output to a file:

```
$ rainbow hello >> text.txt
$ cat -v text.txt
31 - ^[[0;31mhello^[[0m
32 - ^[[0;32mhello^[[0m
33 - ^[[0;33mhello^[[0m
34 - ^[[0;34mhello^[[0m
35 - ^[[0;35mhello^[[0m
36 - ^[[0;36mhello^[[0m
37 - ^[[0;37mhello^[[0m
```

The -v parameter tells cat to make escape characters visible. If you open the file in a text editor, you'll see the escape characters there.

The problem with the rainbow function is that it adds the color escape sequences even when you're writing the results to a file. In most cases, this is *not* going to be what you want. Commands like ls don't include color codes when writing their output to a file.

There is no entirely foolproof way to avoid this issue, but the most common approach is to check whether the output is going to a terminal device with the -t expression of the test or [command (as Chapter 11 explained, [*expression*] and test *expression* are equivalent):

```
if [ -t 1 ]; then
    echo "We are writing to a terminal"
else
    echo "We are not writing to a terminal"
fi
```

The -t test returns success if the provided file descriptor is associated with a terminal. The 1 in this example is the file descriptor for the stdout stream (if this is unfamiliar, refer to Chapter 2).

You could use this test in the rainbow function as follows:

```
rainbow () {
    local message="$1"
    local reset='\e[0m'
    for ((color=31; color<=37; color++))
    do
        color_code="\\e[0;${color}m"
        if [ -t 1 ]; then
            printf "${color} - ${color_code}${message}${reset}\n"
        else
            printf "${color} - ${message}\n"
        fi
    done
}
```

Now when you run

```
$ rainbow test > text.txt
```

the output file won't contain the ANSI escape sequences. To find out more about the -t test, run man test.

As a final formatting tip, you can use the tput ("query terminfo database") command to look up escape sequences in a slightly more user-friendly and readable fashion:

```
bold=$(tput bold)          # Set format to "bold".
green=$(tput setaf 2)      # Set ansi foreground to green.
reset=$(tput sgr0)         # Reset the colors.
echo -e "Do you like ${bold}${green}apples${reset}?"
```

Executing this code in my terminal returns the following output, with the word *apples* in bold green text:

```
Do you like apples?
```

The *~/effective-shell/scripts/common.sh* script includes colorized output and also checks to see whether color codes should be printed, so you can use it as a reference for your own scripts.

Although the tput codes are still not entirely intuitive, they can be more readable than the raw ANSI escape sequences. The tput command will fail if a feature (such as the bold format) is not available, allowing you to build scripts that can adapt to different terminal capabilities.

Checking the Operating System

Different flavors of Unix and Linux are sometimes inconsistent in their behavior. While it's ideal to write scripts that can be used across systems, it's not always possible. Sometimes you need to check for a specific operating system and then take the appropriate action.

You can use a case statement with the uname ("show operating system name") command as follows to check the operating system (Chapter 11 covers case in depth):

```
case "$(uname)" in
    Darwin)
        os="macOS"
        ;;

    Linux)
        os="Linux"
        ;;

    CYGWIN*|MINGW32*|MSYS*|MINGW*)
        os="Windows"
        ;;
```

```
    SunOS)
        os="Solaris"
        ;;

    *)
        echo "Unsupported operating system"
        exit 1
        ;;
esac
echo "Your OS is: ${os}"
```

The *~/effective-shell/scripts/common.sh* script checks to see whether the operating system is macOS. If so, it temporarily aliases the text commands, such as sed, to their GNU equivalents because the macOS versions of the commands are based on BSD and have slightly different parameters. Refer to *common.sh* when writing shell scripts that need to work with both macOS and Linux.

Checking for Installed Programs

There are many different ways to determine whether a command is available. The most correct and portable option is to use command -v as shown here:

```
if ! command -v "curl" >/dev/null 2>&1; then
    echo "'curl' is not installed, please install and try again"
fi
```

When you use command, you silence error output and stdout; otherwise, you'd see either an error message if the command doesn't exist or the details of the command if it does exist.

The *~/effective-shell/scripts/common.sh* script checks to see whether certain GNU versions of tools are installed when it's running on macOS. You can refer to it as a guide if you need to check for the presence of commands in your scripts.

Showing a Menu

The select command prints a menu and allows the user to make a selection. It's not part of the POSIX standard, but it's available in bash and most bash-like shells. The following example uses select to ask a user to pick their favorite fruit from a list:

```
select fruit in Apple Banana Cherry Durian
do
    echo "You chose: $fruit"
    echo "This is item number: $REPLY"
done
```

Running these commands produces the following output:

```
1) Apple
2) Banana
3) Cherry
4) Durian
#? 1
You chose: Apple
This is item number: 1
#? 3
You chose: Cherry
This is item number: 3
#? 4
You chose: Durian
This is item number: 4
#? ^D
```

Notice that select runs just like an infinite loop: after the shell executes the statements in the select body, it prompts for a selection again. The user can tell the shell they're done sending input by pressing CTRL-D, which is the ASCII EOT ("end of transmission") character, or CTRL-C to quit.

You'll normally see select used with a case statement to process the selection.

Running Commands in Subshells

You can run commands in subshells to avoid inadvertently changing the state of your current script. One application for this nice little trick is to change the current directory for a specific command without affecting the current directory for the shell:

```
(mkdir -p ~/new-project; cd ~/new-project; touch README.md)
```

The parentheses indicate that these commands are run in a subshell. As a result, the directory is changed only in the subshell, not in the current shell, which means you don't need to change *back* to the previous directory after the commands have completed.

This sequence of commands creates a new folder (mkdir -p ensures that the command won't fail if the folder exists), changes to that folder, and then creates a new file called *README.md*. The current folder for the shell remains unchanged.

Anti-patterns

Anti-patterns are common practices that should be avoided. This section describes a few you might encounter in the wild and why they're problematic.

Omitting Shebangs

Some shell scripts do not have a shebang (the #! character sequence) at the top. The shebang allows you to be very explicit about *which* shell is required to run your script, so you should always include it.

For example, if you see a shebang like this

```
#!/usr/bin/env sh
```

you would assume that this script can run on *any* POSIX-compliant shell; that is, it is as compatible as possible. However, if you see this

```
#!/usr/bin/env bash
```

you would assume that this script is bash-specific and uses "bash-isms," such as the if [[conditional]] construct.

Finally, if you see a shebang like this

```
#!/usr/bin/env zsh
```

you would expect that this script has been explicitly written for use with the Z shell.

If you omit a shebang in your script, the intended behavior is ambiguous. For example, at the time of writing, if you run a shell script without a shebang from bash, the script will run in a new instance of bash. However, if you run a shell script without a shebang from the Z shell, the Z shell will use sh from your path, which could be a symlink to dash, bash, or another shell, depending on your system.

If you want to experiment, create a script such as the *~/effective-shell/scripts/nobang.sh* script, which looks like this:

```
# nobang: This script shows an anti-pattern of not using a shebang in a shell
# script. It shows the process tree for the shell that runs the script:
pstree $$
```

After running this script from macOS, you should see something like the following output:

```
-+= 00001 root /sbin/launchd
 \-+= 07995 dwmkerr tmux
   \-+= 31195 dwmkerr /bin/zsh
     \-+= 49833 dwmkerr sh ./samples/script/nobang.sh
       \-+- 49834 dwmkerr pstree -p 49833
         \--- 49835 root ps -axwwo user,pid,ppid,pgid,command
```

Although I ran this script from a Z shell session, it was executed with sh, which is the Bourne shell (version 3 on my system).

The only time you should omit the shebang is when you expect the script to be sourced (a topic introduced in Chapter 9 and discussed further in Part IV).

Configuring Options in Shebangs

Sometimes you'll see shell scripts with shebangs that contain options like so:

```
#!/usr/bin/bash -ex

# Script contents below...
```

In this case, the `-ex` flags are passed to the `bash` program, enabling the "exit on error" and "trace" options.

But just because you can specify program arguments in a script's shebang doesn't mean you should. Doing so is risky for two reasons.

First, this pattern requires you to know the path to the shell. If you've read Chapter 9, you know that you should use `#!/usr/bin/env` to search `PATH` for the shell program rather than assume you know where the user has it installed.

Second, not all parameters are handled consistently across operating systems. For example, on some Unix systems, the following shebang will run bash with the `-e` parameter:

```
#!/usr/bin/env bash -e
```

However, on many Unix distributions, only one parameter is passed, in which case the `-e` parameter would be silently ignored. That would be very confusing for anyone reading your code. A workaround to handle these issues is to use the `-S` ("split") parameter for env, but again, this may be confusing for the reader.

Using Complex Logic in Shell Scripts

Although it's been around for decades, the shell has changed remarkably little. This is a testament to the genius of the design of Unix systems and the shell in general.

However, the shell is often *not* the best choice for complex logic or work. Shell scripts are great for automating simple tasks and creating utilities to help you streamline your work, but they come with many challenges. The syntax can be confusing, making scripts work across multiple systems can be challenging, and not many features are available to help you write robust code.

Perhaps the biggest anti-pattern in shell scripts is simply letting them get too large and trying to do too much with them. At a certain point, you'll almost certainly be able to create a more portable, effective, and maintainable solution to your problem by using a dedicated programming language like Python (which is available on almost all systems) or one of the many other languages at your disposal.

This is a topic I'll discuss in detail in Chapter 21, but for now I suggest applying this rule of thumb: as soon as your script starts to get longer than a page or takes more than a few minutes to think through, you're probably reaching the point where a programming language would be a better option.

Summary

This chapter described several useful patterns you can incorporate into your shell scripts to make you an even more effective shell user. You learned how to handle certain user behaviors, add syntax highlighting to shell output, check for the operating system and installed programs, and more. You also saw a few anti-patterns—bad habits you might find in others' scripts but should avoid in your own.

In Part IV, you'll learn how to customize your shell and environment so they're better suited for your particular needs and use cases.

PART IV

BUILDING YOUR TOOLKIT

15

CONFIGURING YOUR SHELL

Once you have the fundamentals of the shell down, you're ready to start customizing it to suit your specific needs and preferences. This chapter introduces the various shell configuration files, explains how they work, and covers the many ways you can configure your shell with the options that work best for you.

Interactive Shells

An *interactive shell* is any shell that has its input, output, and error standard streams (stdin, stdout, and stderr, respectively) connected to a terminal, which really just means that an interactive shell is one you interact with through a keyboard and monitor. When you enter commands using the shell or a terminal emulator like GNOME Terminal or KDE's Konsole, you're running an interactive shell.

The Default Shell Startup File

When an interactive shell starts, one of the operations it performs is to run all of the commands in the file *~/.bashrc*. This *startup file* is what you'll use most often to configure your shell.

The *rc* in the filename stands for "run commands" (some people also refer to it as "run configuration"). This is a convention from the early days of Unix, and you'll find that many tools on Unix and Linux have startup files that end in *rc*. For example, the Vim text editor program loads the *~/.vimrc* file when it starts (Chapter 23 discusses Vim in detail .

The *~/.bashrc* file is in your home directory, so it's your personal bash configuration file. You can use another file, */etc/bash.bashrc*, to configure bash for all users. Having one configuration file that is used globally and another for local, per-user customizations is another common feature of Unix and Linux systems.

The Z shell uses the ~/.zshrc file for per-user configuration and /etc/zsh/zshrc for global configuration. The paths are different, but the concepts are the same. Other shells may use different paths, which you should be able to find in the shell's man pages.

We'll explore some other shell startup files later in the chapter, but for now we'll focus on *~/.bashrc*. Here are some of the commands in the *~/.bashrc* file on a clean Ubuntu installation (to learn how to set up a free Ubuntu virtual machine, see Appendix A):

```
# If not running interactively, don't do anything.
case $- in
    *i*) ;;
      *) return;;
esac

# Don't put duplicate lines or lines starting with space in the history.
# See bash(1) for more options.
HISTCONTROL=ignoreboth

# Append to the history file; don't overwrite it.
shopt -s histappend

# For setting history length, see HISTSIZE and HISTFILESIZE in bash(1).
HISTSIZE=1000
HISTFILESIZE=2000

...

# some more ls aliases
alias ll='ls -alF'
alias la='ls -A'
alias l='ls -CF'

...
```

I've omitted parts of the file in this snippet to focus on the most interesting areas. The first part of the file checks to see if the shell is running interactively. Only interactive shells should be customized, so if the shell isn't running interactively, then return ("exit function or sourced script") is called to stop processing the configuration file. Since this file is *sourced* by the shell—that is, executed by the current shell's environment—you must use return to stop processing it. If you use exit instead, the shell will close as soon as it reads this file on startup, which is definitely not what you want. (For more on sourcing, see Chapter 9.)

Next, the file sets up some of the configuration for the shell's history features, defining variables such as HISTSIZE (the number of commands to store in the history) and setting some shell options with the shopt ("set and unset shell option") command.

The following part of the file defines *aliases*, convenient shorthands for shell commands. For example, la is an alias for ls -A ("list all directories"), saving you a few keystrokes. This is exactly the sort of configuration that makes sense to keep in the *~/.bashrc* file, since users can modify aliases to suit their preferences. But there are many other customizations you can add as well.

Common Startup File Customizations

You can add any commands you like to the *~/.bashrc* file, and they'll be run when the shell starts up. Let's look at some of the most common configurations.

Saving Time with Aliases

You just saw a few built-in aliases, but you can also create your own if you find yourself typing the same series of keystrokes again and again:

```
# Start a web server.
alias serve="python3 -m SimpleHTTPServer 3000"

# Open vim without loading the vimrc.
alias vimnilla='vi -u NONE'

# Run the kubectl command with one character.
alias k='kubectl'

# Quickly go to GitHub repositories.
alias gocode='cd ~/repos/github/dwmkerr'
```

This example creates four aliases: one to run a web server, one to open a text editor without loading any extensions, one to shorten a command name, and one to move to a folder.

You might also use aliases to change the behavior of existing commands. For example, you can change the rm command to automatically ask for confirmation before a file is deleted:

```
# Always run "rm" in interactive mode.
alias rm='rm -i'
```

Keep in mind, however, that the more you customize existing commands, the greater the risk that tutorials and samples you follow may not work as expected, since they'll expect the command's default behavior.

Adding Functions to Streamline Operations

If you regularly run specific sets of commands or more complex operations, you can use functions to add them to your *~/.bashrc* file, like so:

```
# Restart the shell.
restart-shell() {
  exec -l $SHELL
}

# Make a directory (don't fail if it exists) and move into it in one line.
function mkd {
  mkdir -p -- "$1" && cd -P -- "$1";
}

# Cut, but in reverse, for example:
# $ echo "One;Two;Three;Four;Five" | revcut -d';' -f2
# -> Four
function revcut {
  rev | cut "$@" | rev
}
```

This example creates one function that restarts the shell, one that makes a directory and immediately moves to it, and one that works like the cut command in reverse.

You can find out more about functions in Chapter 13.

Creating a Local bin Directory for Custom Commands

Many users find it useful to create a *bin* directory in their home folder to store their own commands and scripts. You can create a local *bin* directory with this command:

```
$ mkdir -p ~/bin
```

You can then update your *~/.bashrc* file to add this directory to the PATH variable (the variable the shell uses to search for executable files), which allows you to run the shell scripts or commands *bin* contains as if they were system-wide executables:

```
# Add the local bin directory to the PATH if it exists.
if [ -d "$HOME/bin" ]; then
    export PATH="$HOME/bin:$PATH"
fi
```

To test this out, you'll add a command from the book's sample files to *bin*. First, install the sample files to your *effective-shell* folder as follows:

```
$ curl effective.sh | sh
```

The sample scripts include a script called common, which shows commonly used commands. Add it to your *bin* directory like so:

```
$ ln -s $HOME/effective-shell/scripts/common.sh $HOME/bin/common
```

You can now run this command like so:

```
$ common
```

This convention ensures that your personal executable scripts or programs are kept separate from the system-provided *bin* folders, such as */usr/local/bin* (which on some systems would require you to have administrative privileges to modify).

Setting Shell Options

The *~/.bashrc* file is the ideal place to configure your shell using *shell options*, settings that control how your shell works. These settings can add new shorthands to navigate folders with the cd command, tweak how the shell history file is managed, and more.

This example uses the shopt command with the -s ("set") parameter to set the autocd ("execute directory names as commands") in your *~/.bashrc* file:

```
shopt -s autocd
```

You can also set this option directly in your shell if you are running interactively:

```
$ shopt -s autocd
```

You can now quickly go to a directory by entering its name and pressing ENTER:

```
$ ~/effective-shell
cd -- /Users/dwmkerr/effective-shell
```

You can unset an option by using the -u ("unset option") parameter:

```
$ shopt -u autocd
```

To list all available options, run shopt with the -p ("print options and status") parameter. Table 15-1 lists some of the most useful options.

Table 15-1: Common Shell Options

Option	Description
autocd	Allows you to enter a directory name as a command to have the shell change (cd) to it
cdable_vars	Allows you to change directory (cd) into a variable, such as repos=~/repos; cd repos
cdspell	Tries to correct typos in the cd command
checkjobs	Shows the status of stopped and running jobs before exiting the shell
cmdhist	Saves multiline commands in the shell history as single entries, rather than one entry per line
dirspell	Tries to correct typos during directory name autocompletion
globstar	Enables the double asterisk (**) pattern for recursive directory matching (for example, **/*.py matches .py files in all subdirectories)
histappend	Appends new entries to ~/.bash_history when the shell exits, rather than overwriting the file

To look up an option in the manual, run man bash and search for the option name.

Configuring Environment Variables

You can set the values of environment variables used by the shell and other tools in your *~/.bashrc* file. For example, you could change your default text editor and add a new folder named *~/commands* to your PATH like so:

```
export EDITOR="nano"
export PATH="$PATH:$HOME/commands"
```

A number of environment variables can change how the shell works, such as the EDITOR variable shown here and the PAGER variable, which sets your default pager. To learn which environment variables you can set to configure a specific tool or command, see the tool's man page.

Sourcing Additional Configuration Files

Another common pattern for the *~/.bashrc* file is to source another configuration file. Say you're storing a set of commonly used functions in a file called *shell-functions.sh*. You could source this file as part of your shell configuration like so:

```
# Load my common shell functions.
source ~/shell-functions.sh
```

In fact, a lot of the shell startup files do exactly this. For example, the default *~/.bashrc* file on Ubuntu has these lines:

```
if [ -f ~/.bash_aliases ]; then
    . ~/.bash_aliases
fi
```

This code uses the -f ("file exists") test to check whether a file named *~/.bash_aliases* exists. If it does, the shell sources it using the dot operator. Dot sourcing is covered in Chapter 9, and tests are detailed in Chapter 11.

Setting Shell Startup Commands

You might always want to run particular commands when you start a shell. For example, say you want to create a temporary folder based on the current date that's linked to *~/today* and updated daily. To do that, you could add the following commands to the *~/.bashrc* file:

```
# Get today's date in the format YYYY-MM-DD.
today=$(date +"%Y-%m-%d")

# Create a path to today's temp folder and then make sure the folder exists.
temp_path="/tmp/${today}"
mkdir -p "${temp_path}"

# Now make a symlink to the folder in your homedir.
ln -sf "${temp_path}" "${HOME}/today"
```

Now, whenever you start a new shell, it creates a folder with today's date in the */tmp* directory, as well as a link to this folder at *~/today*. This configuration is a convenient way to create a temporary working folder for each day that you can go back and refer to in the future if needed.

Avoiding Shell Configuration Pitfalls

There are a few guidelines and best practices to bear in mind when customizing your shell with the *~/.bashrc* file:

Don't print output

It's considered bad practice to print output during shell startup. Avoid running commands like echo or printf. If you call commands that write to stdout, silence the output by piping it to */dev/null*.

Don't run long operations

You might have written a cool script that pulls down information on stocks or weather from a website, ready to show in your shell. But avoid running anything in a startup file that could take a lot of time. Otherwise, you'll encounter a delay every time you start your shell. This can really slow you down, defeating the whole purpose of using the shell.

Be careful not to break things

Don't run so many commands that you might cause errors or failures on startup. Excessive startup commands can make your shell slow and difficult to use, and it can also be hard to debug complex startup logic.

Clean up after yourself

Remember, any variables you set will be set for all shells that read the startup file. If there are variables that you need only while the file is processing, consider using the unset command (covered in Chapter 14) to unset them after startup.

Expect your startup commands to be run multiple times

Write your startup files with the assumption that they will be run multiple times. If you start a new shell from your current shell, your startup files will be loaded again, so make sure they won't cause errors when run multiple times.

In most cases, you'll only need to work with the ~/.bashrc file to configure your shell. However, the shell actually uses a number of different configuration files or startup files, such as /etc/profile, ~/.bash_profile, and ~/.bash_logout. Which files are used depends on whether you're starting an interactive shell, a non-interactive shell, or a login shell. You're familiar with interactive shells by now, so let's look at the other two types.

Non-interactive Shells

Any shell that does not have its stdin, stdout, and stderr attached to a terminal is generally called a *non-interactive shell*. The most common example of non-interactive shells you've seen so far are shells that run shell scripts. Let's take a closer look.

Understanding Shell Script Behavior

The book's sample files include a script called *showpstree.sh* that shows some information about the current process.

To run it, enter its name and press ENTER:

```
$ ./effective-shell/scripts/showpstree.sh
```

NOTE *This script requires a tool called pstree. If pstree is not installed on your system, when you run this script you'll see an error along with instructions on how to install it. For example, if you're running macOS and pstree isn't installed, you'll see this output:*

```
error: pstree not installed, try:
  brew install pstree
```

Follow the instructions to install the tool, and then run the script again

You should see output similar to the following:

```
systemd
  └─sshd
      └─sshd
          └─sshd
              └─bash
                  └─sh ./effective-shell/scripts/showpstree.sh
                      └─pstree -a -s 1675
```

This output is the *process tree* for the shell process in which the script is running—that is, the current process, its parent, its parent's parent, and so on, all the way to the main process, which runs the entire operating system. The process tree will look different depending on what system you're using. We'll focus on the final three processes highlighted in bold:

- The bash shell is the interactive shell that you are currently running. You entered the command to run the *showpstree.sh* script in this shell.

- The sh shell is a new, *non-interactive* shell that the current interactive shell creates to run the *showpstree.sh* script.

- The pstree ("show process tree") command runs in the *showpstree.sh* script.

When you run a shell script using a command like sh, bash, or zsh, it runs in a new, non-interactive shell, and this is a really important point to remember. If the script causes an error, it won't close the current shell you're using, as each script essentially runs in its own "clean" shell. Because this new shell is non-interactive, anything you define in ~/.bashrc won't be loaded, so aliases or other customizations you've added won't be available.

You'll see the following lines in the default ~/.bashrc file in many distributions (including Ubuntu, as you saw at the beginning of the chapter):

```
# If not running interactively, don't do anything.
case $- in
    *i*) ;;
      *) return;;
esac
```

To recap, this case statement checks the current shell parameters (which are stored in the $- variable) to see whether the i ("interactive") parameter is present. If it's not present, the return command runs. This check ensures that even if a non-interactive shell does load the ~/.bashrc file for some reason, it stops reading the file right away.

You could even change the preceding example to display the text INTERACTIVE if the shell is running interactively:

```
# If running interactively, let the user know.
# If not running interactively, don't do anything.
case $- in
    *i*) echo "INTERACTIVE";;
      *) return;;
esac
```

This is a good way to become more familiar with interactive and non-interactive shells, but I recommend deleting this echo command when you're done with it, as shell startup files generally shouldn't show output. (However, showing output can be useful for debugging purposes when you're building and testing your script.) If you need a refresher on how the case statement works, see Chapter 11.

Another way to show a non-interactive shell in action is to simply invoke the shell program with a specified command like so:

```
$ sh -c 'echo $((5 + 5))'
10
```

This example starts the sh program and provides a command via the -c ("command") flag, which launches a non-interactive shell.

Loading a Startup File with BASH_ENV

Why don't non-interactive shells load the ~/.bashrc configuration file by default? First, it doesn't make sense for scripts to rely on user-level customizations. If one user has an alias and refers to it in a script, then the script won't run for another user unless they have the same alias. The second reason is performance: the shell can start much more quickly if it doesn't need to load configurations or customizations before running a script.

If you need to load a startup file for a non-interactive shell, set the BASH_ENV variable to the startup file's path:

```
$ BASH_ENV="~/my_custom_startup_file.sh" bash
```

In general, however, you should avoid this approach, as shell commands and scripts should be written so that they can operate without requiring startup file configuration.

Login Shells

When you log in to a computer with a shell, entering credentials such as a username and password, you're using a *login shell*. Login shells normally run some initial setup of your environment, such as setting the PATH variable, to provide the bare minimum configuration required to work with the system.

For systems that don't have a graphical user interface, any shell you create will be a child of the login shell and thus will inherit the login shell's configuration. For systems with graphical user interfaces, such as KDE and GNOME, when you log in, the desktop manager normally uses the same configuration as for a login shell, setting variables like PATH just as if you had logged in at the command line.

Checking Whether You're in a Login Shell

Not all systems provide you with a login shell by default. You can determine whether your shell is a login shell by examining the 0 variable, which holds the parameters that were used to start the shell. By convention, if the parameter starts with a dash (-), you can assume you're in a login shell. Try it out like so:

```
$ echo "$0"
-bash
```

In this case, the parameter used to start the shell was -bash, indicating that you're in a login shell. If you see something like bash or zsh instead, you're likely in a standard interactive shell that is a child of the login shell.

Run a new bash instance from your login shell to see the difference:

```
$ echo "$0"
-bash
$ bash
$ echo "$0"
bash
$ exit
```

The shell you started in was a login shell. The shell you created with the command bash was a child interactive shell, not a login shell.

Login shells are normally interactive shells (although it's possible to run a non-interactive login shell, it's quite rare). The distinction between login shells and interactive shells more generally is for historical reasons around performance optimization. In the early days of Unix, when executing *any* commands could be time-consuming, the login shell would perform the most essential configuration only once, when a user logged in. Since all subsequent shell processes would inherit the login configuration, they could start more quickly and then load the user-specific configuration.

Loading the Shell Startup Files

When a login shell starts, the shell loads and executes commands from the */etc/profile* file, the profile file containing essential, system-wide configuration. This file is often used to configure settings like the PATH environment variable, which can have different values depending on your operating system.

The shell will then attempt to read each of the following user-specific profile files in order:

1. *~/.bash_profile*
2. *~/.bash_login*
3. *~/.profile*

If the shell finds a file that's readable, it executes that file's commands and doesn't attempt to read the others.

NOTE *Operating systems handle profile loading differently; for example, macOS starts a login shell when you run Terminal, while Linux desktop environments typically load /etc/profile through their display manager. There's a very good discussion on this topic on StackExchange at* https://unix.stackexchange.com/questions/119627/ why-are-interactive-shells-on-osx-login-shells-by-default.

When a login shell closes, it will run any commands in the *~/.bash_logout* file. However, users might forcibly terminate the shell process, which means that you can't be sure this file will always be sourced as the shell exits.

The configuration performed by these startup files varies from distribution to distribution, but in general they will do at least the following:

- Set the PATH variable to include the appropriate folders for tools for your distribution.

- Set the shell prompt, the characters to the left of the cursor prompting you for input (such as ~$ when you're in the home folder, or ~# if you're in the home folder as a superuser—that is, a user with permissions to modify the system with the sudo command).

- Set up autocompletion (the feature that allows you to press TAB to see suggestions when entering commands).

- Load the */etc/bash.bashrc* and *~/.bashrc* files.

There are very few circumstances in which you should change any of these files. Think of them as an essential operating system–specific configuration that makes a login shell functional.

A SHELL CONFIGURATION CHEAT SHEET

The various configuration files can be confusing for many people. But now that you understand the different types of shells, these files are actually quite straightforward.

- When an *interactive* shell starts, it attempts to load the "run commands" (rc) files */etc/bash.bashrc* and *~/.bashrc* (if they exist), which contain the shell configuration for all users and for a specific user, respectively.

- When a *non-interactive* shell starts, it doesn't load any configuration files, unless one has been specified in the BASH_ENV variable.

- In most cases, when you log in to a machine or change user, a *login* shell starts, and the following steps take place:

  1. The shell attempts to load the profile file, which generally is used to implement essential system-wide configuration.

  2. The profile file typically loads the rc files, which apply user-level customizations.

To wrap up this chapter, I'll touch on how to check and change your default shell. While changing your shell isn't something I encourage for novices, you should know how to do it in case you need to access another shell's features or overcome script compatibility issues in your current shell.

Changing Your Shell

To see what your current default shell is, check the */etc/passwd* file like so:

```
$ grep 'dwmkerr' /etc/passwd
dwmkerr:x:1001:1001:Dave Kerr,,,:/home/dwmkerr:/bin/bash
```

The */etc/passwd* file keeps track of the local user accounts on the system. The final item on the line is the current user's shell.

When you log in, your shell is set in the SHELL environment variable. You can write this value out with the echo command:

```
$ echo "My shell is: $SHELL"
My shell is: /bin/bash
```

You have a few ways to change your shell. However, before you do so, make sure that the shell you want to use is in the list of available shells at */etc/shells*:

```
$ cat /etc/shells
# /etc/shells: valid login shells
/bin/sh
/bin/bash
/usr/bin/bash
/bin/rbash
/usr/bin/rbash
/bin/dash
/usr/bin/dash
/usr/bin/tmux
```

If the shell you want to use is *not* listed in */etc/shells*, you'll need to add it; search online for installation instructions for your specific shell.

Once the shell you want to use is in */etc/shells*, you can run the chsh ("change shell") command to change the shell:

```
$ chsh -s /bin/sh dwmkerr
```

The -s ("shell") parameter specifies the shell path, followed by the username you're changing the shell for.

NOTE *On many systems, users can change their own shell as long as it's in the* /etc/shells *list. To change the shell for another user or to use a shell that is* not *in the* /etc/shells *list, you'll need to run the chsh command using sudo.*

You can also change the shell for a user by editing the */etc/passwd* file (you must be using sudo to do this) or by starting the shell from your login shell (for example, by running sh from your bash session).

Here's an end-to-end example showing how you would install zsh and set it for the current user on a Debian-based system:

```
# Elevate privileges to superuser.
sudo su

# Update the apt databases and install "zsh".
apt update -y
apt install zsh

# Add "zsh" to the list of shells.
echo "/bin/zsh" >> /etc/shells

# Return to normal user mode.
exit

# Change the current user's shell to "zsh".
chsh -s "/bin/zsh" $USER
```

Changing your shell is an advanced topic, and not without risk. If you don't properly configure the shell you're changing to, you could lock yourself out of your account. Always test that the new shell works before you set it!

Summary

In this chapter, you learned how to customize your shell configuration with the *~/.bashrc* file. You saw how interactive, non-interactive, and login shells differ, as well as how they load startup files. You can find all of the details on how the shell starts up and loads configuration files by entering man bash and searching for ^INVOCATION.

In the next chapter, we'll take a deeper dive into the command prompt and explore how to customize it to suit your preferences.

16

CUSTOMIZING YOUR COMMAND PROMPT

The previous chapter covered numerous options for configuring certain shell features, and this chapter extends that topic with a specific focus on the *command prompt,* the text shown to the left of your cursor indicating that the shell is waiting for you to type a command. You'll learn how to customize your command prompt to show only the information you want to see, and you'll explore a script that allows you to set a command prompt theme from a list you can extend over time. This script will even handle the differences between bash-like shells and the Z shell, ensuring a consistent command prompt across shells.

Each operating system and Linux distribution comes with its own configuration for the command prompt, but the default often looks something like this:

```
dwmkerr@effective-shell-ubuntu-24:~$
```

This is the prompt on an Ubuntu virtual machine I have set up. If you want to set up a free virtual machine yourself, follow the guide in Appendix A. This prompt consists of the following components:

dwmkerr The name of the current user

@ A separator between the username field and the following field

effective-shell-ubuntu The hostname of the machine

: A colon that separates the hostname from the next field

~ The current working directory

$ The prompt itself (a dollar sign indicates a normal user rather than a root user)

When I change directory, the prompt is updated:

```
dwmkerr@effective-shell-ubuntu-24:~$ cd effective-shell
dwmkerr@effective-shell-ubuntu-24:~/effective-shell$
```

If I change to the root user (or superuser) with the sudo command, the username changes to root and the dollar sign ($) changes to a hash mark (#):

```
dwmkerr@effective-shell-ubuntu-24:~/effective-shell$ sudo su
root@effective-shell-ubuntu-24:/home/dwmkerr/effective-shell#
```

The hash mark is a useful reminder that you're running commands as the root user. You always want to be careful when doing so, as you could easily break features or functions by changing system files.

As useful as these out-of-the-box fields are, however, you might want to customize the prompt to include information that's even more relevant to you. Let's get started!

The Command Prompt Structure

The structure of the command prompt is specified in the PS1 ("Prompt String 1") shell prompt variable. The shell uses this variable to write out the command prompt.

To see the contents of this variable, use echo or printf to write it to the screen:

```
dwmkerr@effective-shell-ubuntu-24:~/effective-shell$ echo $PS1
\[\e]0;\u@\h: \w\a\]${debian_chroot:+($debian_chroot)}\[\033[01;32m\]\u@\h\[\033[0m\]:\
[\033[01;34m\]\w\[\033[00m\]\$
```

This might look extremely complicated, but don't worry: by the time you've finished this chapter, you'll understand what this mess of special characters means.

The Prompt String

You can use the PS1 variable to set your own prompt string like so:

```
dwmkerr@effective-shell-ubuntu-24:~/effective-shell$ PS1="---> "
---> echo "Look at my new prompt!"
---> Look at my new prompt!
```

The shell will use the contents of the PS1 variable to display the prompt. In this example, I've changed the prompt string from $ to --->. As you can see in the echo command, once you set PS1 in the shell, the prompt immediately changes.

Escape Sequences

While simple text works for a basic command prompt, you can also specify escape sequences in the PS1 variable to further customize how the prompt string looks. These are listed in Table 16-1.

Table 16-1: PS1 Escape Sequences

Sequence	Meaning
\a	The special "beep" character that tells the shell to play a beep sound through the speakers
\d	The date in "Weekday Month Date" format (for example, Tue May 26)
\D{format}	The date in a format specified by the format value (for a description, enter man strftime 3)
\e	An ASCII escape character (033) used to print special characters
\h	The hostname up to the first dot (.)
\H	The hostname
\j	The number of jobs currently managed by the shell
\l	The name of the shell's terminal device
\n	A newline character
\r	A carriage return character
\s	The name of the shell (for example, -bash)
\t	The current time in 24-hour HH:MM:SS format
\T	The current time in 12-hour HH:MM:SS format
\@	The current time in 12-hour AM/PM format
\A	The current time in 24-hour HH:MM format
\u	The username of the current user
\v	The version of bash (for example, 5.0)

(continued)

Table 16-1: PS1 Escape Sequences *(continued)*

Sequence	Meaning
\v	The release of bash with the patch level (for example, 5.0.17)
\w	The current working directory, with HOME abbreviated with a tilde (~)
\W	The current working directory name (rather than the entire path, as in \w)
\!	The history number of this command
\#	The command number of this command
\$	The prompt itself (this is a dollar sign unless you're a superuser, in which case the hash mark is used instead)
\nnn	The character corresponding to the octal number nnn, used to show special characters
\\	A literal backslash (\)
\[	The "start of non-printing characters" sequence
\]	The "end of non-printing characters" sequence

Some of these sequences are reasonably self-explanatory, but some are a little more complex. You'll use some of them now to experiment with customizing the prompt.

NOTE *The Z shell uses different sequences. I suggest that you follow this chapter to understand how bash-like shells work, and then you can apply the same techniques using the Z shell. Later in this chapter, I'll introduce a function that automatically converts the prompt into the Z shell format if needed; see "Writing a Shell Script to Customize the Command Prompt" on page 231.*

To change the prompt, simply set the PS1 variable with any escape sequences you choose:

```
dwmkerr@effective-shell-ubuntu-24:~$ PS1='\d \@ \$ '
Sun Jun 06 12:43 PM $
```

This example specifies the \d (current date), \@ (current time in AM/PM format), and \$ (prompt) escape sequences, followed by a space. Note that you have to use single quotes to specify the value of the PS1 variable; otherwise, the shell would see the dollar sign and assume you're trying to use a variable. For a reminder on how quoting works, see Chapter 10

Now say you want to show the number of jobs, the command number, and then the prompt:

```
Sun Jun 06 04:43 AM $ PS1='[\j] (\#) \$ '
[0] (4) $ sleep 10 &
[1] 27598
[1] (5) $ sleep 10 &
[2] 27600
[2] (6) $ sleep 10 &
[3] 27601
[3] (7) $
```

This example sets the \j (current job) sequence and surrounds it with square brackets. Then it specifies the # (command number), surrounded by parentheses, followed by the \$ (prompt). It also starts some background jobs that run the sleep ("wait for a number of seconds") command so that you can see that the number of jobs is changing. The square brackets and the parentheses are simply formatting characters to distinguish between the job number and command number, making the prompt more readable. Again, because you've used single quotes to set the value of the PS1 variable, the shell knows to treat these and the dollar sign as literal characters.

If you're following along and trying this out in your own shell, you might have noticed that there aren't any colors for the new prompts being set; everything is displayed in white. You'll change that next.

Adding Color and Text Formatting to Your Prompt

Earlier in the chapter, you saw that the default prompt on systems like Ubuntu contains lots of special characters. Here it is again:

```
dwmkerr@effective-shell-ubuntu-24:~/effective-shell$ echo $PS1
\[\e]0;\u@\h: \w\a\]${debian_chroot:+($debian_chroot)}\[\033[01;32m\]\u@\h\[\033[00m\]:\
[\033[01;34m\]\w\[\033[00m\]\$
```

You might recognize some of these characters, such as \u for the username and \h for the host. The character sequences that start with \033 or \e are *ANSI escape sequences*. ANSI stands for *American National Standards Institute*, an organization established to set common standards for computing platforms.

In the early days of Unix, each vendor developed their own special characters to control how output was formatted. Since these characters varied from platform to platform, it was challenging to create scripts or functionality that worked across multiple platforms. To deal with this, ANSI defined a common set of codes that could be printed to a terminal to control the output's visual style.

You can use these ANSI escape sequences to format your output. First, you enter \033 or \e, both of which represent the ESCAPE key. The \033 sequence is the ESCAPE key code written in *octal* (base-8) format, and the \e sequence is simply an alternative way of writing the ESCAPE key. The two options have the same result. When a terminal sees them, it knows that the *following* sequence of characters defines the formatting. Table 16-2 shows some of the formats you can use.

Table 16-2: ANSI Formatting Sequences

Sequence	Meaning
Foreground color	
\033[30m	Set foreground to black.
\033[31m	Set foreground to red.
\033[32m	Set foreground to green.
\033[33m	Set foreground to yellow.
\033[34m	Set foreground to blue.
\033[35m	Set foreground to magenta.
\033[36m	Set foreground to cyan.
\033[37m	Set foreground to white (normally shown as light gray).
Foreground color (bold)	
\033[1;30m	Set foreground to bright black (gray, or bold black).
\033[1;31m	Set foreground to bright red (or bold red).
\033[1;32m	Set foreground to bright green (or bold green).
\033[1;33m	Set foreground to bright yellow (or bold yellow).
\033[1;34m	Set foreground to bright blue (or bold blue).
\033[1;35m	Set foreground to bright purple (or bold purple).
\033[1;36m	Set foreground to bright cyan (or bold cyan).
\033[1;37m	Set foreground to bright white (or bold white).
Background color	
\033[0;40m	Set background to black.
\033[0;41m	Set background to red.
\033[0;42m	Set background to green.
\033[0;43m	Set background to brown.
\033[0;44m	Set background to blue.
\033[0;45m	Set background to purple.
\033[0;46m	Set background to cyan.
\033[0;47m	Set background to white (normally light gray).
Background color (bold)	
\033[1;40m	Set foreground to bright black (gray, or bold black).
\033[1;41m	Set foreground to bright red (or bold red).
\033[1;42m	Set foreground to bright green (or bold green).
\033[1;43m	Set foreground to bright yellow (or bold yellow).
\033[1;44m	Set foreground to bright blue (or bold blue).
\033[1;45m	Set foreground to bright purple (or bold purple).
\033[1;46m	Set foreground to bright cyan (or bold cyan).
\033[1;47m	Set foreground to bright white (or bold white).

Notice that each sequence starts with the escape character (the backslash), followed by the [or [1; options, which use the normal color or the bright color, respectively. (How "bright" appears depends on your terminal; in many modern terminals, the bright text is the same color but in bold.) You can also use [0; to clear any changes to the foreground or background before you set the new color. Next, you can choose from eight colors for the foreground, specified by the characters ranging from 30m to 37m. The sequences in the range 40m to 47m set the background color. The sequence 0m resets the colors.

When you write text that uses escape sequences, you need to tell the shell to process them properly. You can use the printf command or the echo -e command to do so, but printf is a better choice since not all systems support the -e parameter for echo:

```
dwmkerr@effective-shell-ubuntu-24:~/effective-shell$ printf "\033[31mRED\033[0m\n"
dwmkerr@effective-shell-ubuntu-24:~/effective-shell$ printf "\033[1;31mBRIGHT RED\033[0m\n"
dwmkerr@effective-shell-ubuntu-24:~/effective-shell$ printf "\033[0;30m\033[42mBLACK ON GREEN
\033[0m\n"
```

These commands output the following text:

```
RED
LIGHT RED
BLACK ON GREEN
```

The colors of the foreground and background should change on each line. The precise formatting will depend on the terminal you use.

With your new knowledge of ANSI escape sequences, you can update the PS1 variable to show a prompt in color. Try the following combination:

```
dwmkerr@effective-shell-ubuntu-24:~/effective-shell$ PS1='\033[34m\u \033[32m\W
\033[37m\$ \033[0m'
```

This example sets the prompt to show the username in blue and the name of the current working directory in green, followed by a white $ prompt symbol. Finally, the reset sequence makes sure that the text you type afterward won't have its color changed. This prompt will be shown in color on modern terminals.

There is one snag here. If you set your prompt this way and press the up and down arrows to cycle through your previously entered commands, your shell prompt might get overwritten. This is because you need to tell the shell that the color and formatting sequences are non-printing characters—that is, that the sequences don't actually produce written text in the terminal.

To deal with this, surround each color sequence with the special characters \[and \] to tell the shell when a non-printing sequence starts and ends, as shown here:

```
PS1='\[\033[34m\]\u \[\033[32m\]\W \[\033[37m\]\$ \[\033[0m\]'
```

Phew! That's a lot of work just to change the color of the prompt. Fortunately, later in this chapter we'll walk through a script that will make it far easier to work with colors and text formatting.

Adding Data to the Command Prompt

When you set the PS1 variable, you're simply setting it to a string. This string could be anything:

```
dwmkerr@effective-shell-ubuntu-24:~$ PS1='-Ready?---> '
-Ready?--->
```

You don't have to limit yourself to the special sequences you've seen so far in this chapter; you can run any commands you'd like to build a command prompt. For example, you could use the ls ("list directory contents") and wc ("word count") commands to count the number of files and folders in the current directory and show that in the prompt:

```
dwmkerr@effective-shell-ubuntu-24:~$ PS1="$(ls -al | wc -l | tr -d '[:space:]') \$ "
32 $
```

This prompt shows that 32 files and folders are in the current directory. The $() notation runs a subshell that lists the contents of the current directory and then pipes them to wc -l, which counts the number of lines. The result is piped into tr -d '[:space:] to remove the whitespace around the line count.

To use the $() notation or any shell variable, you have to use double quotes in the string; otherwise, the shell will write out those characters literally. And because you're using double quotes, you need an extra backslash before the last \$ character to escape it so that the shell doesn't try to treat it as a variable.

However, this PS1 configuration has a subtle bug. Try changing directories as I do here:

```
32 $ cd effective-shell/
32 $ touch newfile{1..10}
32 $
```

Although I changed to the *effective-shell* directory, the count still showed as 32. This was suspicious, so I tried creating 10 new files . . . but the count still shows as 32.

The reason for this is that 32 was the number of files and folders in the current directory at the time I set the PS1 variable. I changed the PS1 variable once, but what I really need is for the shell to count the files *each time* the prompt is shown.

Fortunately, there's a special syntax for this. Add a \ in front of the $ for the subshell like so:

```
32 $ PS1="\$(ls -al | wc -l | tr -d '[:space:]') \\$ "
```

This syntax tells the shell that it should evaluate the subshell *each time* the prompt is shown:

```
32 $ touch newfile{1..10}
42 $
```

Now the prompt shows the correct count. This is where the real power of the PS1 variable comes into play. Because you set PS1 by using the shell itself, you can run *any* commands that you find useful and integrate their output into your command prompt.

Additional Shell Prompt Variables

PS1 isn't the only shell prompt variable you can use to configure your prompt. Table 16-3 lists some others available to you.

Table 16-3: Other Shell Prompt Variables

Name	Purpose
PS2	Indicates a continuation and is set to > by default
PS3	Specifies the prompt used by the select command and is normally not set, so the default #? is used
PS4	Specifies the prompt used when tracing with set -x and is normally set to +
PROMPT_DIRTRIM	Limits the number of directories shown when using \w or \W in your prompt
PROMPT_COMMAND	Specifies the set of commands you want to run before the prompt is shown

Let's take a look at each in more detail.

PS2

If you have a long line of text in the shell, you can start a *continuation* by entering a backslash:

```
$ echo "This is a really really \
> long \
> long line of text"
This is a really really long long line of text
```

When you press ENTER after entering a backslash, you'll see the right angle bracket (>), which reminds you that you're not entering a new command but instead continuing the current command on a new line. To change the > prompt, set the PS2 option:

```
$ PS2="... "
$ echo "This is a really really \
... long \
```

```
... long line of text"
This is a really really long long line of text
```

Now an ellipsis (...) begins each line instead of the right angle bracket. When setting the PS2 option, including a space after the prompt will make your code more readable.

PS3

PS3 allows you to specify the prompt used by the select command:

```
$ PS3="Your choice? : "
$ select fruit in Apples Pears; do echo "$fruit"; done
1) Apples
2) Pears
Your choice? :
```

The PS3 variable isn't set by default. If you don't set it, the select statement uses #? for the prompt.

PS4

When you enable tracing with the -x option, each traced line starts with a plus sign (+) by default:

```
$ set -x
$ echo "The date is $(date)"
++ date
+ echo 'The date is Sun 08 Jun 2025 08:49:07 AM UTC'
The date is Sun 08 Jun 2025 08:49:07 AM UTC
```

To change the + prompt, set the PS4 option:

```
$ PS4='debug-> '
$ set -x
$ echo "The date is $(date)"
debug-> date
debug-> echo 'The date is Sun 08 Jun 2025 08:49:07 AM UTC'
The date is Sun 08 Jun 2025 08:49:07 AM UTC
```

For more about tracing, see "Debugging Shell Scripts with the Trace Option" on page 191.

PROMPT_DIRTRIM

If you set a value in the PROMPT_DIRTRIM variable and then use the \w sequence in a prompt string, the shell won't show the entire contents of the working directory; instead, it will limit the number of folders it shows to the value in PROMPT_DIRTRIM and use an ellipsis for the rest.

For example, if I was in the folder *~/effective-shell/logs/apm-logs* and set my PROMPT_DIRTRIM to 2, my command prompt on Debian would look like this:

```
dwmkerr@effective-shell-ubuntu-24:~/.../logs/apm-logs$
```

Only the last two parts of the path to my working directory are shown. This technique can be helpful to avoid the prompt becoming too long and difficult to read.

PROMPT_COMMAND

You can use the `PROMPT_COMMAND` variable to specify a command or a set of commands to run before the prompt is shown. `PROMPT_COMMAND` is commonly used as follows to save and reload the shell command history before each command is run:

```
PROMPT_COMMAND="history -a; history -c; history -r; $PROMPT_COMMAND"
```

This example uses the `history` ("display or manipulate history list") command three times: first with `-a` to append the lines from the current session to the history file, then with `-c` to clear the shell history in the session, and finally with `-r` to reload it.

For many shells, the command history is updated only when the shell is closed. The change to the `PROMPT_COMMAND` here ensures that even if the shell is terminated unexpectedly, each command you've executed still gets written to the history.

Writing a Shell Script to Customize the Command Prompt

Now you'll put all this new knowledge into action in a script that makes customizing your command prompt far more intuitive. Writing a script will make it much easier to customize your shell prompt for a couple of reasons. First, rather than having to remember each of the color sequences, you can store them in variables to make them easier to refer to. Second, you can run any commands you'd like to show extra information in your prompt. To get started, open your text editor and save a new file as *set_ps1.sh*.

You'll find the full script at *~/effective-shell/scripts/set_ps1.sh*. To install the book's samples, run this command:

```
$ curl effective.sh | sh
```

The *set_ps1.sh* script is quite long, so I'll go through it bit by bit:

```
# Keep track of the original PS1 value.
_original_ps1="${PS1}"

set_ps1() {
    # Foreground colors:
    local fg_black=$(tput setaf 0)     # \033[30m
    local fg_red=$(tput setaf 1)       # \033[31m
    local fg_green=$(tput setaf 2)     # \033[32m
    local fg_yellow=$(tput setaf 3)    # \033[33m
```

```
local fg_blue=$(tput setaf 4)        # \033[34m
local fg_magenta=$(tput setaf 5)     # \033[35m
local fg_cyan=$(tput setaf 6)        # \033[36m
local fg_white=$(tput setaf 7)       # \033[37m

# Background colors:
local bg_black=$(tput setab 0)       # \033[40m
local bg_red=$(tput setab 1)         # \033[41m
local bg_green=$(tput setab 2)       # \033[42m
local bg_yellow=$(tput setab 3)      # \033[43m
local bg_blue=$(tput setab 4)        # \033[44m
local bg_magenta=$(tput setab 5)     # \033[45m
local bg_cyan=$(tput setab 6)        # \033[46m
local bg_white=$(tput setab 7)       # \033[47m
```

First, you store the current value of PS1 in a variable named _original_ps1. This way, if you change the PS1 variable later, you can change t back to its original setting. The underscore (_) in the variable name is a convention indicating that this variable is used internally in the script.

Next, you define a function called set_ps1, using the tput ("query terminfo database") command to get the exact escape sequences for the foreground and background colors. For easy reference, the escape sequences appear as comments to the right of each command, and you store them in local variables with descriptive names (see Chapter 10).

Now you'll get the escape sequences for some of the other formatting options, such as bold (which will be bright on some terminals):

```
# Text styles and reset. Note that on some terminals "bold" will produce
# light colors for bright colors, and on others it will show the text
# in bold.
local bold=$(tput bold)             # \033[1m
local dim=$(tput dim)               # \033[2m
local start_underline=$(tput smul)  # \033[4m
local stop_underline=$(tput mmul)   # \033[24m
local reset=$(tput sgr0)            # \033[0m
```

After this, you use a case statement to set the PS1 variable based on the value of the first parameter you provided to the function:

```
# Depending on the name of the theme provided, set the prompt.
case $1 in
    debian)
        # Debian/Ubuntu style:
        #   \u@\h - username@host (bold/green)
        #   \w - working directory (bold/blue)
        #   \$ - prompt (# if root, otherwise $) (bold/white)
        PS1="\[${bold}${fg_green}\]\u@\h:\[${fg_blue}\]\w\[${fg_white}\]\\$\[${reset}\] "
    ;;

    datetime)
        # A style that shows the date and time:
        #   \D{%Y-%m-%d} - the year/month/date (in white)
        #   \@ - the time (in green)
```

```
          #   \$ - prompt (# if root, otherwise $) (bold/white)
          PS1="\[${fg_white}\]\D{%Y-%m-%d} \[${bold}${fg_green}\]\@\[${fg_white}\]
          \\$\[${reset}\] "
        ;;

    # Add your own themes here!

    *)
          # Restore PS1 to its original value.
          PS1="${_original_ps1}"
        ;;
    esac

    # If in the Z shell, convert the PS1 to use the Z shell format.
    [ -n "$ZSH_VERSION" ] && PS1=$(_to_zsh "$PS1")
}
```

You begin by checking the first parameter of the function $1. If it matches the string debian, you set the PS1 variable to a format like the one used by Debian Linux distributions. If the first parameter matches the string datetime, you set PS1 to a prompt that shows the current date and time. If any other value is used, you reset the PS1 variable to its original value.

Before completing the function, you check whether ZSH_VERSION is set to determine whether the user is in a Z shell. If so, the _to_zsh function converts the PS1 string into the format used by zsh. For readability, I have not included the _to_zsh function in this listing, but you can see how it works by opening the file from the book's samples. Essentially, this function converts bash-specific prompt string constructs into Z shell–compatible ones.

Finally, the } character ends the function definition.

THE Z SHELL AND OH-MY-ZSH

The Z shell differs considerably from bash and bash-like shells in how it handles the PS1 variable. In the Z shell, there's no need for the \[or \] sequences, there are built-in color variables (such as $fg[red] for red), and the special sequences differ (for example, rather than \u for username, the Z shell uses %n). Thus, although the set_ps1 function in set_ps1.sh converts the PS1 string to the Z shell format if needed, this conversion isn't perfect since some sequences don't have a Z shell equivalent. To customize a Z shell prompt, enter man zshmisc and search for PROMPT\ SEQUENCES.

Z shell users might also consider the very popular Oh-My-Zsh project, a collection of themes and plug-ins that add extra aliases, functions, autocompletions, and more to the shell. One of its most popular features is its large assortment of themes for customizing how the prompt looks. Before using Oh-My-Zsh themes, however, be sure you've learned how the fundamentals work so you can understand what's going on under the hood of this package.

(continued)

> You might also realize that you don't need to install an additional package to get the styling you want. As you'll see shortly, my own shell prompt includes information on Git and the working directory (trimmed to show a maximum of three entries), but it requires only a few lines of setup and works consistently in bash-like shells *and* the Z shell. This is very similar to the debian theme you just set in *set_ps1.sh*.

Notice how much easier it is to specify the values for the PS1 string when you've defined the colors and formatting in variables! You still need to wrap the formatting characters with \[and \] to make sure that the shell knows how long the command prompt is, but this is far easier to read than the examples you saw before that provided the ANSI escape sequences.

To use this script, simply source it into your current session and then change the prompt by calling the set_ps1 function:

```
dwmkerr@effective-shell-ubuntu-24:~$ source ~/effective-shell/scripts/set_ps1.sh
dwmkerr@effective-shell-ubuntu-24:~$ set_ps1 datetime
2025-06-08 04:10 PM $ set_ps1 debian
dwmkerr@effective-shell-ubuntu-24:~$
```

This script has a placeholder in the case statement for you to add your own themes for use in your shell. For example, here's one theme I often use:

```
git)
    # A style that shows some Git information

    # Build a string that shows:
    # - The branch (underlined if "main") in green
    # - A red exclamation mark if any local changes are not committed
    # - An indicator of the number of stashed items, if any.
    _git_info() {
        # Git details:
        local git_branch_name="$(git branch --show-current)"
        local git_any_local_changes="$(git status --porcelain=v1 2>/dev/null)"
        local git_stash_count="$(git rev-list --walk-reflogs --count \
            refs/stash -- 2>/dev/null)" # Ignore error when no stashes
        local git_info=""
        if [ "${git_branch_name}" = "main" ]; then
            git_info="${bold}${fg_green}${start_underline}${git_branch_name}${reset}"
        else
            git_info="${bold}${fg_green}${git_branch_name}${reset}"
        fi
        if ! [ -z "${git_any_local_changes}" ]; then
            # Note that you have to be careful to put the exclamation mark
            # in single quotes so that it is not expanded to the last command!
            git_info="${git_info} ${bold}${fg_red}"'!'"${reset}"
        fi
        if [ "${git_stash_count:-0}" -gt 0 ]; then
            git_info="${git_info} ${bold}${fg_yellow}${git_stash_count} in stash${reset}"
```

```
    fi
    printf "${git_info}"
}

# Now show a Debian-style prompt with the Git info above it.
PS1="\$(_git_info)\n\\[${bold}${fg_green}\]\u@\h:\[${fg_blue}\]\w\[${fg_white}\]
\\$\[${reset}\] "
;;
```

Don't worry if you're not familiar with Git; you'll see it in Chapter 18. The takeaway from this snippet is that you can add almost any information you might find useful to your command prompt. When I run set_ps1 git, my prompt looks like this:

```
feat/chapter-16-customizing-your-command-prompt ! 3 in stash
dwmkerr@effective-shell-ubuntu-24:~/repos/github/dwmkerr/effective-shell$
```

My prompt is now spread across two lines: the first shows me the Git branch I'm on, a red exclamation point for any changes I haven't yet saved, and the number of items I have in my stash; the second shows the standard Debian prompt.

Here you can see the power of customizing the command prompt. You can show *exactly* the information you want to see in your day-to-day work.

This code has been slightly simplified for readability, but you can see the original version in the *~/effective-shell/scripts/set_ps1.sh* file. Now you can build your own themes and easily change between them in the shell.

If you want to always source this file into your shell on startup, just add the following to *~/.bashrc* (for more on configuring this startup file, see Chapter 15):

```
$ source "~/effective-shell/scripts/set_ps1.sh"
```

You could also set the default PS1 variable immediately after sourcing the script if you like:

```
$ # Source the set_ps1 function and set the "theme" to Debian.
$ source "~/effective-shell/scripts/set_ps1.sh"
$ set_ps1 "debian"
```

Enjoy playing around with prompt customization! It can be a lot of fun, and the options are almost limitless.

Summary

In this chapter, you learned how to customize the command prompt with the PS1 variable, familiarized yourself with the shell's escape sequences for useful information (such as \u for the current user), and practiced configuring the prompt's text formatting. You also explored a script that makes configuring the command prompt a little more intuitive and manageable.

In the next chapter, you'll see some sensible ways to organize files like the _set_ps1.sh script and the ~/.bashrc file so that you can easily manage your customizations and share them across different machines.

For further information on controlling the command prompt, run man bash and search for ^PROMPTING on bash-like shells, or run man zshmisc and search for PROMPT\ SEQUENCES on the Z shell.

17

MANAGING YOUR DOT FILES

As you build up more and more customizations for your shell and environment, it's increasingly important to find a way to manage them effectively. In this chapter, you'll learn how to organize your configuration files (also known as dot files) so that you can easily make changes over time and build up a library of scripts and features for your preferred shell. In addition, you'll see how you can use your dot files across different shells.

I'll begin by discussing how to manage your customizations for bash, but we'll also go over solutions that work across many shells. This includes the Z shell. So if you're a Z shell user, don't worry: all of this guidance will apply to your environment as well.

In this chapter you'll be creating some files and folders, but if you just want to see the results, install the samples. You can find them in the *~/effective-shell/dotfiles* folder.

To install the samples to the ~/*effective-shell* folder, run this command:

```
$ curl effective.sh | sh
```

Dot Files Defined

Any file or folder on your system that starts with a dot (.) is a *dot file*. On many systems, dot files are hidden by default. This means that they won't show up when you run commands like ls unless you provide flags, such as -a ("show all files and folders"). In desktop environments such as GNOME, KDE, and macOS, dot files are hidden by default.

Dot files are often used "behind the scenes" as configuration or system files. This is why they're hidden by default: everyday users shouldn't have to worry about dot files or their contents.

You'll often see dot files in your home directory, where the dot marks them as hidden to distinguish them from your personal files and folders. When there are configuration files *outside* your home directory, the dot isn't normally used, because it's clear from the folder in which the file resides that it's a configuration file.

As an example, a user's personal bash configuration is stored in ~/*.bashrc*, but the global bash configuration applied to *all* users is stored in */etc/bash.bashrc*. The second configuration file doesn't need the dot, because the */etc* folder is where configuration is kept; thus, there's no need to differentiate it from the user's personal files.

Nowadays, when someone says "my dot files," they typically mean the configuration files in their home directory, like ~/*.bashrc*. In a sense, your dot files are a bit like your personal settings for your computer. On a desktop environment, your settings might control your theme or wallpaper. On a shell, your settings will be files like ~/*.bashrc* for your shell configuration, ~/*.ssh/config* for your SSH configuration (see Chapter 22), and so on.

You'll likely change your dot files over time to suit your preferences, so we'll look at some sensible ways to organize and structure them. You'll need to be able to easily distinguish between them and the default configuration provided by the system, so let's begin by reviewing that.

The Default Shell Dot File

On many platforms, the default ~/*.bashrc* file will contain a number of customizations out of the box. Let's take a look at a few snippets from the ~/*.bashrc* file that comes with Ubuntu 20 as an example (the contents of your own machine's ~/*.bashrc* file may differ depending on your distribution). Some of this may be familiar to you from Chapter 15.

There are a number of options here that relate to the shell history: making it slightly larger than the default, appending to the history file rather than overwriting it, and so on:

```
# Don't put duplicate lines or lines starting with space in the history.
# See bash(1) for more options.
HISTCONTROL=ignoreboth

# Append to the history file; don't overwrite it.
shopt -s histappend

# For setting history length, see HISTSIZE and HISTFILESIZE in bash(1).
HISTSIZE=1000
HISTFILESIZE=2000
```

In the following snippet, the shopt -s globstar command has been commented out so that users can quickly uncomment it to enable pathname expansion across subdirectories:

```
# If set, the pattern "**" used in a pathname expansion context will
# match all files and zero or more directories and subdirectories.
# shopt -s globstar
```

This rather complex-looking code determines whether the shell supports color, and if so, updates the command prompt appropriately:

```
# Set a fancy prompt (non-color, unless you know you want color).
case "$TERM" in
    xterm-color|*-256color) color_prompt=yes;;
esac

# Uncomment for a colored prompt, if the terminal has the capability; turned
# off by default to not distract the user: the focus in a terminal window
# should be on the output of commands, not on the prompt.
# force_color_prompt=yes

if [ -n "$force_color_prompt" ]; then
    if [ -x /usr/bin/tput ] && tput setaf 1 >&/dev/null; then
        # We have color support; assume it's compliant with ECMA-48
        # (ISO/IEC-6429). (Lack of such support is extremely rare, and such
        # a case would tend to support setf rather than setaf.)
        color_prompt=yes
    else
        color_prompt=
    fi
fi

if [ "$color_prompt" = yes ]; then
  ❶ PS1='${debian_chroot:+($debian_chroot)}\[\033[01;32m\]\u@\h\[\033[00m\]:\[\033[01;34m\]\w\
    \[\033[00m\]\$ '
else
    PS1='${debian_chroot:+($debian_chroot)}\u@\h:\w\$ '
fi
unset color_prompt force_color_prompt
# Enable color support of ls, and also add handy aliases.
if [ -x /usr/bin/dircolors ]; then
    test -r ~/.dircolors && eval "$(dircolors -b ~/.dircolors)" || eval "$(dircolors -b)"
    alias ls='ls --color=auto'
```

```
      #alias dir='dir --color=auto'
      #alias vdir='vdir --color=auto'

      alias grep='grep --color=auto'
      alias fgrep='fgrep --color=auto'
      alias egrep='egrep --color=auto'
fi
```

> The debian_chroot variable is set when you've run the chroot ("change root") command as a superuser ❶. The chroot command allows you to create an isolated filesystem tree to run programs in a container-like environment sometimes called a *jail*. This is an advanced topic and beyond the scope of this book, but the debian_chroot command in the PS1 variable helps make it clear that you're running in a "changed root" environment in the shell.
>
> If the shell supports color, the following aliases for ls display its output in color:

```
# Some more ls aliases:
alias ll='ls -alF'
alias la='ls -A'
alias l='ls -CF'

# Add an "alert" alias for long-running commands like so:
#   sleep 10; alert
alias alert='notify-send --urgency=low -i "$([ $? = 0 ] && echo terminal || echo error)"
"$(history|tail -n1|sed -e '\''s/^\s*[0-9]\+\s*//;s/[;&|]\s*alert$//'\'')"'

# Alias definitions:
# You may want to put all your additions into a separate file like
# ~/.bash_aliases, instead of adding them here directly.
# See /usr/share/doc/bash-doc/examples in the bash-doc package.

if [ -f ~/.bash_aliases ]; then
    . ~/.bash_aliases
fi
```

> The configuration file adds other aliases as shortcuts for useful commands and also sources the *~/.bash_aliases* file if it exists. A number of other configuration commands are likely to be set in the file, such as for the bash autocompletion feature.
>
> You could add your own customizations to this file (as discussed in Chapter 15), and many people do. However, if you keep your changes in your own configuration file instead, then you can easily differentiate them from the out-of-the-box configuration settings. Let's walk through how to create this file.

Creating Your Own Dot Files

Keeping your shell customizations in your own dot file not only helps you distinguish between your personal configuration settings and those provided by the system, but it also makes it easier to share the file across different machines. All you need to do is copy the file to each machine you want it on and source it from the *~/.bashrc* file.

Another great benefit is that you can then source your dot file in *different* shells if you want to, or you can check in the dot file for the shell type and then load a configuration specifically for that shell.

Creating the Dot Files Folder

It's entirely possible (and quite likely) that over time you'll build up a collection of many dot files—some might be used for the shell, such as a file to set your favorite aliases or functions, and some might be for other tools—so you'll need a way to keep things organized. I'll show you a technique to manage your dot files that I've found useful. As I walk through the process, feel free to customize or adapt it to suit your preferences.

First, create a folder called *~/dotfiles* for your personal configuration files:

```
$ mkdir ~/dotfiles
```

Keeping your dot files in a single folder will make it easier for you to package them up and share them, track changes to them, and update them later.

Creating shell.sh

Now you're ready to create your own shell configuration file in the *dotfiles* folder:

```
$ touch ~/dotfiles/shell.sh
```

You can call this file whatever you like; it really comes down to personal preference. But here are a few points about the name I have suggested, *shell.sh*:

- I haven't put a dot in front of the name. This is because I don't actually want this file to be hidden within the *~/dotfiles* folder; I want to see this file when I look in the folder.

- I haven't used the name of a shell program in this file. I want to make this file work with *any* shell that I regularly use. Whether I'm using zsh, bash, or sh, this file should still be able to load.

- I've put *.sh* at the end of the filename. This isn't really needed or even common in the world of Linux or Unix, but it makes it immediately clear to the reader (or any program that opens the file) that this is a shell script.

Adding Custom Configuration

Now you'll edit the *~/dotfiles/shell.sh* file to add some configuration that might be useful for your shell:

```
# There's no shebang in this script. This script sets the preferred shell
# configuration and should be able to be sourced from any bash-like shell or
# from the Z shell.

# If the shell is not running interactively, do not continue loading this file.
case $- in
    *i*) ;;
      *) return;;
esac
```

The file starts with a comment clearly explaining why it doesn't have a shebang and that it should be available for sourcing from any bash-like shell or the Z shell. Then you perform a quick check on the parameters the shell was started with, which are available in the $- ("shell options") parameter, to see if the i ("interactive") parameter is set. (See Chapter 13 for more on shell options.) If the interactive parameter isn't set, you call return to stop loading the script.

It's standard to change the shell configuration only when you're running interactively; non-interactive shells should not be customized like this (for an explanation of why, refer to Chapter 15).

Setting the Preferred Editor

Next, you'll set your preferred editor:

```
# Set your editor. Some tools use VISUAL and some use EDITOR.
VISUAL=nano
EDITOR=nano
```

The shell and command line programs use two variables to run an editor. The first variable is EDITOR, which originally referred to a *line mode* editor—that is, one that doesn't take up the whole screen. This was useful in the days of printed output before screens were used. The second variable, VISUAL, specifies the editor to use for full-screen terminal editing. Some programs use EDITOR and others use VISUAL, so it's best to set both.

I've used the nano editor in this example as it's available on many distributions and is a little easier than vi or emacs, but you can use whatever you like. For my personal dot files, I use Vim, which you'll see in detail in Chapter 23.

At this stage, you can start to go a bit over the top. For example, here's an alternative way to set the editor to the first one available in an array of your preferred editors:

```
# Set your preferred editor to the first one available in the following array.
preferred_editors=(nano vi)
for editor in ${preferred_editors[@]}; do
    if command -v "${editor}" >/dev/null 2>&1; then
```

```
        # Note that VISUAL can be a full-screen terminal editor. On legacy
        # systems EDITOR was normally a line mode editor, but there is
        # generally no need to differentiate them anymore.
        VISUAL="$(command -v ${editor})"
        EDITOR="${VISUAL}"
        break
    fi
done
unset editor preferred_editors
```

This script specifies an array of editors, checks each to see if it's loaded, sets it if so, and looks for the next editor in the list otherwise. (For a reminder on how to check whether a command is available, see "Checking for Installed Programs" on page 200.) This is completely excessive and unnecessary. But the great thing about your dot files is—they're yours! If you want to do this, that's absolutely fine. If you want to check to see if Sublime Text or Visual Studio Code is installed and use that, it's not a problem. This is your personal configuration file, so do what works for you.

Cleaning Up Variables and Configuring Keyboard Shortcuts

Notice that in *shell.sh*, I clean up every shell variable after I use it with unset (discussed in Chapter 14). This is a good habit to get into: try to leave the environment as pristine as possible after sourcing the file.

Another useful option to set is stty -ixon:

```
# Allows you to use Ctrl-S to perform forward search by disabling the start
# and stop output control signals, which are not needed on modern systems.
stty -ixon
```

This command tells the terminal driver that you don't need to control transmission with the CTRL-S (start) and CTRL-Q (stop) commands, meaning you can instead use CTRL-S to perform a forward search of the shell command history.

Working with Folders

Now you'll configure some sensible settings for working with folders:

```
# Set a shell option, but don't fail if it doesn't exist.
safe_set() { shopt -s "$1" >/dev/null 2>&1 || true; }

# Set some options to make working with folders a little easier. Note that
# you send all output to "/dev/null" since startup files shouldn't write to
# the terminal and older shells might not have these options.
safe_set autocd         # Enter a folder name to change (cd) to it.
safe_set cdspell        # Fix minor spelling issues with "cd".
safe_set dirspell       # Fix minor spelling issues for commands.
safe_set cdable_vars    # Allow "cd varname" to switch directory.

# Uncomment the following to be able to change (cd) to directories that are
# not just relative to the current location. For example, if the following
```

```
# was uncommented, you could do "cd my_project" from anywhere if my_project
# is in the repos folder.
# CDPATH="~:~/repos"
```

If you run this script on an older shell, some of these options might not be available. This is why you've created a safe_set function that will execute if the shopt function fails and will pipe any output to */dev/nul*. You can use these settings or remove them—it's up to you. I've also left a comment on how to use the CDPATH shell variable so that you can change directory (cd) to relative folders outside of your current path. Be careful with this option, though, as it can be a bit confusing: if you forget the CDPATH settings you have saved, you might be surprised when you change to a directory based on the customized CDPATH.

Setting Shell History Options

Finally, you'll set some common shell options and variables to fine-tune how the history works:

```
# Configure the history to make it large and support multiline commands.
safe_set histappend                      # Append to instead of overwrite the history file.
safe_set cmdhist                         # Record multiline commands as one entry only.
PROMPT_COMMAND='history -a'              # Before prompting, save the history.
HISTSIZE=10000                           # Store up to 10,000 commands per session.
HISTFILESIZE=100000                      # Store up to 100,000 commands for all sessions.
# HISTCONTROL="ignorespace:ignoredup"    # Uncomment to ignore duplicate commands or
                                         # commands starting with a space.
# HISTIGNORE="ls:history"                # Uncomment to not record certain commands.
# HISTTIMEFORMAT='%F %T '                # Uncomment to add a timestamp for commands.
```

At this stage, you've got a sensible set of basic options for your shell that should work in bash or bash-like shells, as well as in the Z shell.

Now we'll look at how to test this file before you source it.

Testing the Shell Dot File

Fortunately, there's a really easy way to test that the shell dot file runs without errors. From your shell, run the following command:

```
$ sh -iex ~/dotfiles/shell.sh
+ case $- in
+ EDITOR=vi
+ VISUAL=vi
+ safe_set autocd
+ shopt -s autocd
...
```

You're running a shell program (in this case, sh) and passing three flags: i to make the shell interactive (the script runs only in interactive shells, so you need this flag to test it), e to cause the shell to exit if a command fails, and x to set the tracing output.

By running this script in a shell this way, you can see *exactly* what's being run. If there's an error, you'll see the tracing stop at the point where it occurs. You could perform the same test with other shells, such as bash or zsh.

This is a great way to verify that the script works as expected before you commit to sourcing it as part of your shell startup—which you'll do next.

Sourcing the Shell Dot File

Rather than having your shell startup file load the dot files from the *~/dotfiles* folder, you'll create a symlink in your home directory that points to your *~/dotfiles/shell.sh* file (later on, you'll see this makes it a little easier to load):

```
$ ln -sf "$HOME/dotfiles/shell.sh" "$HOME/.shell.sh"
```

Note the use of the -f ("force") flag to force the creation of the symlink even if one already exists at this location.

Now all you need to do is add the following lines to your *~/.bashrc* (or for the Z shell, *~/.zshrc*) file:

```
# Source shell configuration if it exists.
[ -r ~/.shell.sh ] && source ~/.shell.sh
```

This command performs the -r ("does file exist and is it readable?") test to check whether you have a *~/.shell.sh* file. If the file exists, the command sources it.

You're going to make a couple more changes and then bring this all together by creating one final script that performs the preceding steps for you. If this is enough dot file configuration for you, feel free to stop now. But if you'd like to go deeper, we'll look at loading additional files next.

Sourcing Files from a Folder

Linux and Unix systems commonly store multiple configuration files for a program in a dedicated folder in the user's home directory (although many distributions now prefer using *~/.config* or *~/.local* instead of littering the home directory). This pattern became popular as configuration files grew larger and more complex, and system designers needed a way to spread their configuration across multiple files. The convention is to append a *.d* (for *directory*) to the folder name to differentiate it from the configuration files it contains.

Table 17-1 shows some common examples of configuration files and folders.

Table 17-1: Common Configuration File Examples

Configuration file	Configuration directory	Description
/etc/crontab	/etc/cron.d	Configuration for scheduled tasks
/etc/bash_completion	/etc/bash_completion.d	Configuration for bash autocomplete
/etc/sudoers	/etc/sudoers.d	Configuration for superusers

You'll follow this practice for your shell configuration. Say you want to customize your command prompt when you start the shell. You could put the *set_ps1.sh* file (from Chapter 16) in your shell configuration folder, load it, and then use it to set the PS1 variable in your shell configuration file, *shell.sh*.

First, make a folder to hold your shell configuration files:

```
$ mkdir ~/dotfiles/shell.d
```

Then copy over your *~/effective-shell/scripts/set_ps1.sh* file:

```
$ cp ~/effective-shell/scripts/set_ps1.sh ~/dotfiles/shell.d
```

Now update the *shell.sh* file to source all of the files in the *~/.shell.d* folder (the new code is shown in bold):

```
# If the shell is not running interactively, do not continue loading this file.
case $- in
    *i*) ;;
      *) return;;
esac

# Source any files in your ~/.shell.d folder.
if [ -d ~/.shell.d  && -x ~/.shell.d ]; then
    for shellfile in ~/.shell.d/*; do
        [ -r "$shellfile" ] && source "$shellfile"
    done
    unset shellfile
fi
```

After testing to see whether the shell is interactive, you use the -d test to ensure that *.shell.d* exists and is a directory and the -x test to ensure the directory can be searched. As long as these two tests pass, you loop through each file in the directory. Then, using the -r test, you determine whether the file can be read, and source it if so.

At the end of the *shell.sh* file, you can now call the set_ps1 function to set your theme:

```
# Set the theme. Do not fail if the function doesn't exist.
set_ps1 "debian" || true
```

Finally, create a symlink in your home directory for the shell configuration files:

```
$ ln -sf "$HOME/dotfiles/shell.d" "$HOME/.shell.d"
```

Congratulations! You've successfully created a *dotfiles* folder to store your configuration, added symlinks in your home directory that point to it, and updated your *~/.bashrc* or *~/.zshrc* files to load your shell configuration.

To see the new links you've created, run the ls command like so (I've abbreviated the output to make it more readable):

```
$ ls -al ~ | grep shell
lrwxr-xr-x    dwmkerr  .shell.d -> /home/dwmkerr/dotfiles/shell.d
lrwxr-xr-x    dwmkerr  .shell.sh -> /home/dwmkerr/dotfiles/shell.sh
```

Now you'll combine all this functionality into a script that installs the dot files locally for you.

A Dot File Installation Script

You can easily use a shell script to run the manual steps you just performed to set up the links for your dot files:

```
#!/usr/bin/env sh

# This script installs the dot files locally. Note that it should be run
# from the dotfiles folder so that the links are set properly.

# Create links for the shell configuration.
ln -sf "$PWD/shell.sh" "$HOME/.shell.sh"
ln -sf "$PWD/shell.d" "$HOME/.shell.d"

# Source your shell configuration in any local shell config files.
config_files=(~/.bashrc ~/.zshrc)
for config_file in ${config_files[@]}; do
    # Skip config files that don't exist.
    [ -r "${config_file}" ] || continue

    # If you don't have the "source ~/.shell.d " line in your config, add it.
    source_command="[ -r ~/.shell.sh ] && source ~/.shell.sh"
    if ! grep -q -F "${source_command}" "${config_file}"; then
        echo ".shell.sh is not sourced in '${config_file}' adding now..."
        echo "${source_command}" >> "${config_file}"
    fi
done
```

This script creates the symlinks to your dot files and loops through a set of shell configuration files, adding a line to source *~/.shell.sh* in the configuration file if it doesn't exist.

The grep -q command searches through the shell configuration file for the line that sources your dot file. It returns 0 if it finds a result and 1 otherwise, meaning you can easily use it in an if statement. The -F ("fixed strings") flag tells grep that it can treat the string you're matching against as a plaintext string; it doesn't need to interpret the dots or square brackets as special characters for matching.

Run this script from the *~/dotfiles* folder as follows:

```
$ cd ~/dotfiles
$ ./install.sh
.shell.sh is not sourced in '/home/dwmkerr/.bashrc' adding this now...
```

And that's it! You now have a *~/dotfiles* folder with your configuration, a sensible set of options for the shell, and the ability to quickly configure your dot files for different shells.

In addition to the dot files you've just created, you can find this installation script in the *~/effective-shell/dotfiles* folder with the book's sample files.

Summary

This chapter has demonstrated some sensible configuration settings for shells. You learned how to keep your own settings separated from the system-provided configuration file as well as how to manage your configuration files and folders in a *dotfiles* folder. You also ran a simple script to install the dot files for the local user.

The next chapter will introduce Git, a version control tool you can use to easily manage changes to files like dot files over time. Git will also enable you to share your dot files across machines.

18

CONTROLLING CHANGES WITH GIT

Git is a popular version control tool you can use to manage changes to text, code, or any other type of file you might be working with. Many developers and teams use Git as a tool to allow users to contribute, collaborate, and publish their projects. In this chapter, we'll look at Git operations that allow you to quickly and easily work with Git *repositories*, which are virtual storage spaces for your projects. You'll use the *dotfiles* folder (introduced in the previous chapter) to track and manage changes with Git from the command line.

Before diving into the specifics of working with Git, let's go a little deeper into what exactly it is and how it came to be.

What Is Git?

Any files or folders you work with regularly, such as your personal configuration files (dot files), will change over time—things get added, deleted, updated, moved around, and so on. Git is a *version control system* that allows you to track such changes, maintaining a history of the changes that have been made: when, by whom, and why. You can also maintain multiple *branches* of your files and folders—that is, working environments where you can make changes without affecting the current "main" set of files.

Git was written by Linux creator Linus Torvalds in 2005 and has since been enhanced by many others. "Git" is slang for an annoying person; Torvalds has joked that he always names projects after himself, first Linux and then Git. There were many version control systems around before Git, such as CVS (Concurrent Versions System) and SVN (Subversion, a system similar to CVS but with some improvements). There were also a number of proprietary and commercial solutions.

In recent years, Git has become the most widely used version control system globally, and many highly popular software collaboration systems—such as GitHub, GitLab, and Bitbucket—use Git as their underlying version control system and add other features on top.

Creating a Git Repository

All of the information about a set of files or folders for which you're tracking changes is stored in a Git repository. In this section, you'll create a Git repository to track changes to your *dotfiles* folder (discussed in Chapter 17), which stores simple shell configurations. You can read about how to create this folder in Chapter 17, or you can download the book's sample files to get a copy of it.

To install the samples to the *~/effective-shell* folder, run the following command:

```
$ curl effective.sh | sh
```

Then you can copy the *~/effective-shell/dotfiles* folder to your home directory, where you'll create your Git repository and start using the Git commands, by running the following command:

```
$ cp -r ~/effective-shell/dotfiles ~/dotfiles
```

Whether you installed the *~/dotfiles* folder from the book's samples or have your own version from the previous chapter, move into it in your home directory like so:

```
$ cd ~/dotfiles
```

Now create a Git repository with the git init ("initialize Git repository") command and choose a branch name for it with the git checkout command:

```
$ git init
Initialized empty Git repository in /home/dwmkerr/dotfiles/.git/
$ git checkout -b main
```

You'll see the git checkout command in detail soon. For now, it's enough to know that you've initialized a new Git repository and chosen the name main for the first branch. You can name it anything you want, but you might want to call it main to follow along with the chapter and because the name main or master is the convention for the primary branch.

If you're using Git 2.2 or later, you can initialize a repository and set the branch name with a single command:

```
$ git init -b main
```

If you get the error message error: unknown switch 'b', it means you're using a version of Git earlier than 2.2 that doesn't support the -b ("initial branch name") flag. Search online for "how to install Git" to get the latest version.

Adding and Resetting Changes to the Index

You now have an empty Git repository, so you can use the git status ("show the working tree status") command to show some information on the files in the *working tree*, which is the folder that Git is tracking changes to (in your case, *~/dotfiles*):

```
$ git status
On branch main

No commits yet

Untracked files:
  (use "git add <file>..." to include in what will be committed)
        install.sh
        shell.d/
        shell.sh

nothing added to commit but untracked files present (use "git add" to track)
```

First, git status tells you the name of the branch you're on. Next, it tells you there are no *commits*, or tracked sets of changes, and then lists three files that are untracked: the *install.sh* and *shell.sh* files and the *shell.d* folder.

Since you want to use Git to track changes to these files, you need to add them to the repository. To do that, use the git add ("add file contents to index") command:

```
$ git add .
```

The git add command takes a list of filepaths. Here, you've used the dot folder to represent the entire current directory. Now take a look at the status again:

```
$ git status
On branch main

No commits yet

Changes to be committed:
  (use "git rm --cached <file>..." to unstage)
        new file:   install.sh
        new file:   shell.d/set_ps1.sh
        new file:   shell.sh
```

Git tells you that you have three new files ready to be *committed*. At the moment, these files are in the *index*, or staging area, which refers to the set of changes you're preparing to commit. These changes are not yet stored in the repository. When you add files to the index, you're "staging" changes, and when you remove files from it, you're "unstaging" changes.

Think of the index as a holding area where you can build up a set of changes that you eventually want to record in the repository. You can add more files to the index before saving, or committing, them to the repository.

Figure 18-1 visualizes what you've done so far.

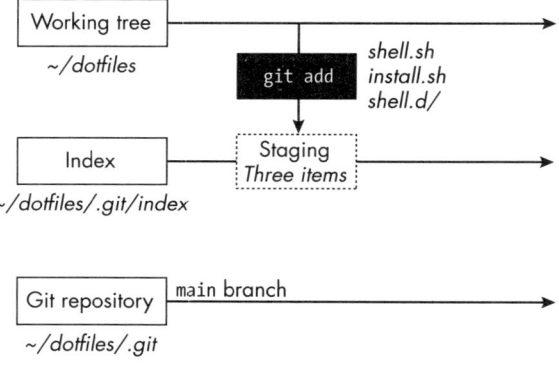

Figure 18-1: The git add command tells Git to track changes in the working tree and adds them to the index.

To recap: your working tree is the folder associated with your Git repository (*~/dotfiles*), and your index is initially empty. When you ran the git add command, you told Git you wanted to add three files to the repository. At this point, your index has three files in it, but your repository doesn't have any commits recorded yet.

What if you realize that you don't want to add one of these files to the repository after all? To remove a file from the index—that is, to unstage it—you use the git reset ("reset changes") command. Try resetting the *~/dotfiles/shell.d/set_ps1.sh* file and then check the status:

```
$ git reset shell.d/set_ps1.sh
$ git status
On branch main

No commits yet

Changes to be committed:
  (use "git rm --cached <file>..." to unstage)
        new file:   install.sh
        new file:   shell.sh

Untracked files:
  (use "git add <file>..." to include in what will be committed)
        shell.d/
```

The git reset command has removed a change from the index, telling Git that you don't want to stage the *shell.d/set_ps1.sh* file. Git now tells you there are two files in the index and one that isn't tracked.

Figure 18-2 shows this step.

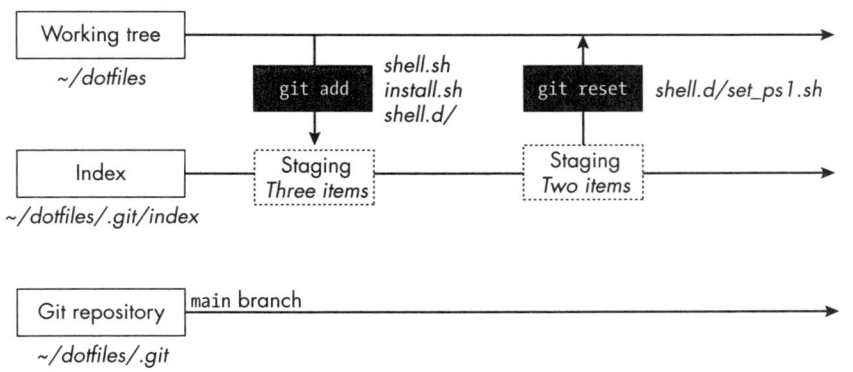

Figure 18-2: The git reset command removes items from the index but does not affect the working tree.

You can also reset changes with the git rm --cached ("remove changes from index") command. However, I think this is a little harder to work with, as you have to remember to use the --cached flag to tell Git that you're removing from the index and not from the repository. You'll see the git rm command a little later in the chapter.

Remember, at this point you haven't changed a single file! Nothing you've done has changed the content of any of the files in the working tree.

The only thing that has changed in the Git repository is the index: the current set of files that you're staging.

To save these changes, you need to commit them.

Committing Changes

Once you're happy with the set of changes in the index, you commit them as follows:

```
$ git commit
```

Now your shell editor will open, prompting you to enter a message describing your changes:

```
# Please enter the commit message for your changes. Lines starting
# with "#" will be ignored, and an empty message aborts the commit.
#
# On branch main
#
# Initial commit
#
# Changes to be committed:
#       new file:   install.sh
#       new file:   shell.sh
#
# Untracked files:
#       shell.d/
#
```

Type a short description like this one:

```
add the "install" and "shell" scripts
# Please enter the commit message for your changes. Lines starting
# with "#" will be ignored, and an empty message cancels the commit.
#
# On branch main
#
# Initial commit
#
# Changes to be committed:
#       new file:   install.sh
#       new file:   shell.sh
#
# Untracked files:
#       shell.d/
#
```

Below the cursor is some information starting with a hash mark (#); these are comments Git conveniently provides to tell you the status of the index, so they won't be stored in the commit message.

If you are using the nano editor, save the file with CTRL-W and close the editor with CTRL-X. If you're using a different editor, use the corresponding save and close commands instead.

After closing the editor, you'll see a confirmation below the git commit command:

```
$ git commit
[main (root-commit) 01e7a10] add the "install" and "shell" scripts
 2 files changed, 90 insertions(+)
 create mode 100755 install.sh
 create mode 100644 shell.sh
```

This message tells you that two files have changed and 90 lines have been added. It also lists the files you've added. At this point you've made your first commit, as shown in Figure 18-3.

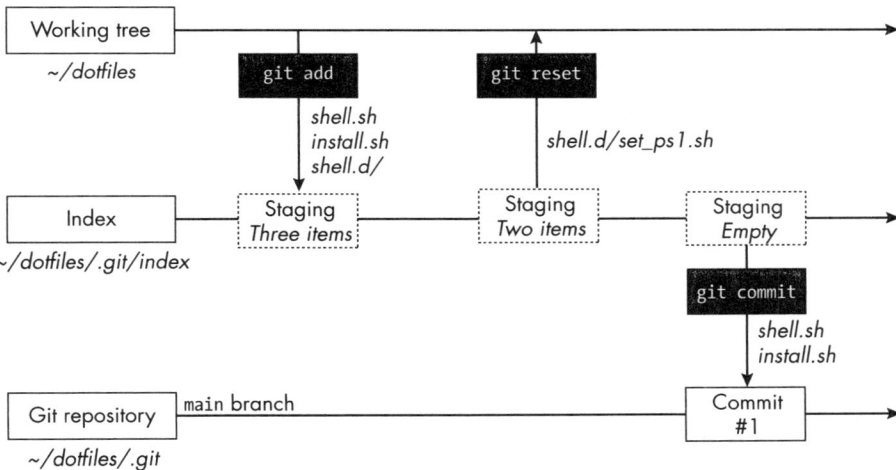

Figure 18-3: The git commit command commits changes to the repository.

You've staged a set of changes and then committed them, so now you have a single commit in your repository. Your files are *still* unchanged, but the Git repository now has a single commit in it that tracks the two files you added.

Now run git status again:

```
$ git status
On branch main
Untracked files:
  (use "git add <file>..." to include in what will be committed)
        shell.d/

nothing added to commit but untracked files present (use "git add" to track)
```

The git status command tells you you're still on the main branch and that there's one file that isn't tracked. Now create a second commit with git add to add the *shell.d/set_ps1.sh* file back to the index. When you run the git commit command, enter a message with the -m ("commit message") parameter to describe the commit:

```
$ git add .
$ git commit -m "add the 'shell.d' folder"
[main d7e1bb9] add the 'shell.d' folder
 1 file changed, 228 insertions(+)
 create mode 100644 shell.d/set_ps1.sh
```

Using the -m parameter for the git commit command allows you to provide a commit message inline, so Git knows it doesn't need to open your editor.

With this second commit, your timeline will look like Figure 18-4.

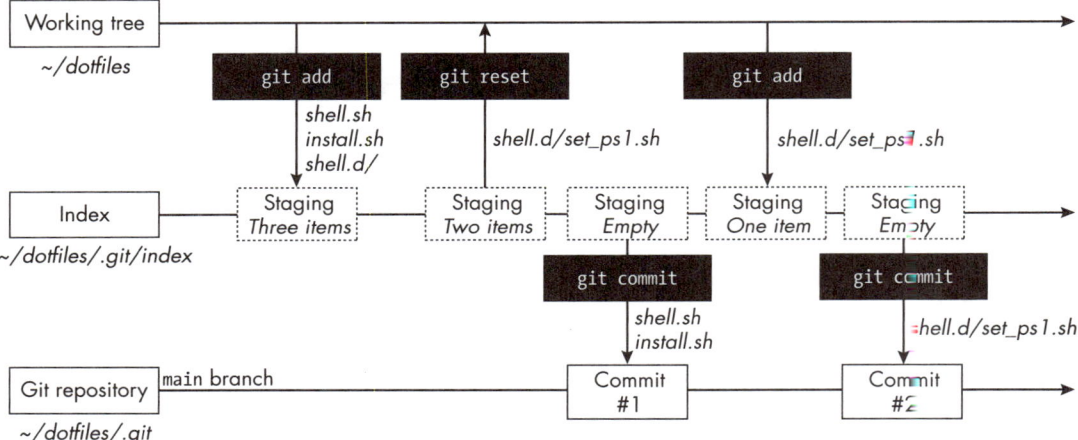

Figure 18-4: Making a second commit to add shell.d/set_ps1.sh back to the index

Run git status one more time to confirm that everything in the working tree is tracked in Git:

```
$ git status
On branch main
nothing to commit, working tree clean
```

The concepts of the index, the working tree, and the Git repository itself can take a bit of getting used to. If you haven't used Git before and this seems like a lot to take on board, don't worry. People often find Git quite challenging at first. As you use it more, all these concepts will become more familiar and intuitive.

CONVENTIONS FOR COMMIT MESSAGES

You can use any text you like for a commit message. However, there are a couple of best practices to bear in mind:

- Try to keep the first line—known as the *subject line*—to 50 characters or fewer. Keeping it short will make it easier to look through the log of changes later and see what each commit means.

- If you want to add more detail, leave a blank line after the subject line and then include as much text as you like. Common convention is to wrap the text at 80 characters so that it will fit in a typical shell window.

There are many articles available online with further guidance on writing your commit messages. You can explore these articles as you get more familiar with Git. My primary recommendation is to make sure that your commit message makes sense; it should describe what the change is and (ideally) the reason for it. Over time, it's easy to forget why you made certain changes, so writing clear commit messages will save you a lot of time in the long run and make it easier for others to work with your repository.

Working with Branches

Branches provide a convenient way to work on a set of changes and record these changes with commits, without affecting the primary (main or master) and other branches. Your branch can then be merged back to the primary branch.

When others work in your repository, they also typically work in a branch and later submit a request to merge it into the primary branch. This section will take a closer look at branches and how these processes work.

Creating Branches

The commits you've made so far have been on the main branch. You can create new branches and make commits on them in order to save a series of changes that are isolated from the main branch.

You can create branches with the git branch ("list, create, or delete branches") command or the git checkout ("switch branches or restore working tree") command:

```
$ git checkout -b aliases
Switched to a new branch 'aliases'
$ git status
On branch aliases
nothing to commit, working tree clean
```

Here you're using the git checkout command to switch to another branch. The -b ("new branch") option tells Git that you want to create a new branch, and you've specified aliases as its name. Running the git status command shows the new branch name.

Now create a new file that includes an alias for the git status command, and then run git status to check the status of the working tree:

```
$ echo 'alias gs="git status"' >> ./shell.d/git_aliases.sh
$ git status
On branch aliases
Untracked files:
  (use "git add <file>..." to include in what will be committed)
        shell.d/git_aliases.sh

nothing added to commit but untracked files present (use "git add" to track)
```

Excellent! You have a new file, *shell.d/git_aliases.sh*, and Git knows that it is not currently tracked. Stage this file and then commit it as follows:

```
$ git add .
$ git commit -m "add alias 'gs' for 'git status'"

[aliases f61369d] add alias 'gs' for 'git status'
 1 file changed, 1 insertion(+)
 create mode 100644 shell.d/git_aliases.sh
```

If you were to load your new *shell.d/git_aliases.sh* configuration file into your shell, you would now be able to use gs as an alias (shorthand) for git status. For more on assigning aliases and loading configuration files, see Chapter 15.

Your current series of commits looks like Figure 18-5.

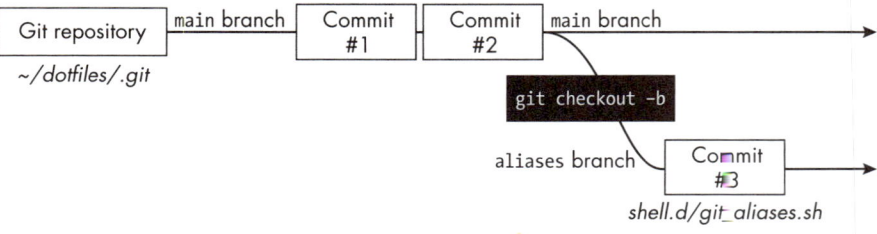

Figure 18-5: The git checkout -b command creates a new aliases branch to which you commit the git_aliases.sh file.

Your new *~/dotfiles/shell.d/git_aliases.sh* file has been committed to the aliases branch.

You can switch branches simply by passing the name of the branch you want to switch to as the parameter to the git checkout command. Switch back to the main branch and then use the tree command to view your working tree:

```
$ git checkout main
Switched to branch 'main'
$ tree
.
├── install.sh
├── shell.d
│   └── set_ps1.sh
└── shell.sh
```

When you look at your working tree back on the main branch, you can see that the *git_aliases.sh* file isn't there. This is because the commit you just made was on the alias branch instead. To get back to that branch, just run git checkout with aliases as the parameter, and then run tree again:

```
$ git checkout aliases
Switched to branch 'aliases'
$ tree
.
├── install.sh
├── shell.d
│   ├── git_aliases.sh
│   └── set_ps1.sh
└── shell.sh
```

And there's the *git_aliases.sh* file!

You can always go back to the last branch you were on by running git checkout - (just like you can use cd - to change to the last directory you visited).

Now add another alias to the file and commit it:

```
$ echo 'alias gcm="git checkout main"' >> ./shell.d/git_aliases.sh
$ git add .
$ git commit -m "add alias 'gcm' for 'git checkout main'"
[aliases b9ae0ad] add alias 'gcm' for 'git checkout main'
 1 file changed, 1 insertion(+)
```

Here you've added the alias gcm for the get checkout main command. Your branches should now look like Figure 18-6.

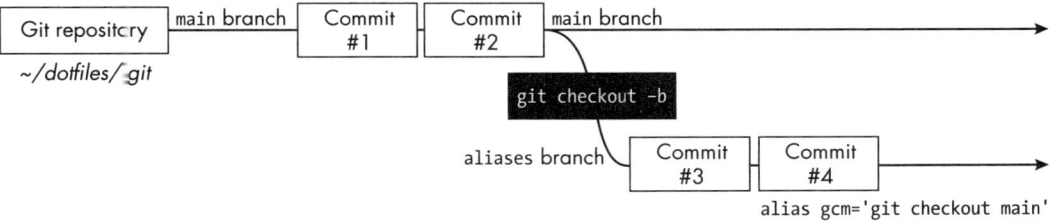

Figure 18-6: Adding two commits to the aliases *branch*

You can create as many branches as you'd like. Just remember that when you run git checkout -b, you branch from the *current* branch (and in fact, the current HEAD, which you'll see a little later).

If you want to create a branch without switching to it, run git branch *new_branch*. This command will create a branch from your current position but won't move into it.

Performing Fast-Forward Merges

Sometimes you'll want to take the changes from one branch and bring them into another. To do this, you use the git merge ("join two or more branches") command.

To merge the changes from the aliases branch into the main branch of the repository, first you check out the branch you want to merge into, and then you run git merge:

```
$ git checkout main
$ git merge aliases
Updating d7e1bb9..b9ae0ad
Fast-forward
 shell.d/git_aliases.sh | 2 ++
 1 file changed, 2 insertions(+)
 create mode 100644 shell.d/git_aliases.sh
```

When you run the git merge command, Git tells you what *type* of merge it has performed. In this case, it's a *fast-forward* merge, which is the simplest type. When Git tries to merge the two branches, it sees that each of the commits on the aliases branch can be applied sequentially to the main branch, as shown in Figure 18-7. In other words, the aliases branch's commits follow directly after the main branch's commits, with no diverging changes.

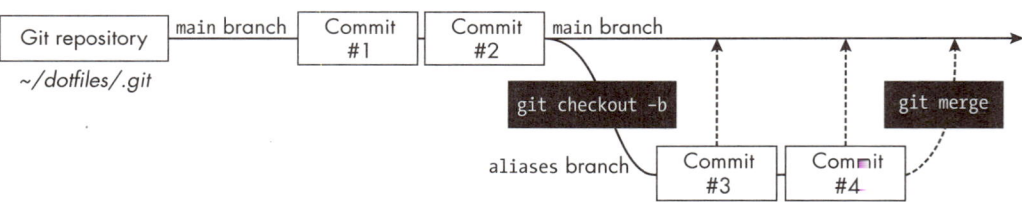

Figure 18-7: How Git prepares for a fast-forward merge

Once the merge is complete, your branches should look like Figure 18-8.

Figure 18-8: The result of the fast-forward merge

The main and aliases branches now contain the same set of commits.

With the simplest merge case behind us, we'll now look at a slightly more complicated merge scenario: merging branches that have diverged.

Performing Recursive Merges and Handling Diverged Branches

Now you'll be creating a set of commits where your branches have *diverged*— that is, each branch has its own new commits. First, check out a new branch called more_aliases, and add two new empty files, *shell.d/bash_aliases.sh* and *shell.d/zsh_aliases.sh*, as separate commits:

```
# Create a branch called "more_aliases," add a file to it, then commit.
$ git checkout -b more_aliases
$ touch ./shell.d/bash_aliases.sh
$ git add .
$ git commit -m "add a file to store 'bash' aliases"

# Create another file, add it, then commit.
$ touch ./shell.d/zsh_aliases.sh
$ git add .
$ git commit -m "add a file to store 'zsh' aliases"
```

Now go back to your main branch and change a file:

```
# Go back to the "main" branch, and add and commit another file.
$ git checkout main
$ echo 'alias gm="git merge"' >> ./shell.d/git_aliases.sh
$ git commit -a -m "add the 'gm' alias for 'git merge'"
```

You've added a new alias called gm to the *shell.d/git_aliases.sh* file. Adding the -a ("all changes") flag to the git commit command allows you to add the changes to the index and commit them in a single command.

Your branches now look like Figure 18-9.

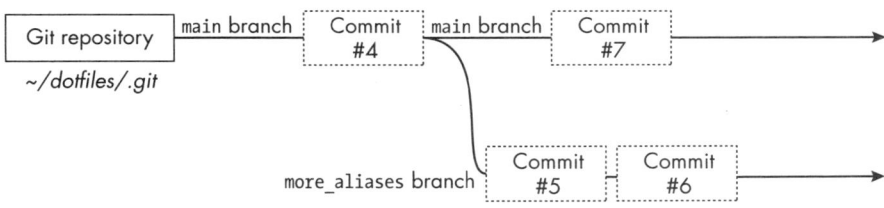

Figure 18-9: Two diverged branches: main and more_aliases

Merge the more_aliases branch into the main branch as you did before:

```
$ git merge more_aliases
```

Since Git will be creating a new commit on the main branch that brings in the changes from the bash_aliases branch, your shell editor will open and show a default commit message:

```
merge branch 'more_aliases'
# Please enter a commit message to explain why this merge is needed,
# especially if it merges an updated upstream into a topic branch.
```

```
#
# Lines starting with "#" will be ignored, and an empty message will abort
# the commit.
```

The default commit message simply explains that this commit merges the branch named more_aliases. Change it or leave it as is, and then save the file. You should see the following output:

```
$ git merge more_aliases
Merge made by the 'recursive' strategy.
 shell.d/bash_aliases.sh | 0
 shell.d/zsh_aliases.sh  | 0
 2 files changed, 0 insertions(+), 0 deletions(-)
 create mode 100644 shell.d/bash_aliases.sh
 create mode 100644 shell.d/zsh_aliases.sh
```

Git now tells you that you've made a merge. Your branches should look like Figure 18-10.

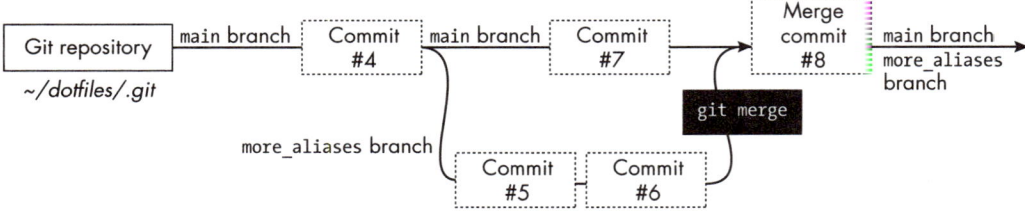

Figure 18-10: The result of a recursive merge of two diverged branches

At this stage, the main and more_aliases branches have the full set of changes that you made to *each* branch. Git merged the two branches and created a new commit that joins them.

The difference between a fast-forward merge and a recursive merge can be summarized as follows: in a fast-forward merge, the primary branch simply moves forward to include another branch's commits, creating a linear history, whereas a recursive merge combines parallel changes from both branches into a new merge commit, creating a more complex, nonlinear history.

The Git Log

In the figures you've seen so far, each commit is numbered to make the process easier for you to follow. In reality, Git doesn't use a number for commits; instead, it uses a *Secure Hash Algorithm* (*SHA*), or simply *hash*, a sequence of letters and numbers that uniquely identify each commit. The SHA will become increasingly important as you use it more and more throughout this chapter to reference exact commits.

To see the log of commits and their SHAs (highlighted in bold in the following example), use the git log ("show commit logs") command:

```
$ git log
commit 138b40418d5658bc64421e7bcf2680c8339f8350 (HEAD)
Merge: a95bd90 a51ae1a
Author: Dave Kerr <dwmkerr@gmail.com>
Date:   Tue Jun 10 21:00:28 2025 +0800

    Merge branch 'more_aliases'

commit a95bd90e3656b2e55b8708193d387c80c282a6ad
Author: Dave Kerr <dwmkerr@gmail.com>
Date:   Tue Jun 10 21:00:22 2025 +0800

    add the 'gm' alias for 'git merge'

commit a51ae1aa42432c2f391ca782c1c20b3793c232ab (more_aliases)
Author: Dave Kerr <dwmkerr@gmail.com>
Date:   Tue Jun 10 20:53:01 2025 +0800

    add a file to store 'zsh' aliases
```

You can see that the log shows each commit, its SHA, the branch it was on, the message, the date, and more.

To see a more compact log, use the --oneline ("show one line per commit") flag as follows. Again, the SHA is highlighted in bold. In the compact log, only the first seven characters of the SHA are shown:

```
$ git log --oneline
138b404 (HEAD) Merge branch 'more_aliases'
a95bd90 add the 'gm' alias for 'git merge'
a51ae1a (more_aliases) add a file to store 'zsh' aliases
63ea74f add a file to store 'bash' aliases
b9ae0ad (aliases) add alias 'gcm' for 'git checkout main'
f61369d add alias 'gs' for 'git status'
d7e1bb9 add the 'shell.d' folder
01e7a10 add the 'install' and 'shell' scripts
```

When you run this command yourself, it will be a little easier to read, as the output uses different colors for the SHAs and the branch names.

You can even see a graph view, showing the branches you've made and when they branched off and were merged back, by passing the --graph ("show commit graph") flag:

```
$ git log --oneline --graph
*   138b404 (HEAD) Merge branch 'more_aliases'
|\
| * a51ae1a (more_aliases) add a file to store 'zsh' aliases
| * 63ea74f add a file to store 'bash' aliases
* | a95bd90 add the 'gm' alias for 'git merge'
|/
* b9ae0ad (aliases) add alias 'gcm' for 'git checkout main'
* f61369d add alias 'gs' for 'git status'
* d7e1bb9 add the 'shell.d' folder
* 01e7a10 add the 'install' and 'shell' scripts
```

Each commit is shown with an asterisk (*). Notice when you created the more_aliases branch and when you merged it back in, indicated by the backslash (\) and forward slash (/), respectively.

The Git log is a very useful tool to help you understand the changes that have happened in the repository.

Resolving Conflicts

One of the most important features of any version control system is the ability to manage *conflicts*, or changes that contradict each other for some reason. When conflicts occur between a set of changes, Git cannot merge them until you manually intervene to tell it which of the changes takes precedence.

Here are a few common scenarios that might lead to merge conflicts:

- In one branch a file is deleted, and in another branch the file is changed. When Git merges the changes, should it delete the file or keep the version with the changes?

- In one branch a file is edited, and in another branch the same part of the file is edited but in a different way. Which edit should Git keep? Or should it keep both?

- In one branch you've added content to the end of a file, and in another branch you've added different content at the end of the same file. Which of these changes should come first?

A lot of the time, you can avoid conflicts by making sure that you don't keep branches for too long. If other people are merging changes into the main branch while you're working on another branch, you are "drifting" from the main branch. You should either regularly update your branch with the changes in main or merge your changes into main.

Version control systems have many different ways to manage conflicts. To see how Git does it, you'll intentionally cause a conflict.

First, create a branch that adds a new alias to the *git_aliases.sh* file:

```
# Create a "glog_alias" branch and commit a file.
$ git checkout -b glog_alias
$ echo 'alias glog="git log --graph --oneline"' >> ./shell.d/git_aliases.sh
$ git commit -a -m "add the 'glog' alias"
```

Now go back to main and add an alias with the same name:

```
# Go back to "main" and commit a change to the same file as the last one.
$ git checkout main
$ echo 'alias glog="git log"' >> ./shell.d/git_aliases.sh
$ git commit -a -m "add the 'glog' alias"
```

You've changed the *shell.d/git_aliases.sh* file in two branches, so if you try to merge them, you'll get a conflict message:

```
$ git merge glog_alias
```

```
Auto-merging shell.d/git_aliases.sh
CONFLICT (content): Merge conflict in shell.d/git_aliases.sh
Automatic merge failed; fix conflicts and then commit the result.
```

When Git cannot automatically consolidate the changes into a single merge commit, it terminates the merge process. No new commits have been made, so the conflicting files with their changes remain in the index. Now you have to manually fix these files.

Check the current status:

```
$ git status
On branch main
You have unmerged paths.
  (fix conflicts and run "git commit")
  (use "git merge --abort" to abort the merge)

Unmerged paths:
  (use "git add <file>..." to mark resolution)
        both modified:   shell.d/git_aliases.sh

no changes added to commit (use "git add" and/or "git commit -a")
```

Git shows that you're currently in the process of trying to fix a merge conflict. It tells you that you need to fix the *shell.d/git_aliases.sh* file, then use git add to stage the changes and commit the result.

When you open the *shell.d/git_aliases.sh* file in an editor, you'll see the changes, along with some special sequences (highlighted in bold):

```
alias gs="git status"
alias gcm="git checkout main"
alias gm="git merge"
<<<<<<< HEAD
alias glog="git log"
=======
alias glog="git log --graph --oneline"
>>>>>>> glog_alias
```

The <<<<<< HEAD line is shown before changes in the current branch, the ======= line is a separator, and the >>>>>> glog_alias line indicates that everything after the ======= line reflects the changes in the glog_alias branch. Many modern editors will immediately recognize the sequence of symbols that Git uses to indicate conflicts and highlight them.

You can see why Git hasn't been able to merge these changes: each branch has a new line, and Git doesn't know which one is correct. Rather than assuming that the most recent change should take priority, Git asks you to choose.

In your editor, update the file to look like this:

```
alias gs="git status"
alias gcm="git checkout main"
alias gm="git merge"
alias glog="git log --graph --oneline"
```

You've chosen the version of the glog alias in the glog_alias branch. You could have chosen the version in the main branch instead or replaced this content with a new line. Here's how you could rename the glog alias for the glog_alias branch instead of deleting glog for the main branch:

```
alias gs="git status"
alias gcm="git checkout main"
alias gm="git merge"
alias glog="git log"
alias ggraph="git log --graph --oneline"
```

You can make any changes you like—just be sure to remove the lines that start with <<<, ===, and >>>. You don't even have to use the changes from one of the branches; you could remove the lines altogether or add completely new ones. As long as you change the file so that the merged result makes sense, Git can proceed.

Now you can use git add to mark the file as resolved:

```
$ git add shell.d/git_aliases.sh
```

Run **git commit**, and the editor will open, showing a sensible default commit message:

```
Merge branch 'glog_alias'

# Conflicts:
#       shell.d/git_aliases.sh
#
# It looks like you may be committing a merge.
# If this is not correct, please run
#       git update-ref -d MERGE_HEAD
# and try again.


# Please enter the commit message for your changes. Lines starting
# with "#" will be ignored, and an empty message aborts the commit.
#
# On branch main
```

The message is just like the earlier merge commit message, but the comments show a little more information (the files that were in conflict). Save the file and close the editor to complete the commit.

Your Git log will now show this new merge commit:

```
$ git log --graph --oneline
*   2532277 (HEAD -> main) Merge branch 'glog_alias'
|\
| * a8cbb15 (glog_alias) add the 'glog' alias
* | 31548e4 add the 'glog' alias
|/
*   138b404 Merge branch 'more_aliases'
|\
| * a51ae1a (more_aliases) add a file to store 'zsh' aliases
| * 63ea74f add a file to store 'bash' aliases
* | a95bd90 add the 'gm' alias for 'git merge'
|/
* b9ae0ad (aliases) add alias 'gcm' for 'git checkout main'
* f61369d add alias 'gs' for 'git status'
* d7e1bb9 add the 'shell.d' folder
* 01e7a10 add the 'install' and 'shell' scripts
```

Dealing with conflicts can be extremely complicated. We've only scratched the surface here, but a wealth of information is available online if you'd like to go deeper.

GIT WORKFLOWS

Git has a number of workflows that you can use to combine changes across branches. There are workflows that allow you to create a single, coherent history between two branches rather than creating a merge commit, options to "squash" all of the commits from one branch into another, and more.

Going into them is beyond the scope of this book, but it's useful to know that you have a lot of resources available to you for controlling how branches are merged. As you become more familiar with the basics of Git, I recommend searching online for "Git merge strategies" or "Git workflows." You'll find many articles that go into further detail.

Managing Files in Your Repository

Now that you've seen how to create a repository, add files, work with branches, and manage merges, we'll take a look at some of the other common operations you might do with the files in your repository.

Deleting Files

It's quite simple to remove files from your Git repository. You can either ask Git to do it for you or just delete the file yourself and then tell Git that you've done so.

Let's see both ways in action. First, use the `git rm` ("remove files from the working tree and index") command:

```
$ git rm install.sh
rm 'install.sh'
```

This removes the file from your working tree and stages it for deletion at the same time, which you can confirm with `git status`:

```
$ git status
On branch main
Changes to be committed:
  (use "git restore --staged <file>..." to unstage)
        deleted:    install.sh
```

The deletion is only in the index at this point, so you need to run `git commit` to commit it.

Sometimes you'll have already deleted files outside of Git (using `rm` or another tool):

```
$ rm install.sh
$ git status
On branch main
Changes not staged for commit:
  (use "git add/rm <file>..." to update what will be committed)
  (use "git restore <file>..." to discard changes in working directory)
        deleted:    install.sh
```

At this point, Git knows the file is missing, but the deletion isn't yet staged, because you haven't explicitly told Git that you want to remove this file as part of your commit. To confirm that you want to remove the file, you'll still need to run the `git rm` command:

```
$ git rm install.sh
```

You could also run `git add install.sh`, which is like saying, "Stage my change to *install.sh*"; that is, you're *adding* a change to the index. (I often just run `git add .` to add all of my changes, including deletions, to the index.)

Now you can make any other changes you like, stage them, and then commit.

Restoring and Renaming Files

To restore a file that's been modified or deleted but not yet committed, you can use `git checkout HEAD` *filepath* like so:

```
$ git checkout HEAD install.sh
```

`HEAD` tells Git you want to check out the file from the current commit (in this case, the most recent commit on `main`).

Another method for restoring a file uses git reset:

```
$ git reset .
Unstaged changes after reset:
D       install.sh
$ git checkout .
Updated 1 path from the index
```

First, git reset . resets all of the changes to the index, and then git checkout . checks out all of the files in the current commit. Be careful with this approach, however, as it will also reset any other changes you've made. I prefer the first method as it is more explicit and restores only one file.

What if you want to rename a file? Try renaming the *install.sh* file to *install_dotfiles.sh* like so and then check its status:

```
$ mv install.sh install_dotfiles.sh
$ git status
Changes not staged for commit:
  (use "git add/rm <file>..." to update what will be committed)
  (use "git restore <file>..." to discard changes in working directory)
        deleted:    install.sh

Untracked files:
  (use "git add <file>..." to include in what will be committed)
        install_dotfiles.sh

no changes added to commit (use "git add" and/or "git commit -a")
```

You've renamed the *install.sh* file, but when you run git status, Git tells you that the file is missing and there's a new untracked file. But Git is smart enough to know when you move a file, so if you run git add . to add all changes in the working tree to the index, Git will recognize that you haven't deleted and added a file but instead renamed it:

```
$ git add .
$ git status
On branch main
Changes to be committed:
  (use "git restore --staged <file>..." to unstage)
        renamed:    install.sh -> install_dotfiles.sh
```

Now restore the *install_dotfiles.sh* file by renaming it back to *install.sh* and add these changes:

```
$ mv install_dotfiles.sh install.sh
$ git add .
$ git status
On branch main
nothing to commit, working tree clean
```

You can also use the git mv ("move or rename a file") command to move or rename a file and stage the changes in one go:

```
$ git mv install.sh install_dotfiles.sh
Changes to be committed:
  (use "git restore --staged <file>..." to unstage)
        renamed:    install.sh -> install_dotfiles.sh
```

You can also revert the name change with git mv:

```
$ git mv install_dotfiles.sh install.sh
$ git status
On branch main
nothing to commit, working tree clean
```

These commands work equally well with folders or lists of files and folders.

Restoring Your Working Tree

You've already seen how to use the git checkout command to switch branches, but you can also use it to restore your working tree to a certain point in your commit history. This is extremely useful if you want to see how your files looked at an earlier point in time or restore your files to a previous state.

Take a quick look at your Git log so far:

```
$ git log --graph --oneline
*   2532277 (HEAD -> main) Merge branch 'glog_alias'
|\
| * a8cbb15 (glog_alias) add the 'glog' alias
* | 31548e4 add the 'glog' alias
|/
*   138b404 Merge branch 'more_aliases'
|\
| * a51ae1a (more_aliases) add a file to store 'zsh' aliases
| * 63ea74f add a file to store 'bash' aliases
* | a95bd90 add the 'gm' alias for 'git merge'
|/
* b9ae0ad (aliases) add alias 'gcm' for 'git checkout main'
* f61369d add alias 'gs' for 'git status'
* d7e1bb9 add the 'shell.d' folder
* 01e7a10 add the 'install' and 'shell' scripts
```

The Git log shows the first 7 characters of the SHA for each commit. You can check out any commit by providing its SHA this way. You don't need to enter all 40 characters of the SHA, only enough to uniquely identify it (4 or 5 is generally plenty).

Notice that the most recent commit is marked with the text HEAD. Earlier in the chapter, HEAD meant the most recent commit of a branch, but in this context HEAD refers to where Git is currently "pointing."

Figure 18-11 visualizes your Git log, with the commits, branches, and HEAD, as it appears currently.

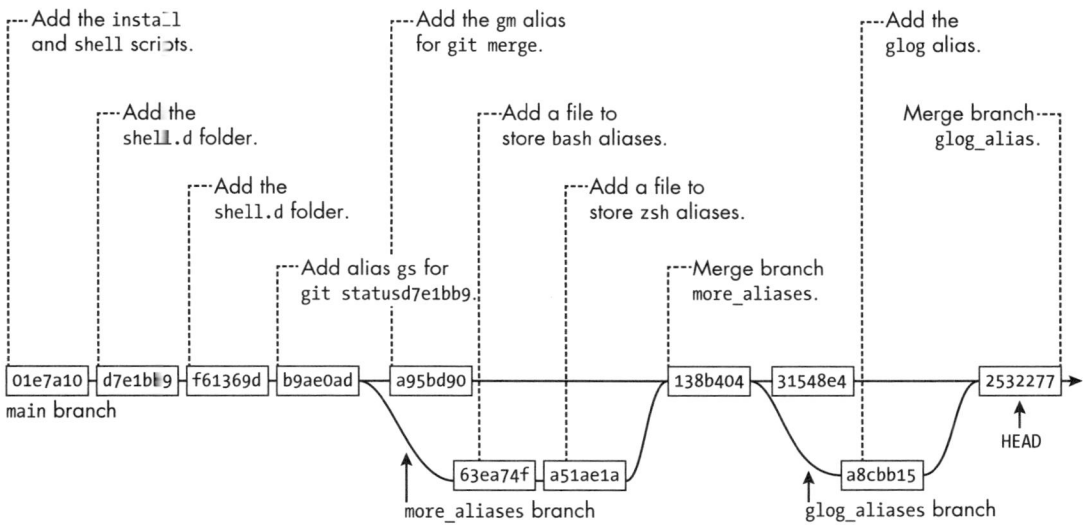

Figure 18-11: The commits, branches, and HEAD of your current Git log

To restore the working tree to the state of any of these commits, run git checkout *commit_sha*, as in this example (remember, you only need to enter enough characters from the SHA for it to be uniquely identified):

```
$ git checkout f61369d
Note: switching to 'f61369d'.

You are in 'detached HEAD' state. You can look around, make experimental
changes, and commit them, and you can discard any commits you make in this
state without impacting any branches by switching back to a branch.
```

This snippet moves your HEAD to the third commit in your repository. If you look at the files in your working tree now, you'll see that they're in the exact state they were in when you made your third commit. The HEAD has moved where indicated in Figure 18-12.

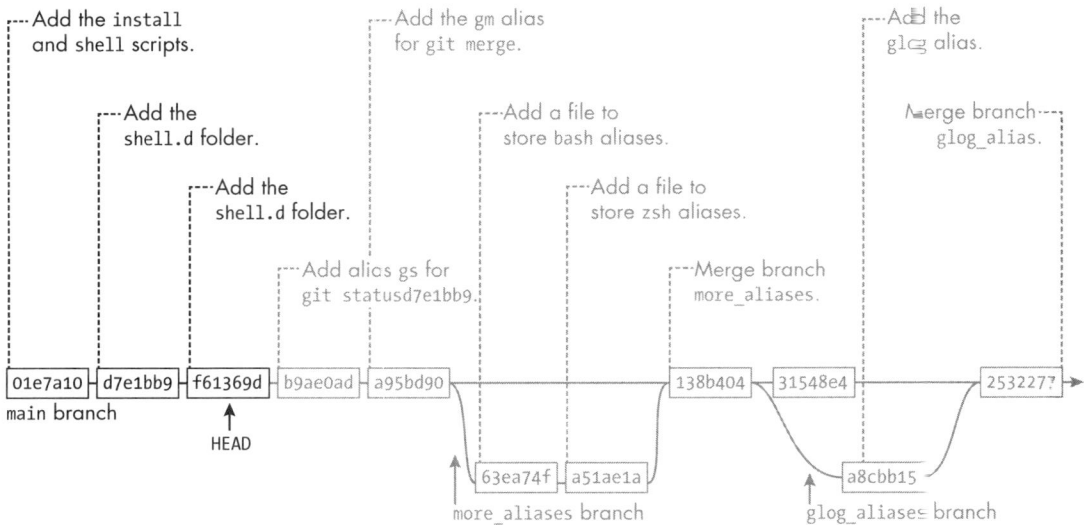

Figure 18-12: A detached HEAD in the current Git log

The warning that you're in "detached HEAD state" sounds more sinister than it is! It's telling you that your current position in the history is not at the "tip" of a branch, so you won't be able to make a new commit without starting a new branch first.

To move back to the tip of a branch, use git checkout *branch*:

```
$ git checkout main
```

Now you're back at the tip of your main branch.

Git has a very convenient syntax you can use to move backward. Specify a branch name, SHA, or HEAD, and then use a tilde (~), followed by the number of commits you want to move backward:

```
$ git checkout HEAD~1
```

This command moves the HEAD backward one commit. This is useful if you realize you've made a mistake in a recent commit and need to go backward to fix it.

Remember, running git checkout *branch* moves the HEAD to the tip of the branch by default.

Git Command Quick Reference

You've seen a lot of commands in this chapter, so I've summarized them in Table 18-1 as a quick reference for you.

Table 18-1: Common Git Commands

Command	Description
`git init`	Initialize a new Git repository.
`git status`	Show the status of the working tree and index.
`git add files`	Stage *files*. You can use patterns and wildcards.
`git reset files`	Unstage *files*. You can use patterns and wildcards.
`git rm --cached files`	Unstage *files*. You can use patterns and wildcards.
`git commit`	Create a commit from the current index. The shell will open for the commit message.
`git commit -m 'message'`	Create a commit with the given message.
`git commit -a`	Stage and commit all changes in the working tree.
`git checkout branch`	Check out a branch.
`git checkout -b branch`	Create and check out a new branch named *branch*.
`git branch name`	Create a branch named *name*, but do not change the current branch.
`git branch -m new_name`	Change the current branch name to *new_name*.
`git merge branch`	Merge the branch named *branch* into the current branch.
`git log`	Show the commit log.
`git log --oneline --branch`	Show the log of commits, one line per commit, with the branch graph.
`git rm files`	Stage the removal of *files*. You can use patterns and wildcards.
`git mv source destination`	Stage the movement of *source* to *destination*.
`git checkout 8342bec`	Check out the commit that has an SHA starting with 8432bec.
`git checkout HEAD~1`	Move the current HEAD back one commit.
`git checkout branch~3`	Check out *branch*, then move back three commits from the tip of the *branch*.

You'll encounter some of these again in Chapter 19, where you'll extend your Git skills with GitHub, an online Git collaboration platform.

Summary

In this chapter, we've looked at some of the core concepts behind Git, such as the repository, the working tree, and the index. You saw how to stage, unstage, and commit changes; create and merge branches; deal with conflicts; and remove and rename files.

In the next chapter, you'll learn how to work with remote repositories, which allow you to share your changes publicly, collaborate with other users on projects, and download your customizations to other machines you use.

19

MANAGING REMOTE GIT REPOSITORIES AND SHARING DOT FILES

In this chapter, you'll learn how to upload a local Git repository to a remote repository. You'll use the popular site GitHub to host your repository. GitHub allows you to share your repositories, collaborate with other users, and access your code across different machines. To explore some of its capabilities, you'll set up a repository for your dot files so that you can quickly set up any machine with your personal configuration.

To follow along with the code in this chapter, be sure to install the sample files or refer to the previous chapter for instructions on creating a local Git repository.

Run the following command to install the samples to the ~/effective-shell folder:

```
$ curl effective.sh | sh
```

First, copy the version of the *dotfiles* folder from Chapter 18 to your home directory and then change the current directory to *dotfiles*:

```
$ cp -r ~/effective-shell/repositories/chapter-19-dotfiles ~/dotfiles
$ cd ~/dotfiles
```

This folder contains the Git repository with the exact set of changes from the previous chapter.

Getting Started with GitHub

If you followed along with Chapter 18, so far all of the changes you've made are stored in a *local* Git repository. In other words, the repository's files are stored on your local machine in a folder named *.git* wherever you initialized the repository. You'll never need to directly access the files in this folder; you'll always use the git command to work with the repository.

A remote Git repository (often just called a *remote*), in contrast, is located on another machine. You can send and retrieve your changes to and from a remote repository as a backup method. You can share this remote with other people so that they can collaborate on it, or you can download it to other machines you work on.

A number of services allow you to host public repositories (which anyone can view) and private repositories (which have more restricted access).

To see how remotes work, you'll create a repository in GitHub, an extremely popular Git provider and online collaboration platform that is free for individuals to use.

Creating a Repository

First, you'll need to sign up for a GitHub account at *https://github.com*. Once you've done that, click the arrow by the plus sign at the top right, as shown in Figure 19-1 (note that your home page might look different, depending on the type of GitHub account you have, but the plus sign should be in the same place).

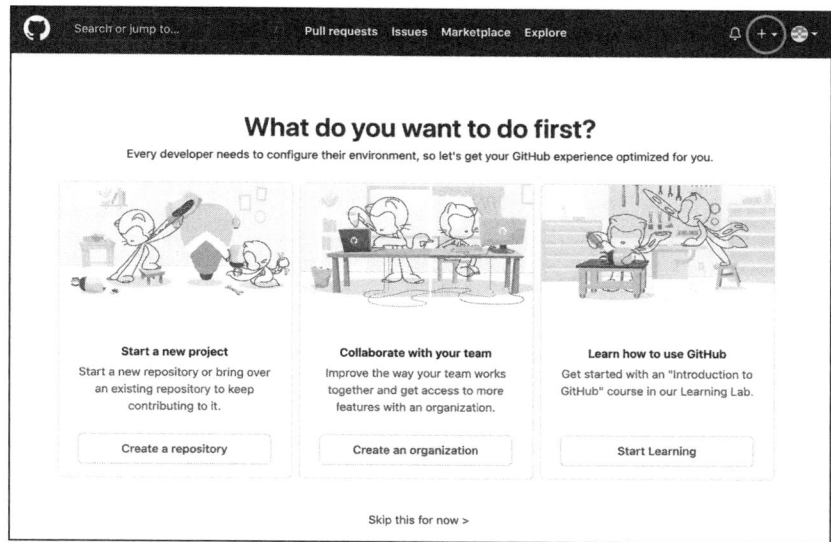

Figure 19-1: GitHub's opening page gives you the option to create a repository.

Choose **Create a Repository**. You'll be asked to provide a name for your repository. Since I'm going to use this repository to host my dot files, I've chosen *dotfiles* (see Figure 19-2).

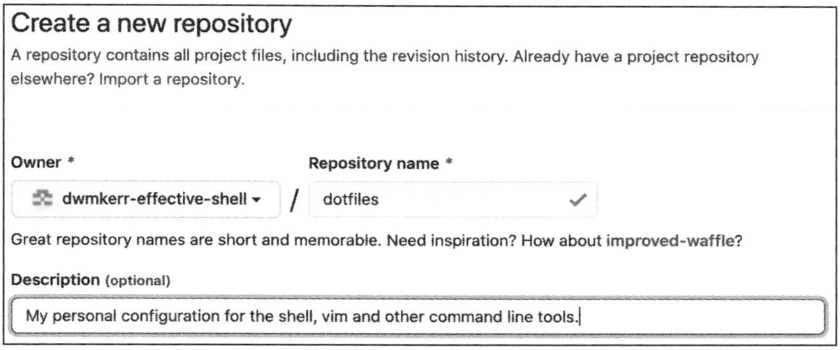

Create a new repository

A repository contains all project files, including the revision history. Already have a project repository elsewhere? Import a repository.

Owner *

  🔲 dwmkerr-effective-shell ▾

Repository name *

  dotfiles   ✓

Great repository names are short and memorable. Need inspiration? How about improved-waffle?

Description (optional)

My personal configuration for the shell, vim and other command line tools.|

Figure 19-2: Naming the new repository

If you don't want members of the public to be able to see your repository, choose **Private** (not pictured).

If you already have a local repository, don't check any of the boxes under Initialize This Repository With. You want to create an *empty* repository that you'll then push your changes to.

Once you're finished, click **Create Repository** at the bottom. You should see some commands for configuring your local repository to point to your new remote (see Figure 19-3).

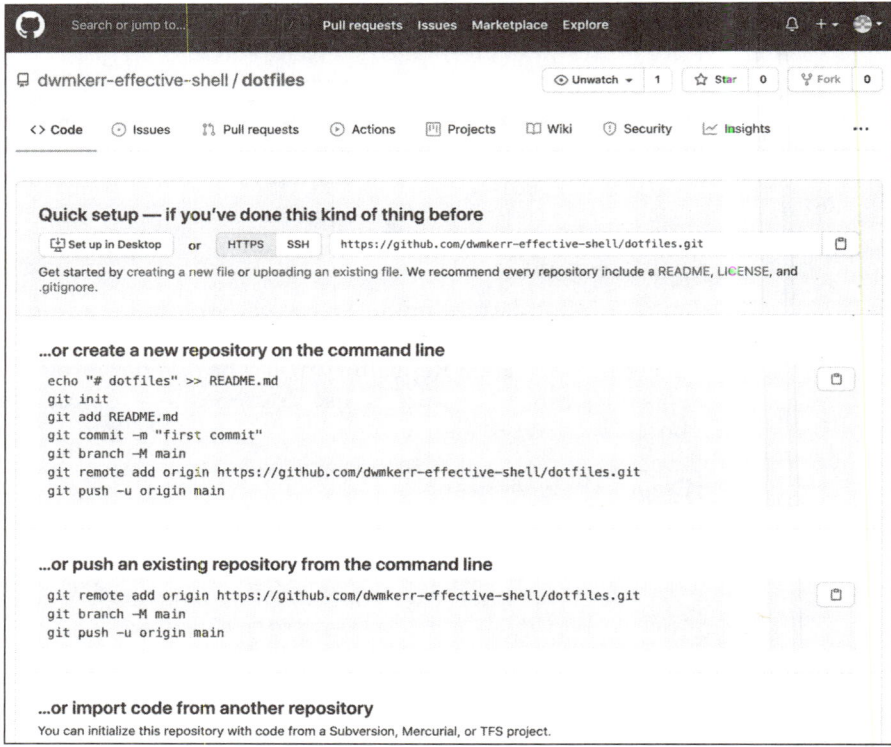

Figure 19-3: The setup page for the new repository

Since you already have a repository, you'll follow the instructions in the section that has the heading ". . . or push an existing repository from the command line." Click the clipboard icon to copy the commands. Then paste them in your shell to run them from the *~/dotfiles* folder like so:

```
$ git remote add origin https://github.com/dwmkerr-effective-shell/dotfiles.git
$ git branch -m main
$ git push -u origin main

Username for 'https://github.com': dwmkerr+effective-shell@gmail.com
Password for 'https://dwmkerr+effective-shell@gmail.com@github.com':
Enumerating objects: 39, done.
Counting objects: 100% (39/39), done.
Delta compression using up to 16 threads
Compressing objects: 100% (36/36), done.
Writing objects: 100% (39/39), 12.83 KiB | 1.83 MiB/s, done.
Total 39 (delta 7), reused 0 (delta 0), pack-reused 0
remote: Resolving deltas: 100% (7/7), done.
To https://github.com/dwmkerr-effective-shell/dotfiles.git
 * [new branch]      main -> main
Branch 'main' set up to track remote branch 'main' from 'origin'.
```

The first command tells Git that you'd like to add a new remote called origin at the provided address. The remote in this case is the repository you've just created in GitHub. The second command renames the current branch to main, but because your current branch is already called main, nothing has changed and no output is displayed. Finally, the third command pushes your main branch to the origin remote. You'll see what the -u ("set upstream") flag does shortly. When you run this command, you'll be prompted for your username and password before the local changes are pushed to the remote repository.

> ### USING SSH KEYS INSTEAD OF PASSWORDS
>
> To keep this example simple, I've authenticated with a username and password. However, I strongly recommend that you set up an SSH (Secure Shell Protocol) key as soon as possible to authenticate with GitHub. SSH keys are far more secure than usernames and passwords.
>
> GitHub has an excellent guide on how to set up SSH keys at *https://docs.github.com/en/github/authenticating-to-github/connecting-to-github-with-ssh*. I also discuss how to do so in Chapter 22.

Now refresh your browser, and you should see your *dotfile* repository with all of the changes you've made so far (see Figure 19-4).

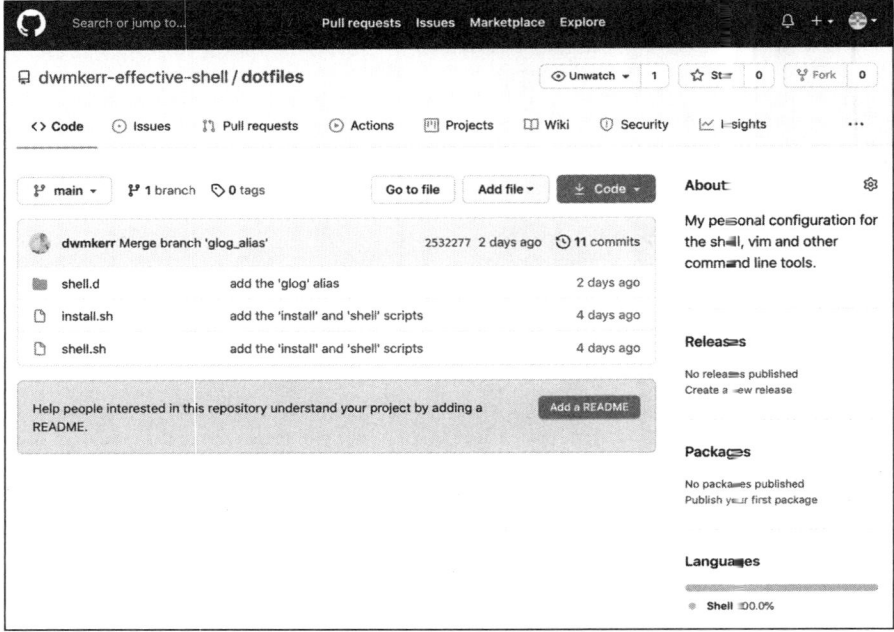

Figure 19-4: The initial view of the dotfiles repository with all changes implemented

You can view all of the files and folders you've created, your commit history, your log messages, and more.

Before you make too many changes, though, you need to be aware of three important commands when working with remotes: git push, git fetch, and git pull.

Pushing Changes

You've already used the git push command once. This command pushes the changes you've made locally to a remote. It's a common convention to call the primary remote that you work with origin, but you can use any name you want. You can also have multiple remotes. For example, you could sign up with *GitLab*, another Git services provider, create a repository there, and add it as a remote called gitlab.

You can show your remotes with the git remote ("managed remote repositories") command like so:

```
$ git remote -v
origin  https://github.com/dwmkerr-effective-shell/dotfiles.git (fetch)
origin  https://github.com/dwmkerr-effective-shell/dotfiles.git (push)
```

Running git remote with the -v ("verbose") parameter will show each remote, along with the address used when you push changes and when you fetch changes (which we'll look at next).

Earlier, you used this command to push your changes:

```
$ git push -u origin main
```

The -u ("set upstream") option tells Git that you want to associate your local main branch with the remote main branch. This way, you don't need to specify the remote name for each subsequent git push command: Git knows to push changes to the upstream branch called main in the origin remote.

Fetching Changes

The git fetch ("get remote changes") command downloads all of the changes that have been made to the remote. It does *not*, however, change your local branch or working copy. It just means that Git is aware of the most recent changes to the remote. To see what I mean, run the command:

```
$ git fetch
```

There won't be any output, because the remote hasn't changed. Now you'll make a change to the remote to see how git fetch works. Open the repository in the GitHub website. You should see a message suggesting that you add a README file, as shown in Figure 19-5.

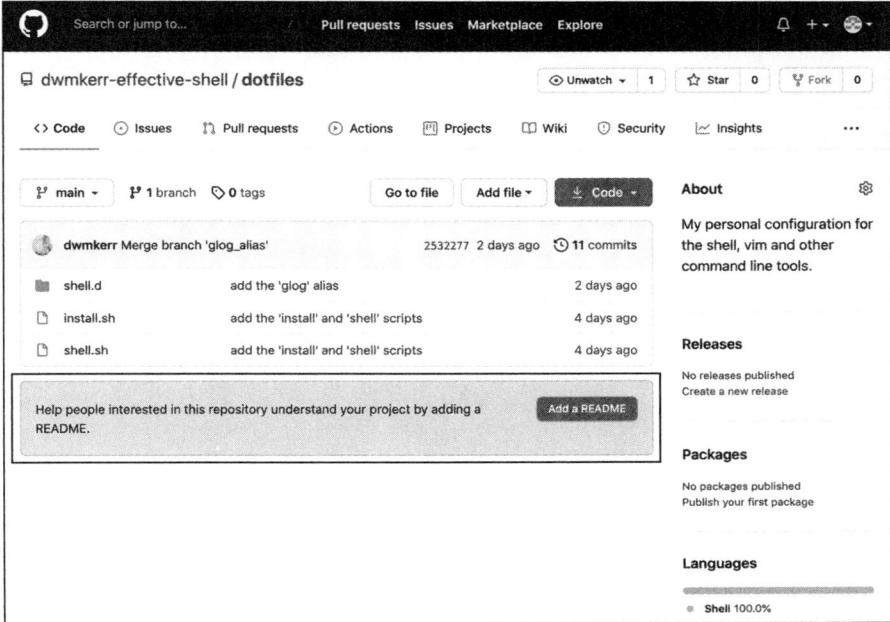

Figure 19-5: GitHub's message prompting you to add a README file

Click **Add a README** and add a description of your project.

By convention, if a repository has a file named *README.md*, then the contents of this file will be shown on the repository home page; it typically includes instructions on how to use the repository. The *.md* file extension refers to Markdown, a plaintext language that allows you to add styles like headings, bullets, and code formatting (search online for "GitHub Flavored Markdown" to find out about the syntax). The contents of the *README.md* file are shown in Figure 19-6.

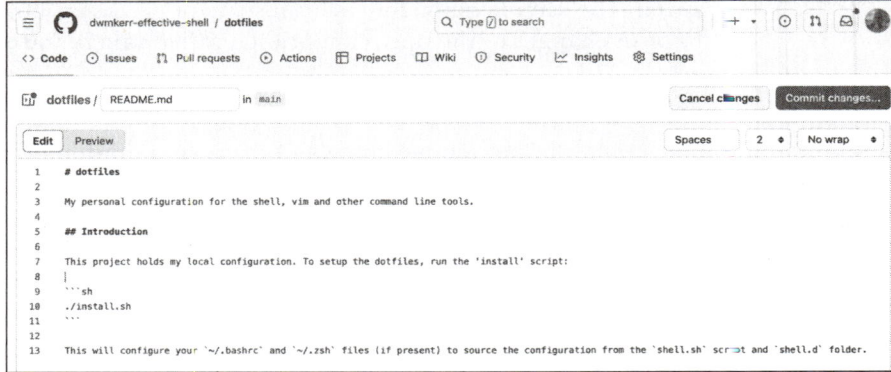

Figure 19-6: The contents of the README Markdown file

Once you're happy with the file's content and styling (you can click Preview to see how it will look, as shown in Figure 19-7), scroll down to add a commit message.

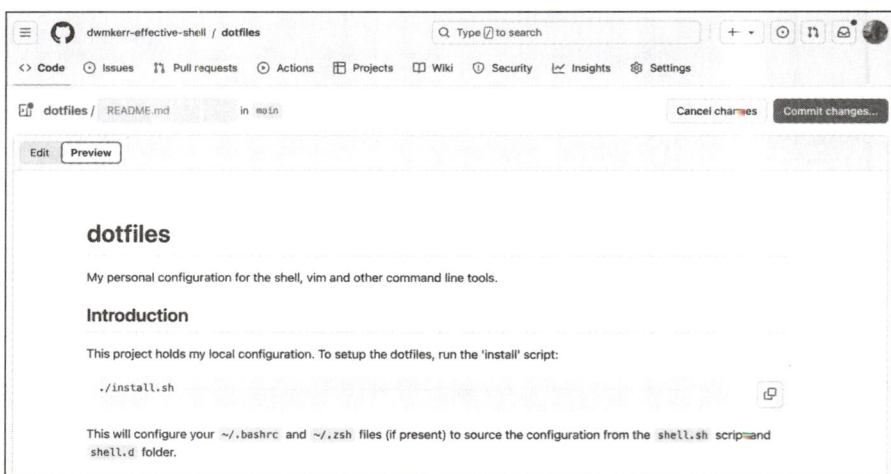

Figure 19-7: The GitHub README commit page

Finally, click **Commit New File**, and you'll be taken back to the repository page, where you should see the *README.md* file (see Figure 19-8).

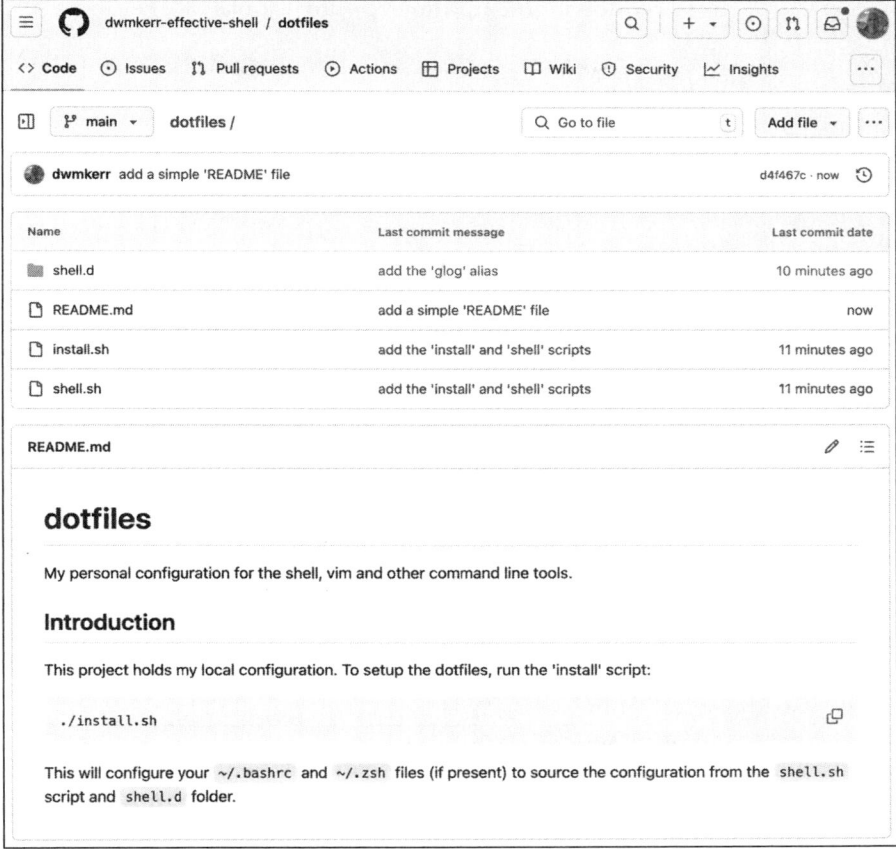

Figure 19-8: The dotfiles *repository home page with your updated* README.md *file*

You've created a commit on the origin remote, so when you run git fetch now, you should see that the remote has changed:

```
$ git fetch
remote: Enumerating objects: 4, done.
remote: Counting objects: 100% (4/4), done.
remote: Compressing objects: 100% (3/3), done.
remote: Total 3 (delta 0), reused 0 (delta 0), pack-reused 0
Unpacking objects: 100% (3/3), 962 bytes | 240.00 KiB/s, done.
From https://github.com/dwmkerr-effective-shell/dotfiles
   2532277..4a28994  main       -> origin/main
```

When you run git fetch, Git looks at the upstream branch associated with the current branch and checks to see if there are any changes. If so, it downloads the information about those changes but doesn't change your local copy or working tree. If you run git log, you won't see the new commit that includes the *README.md* file, because you haven't yet checked out this commit.

At the moment, your repository looks like Figure 19-9.

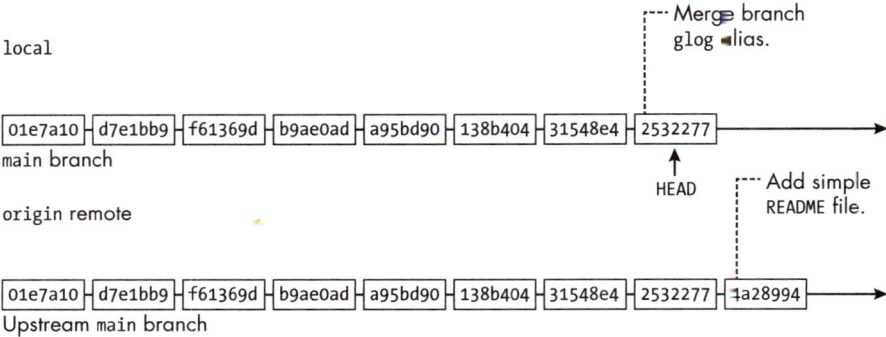

Figure 19-9: The current local main and upstream main branch

The local branch HEAD is still exactly where it was before you ran git fetch. However, because you ran git fetch, Git knows that your upstream branch has changed. In fact, it even told you what the changes are: notice that the message includes the text 2532277..4a28994 main -> origin/main, which means "new commits from 532277 to 4a28994 have been fetched for main," which tracks origin/main.

To update your local branch with this (and any other) new commits, merge these changes:

```
$ git merge origin/main
```

You can also directly bring any changes from the remote into your local branch without fetching first with the git pull command, which we'll look at next.

Pulling Changes

The git pull ("download from remote") command integrates the changes from a remote into the current branch. Because you've already told Git what the upstream branch for the main branch is, running git pull without any parameters will move to the latest commit:

```
$ git pull
Updating 2532277..4a28994
Fast-forward
 README.md | 13 +++++++++++++
 1 file changed, 13 insertions(+)
 create mode 100644 README.md
```

The git pull command tells you what commit you've moved from and to and gives a summary of the files that have changed. You can see that a file named *README.md* has been created, which you can confirm by checking your local files as follows:

```
$ ls
README.md  install.sh  shell.d  shell.sh
```

Finally, check the graph view of your commit log:

```
$ git log --graph --oneline
* 4a28994 (HEAD -> main, origin/main) add a simple 'README' file
*   2532277 Merge branch 'glog_alias'
|\
| * a8cbb15 (glog_alias) add the 'glog' alias
* | 31548e4 add the 'glog' alias
|/
*   138b404 Merge branch 'more_aliases'
|\
| * a51ae1a (more_aliases) add a file to store 'zsh' aliases
| * 63ea74f add a file to store 'bash' aliases
* | a95bd90 add the 'gm' alias for 'git merge'
|/
* b9ae0ad (aliases) add alias 'gcm' for 'git checkout main'
* f61369d (more_changes) add alias 'gs' for 'git status'
* d7e1bb9 add the 'shell.d' folder
* 01e7a10 add the 'install' and 'shell' scripts
```

You can see that your HEAD is at the tip of the main branch, and that this is also the tip of the origin remote's main branch.

You can pull any branch into your current branch—just provide the name of a remote and the name of a branch:

```
git pull remote_name branch_name
```

If you don't provide any parameters to git pull, it will pull from the upstream branch. But you can also use git pull to merge other branches into your current branch.

Congratulations! If you've followed along with this chapter and the previous one, you've now created a local repository, staged and unstaged changes to and from the index, created commits, created branches, handled merging and merge conflicts, and set up a remote and synchronized changes with it. Now we'll look at how you can share your repository with other GitHub users or other machines.

Sharing Your Dot Files

Hosting your dot files on GitHub is a very convenient way of making them accessible anywhere and to anyone you wish. Making your GitHub *dotfiles* repository public will allow people to copy your code or propose changes. When you create a new repository with your GitHub account, it is public by default. You can also make your repository private, meaning that only you and collaborators you invite can see and make changes to it.

You might also want to share your repository to another machine so that your custom configuration settings will carry over. To clone your *dotfiles* repository onto another machine, use this one-line command:

```
$ git clone git://github.com/your_username/dotfiles.git
```

The git clone ("download a repository") command downloads the repository into the current folder. If your repository is private, you'll have to authenticate to be able to do this, but if your repository is public, you or anyone else can download your dot files.

Once you've downloaded your dot files, simply run the *install.sh* script from the *dotfiles* folder to set up the shell startup files on the new machine.

Search online for "dot files," and you'll find many articles on the topic as well as users who have shared their dot files online—look to these for inspiration!

Collaborating with Other Users

Forking and pull requests are features offered by popular Git hosting services like GitHub, Bitbucket, and GitLab. They're not actually Git features but have become so widely used that you're likely to hear them referred to as such when working with online Git repositories.

Forking

A *fork* is a copy of a Git repository. Typically, you fork a repository if you want to make a copy of someone else's code and work on it yourself.

I've created a simple *dotfiles* repository on GitHub that you can use as a starting point for your own dot file configuration. You'll use this to see how forking works.

First, open up the GitHub project that you'd like to fork, which in this case is at *https://github.com/effective-shell/dotfiles*. Click **Fork** at the top right of the screen (see Figure 19-10).

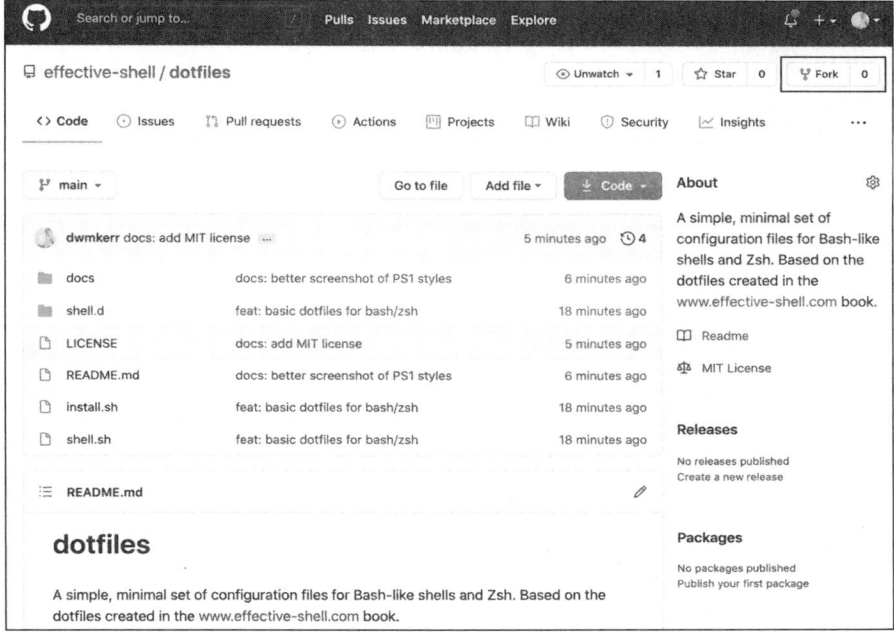

Figure 19-10: The effective-shell/dotfiles *repository with the Fork option shown at the top right*

When you click Fork, GitHub will create a copy of the repository in your own account. You can now clone this repository, make changes to it, and work on it as if it were your own. The original repository is tracked by GitHub, meaning that you can update from it at any time.

Making Pull Requests

If you make some improvements to the forked *dotfiles* repository and want to share them back, you can click Create Pull Request. A *pull request* is a request to merge a set of changes from one branch into another or from one fork into the original repository.

Typically, when you open a pull request, the project maintainer will review the changes, make suggestions, or discuss your proposal and then either merge the pull request or reject it. In Figure 19-11, I am opening a pull request from my clone of the *dotfiles* repository to the original *dotfiles* repository to add an uninstall script.

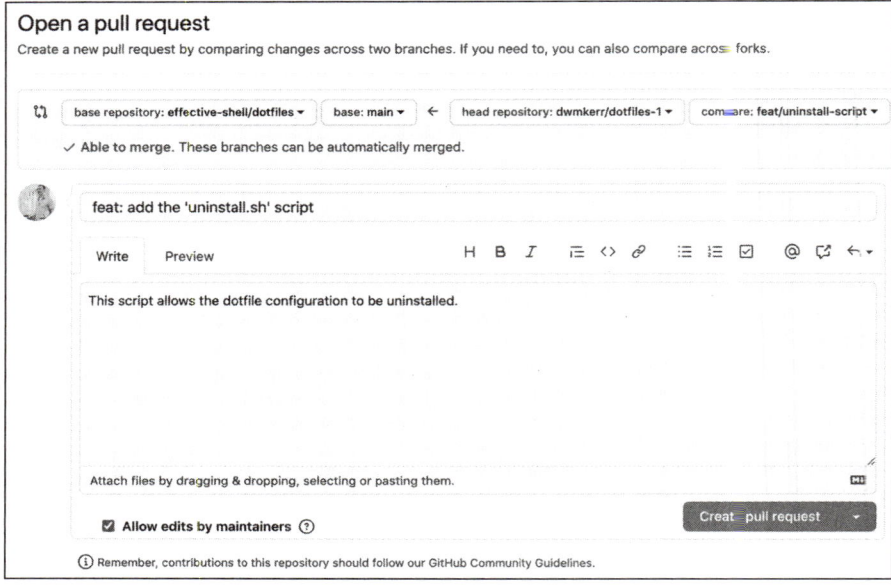

Figure 19-11: Opening a pull request to add an uninstall.sh *file*

This model of forking and making pull requests is really just a nice user interface on top of Git's underlying capabilities to track remotes and manage branches. Services like GitHub offer functionality to discuss changes, run arbitrary pipelines that project maintainers might create to test the code, and more.

GitHub has become a remarkably popular site for people to collaborate on projects together. At the time of writing, the *microsoft/vscode* repository for the popular Visual Studio Code open source editor has had contributions from more than 19,000 individuals!

Writing a Shell Function to Open a Pull Request

When you push a branch to a remote on GitHub, GitLab, Bitbucket, or a number of other Git services providers, you'll see a message in the command prompt with a link to open a pull request:

```
$ git push -u origin fix/fix-shell-configuration
...
remote:
remote: Create a pull request for 'fix/fix-shell-configuration' on GitHub by visiting:
remote:        https://github.com/dwmkerr/dotfiles/pull/new/fix/fix-shell-configuration
...
```

You can write a shell function that runs the git push command, reads its output, and, if it finds a web address, opens it in a browser. In fact, the *dotfiles* repository at *https://github.com/effective-shell/dotfiles* does exactly this—just run the command gpr to open a pull request!

The gpr function is actually quite straightforward, as you can see in the following code (note that some of the comments and syntax formatting code have been removed for legibility):

```
gpr() {
    # Get the current branch name, or use HEAD if you cannot get it.
    branch=$(git symbolic-ref -q HEAD)
    branch=${branch##refs/heads/}
    branch=${branch:-HEAD}

    # Pushing takes a little while, so let the user know you're working.
    printf "Opening pull request for ${branch}...\n"

    # Push to origin, grabbing the output but then echoing it back.
    push_output=`git push origin -u ${branch} 2>&1`
    printf "\n${push_output}"

    # If there's anything that starts with http, it's a good guess it'll be a
    # link to GitHub/GitLab/whatever. So open the first link found.
    link=$(echo ${push_output} | grep -o 'http.*' | head -n1 | sed -e 's/[[:space:]]*$//')
    if [ ${link} ]; then
        printf "\nOpening: ${GREEN}${link}${RESET}..."
        python3 -mwebbrowser ${link}
    fi
}
```

This snippet first gets the name of the current branch, or HEAD if you can't work the name out. (Technically, it gets the reference for HEAD or exits with a nonzero status and no output if HEAD refers to a detached state; the two commands that follow in the script then clean up this output.) It then runs the git push origin command and records the output of the command into a variable called push_output.

Once the push command has completed, this function writes its output to the screen, uses grep and sed to search for the first hyperlink, and then opens the link in a browser with Python.

NOTE   *Another option worth exploring if you use GitHub regularly is GitHub CLI, called gh, which allows you to open a pull request directly in GitHub. The program offers many other ways to work with GitHub from the command line. You can find GitHub CLI at* https://cli.github.com.

I use the gpr function many times every day, and it has been a real time-saver.

Showing Git Information in the Command Prompt

Chapter 16 covered how to customize the command prompt by setting the PS1 variable. As you start using Git more, you might find it convenient to show some information about the repository in your prompt.

For example, as I am writing this chapter, my command prompt looks like this (but with syntax highlighting applied):

```
github/dwmkerr/effective-shell feat/managing-git-remotes ! 1 in stash
$
```

I spread my prompt over two lines, with the prompt indicator as the only character on the second line to keep my cursor from becoming too indented. Here's the breakdown of each component:

github/dwmkerr/effective-shell   Indicates my current folder and up to two parent folders in blue

feat/managing-git-remotes   Indicates my current Git branch (if I am in a Git repository) in green

!   Appears in red if I have uncommitted changes

1 in stash   Appears in yellow if I have anything in my Git stash

NOTE   *A Git* stash *is a temporary storage space that saves your uncommitted changes so you can switch to a different task and come back to them later. Stashes are a more advanced feature and will be discussed briefly later in the chapter.*

You can try out this style of command prompt by calling the set_ps1 function:

```
$ source ~/dotfiles/shell.d/set_ps1.sh
$ set_ps1 dwmkerr
```

The style name is dwmkerr since it's my personal configuration, but feel free to create your own. To change back to your previous prompt, just run set_ps1 again without any parameters.

If you're interested in showing Git information in your command prompt, take a look at the *set_ps1.sh* file to see the full details. The following snippet shows how to get this Git information:

```
_git_info() {
    # Don't write anything if you're not in a folder tracked by Git.
❶  if ! [ "$(git rev-parse --is-inside-work-tree 2>/dev/null)" == "true" ]
    then
        return
    fi

    # Get the branch name, changes, and number of stashes.
❷  local git_branch_name="$(git branch --show-current)"
❸  local git_any_local_changes="$(git status --porcelain=v1 2>/dev/null)"
❹  local git_stash_count="$(git rev-list --walk-reflogs --count \
```

```
            refs/stash -- 2>/dev/null)" # Ignore error when no stashes.
    local git_info=""
    if [ "${git_branch_name}" = "main" ]; then
        git_info="${fg_green}${start_underline}${git_branch_name}${reset}"
    else
        git_info="${fg_green}${git_branch_name}${reset}"
    fi
    if ! [ -z "${git_any_local_changes}" ]; then
        # Make sure to put the exclamation mark in single quotes
        # so that it is not expanded to the last command!
        git_info="${git_info} ${fg_red}"'!'"${reset}"
    fi
    if [ "${git_stash_count:-0}" -gt 0 ]; then
        git_info="${git_info} ${fg_yellow}${git_stash_count} in stash${reset}"
    fi
    printf "${git_info}"
}
```

First, git rev-parse ❶ checks whether you're in a folder that is part of
a Git working tree. If you're not in a Git working tree, nothing is shown.
Next, git branch --show-current gets the current branch name ❷. In the following line, git status checks to see if there are any changes ❸, using the
--porcelain=v1 option to generate a machine-readable status (which is easier
to use in scripts). Then, the git rev-list command checks the number of
stash revisions ❹. As you can see, there are many advanced Git commands
available to get data about a repository.

The rest of the script is formatting only: underlining the branch name
if it's the main branch, showing the exclamation mark if you have changes,
and so on.

NOTE *This example uses the snippet "'!'" to write an exclamation mark in the output. The
double quotes indicate that you're creating a string, and the single quotes around the
exclamation point tell the shell to treat it literally. Without the single quotes, the shell
interprets an exclamation point as "rerun last command."*

If you'll be using Git a lot, feel free to use this script as a starting point
for your own command prompt customizations.

Diving Deeper into Git

Git has a reputation for being complicated or overwhelming, but this is
somewhat unfair. Version control of files is itself an inherently complex
topic; no matter what tool you use, there are always challenges with managing changes across environments, dealing with conflicts, integrating work,
and the like. The basic Git functionality is *incredibly* good at making 99 percent of this work simple and straightforward, and Git gives you the tools to
make the other 1 percent at least manageable.

But we've only scratched the surface of Git in this chapter. It's an amaz-
ingly powerful tool, and I can't recommend highly enough that you take the
time to really learn how the commands work. Many people use a graphical

tool to work with Git, and this is perfectly fine if it works for you. But to be an *effective shell* user, you should spend some time using the command line to get familiar with the core Git commands.

Once you're feeling more confident with those commands, I suggest learning about the following topics:

- The `.gitignore` file, a special file you can use to tell Git not to track certain changes
- The `.gitconfig` file, Git's own dot file, which you can use to fine-tune Git configuration
- *Tags*, labels you can add to commits to track releases for projects or other metadata
- The `git diff` command, which lets you see changes between branches, commits, the index and the working tree, and more
- The `git stash` command, which lets you temporarily save and reset any changes to the working tree without having to create a branch or commit; stashes are useful if you need to quickly go back to a "clean" working tree (perhaps to work on another branch) and then bring the changes back later
- The `git clean` command, which helps you remove unneeded files from your working tree
- *Interactive staging* for files, parts of files (called *hunks*), or even individual lines directly from the shell, which can be invaluable for making sure that exactly the right changes are going into the index
- *Patch staging* or checkout with the `git add -p` command, which allows you to review and edit changes interactively as you stage them
- Merge strategies such as *squashing* (combining multiple commits into one), which can be very useful when you're working with branches
- *Rebasing*, a merge workflow that can also help in other scenarios, such as having multiple people working on a repository and integrating complex changes
- *Commit and tag signing*, a great solution for security-sensitive users that allows you to use special keys to sign your commits and improve your repository security
- GitHub flow, a common workflow used with GitHub projects (see *https://docs.github.com/en/get-started/using-github/github-flow*)

Many articles and online books on Git are available. I also recommend the excellent book *Pro Git* by Scott Chacon and Ben Straub (Apress, 2014).

Git at a Glance: A Recap of Key Concepts and Commands

To wrap things up, I'll summarize what you've learned throughout the chapter. First, Figure 19-12 offers an overview of a typical Git workflow.

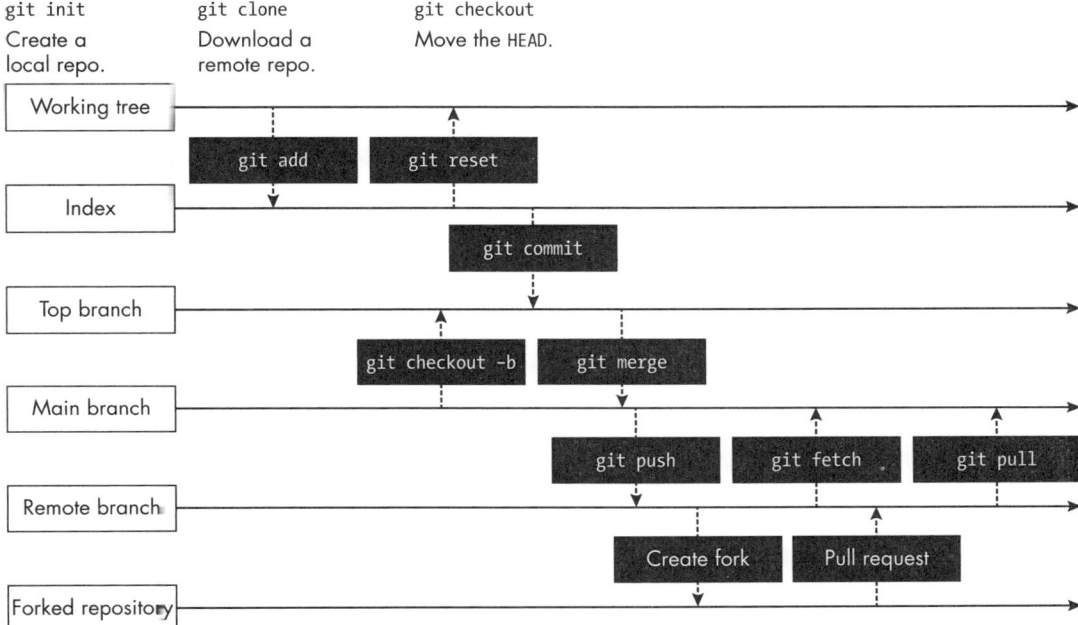

Figure 19-12: A typical Git workflow

The key concepts introduced in this chapter including the following:

Working tree   The folder you're working in and tracking changes to

Index   The staging area for building commits

Repository   The full set of all commits, branches, and metadata

Fork   A copy of an entire repository, including its history and all branches

Pull request   A request to merge one branch into another, or a branch in a fork to the upstream branch

Finally, Table 19-1 summarizes the core commands you'll use to work with Git.

Table 19-1: Core Git Commands

Command	Description
git init	Creates a local repository
git clone	Downloads a remote repository or creates a new copy of a local repository
git add	Stages a change from the working tree to the index
git reset	Unstages a change from the index
git commit	Creates a new commit
git checkout -b	Creates a new branch
git merge	Merges a branch into the current branch
git checkout	Moves the current HEAD to a new branch or commit
git push	Pushes changes to an upstream branch
git fetch	Retrieves information about changes to a remote
git pull	Downloads and merges changes from a remote

For everything else Git, see the manual at *https://git-scm.com/docs*.

Summary

In this chapter, you saw how to use GitHub to host a remote repository; how to push, fetch, and pull changes; and how remotes work. You also learned about making pull requests, creating forks, and showing Git information on the command line. And you were introduced to some of the more advanced topics that you might want to explore as you continue to use Git.

Although we've only scratched the surface of what Git can do, you should now have the tools to work with repositories, share content like your dot files, collaborate with others, and manage your own changes.

This concludes Part IV, where you've added to your shell toolkit several customizations and configurations that you can share across machines or with other users. In the next part of the book, we'll look at some advanced techniques that can help you level up your skills as a shell user.

PART V

ADVANCED TECHNIQUES

20

SHELL EXPANSION

When the shell receives a command from the user or from a shell script, it splits the command into words and performs several operations that determine how the command is interpreted. Collectively, these operations are known as *shell expansion*. Although you've probably already encountered many of these operations in action throughout the book, seeing all of them together in one place will help you better understand what exactly the shell does with the commands you give it.

Using shell expansion techniques can make your workflow more efficient. For example, you can use brace expansion to create multiple files with fewer keystrokes, or use pathname expansion to delete all files with names that start with the same letters. I'll introduce the full set of shell expansion operations in this chapter along with practical examples on how to use them.

Shell Expansion Operations

The shell performs its seven expansion operations in the following order:

Brace expansion   Expands values between braces, such as file{1..3} into file1 file2 file3

Tilde expansion   Expands the tilde (~) into the full path for the home directory, such as *~/effective-shell* into */home/dwmkerr/effective-shell*

Parameter expansion   Expands terms that start with a dollar sign ($) into parameter values, such as $HOME into the value of the variable named HOME

Command substitution   Evaluates the contents of $(*command*) sequences, which are used to run commands in a subshell

Arithmetic expansion   Evaluates the contents of $((*expression*)) sequences, which are used to perform basic mathematical operations

Word splitting   Splits up text and input into "words," or sequences of text that you can run operations such as loops over

Pathname expansion   Expands wildcards and special characters in pathnames, such as *file*.txt* into *filename.txt* and *fileserver.txt*

This order of operations is important to keep in mind, as it affects how the command is executed. I'll talk more about this in "Pathname Expansion" on page 309.

For more information on these operations in the man pages, run man bash and search for the text ^EXPANSION.

Brace Expansion

Brace expansion, the first shell expansion operation performed, expands a simple expression representing a sequence or range of characters.

The following example expands a set of words or characters:

```
mkdir /tmp/{one,two,three}

# The line above is expanded to:
mkdir /tmp/one /tmp/two /tmp/three
```

Brace expansion provides an efficient way to perform operations on multiple files or folders at once.

You can also create sequences of numbers or characters:

```
touch file{1..5}.txt

# The line above is expanded to:
touch file1.txt file2.txt file3.txt file4.txt file5.txt
```

As well as specifying the start and end of a sequence, you can specify an increment. You might see this type of expansion used in for loops:

```
for x in {0..10..2}; do print $x; done

# The line above is expanded to:
for x in 0 2 4 6 8 10; do print $x; done
```

With its ability to create sequences, handle multiple paths, and generate file patterns, brace expansion can save you some keystrokes and help prevent errors in your shell scripts.

Tilde Expansion

If a word starts with a tilde, the shell performs tilde expansion to expand ~ into the value of the HOME variable:

```
cd ~/effective-shell

# The line above is expanded to:
cd $HOME/effective-shell

# This is subsequently expanded to the user's home directory, for example:
cd /home/dwmkerr/effective-shell
```

You can change the HOME variable to another location if you prefer, and the tilde will expand to that value. If you unset the HOME variable, the tilde will always expand to the current user's home directory configured by the system (typically in the */etc/passwd* file, discussed in Chapter 15):

```
unset HOME
cd ~/effective-shell

# The line above is expanded to the system-defined home directory:
cd /home/dwmkerr/effective-shell
```

Whether using the default HOME path or a custom value, tilde expansion gives you a useful shorthand for referencing home directories in your shell commands and scripts.

Parameter Expansion

The dollar sign indicates that the shell is going to perform parameter expansion, which expands variables or the parameters of a script. (With slight alterations, the dollar sign can also be used to indicate command substitution or arithmetic expansion, as you'll see shortly.)

In its simplest form, parameter expansion replaces the name of a variable or parameter with its value:

```
fruit=apples
echo "I like $fruit"

# The line above is expanded to:
echo "I like apples"
```

When using parameter expansion, it's a good idea to surround the parameter name with braces to be as unambiguous as possible:

```
echo "My backup folder is: ${HOME}_backup"

# The line above is expanded to:
echo "My backup folder is: /home/dwmkerr_backup"
```

Here's the same operation without the braces:

```
echo "My backup folder is: $HOME_backup"

# The line above is expanded to:
echo "My backup folder is: "
```

The expansion doesn't work as expected in this case, because the shell is trying to expand a parameter with the name HOME_backup rather than using a parameter named HOME and then adding the text _backup to its value. The braces used in the first example remove any ambiguity, making it clear to the shell that the parameter name is HOME.

A number of additional features are available to make parameter expansion even more convenient.

Set Default Values

The expression ${*parameter*:-*default*} will expand to the value of *parameter*, but if that value isn't set, the *default* value is used instead. This is handy when you want to provide a "default" value for the shell to use if a parameter is not set:

```
$ backup_location=${BACKUP_DIR:-~/backup}
$ echo "Backing up to: ${backup_location}"
Backing up to: /home/dwmkerr/backup
```

In this example, if BACKUP_DIR isn't set, then backup_location will be set to the default value provided, which is *~/backup*. Notice that the first line of this example also uses tilde expansion to specify the user's home directory.

Assign Default Values

The expression ${*parameter*:=*default*} will expand to the value of *parameter*, but if that value isn't set, the *default* value is used instead. In this case, *parameter* is also set to *default*, so the expression works just like the previous one but sets the parameter at the same time.

```
$ : ${BACKUP_DIR:=~/backup}
$ echo "Backing up to: ${BACKUP_DIR}"
Backing up to: /home/dwmkerr/backup
```

In this example, the first line starts with a colon (:), which is a shell expression for "no operation," and it means "Don't try to execute the result of the following command but do expand it." If the variable BACKUP_DIR isn't set, it will be set to the default value provided, which is *~/backup*.

Display an Error If a Value Is Null or Unset

The expression ${*parameter*:?*message*} tells the shell to expand to the value of *parameter*, but if that value is null or unset, to instead write *message* to stderr and exit (unless the shell is interactive, in which case the shell isn't closed).

You can use this operation to put a guard in place to ensure that a script exits if a value isn't set. To try it out, you'll need to unset the BACKUP _DIR parameter if you set it in the previous example:

```
$ unset BACKUP_DIR
```

Now run the following:

```
$ backup_location=${BACKUP_DIR:?Please set BACKUP_DIR to use this script}
bash: BACKUP_DIR: Please set BACKUP_DIR to use this script
```

This script copies the *~/effective-shell* folder to the folder set in the BACKUP _DIR parameter. However, because BACKUP_DIR is no longer set, the script will exit, set the error status, and show an error message telling you to set the variable.

Use an Alternate Value

The expression ${*parameter*:+*alternate*} expands to an empty string if *parameter* is null or unset. If *parameter* has a value, the value of *alternate* is used instead. You will often see this kind of expression used to conditionally add parameters to commands:

```
$ SHOW_HIDDEN=1
$ ls ${SHOW_HIDDEN:+-a} ~
.bash_rc
...
```

In this case, if the SHOW_HIDDEN parameter has been set, its value is replaced with the string -a in the ls ~ command to list all files in the user's home folder, including hidden files. The alternate value expression is a convenient way to translate a variable into a parameter or flag.

Specify Offset and Length

The ${*parameter*:*offset*} expression tells the shell to expand only a subset of a parameter's value. In this case, the shell will expand the value of *parameter* but skip *offset* number of characters from the beginning:

```
$ echo "My home folder name is: ${HOME:6}"
My home folder name is: dwmkerr
```

Only my home folder name (*dwmkerr*) is displayed now, rather than the full path (*/home/dwmkerr*). You can also specify how many characters should be used by providing a *length* value in the expression ${*parameter*:*offset*:*length*} like so:

```
$ error_message="file not found: did you enter the right path?
$ echo "${error_message:0:14}"
file not found
```

Now, the first 14 characters of the parameter error_message will be shown.

The *offset* and *length* values can also be used with arrays:

```
$ days=("Monday" "Tuesday" "Wednesday" "Thursday" "Friday" "Saturday"
"Sunday")
$ echo "${days[@]:2:3}"
Tuesday Wednesday Thursday
```

However, when using this technique with arrays, you must specify the array name followed by [@] to indicate that you want to work with all of the members of the array. Otherwise, the expression would use only the first element of the array.

Expand Variable Names

The ${!*name**} expression evaluates to the name of every parameter that starts with the text *name*. You can use this expression to find the full set of parameters that match a certain pattern.

How might this be useful? To tidy up scripts, for one thing. This example shows how the script that downloads the book's sample files creates some variables and then tidies up after itself:

```
_es_download_folder=~/downloads
_es_backup_folder=~/backups
_es_download_address=https://effective-shell.com/downloads/effective-shell-samples.tar.gz

# (For brevity, the code that downloads and installs the samples is omitted.)

# Now clean up any variables you created.
for var_name in ${!_es_*}
do
```

```
      echo "Clearing up: ${var_name}..."
      unset ${var_name}
done
```

Any variable created in this script that starts with _es_ will be automatically cleaned up at the end of the script. The output of this script will look similar to the following:

```
Cleaning up: _es_download_folder...
Cleaning up: _es_backup_folder...
...
```

This is a rather advanced technique but a useful one for keeping your scripts organized and easier to maintain.

Expand an Array

Array expansion is partly covered in Chapter 10. The expression ${!array[@]} expands to the indices (or keys, in the case of an associative array) for each item in an array:

```
$ days=("Monday" "Tuesday" "Wednesday" "Thursday" "Friday" "Saturday"
"Sunday")
$ echo "${!days[@]}"
0 1 2 3 4 5 6
```

Now, you can loop over or perform other operations on the indices of the array.

Find the Length of a Parameter or an Array

The ${#parameter} expression expands to the length of the value in the parameter named *parameter*:

```
$ word="Supercalifragilisticexpialidocious"
$ echo "Length of word: ${#word} characters"
Length of word: 34 characters
```

You can also use this expression to find the length of an array; simply append [@] like so:

```
$ days=("Monday" "Tuesday" "Wednesday" "Thursday" "Friday" "Saturday"
"Sunday")
$ echo "There are ${#days[@]} days in the array"
There are 7 days in the array
```

You may have noticed a pattern by this point: you can perform many parameter expansions on an array simply by appending [@] to the parameter name. The [@] translates to "all of the array members," so without it, the shell uses only the first element of the array.

Remove a Pattern from the Beginning

You can use the ${*parameter#pattern*} expression to expand the value of *parameter*, removing *pattern* from the front of its value:

```
$ address=https://effective-shell.com
$ echo "Address: ${address#https://}"
Address: effective-shell.com
```

To tell the shell to remove as many sequential matches of *pattern* as possible, use the ${*parameter##pattern*} expression. This strips out all the characters up to a certain point in a parameter:

```
$ folder=/home/dwmkerr/backups/2025-4-19
$ echo "Today's backup folder is: ${folder##*/}"
Today's backup folder is: 2025-4-19
```

Notice this example uses an asterisk (*) in the pattern, telling the shell to strip as many possible characters from the beginning of the parameter until it finds the final forward slash (/).

Remove a Pattern from the End

The ${*parameter%pattern*} expression works exactly like the preceding expression but removes text from the end of a parameter instead:

```
$ echo "My working directory is: ${PWD}"
My working directory is: /home/dwmkerr/repos/github/dwmkerr/effective-shell
$ echo "My parent folder is: ${PWD%/*}"
My parent folder is: /home/dwmkerr/repos/github/dwmkerr
```

Again, the * wildcard in the pattern tells the shell to remove all of the text from the end of the parameter, up to and including the first forward slash (/) it finds.

To remove as many matches as possible, use the expression ${*parameter %%pattern*} like so:

```
$ archive=effective-shell.tar.gz
$ echo "Name of archive is: ${archive%%.*}"
Name of archive is: effective-shell
```

Notice that the character removal doesn't stop at the first period (.); the shell removes as many characters as possible until it finds the *last* period.

NOTE *One way to remember that the hash mark (#) pattern removes from the beginning and the percent sign (%) pattern removes from the end is to look at the keyboard: the # is on the left and the % is on the right.*

Replace a Pattern

You can replace a pattern in a parameter with the expression ${*parameter*/ *pattern*/*string*} as follows:

```
$ message="Hello Dave"
$ echo "${message/Hello/Goodbye}"
Goodbye Dave
```

There are pattern replacement options that can control things like the number of replacements performed and how arrays are treated. I wouldn't recommend making overly complex replacements using these types of expressions, however, as they can be quite challenging for readers to parse and can also vary from shell to shell. Instead, use a command like tr or sed to make what's going on very clear.

Convert to Lowercase or Uppercase

You can use the ${*parameter*^^} expression to convert the value of *parameter* to uppercase or ${*parameter*,,} to convert it to lowercase:

```
$ message="Hello Reader"
$ echo "${message^^}"
HELLO READER
$ echo "${message,,}"
hello reader
```

You can find alternative ways to manipulate text in Chapters 6 and 7.

Use Parameter Indirection

To get the value of a parameter that has an arbitrary name, you can use the ${!*parameter_name*} expression:

```
$ parameter_name="HOME"
$ echo "${!parameter_name}"
/home/dwmkerr
```

This example returns the value of the parameter whose name is stored in parameter_name. This expression can be very useful if you are writing scripts that will work with arbitrary or variable parameter names.

For more examples of using parameter expansion with the parameters of functions or scripts, see Chapter 10.

Command Substitution

Command substitution, the second form of expansion that starts with a dollar sign, instructs the shell to run a specific command. The syntax is simply $(*command*).

You've seen command substitution throughout the book. In this example, it is used to expand the date command to print the current date:

```
$ echo "The date is: $(date)"
The date is: Tue Feb 25 16:49:07 +08 2025
```

Your scripts or commands may be easier to manage if you store the results of a command in a variable like so:

```
$ archives=$(find ~/downloads -type f -name "*.tar.gz")
```

Here you're storing the results of the find operation in the parameter named archives.

You might see an alternative syntax for command substitution in which the command is surrounded by backticks (`) instead of parentheses:

```
$ archives=`find ~/downloads -type f -name "*.tar.gz"`
```

However, I suggest avoiding the backtick syntax because it doesn't allow you to easily nest commands like so: *result=$(command1 $(command2))*.

Arithmetic Expansion

The final form of shell expansion that starts with a dollar sign is arithmetic expansion, which can be used to perform simple arithmetic operations:

```
$ echo "The result of 23*4 is: $((23*4))"
The result of 23*4 is: 92
```

Arithmetic expansion is covered in detail in Chapter 10.

Word Splitting

Word splitting is the process by which the shell attempts to split the result of parameter expansion, command substitution, and arithmetic expansion into separate items, or *words*. The shell applies word splitting to any expansion that starts with a dollar sign and does *not* appear within double quotes. This rule can cause confusion, so let's take a look at word splitting in detail and see when it's useful and when it can be problematic.

To show word splitting in action, this script prints a set of days:

```
days="Monday Tuesday Wednesday      Thursday Friday    Saturday Sunday"
for day in "$days"
do
    echo "${day}"
done
```

Notice that there are different numbers of space characters between each day in the days variable.

Here's the output of this script:

```
Monday Tuesday Wednesday     Thursday Friday   Saturday Sunday
```

The expression for day in "$days" uses shell parameter expansion to expand the days parameter. Because $days appears in quotes, the shell preserves the spaces between the days instead of applying word splitting. When it loops through the days parameter, it sees only one value: the original line of text, including the spaces.

This version of the script does *not* surround $days in quotes:

```
days="Monday Tuesday Wednesday     Thursday Friday   Saturday Sunday"
for day in $days
do
    echo "${day}"
done
```

Its output is as follows:

```
Monday
Tuesday
Wednesday
Thursday
Friday
Saturday
Sunday
```

In this case, word splitting has occurred. The shell is performing the following operations:

1. It searches through each character in the input.

2. Every time it encounters the separator character set in the IFS ("internal field separator") special variable, it splits the word.

3. If there are multiple instances of a separator character, it uses the first and skips all of the additional characters.

Word splitting and the IFS variable are discussed in Chapter 12, but let's see them in action by breaking down exactly what the shell is doing in this example.

By default, the IFS variable is set to <space><tab><newline>, meaning those are the characters the shell will use to split an expression into words. When there are multiple instances of these characters in a row (such as the five spaces after the Wednesday value), the shell treats them as a single delimiter and applies the splitting accordingly.

The fact that the shell uses spaces, tabs, and newlines as internal field separators can sometimes cause confusion, particularly if you have a list of files as a parameter value:

```
programs="/usr/bin/bash /usr/bin/zshell /usr/bin/new shell"
for program in $programs
do
    echo "${program}"
done
```

This script outputs the following:

```
/usr/bin/bash
/usr/bin/zshell
/usr/bin/new
shell
```

The final value in the programs variable, /usr/bin/new shell has a space in its name, so it has been split into two words. You could avoid this issue by temporarily changing the value of IFS to a different character and separating your parameter value accordingly:

```
programs="/usr/bin/bash;/usr/bin/zshell;/usr/bin/new shell"
OLDIFS=$IFS
IFS=';'
for program in $programs
do
    echo "${program}"
done
IFS=$OLDIFS
```

Here's the output:

```
/usr/bin/bash
/usr/bin/zshell
/usr/bin/new shell
```

This script separates the programs with a semicolon (;), saves the original value of IFS into a parameter called OLDIFS, changes IFS to use the semicolon as a separator, runs the loop (which correctly splits the programs and preserves the space in the last program name), and then changes IFS back to its original value.

NOTE   *Other programs or commands might expect IFS to be set to the default value, so change it only when you must, and always make sure to revert it to its original value immediately afterward.*

If you look at the contents of the PATH variable, which specifies the locations where the shell should search for commands, you can see that they are actually separated by colons:

```
$ echo $PATH
/usr/local/sbin:/usr/local/bin:/usr/sbin:/usr/bin:/sbin:/bin:/usr/games:/usr/local/games
```

The results you see will vary depending on your operating system. But the fact that they are separated by colons means that you can easily change IFS to a colon character to get each path, even if it contains spaces:

```
OLDIFS=$IFS
IFS=":"
for path in $PATH
do
        echo "${path}"
done
IFS=$OLDIFS
```

The output of this script should look something like this:

```
/usr/local/sbin
/usr/local/bin
/usr/sbin
/usr/bin
/sbin
/bin
/usr/games
/usr/local/games
```

You'll learn a little more about how the shell can sometimes split up a filename with spaces (or even newlines) in the path when we look at the final shell expansion operation: pathname expansion.

Pathname Expansion

When the shell encounters an asterisk, a question mark, or an open square bracket ([) at the beginning of an expression, it knows to apply pathname expansion, the expansion that occurs when you use wildcards or patterns in shell scripts to expand a list of paths:

```
$ ls ~/downloads/*.tar.gz
/home/dwmkerr/downloads/aspnetcore-runtime-3.1.18-osx-x64 (1).tar.gz
/home/dwmkerr/downloads/aspnetcore-runtime-3.1.18-osx-x64.tar.gz
/home/dwmkerr/downloads/dotnet-sdk-3.1.412-osx-x64.tar.gz
/home/dwmkerr/downloads/effective-shell-playground.tar.gz
/home/dwmkerr/downloads/effective-shell-samples (1).tar.gz
/home/dwmkerr/downloads/effective-shell-samples (2).tar.gz
/home/dwmkerr/downloads/effective-shell-samples.tar.gz
```

This script shows all of the files in the *~/downloads* folder that match the pattern **.tar.gz*. The results you see will depend on what you have in your own *~/downloads* folder.

Remember that the shell performs all of the types of expansion described in this chapter *in order*. This means that word splitting is performed *before* pathname expansion—so if you loop through the results of an expanded path, word splitting will not be performed on those results. You can see this in the following script:

```
for $path in ~/downloads/*.tar.gz
do
    echo "${path}"
done
```

Here's the output:

```
/home/dwmkerr/downloads/aspnetcore-runtime-3.1.18-osx-x64 (1).tar.gz
/home/dwmkerr/downloads/aspnetcore-runtime-3.1.18-osx-x64.tar.gz
/home/dwmkerr/downloads/dotnet-sdk-3.1.412-osx-x64.tar.gz
/home/dwmkerr/downloads/effective-shell-playground.tar.gz
/home/dwmkerr/downloads/effective-shell-samples (1).tar.gz
/home/dwmkerr/downloads/effective-shell-samples (2).tar.gz
/home/dwmkerr/downloads/effective-shell-samples.tar.gz
```

Note that the spaces in the pathnames have been preserved. Because pathname expansion happens after word splitting, the expanded paths are left as is.

In addition to using the asterisk as a wildcard character, you can use the question mark, which means "any single character," for pathname expansion. You can also use expressions such as [abc] to match on a range of characters. For details on using these special characters, run man bash.

One feature of pathname expansion that might surprise you is what happens if the shell finds *no files* that match the pattern, as in this example:

```
$ echo ~/effective-shell/*.txt
/home/dwmkerr/effective-shell/*.txt
```

There are no files in the *~/effective-shell* folder that match the pattern *.txt*, so the shell has left the wildcard expression as is. This is why you should always check the results of the expansion before assuming the shell has found a file!

For example, to run the touch command on a set of files and handle the case where no files are found, you could do the following:

```
for file in ~/effective-shell/*.txt; do
    # If the file or folder doesn't exist, skip it.
    if ! [ -e "$file" ]; then continue; fi
    touch "$file"
done
```

This script first checks to see whether the file or folder exists with the -e ("exists") test. If the file or folder doesn't exist, the shell skips through the loop. For more examples of this pattern, see Chapter 12.

Pathname expansion has limitations, so if you need a more sophisticated way to search for a set of files, consult Chapter 3.

Summary

This chapter went into the lower-level details of how shell expansion works, exploring the seven types of expansion the shell performs on the input it is provided.

With this additional knowledge on shell expansion, I hope you'll be more comfortable with topics like word splitting and how empty results from filename expansion are treated, both of which are often sources of confusion for shell users.

In the next chapter, we'll examine some of the limitations of shell scripting and useful alternatives you should become familiar with.

21

ALTERNATIVES TO SHELL SCRIPTING

Sometimes being an effective shell user means recognizing when a shell script is *not* the right tool for the job and you need a more powerful programming language instead. In this chapter, we'll look at scenarios where shell scripting may not be ideal, explore the pros and cons of alternative approaches, and identify what constitutes a shell-friendly tool. Then you'll create a real-world tool to look up a word's definition using an online dictionary. This type of tool would be complex to produce with a shell script but is a snap with the Python programming language.

When to Avoid Shell Scripting

Shell scripts often can't be beat as a quick way to solve a simple problem. When you add in the handy tools that you've seen across this book, such as sed for advanced text manipulation, they can be even more powerful. But there are some scenarios where you might want to avoid using a shell script:

- If the problem you're solving requires complex logic that would be better handled by a full programming language
- If a program needs to be used or maintained by others who may not be very familiar with shell scripting
- If you need portability across different systems, since complex scripts may rely on tools that aren't available everywhere

Shell scripts are occasionally the *only* sensible tool to use. For example, if you wanted to show the shell's options and let the user toggle them on and off, a shell script would be ideal. In that scenario, a script written in Python or another programming language would be needlessly complex since it wouldn't have direct access to the shell environment.

But in general, as soon as a shell script gets longer than about a page of code, you're at a good point to consider using an alternative tool.

Choosing a Programming Language

There are hundreds of programming languages that can help you solve technical problems. But, as just mentioned, not all of them are ideal alternatives to a shell script. Before proceeding with a programming language, ask yourself the following questions:

- Is the language designed for handling the kind of problem I want to solve? Does it support console-based input and output? Is it easy to write shell-style tools in this language?
- Is the language simple and popular? Can others understand or adapt the script without too much intervention?
- Is the programming language going to be available on almost any machine? Simple shell scripts run almost anywhere without the need for other tools. Will the language offer this functionality?

Based on the answers, some candidates jump to mind as alternatives for shell scripts:

Python   The Python language is installed by default on almost every Linux system, highly popular, and simple to use and read. It also works well for input-process-output programs.

Node.js   While Node.js is a runtime environment and not a language itself, it uses the popular JavaScript language and is event-driven, meaning it can be very fast. But the version installed across systems varies considerably, and this can cause headaches for script sharing.

Ruby   Also installed on many systems by default, Ruby is a simple language that is highly popular but perhaps less well known than Python.

Go   Go is a widely used language with simple syntax and built-in concurrency. Its self-contained binaries run uniformly across platforms, making it a robust alternative for command line tools once its toolchain is installed.

C   The C language is great for working with low-level system libraries, and most platforms have a C compiler installed. But it requires compilation, may behave quite differently on different systems, and is fairly complex for others to use.

Perl   Installed almost universally on any system, Perl is a very powerful language. It's not as popular as it used to be, however, so it's perhaps less likely to be understood by other users.

Now, when you're writing *complex* tools or programs, the criteria will change. You want to use a language and platform that really suit the problem you're solving or that are already being used by your team. For more complex programs that will be used in the shell and have a lot of functionality—options, parameters, and so on—languages like Rust, Java, and C# are often popular choices, in addition to the languages already mentioned.

But since in this chapter we're looking at alternatives for writing simple tools that work well in the shell, we're going to stick to one of the common choices: Python. Given its almost universal presence on systems, its huge (and increasing) popularity, and its robust standard library (which allows you to use many features without requiring users to download additional packages), Python is an excellent choice for writing shell-friendly tools.

Characteristics of Shell-Friendly Tools

When you're writing a tool for the shell, following the conventions set by *other* shell tools will make your tool more intuitive for others to use. It will also allow users to combine your tool with other tools (for example, with piping) to build more complex workflows.

The following capabilities make for a shell-friendly tool:

Reading from standard input   This allows you to pipe inputs from *other* tools into your programs (see Chapter 2 for more on pipelines). You also want to be able to read and process line by line in case the input is very large.

Writing to standard output   This sounds obvious, but it means making sure that your output can be read by a human operator and (ideally) be processed by other tools, such as cut, sed, and rev. It also means thinking about how color will or will not be used in output and avoiding superfluous output (such as titles and version numbers) that makes processing more difficult.

Specifying options using sensibly defined flags   There are many conventions for flags and parameters, and adhering to them (rather than inventing your own) will make your tool easier to use. For example, the -h flag is commonly used to show help. For a detailed description of how options should be specified for GNU tools, see *http://www.gnu.org/prep/standards/html_node/Option-Table.html#Option-Table*.

Running on different systems   Shell users are used to being able to use tools like grep and sed in a similar way across platforms. A well-written tool should provide the same kind of cross-platform portability.

Handling errors by using shell idioms   Shell-friendly tools use 0 as a status code to indicate success and define error codes in their documentation so that users know how to handle exceptional circumstances; your tool should do the same.

Many other conventions and practices may apply, but these are some of the fundamentals.

Writing a Dictionary Lookup Tool in Python

To practice writing a shell-friendly tool, you're going to create a simple program that reads a word and shows its definition, using the Free Dictionary API (*https://dictionaryapi.dev*).

This is a good example of a tool that would be overly complex to write with a shell script. You need to handle input, parse and process it, make HTTP requests to download pages from the internet, parse and process those requests, format the output, and provide some options for the user to control how the output looks. A highly experienced shell programmer could likely create this tool with a shell script without breaking a sweat, but it would be much harder for a less experienced scripter. In contrast, Python is easy to write and read, has a wealth of online learning resources, and is available on almost any platform.

The requirements for the tool are as follows:

1. Allow the user to provide a set of words from a text file or standard input.
2. Look up the definitions of those words.
3. Write the words and their definitions to standard output, giving the user the option to format how this output looks.
4. Offer help to the user on how to use the tool.

You'll stick to "raw" Python, using only the standard library so that users won't have to install any packages to make this tool work.

All of the files you'll see in this section are in the *~/effective-shell/programs/ lookup* folder. To install the sample files to your *~/effective-shell* folder, run this command:

```
$ curl effective.sh | sh
```

Before proceeding, you'll need to make sure you have Python installed. There are two commonly used versions of Python. Python 3 is the latest version at the time of writing and what you'll use for this script. Python 2 was *sunsetted* (support and improvements were discontinued) in January 2020. Many people still use it, and a lot of code is written in it, but where possible, you should update Python 2 code to Python 3.

Check that Python 3 is installed by running the following:

```
$ python3 --version
```

NOTE *In general I recommend making it clear that you're using Python 3 by running the python3 command, as in this example. On many systems, the python command points to python3 by default, but it is safer to be explicit.*

Otherwise, the command outputs the currently installed version of Python on your system. If you see a message like command not found: python3, then you need to install Python. Go to *https://www.python.org/downloads/* for instructions.

Defining the Tool's Basic Structure

As explained in Chapter 2, shell tools take input, process it, and produce output. You'll start with this input-process-output structure to create a first draft of the tool. This version won't perform any processing—it'll just take the input and produce simple output—but it will give you a working starting point to which you can incrementally add more features in later versions.

At this stage, I'll share the code in the form of snippets. View the files in the *~/effective-shell/programs/lookup/* folder o see the full code as it evolves. Open a text file, save it as *lookup-v1.py*, and enter the code in Listing 21-1.

lookup-v1.py

```
import sys

# Read standard input until nothing is left to read.
while True:
    # Read a line of input.
    word = sys.stdin.readline()

    # If the user presses Ctrl-D to end transmission, readline returns an
    # empty string and you can stop reading.
    if not word:
        break

    # If the input is an empty line or whitespace, skip it.
    if word.isspace():
        continue

    # Add the word to your list of lookups, and strip any whitespace from
    # the beginning and end of it. For now, you don't have a definition.
    word = word.strip()
    definition = ''

    # Write the result.
    print("{} - {}".format(word, definition))
```

Listing 21-1: Creating the structure for the dictionary tool

Now, to test the program, you'll run it, type some words, and then press CTRL-D to signal end of transmission (that you've finished entering input):

```
$ python3 ~/effective-shell/programs/lookup/lookup-v1.py
$ one
one -
$ two
two -
$ three
three -
```

The program successfully reads your input and writes out a result for each word. (Note that you can also press CTRL-C to close the program.)

You can also test that the program can receive input piped from a file:

```
$ cat ~/effective-shell/data/words.txt | python3 ~/effective-shell/programs/lookup/lookup-v1.py
louche -
liana -
lieder -
Manchu -
Nankeen -
naevi -
Ness -
```

You have a program that can read from standard input, either interactively or from a file! Now let's break down the code section by section.

First, you create a loop that will run continuously, reading lines from standard input:

```
while True:
    # Read a line of input.
    word = sys.stdin.readline()
```

If the input is completely empty, you've either reached the end of the file piped to stdin or the user has entered input directly and signaled the end of transmission with CTRL-D:

```
if not word:
    break
if word.isspace():
    continue
```

If the input is just whitespace, such as a newline or tab, you skip it.

Now you record the value of the word stripped of any surrounding whitespace and set the definition to an empty string, which you'll fill in later:

```
stripped_word = word.strip()
definition = ''
```

Then you write out the word, a hyphen surrounded by spaces, and the definition:

```
print(stripped_word, "-", definition)
```

In the next version of the script, you'll download the definition from the online dictionary.

Downloading the Definition

Now that you've got the list of words, you can download the definition of each one from the Free Dictionary API. This site searches a number of online dictionaries, including Wiktionary.

Add the new function shown in Listing 21-2 and then save your updated script as *lookup-v2.py*.

```
import json
import subprocess
import urllib.parse

def search_for_word(word):
    # Encode the word for HTML.
    encoded_word = urllib.parse.quote(word.encode("utf8"))

    # Construct the URL required to load the definition.
    url = "https://api.dictionaryapi.dev/api/v2/entries/en/{}".format(encoded_word)
```

```
command = ["curl", url]

# Run the "curl" command to retrieve the definition.
result = subprocess.run(command,
                        stdout=subprocess.PIPE,
                        stderr=subprocess.PIPE,
                        text=True)

# If there was an error, show it as the definition.
if result.returncode != 0:
    return "error: " + result.stderr

# Now try to parse the data.
data = json.loads(result.stdout)

# Grab the first value from "meanings". If it doesn't exist in the response,
# then the word was not found.
try:
    return data[0]["meanings"][0]["definitions"][0]["definition"]
except KeyError:
    return "definition not found!"
```

Listing 21-2: Adding the definition lookup functionality

This script uses a fairly rough-and-ready way to get the definition of a word from an online resource. In a nutshell, it does the following:

1. Builds the correct URL needed to use the Free Dictionary API to search for the word
2. Sends a request to the dictionary API, using the curl tool to look up the word
3. Decodes the response, returning either the definition or the text definition not found! if no definition was found

With this new function, you can update the main loop of your program to look like this:

```
# Strip whitespace from the word and find the definition.
stripped_word = word.strip()
definition = search_for_word(stripped_word)

# Write the result.
print(stripped_word, "-", definition)
```

Pass some test words into the program. Your output should look like this:

```
$ cat ~/effective-shell/data/words.txt | python3 ~/effective-shell/programs/lookup/lookup-v2.py
louche - To make (an alcoholic beverage, e.g. absinthe or ouzo) cloudy by mixing it with water,
due to the presence of anethole.
This is known as the ouzo effect.
liana - A climbing woody vine, usually tropical.
lieder - An art song, sung in German and accompanied on the piano.
Manchu - definition not found!
Nankeen - A type of cotton cloth originally from Nanking in China.
naevi - A pigmented, raised, or otherwise abnormal area on the skin...
Ness - A promontory; a cape or headland. (Frequently used as a suffix in placenames.)
```

Pretty cool—your program can find a reasonable definition for most of the words in the test dataset!

You can find this version in its entirety at *~/effective-shell/programs/lookup/lookup-v2.py*.

WHY CURL?

This program uses the `curl` command to download the definition of a word from the dictionary API. You might be wondering why it doesn't use the native Python capabilities, such as the `urllib` library, to make the request to download the word. Originally this sample *did* use `urllib`, but recently the Free Dictionary API was updated in a way that makes using `urllib` a lot more complex. Rather than complicating the sample tool or using third-party libraries, you're instead calling the `curl` command, which keeps the code simple.

For your own programs, I recommend looking at the `urllib`, `urllib2`, or `requests` modules as more "Pythonic" ways to make HTTP requests.

Your program is working quite well, but you can improve on it by making the output a little friendlier to read.

Formatting the Output

To make the output more readable, you can show the word in a different color than the definition, separate the definition with a colon (which will make it easier for you to process it with other tools), and even limit the definition's length so that it fits on the screen. For the last item, you'll give the user the option to provide a *crop* value—a maximum number of characters for each output line. You'll use a special module in Python called argparse to specify and parse the crop argument.

Add the code in Listing 21-3 to the beginning of your script and rename it *lookup-v3.py*.

lookup-v3.py

```
import argparse

parser = argparse.ArgumentParser()
parser.add_argument(
    '-c', '--crop',
    help='crop the output line length',
    type=int,
    nargs='?',
    const=80,          # Default value if -c is supplied
    default=None)      # Default value if -c is not supplied
args = parser.parse_args()
```

Listing 21-3: Defining the crop argument with argparse

This code defines an optional argument named crop that can be provided with or without a number. You'll see it in action shortly.

NOTE   *The argparse module is very sophisticated and can handle many different types of arguments and options. To learn more about it, see its documentation at https:// docs.python.org/3/library/argparse.html.*

Now add a function that writes the dictionary definition in a nicer way, as shown in Listing 21-4.

```
def write_definition(word, definition):
    # Check if stdout is a terminal, and if it is, color the output.
    is_terminal = sys.stdout.isatty()

    # Separate the word and the definition with a colon and a space.
    separator = ": "

    # If the "crop" argument is set, use it.
    if args.crop:
        output_length = len(word) + len(separator) + len(definition)
        if output_length > args.crop:
            # You need to chop some letters off the end of the definition,
            # but leave space for '...' to indicate the output is cropped.
            new_length = len(definition) - 3 - (output_length - args.crop)
            definition = definition[:new_length] + '...'

    # If in a terminal, make the word green and the separator white.
    if is_terminal:
        word = "\033[92m" + word + "\033[0m"
        separator = "\033[37m" + separator  + "\033[0m"

    # Write out the word, separator, and definition.
    print(word + separator + definition)
```

Listing 21-4: Formatting the code output with color and punctuation

The `write_definition()` code first checks to see whether stdout is a terminal. This is useful because if the user is in a terminal, you can show color codes, but if the output is something like a file, you can skip them (since they would look messy in the resulting file). Then, if the user specifies a value for the crop argument, you do some arithmetic to shorten the definition if needed.

The weird-looking character sequences such as /033[92m are ANSI control codes to set the output color; you can read all about them in Chapter 14.

Finally, you can update your main loop to call the `write_definition()` function, as shown in Listing 21-5.

```
# Strip whitespace from the word and find the definition.
stripped_word = word.strip()
definition = search_for_word(stripped_word)

# Write the result.
write_definition(stripped_word, definition)
```

Listing 21-5: Updating the main loop to call the `write_definition` function

Your program can now look up definitions, print the output in color, and crop the output as needed:

```
$ cat ./effective-shell/data/words.txt | python3 ./effective-shell/programs
/lookup/lookup-v3.py -c 60
louche: To make (an alcoholic beverage, e.g. absinthe or ...
liana: A climbing woody vine, usually tropical.
lieder: An art song, sung in German and accompanied on th...
Manchu: definition not found!
Nankeen: A type of cotton cloth originally from Nanking i...
naevi: A pigmented, raised or otherwise abnormal area on ...
Ness: A promontory; a cape or headland. (Frequently used ...
```

An added benefit of using the `argparse` module is that your program automatically gets a `--help` or `-h` option so the user can find instructions:

```
$ python3 ./samples/programs/lookup/lookup-v3.py -h
usage: lookup-v3.py [-h] [-c [CROP]]

optional arguments:
  -h, --help            show this help message and exit
  -c [CROP], --crop [CROP]
                        crop the output line length
```

We've really just scratched the surface of what you can do here. You can find this version of the program in full at *~/effective-shell/programs/lookup/lookup-v3.py.*

Installing the Lookup Tool

The great thing about a Python script like the one you just built is that it is stand-alone. Anyone can install it on their system with very little effort.

All you need to do is first tell the shell that it can execute the script using the python3 program. To do this, put a shebang at the top of the file like so:

```
#!/usr/bin/env python3

# ...the rest of the code goes here but has been omitted for brevity.
```

This shebang uses the env program to locate the python3 program. This is important, as python3 might be installed in different locations on different systems. You can read more about how to use env in shebangs in Chapter 9.

Now that you have a shebang, you can make the file executable using the chmod program and link to it from your local *bin* folder:

```
$ chmod +x ~/effective-shell/programs/lookup/lookup.py
$ sudo ln -s ~/effective-shell/programs/lookup/lookup.py /usr/local/bin/lookup
```

To review how to use the chmod and ln tools to install scripts, see Chapter 9.

You're putting the symlink to the tool in the folder */usr/local/bin* as this folder is conventionally used to store user-installed programs (rather than */usr/bin*, which is where programs installed by package managers will go).

NOTE *Administrator privileges are required to install programs to the */usr/local/bin *folder. Some users prefer to create a folder in their home directory, such as ~/*bin, *and then keep their personal programs there. The ~/*bin *folder is then added to the *PATH *variable in the shell configuration file. See "Creating a Local bin Directory for Custom Commands" on page 210 for more details.*

With the tool now installed, you can run it like so:

```
$ lookup -c -- effective shell
effective: A soldier fit for duty
shell: A hard external covering of an animal.
```

The final version of the script, *lookup.py*, includes some additional features, one of which is the -- ("end of options") marker, the Linux convention to indicate that the list of flags is complete and that what follows is the list of positional parameters. If you didn't include this marker, the tool would think that you're providing effective as the value of the -c flag. Many Linux tools support this separator; enter man bash to find out more.

Improving the Lookup Tool

One of the fun aspects of coding is thinking about all of the exciting features you can add! The final version of the script, which is in the *~/effective-shell/programs/lookup/lookup.py* file, includes the following features:

More robust error handling   Adds exception handlers in the key places where the program might fail

Graceful handling of CTRL-C   Ensures the program closes cleanly on CTRL-C without a noisy error message (see KeyboardInterrupt in the code for this)

More detailed help   Includes examples in the help text (see argparse in the code)

Ability to look up multiple words   Allows you to provide multiple words as parameters to the lookup command and get a definition for each one

Here are a few other features I considered including that you could add as a coding and learning exercise:

A browse flag   Opens the user's browser to the full definition online

Man pages   Installs a man page for the tool, meaning a user could run man lookup

Clearer interactive mode   Shows a prompt and instructions when stdin is a terminal, meaning the user is interactive

A --verbose flag   Shows detailed error messages

If you find yourself writing more complex command line tools in Python, check out Click (*https://click.palletsprojects.com/en/8.0.x/*), a popular package among Python developers that's used by several large and well-established projects. The Typer package (*https://typer.tiangolo.com*) is also worth exploring.

Summary

This chapter examined when and why you might consider alternatives to shell scripts. You learned what makes a tool shell-friendly and used the highly accessible and popular Python programming language to write a simple but useful dictionary tool.

In the next chapter, you'll learn how to use the shell to connect to and work on machines besides your local computer, such as those in the cloud or on a network. This gives you the convenience and flexibility of accessing files and features that aren't available to you locally, and allows you to manage and administer other machines.

22

THE SECURE SHELL

So far you've been using the shell to operate on your local machine. But you can also use the *Secure Shell (SSH) protocol* to open a secure network connection to a remote machine and use the shell to work on that machine.

In this chapter, you'll learn how to set up the credentials and keys required for secure remote connections, how to create a virtual machine in the cloud, and how to connect to that machine from your local computer using the ssh program. I'll also show you how to configure SSH to make it easier to work with.

What Is SSH?

SSH is a protocol that has been used for decades to establish a secure connection to a remote machine, either on your network or across the internet. The ssh program is the "secure shell" that helps you establish SSH connections, manage credentials, and open a shell on a remote machine.

To use SSH, you'll need a private key and a public key, known as a *key pair*, to manage authentication. A detailed description of key pairs, cryptography, and the mechanics of SSH is beyond the scope of this book, but if you're interested in learning more, I highly recommend *Applied Cryptography: Protocols, Algorithms, and Source Code in C* by Bruce Schneier (Wiley, 2015). All you need to know for the purposes of this chapter is how to create a key pair and use it to authenticate to a remote machine.

Creating a Key Pair

You'll use the OpenSSH authentication key utility ssh-keygen to create a key pair to communicate with a server on Amazon Web Services (AWS). AWS is a cloud services provider you'll use to create a free virtual machine to connect to. AWS requires that you use a particular format known as *Privacy Enhanced Mail (PEM)*. To specify the PEM format, move to the *~/.ssh* folder, which is where users often store their SSH keys:

```
$ cd ~/.ssh
```

Then run the command ssh-keygen with the -m ("key format") parameter to set PEM as the format like so:

```
$ ssh-keygen -m PEM
```

When you run this command, you'll be asked where you'd like to save the file. Keep the default location (the *~/.ssh* folder) but name the key pair *effective-shell*:

```
Generating public/private rsa key pair.
Enter file in which to save the key (/home/dwmkerr/.ssh/id_rsa): effective-shell
Enter passphrase (empty for no passphrase):
```

When prompted to provide an optional passphrase, simply press ENTER twice to skip it. Since you won't be using the server or the key for any particularly sensitive data in this chapter's exercises, you don't need a passphrase. In the future, however, be sure to add a passphrase if you're creating keys to encrypt sensitive data. You'll be required to enter that passphrase each time you load the key; this added security measure ensures that if someone were to steal your private key, they would need your passphrase to open it.

Once you've pressed ENTER twice, you'll see the final output:

```
Your identification has been saved in effective-shell
Your public key has been saved in effective-shell.pub
The key fingerprint is:
SHA256:HcqIl3ZhRz9jvhYO3g64FEYT3mAoDc6P4mnh4aKuYO8 dwmkerr@macbook
The key's randomart image is:
```

```
+---[RSA 3072]----+
|    .o .+ .       |
|    o. oo = .     |
|     o.  * + =    |
|      + * * + o   |
|     + o * S o    |
|     + = o + + o  |
|    . *E    o =   |
|    o+.    . . +  |
|    *o..     .  . |
+----[SHA256]-----+
```

NOTE *The* randomart *is designed to provide a more user-friendly way to identify a key. If you have many keys, the randomart supposedly makes it easier to pick the one you want. That said, I've yet to meet anyone who remembers their randomart, so you can safely ignore it for now!*

You should have two new files, your public key and your private key:

```
$ ls | grep effective
effective-shell
effective-shell.pub
```

The public key is the file with the *.pub* extension. You'll be sharing this key with a virtual machine in the cloud. Let's look at how to set that up.

Setting Up an AWS Account

You'll create the virtual machine with AWS, which is probably the most popular cloud services provider. If you already have an AWS account, you can skip to the next section. If not, keep reading.

Go to *https://aws.amazon.com/free/* and click **Create a Free Account**, as shown in Figure 22-1.

Figure 22-1: Signing up for a free AWS account

When you sign up, you'll be asked to provide several personal details, as well as credit card details. Make sure you select the Basic Support Plan, which is free.

Once you've signed up successfully, you should see the "Congratulations!" message shown in Figure 22-2. Click **Go to the AWS Management Console**.

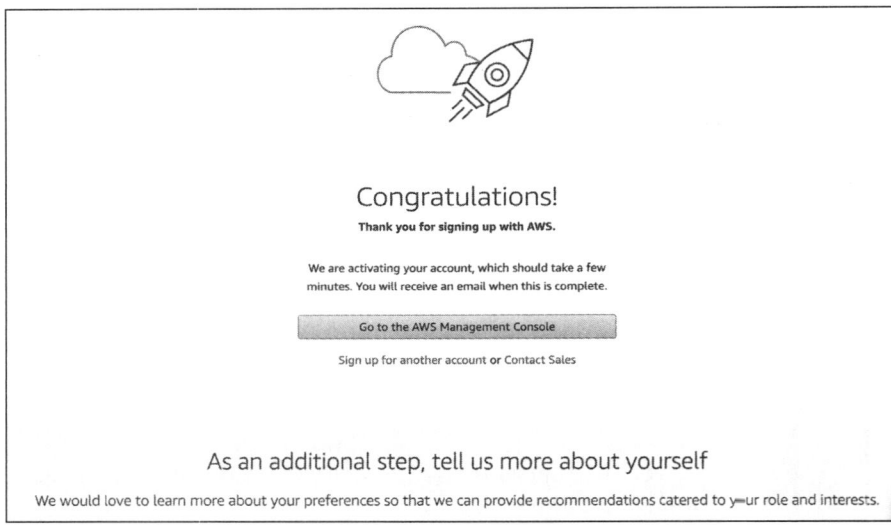

Figure 22-2: After activating your account, go to the Management Console

You'll be asked for your password again, and after providing it, you'll officially have an AWS account that you can use to run services in the cloud. Now you'll create a virtual machine to connect to.

Creating a Virtual Machine on AWS

Using the search bar in the AWS Management Console, search for "EC2." This is the name AWS uses for its virtual machine services. You should be taken to the EC2 dashboard, where you'll upload your public key so that you can use it when creating your virtual machine. Select **Key Pairs** as shown in Figure 22-3.

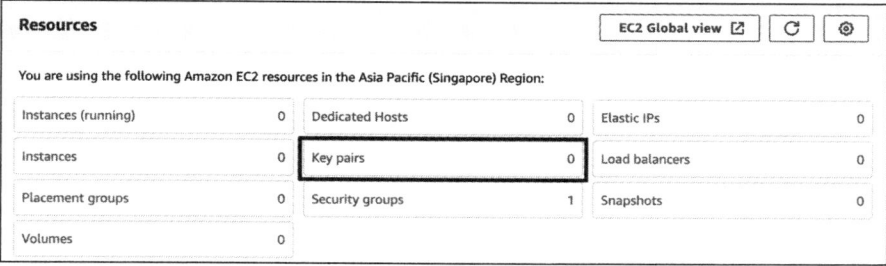

Figure 22-3: Preparing to upload your key pair from the EC2 dashboard

On the page that opens, choose **Actions ▶ Import Key Pair**, as shown in Figure 22-4.

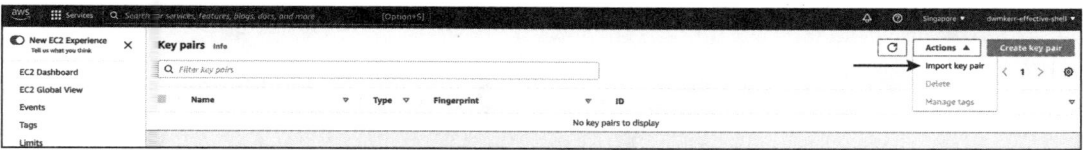

Figure 22-4: Importing the key pair

Give the key pair a sensible name like *effective-shell*, and upload your public key file, which will be in *~/.ssh/effective-shell.pub* if you've been following along so far. Alternatively, you can open that file on your local machine, copy its contents, and paste them as shown in Figure 22-5.

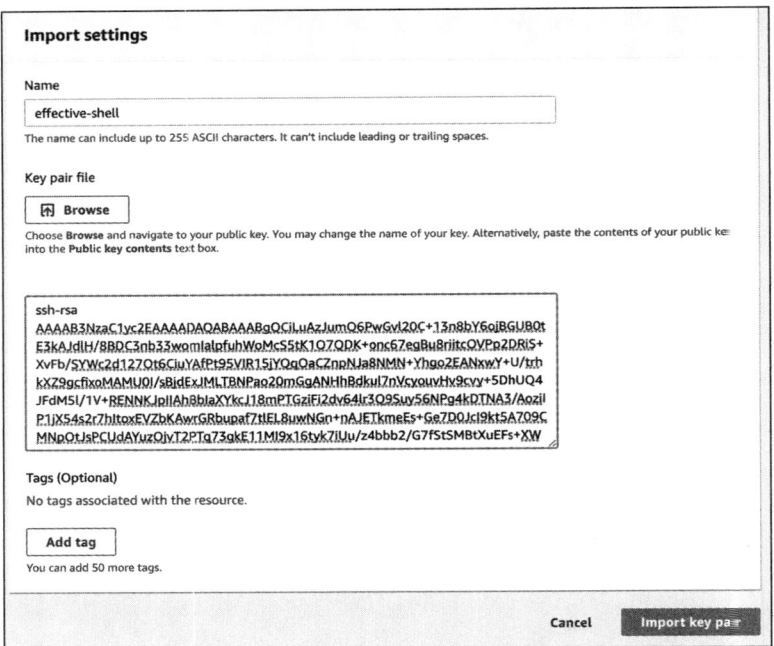

Import settings

Name

effective-shell

The name can include up to 255 ASCII characters. It can't include leading or trailing spaces.

Key pair file

[⊞ Browse]

Choose **Browse** and navigate to your public key. You may change the name of your key. Alternatively, paste the contents of your public key into the **Public key contents** text box.

ssh-rsa
AAAAB3NzaC1yc2EAAAADAQABAAABgQCiLuAzJumQ6PwGvl20C+13n8bY6ojBGUB0t
E3kAJdlH/8BDC3nb33womlalpfuhWoMcS5tK1Q7QDK+onc67egBu8riitcQVPp2DRiS+
XvFb/SYWc2d127Qt6CiuYAfPt95VIR15jYQqOaCZnpNJa8NMN+Yhgo2EANxwY+U/trh
kXZ9gcfixoMAMU0I/sBjdExJMLTBNPao20mGgANHhBdkul7nVcyouvHv9cvy+5DhUQ4
JFdM5l/1V+RENNKJplIAh8blaXYkcJ18mPTGziFi2dv64lr3Q9Suy56NPg4kDTNA3/Aozil
P1jX54s2r7hltoxEVZbKAwrGRbupaf7tIEL8uwNGn+nAJETkmeEs+Ge7D0JcI9kt5A709C
MNpOtJsPCUdAYuzOjvT2PTq73gkE11MI9x16tyk7lUu/z4bbb2/G7fStSMBtXuEFs+XW

Tags (Optional)

No tags associated with the resource.

[Add tag]

You can add 50 more tags.

[Cancel] [Import key pair]

Figure 22-5: Pasting your public key

Click **Import Key Pair**, and you'll be returned to the EC2 dashboard. From there, choose **Launch Instance**, as shown in Figure 22-6. An *instance* refers to a virtual server in the cloud.

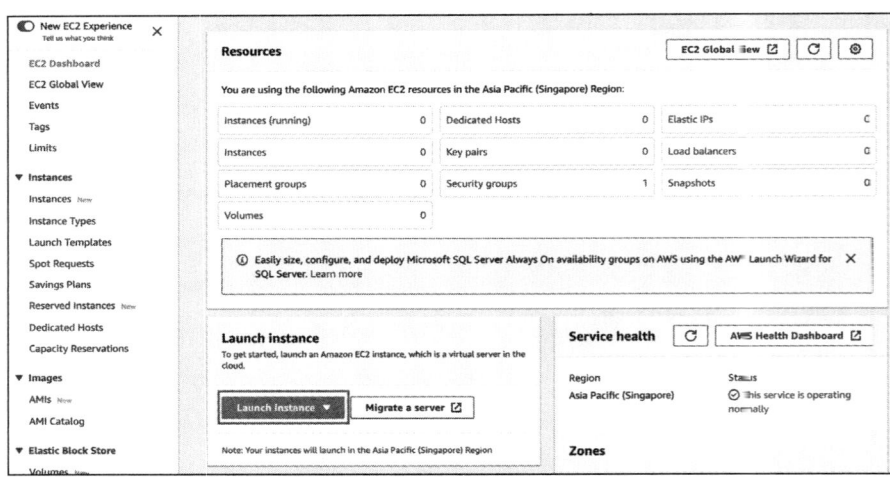

Figure 22-6: Launching a virtual server in the cloud

Next, you'll need to specify some details for the virtual machine that AWS is creating for you.

Choose an Amazon Machine Image

First, choose the appropriate Amazon Machine Image (AMI) for your version of Linux. Be sure to select one that is labeled as "Free Tier Eligible."

Choose an Instance Type

Make sure the default instance type, t2.micro, is selected. This is free-tier eligible and more than powerful enough for your needs.

Click **Review and Launch** since you won't need to configure any of the advanced options.

Review the Instance Launch

You'll see the warning "your security group is open to the world" on the Review Instance Launch page, informing you that anyone who knows the address of your instance can try to connect to it. Since you're not putting anything sensitive on your instance, you can safely ignore this warning.

Click the **Launch** button on the bottom right, and another screen should pop up. Don't dismiss this screen—this is where you'll choose your key pair! Make sure the key pair you just imported is selected, as shown in Figure 22-7.

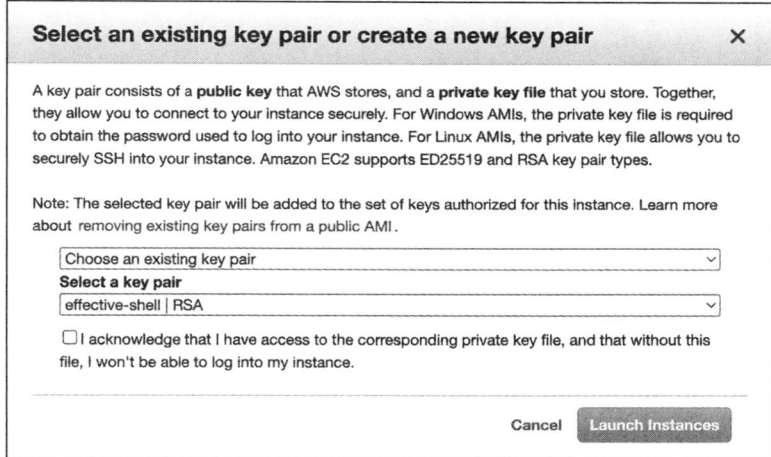

Figure 22-7: Selecting your key pair before launching your virtual machine

You'll be required to select the checkbox labeled "I acknowledge that I have access to the private key." AWS is warning you that if you don't have the private key associated with the public key you've uploaded, you can't connect to the instance.

Select the box and then click **Launch Instances**.

Launching the instance will take a few seconds. Click the **View Instances** button when it's done.

Select the checkbox next to this new instance, as shown in Figure 22-8.

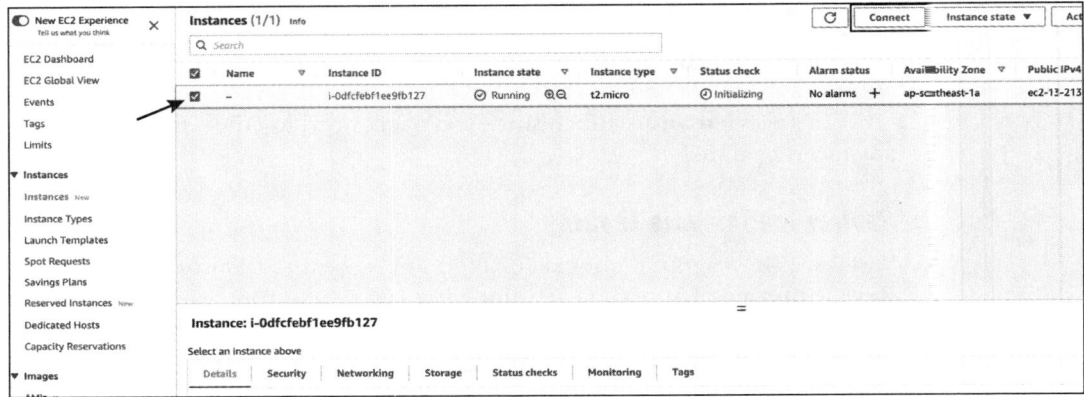

Figure 22-8: Selecting the virtual machine to connect to

Once you've selected the instance, click the **Connect** button. In the screen that pops up, choose **SSH Client** (see Figure 22-9).

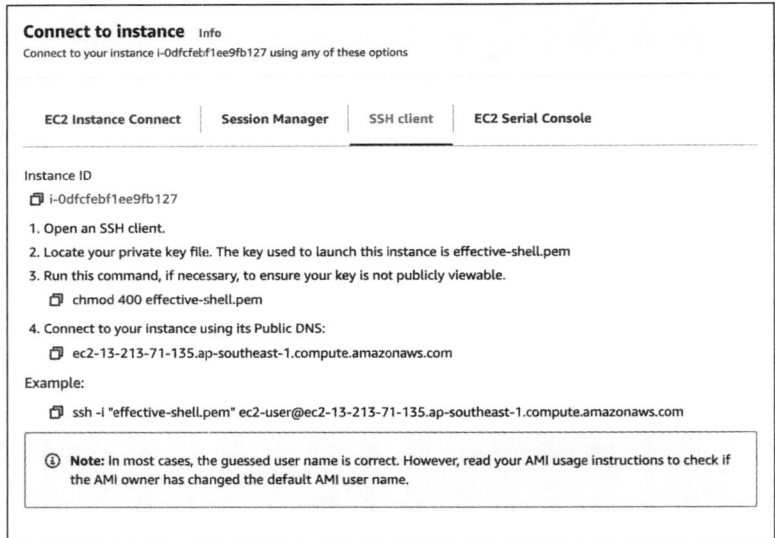

Figure 22-9: Instructions for connecting to the virtual machine

Keep this browser window open, as it contains the details you need for the next steps.

> **SHUT DOWN YOUR VIRTUAL MACHINE**
> **WHEN YOU'RE DONE!**
>
> When you've finished experimenting with your virtual machine, power it
> down by selecting it in the AWS Console and choosing **Instance State ▸ Stop
> Instance**. When you're completely finished with the instance, choose **Instance
> State ▸ Terminate**. You shouldn't be billed for this instance, as it's in the free tier,
> but better safe than sorry!

Using SSH to Connect to a Virtual Machine

In the SSH Client tab of the Connect to Instance page shown in Figure 22-9,
you should see the address of the machine you've created. AWS gives you
some hints here about how to connect, even showing the specific command
you'll run with ssh.

Using the details for my new virtual machine, I would run this
command:

```
ssh -i ~/.ssh/effective-shell ec2-user@ec2-13-213-71-135.ap-southeast-1.compute.amazonaws.com
```

This includes three pieces of information:

- The credentials for the user I'm connecting with, indicated by the -i
  ("identity file") flag, which provides my private key file
- The username for that user, which is the ec2-user part of the command
  before the @
- The hostname, or address of the machine, which follows the @

Now run the ssh program from your own shell to open a connection to
your virtual machine.

When I run this command, I get the following warning:

```
The authenticity of host 'ec2-13-213-71-135.ap-southeast-1.compute.amazonaws.com
(13.213.71.135)' can't be established.
ED25519 key fingerprint is SHA256:8wq6Xu4xEk/BO3diae+BWUFTTKunzvCz4XidFYpl6F8.
This key is not known by any other names
Are you sure you want to continue connecting (yes/no/[fingerprint])?
```

My SSH client tells me that I haven't connected to this machine before
and asks me to confirm that I want to proceed. Once I confirm, my SSH client will record the machine's IP address and hostname so that when I connect in the future, it will recognize the machine. If the IP address changes,
my SSH client will warn me—a useful security feature to protect against
someone swapping the machine you're connecting to for another one!

Type **yes** and press ENTER to continue connecting, and you should see bash running in your AWS Linux virtual machine:

```
Warning: Permanently added 'ec2-13-213-71-135.ap-southeast-1.compute.amazonaws.com' (ED25519)
to the list of known hosts.

    _|  _|_  )
    _|  (     /   Amazon Linux 2 AMI
   ___|\___|___|

https://aws.amazon.com/amazon-linux-2/
[ec2-user@ip-172-31-23-196 ~]$
```

If you see this welcome message from AWS, you're successfully running a shell on your virtual machine via the ssh program from your local machine!

You can see the shell being used currently by checking the SHELL variable:

```
[ec2-user@ip-172-31-23-196 ~]$ echo $SHELL
/bin/bash
```

Now you're ready to run any commands that you like on this machine. At this point, you might install programs, manipulate files, and more. When you're ready to disconnect, run the exit command to close the connection to the virtual machine.

Now let's look at some things you can do with SSH to make accessing these machines even easier.

Dealing with Key Permission Errors

When you try to use a private key to connect to a virtual machine, you might see an error message like this:

```
@@@@@@@@@@@@@@@@@@@@@@@@@@@@@@@@@@@@@@@@@@@@@@@@@@@@@@@@@@@@@@@
@        WARNING: UNPROTECTED PRIVATE KEY FILE!           @
@@@@@@@@@@@@@@@@@@@@@@@@@@@@@@@@@@@@@@@@@@@@@@@@@@@@@@@@@@@@@@@
Permissions 0644 for 'my-key.pem' are too open.
It is recommended that your private key files are NOT accessible by others.
This private key will be ignored.
bad permissions: ignore key: my-key.pem
Permission denied (publickey).
```

In this case, the server is warning you that other users could open your private key. You can verify this vulnerability by checking the file permissions like so:

```
$ ls -al
-rw-r--r--    1 dwmkerr    1103 Apr 19 12:02 my-key.pem
```

The permissions are `-rw-r--r--`, which translates to the following:

-rw Read and write for the owner, which is the dwmkerr user

-r- Read to the group the owner belongs to, which is the dwmkerr group

-r-- Read to all users

This is not ideal: other users on the system would be allowed to open the file, and members of the same group would be allowed to read the file as well. There's a quick fix for this, fortunately. Set the permissions to read and write for the owner only:

```
$ chmod 400 my-key.pem
$ ls -al
-rw-------    1 dwmkerr  dwmkerr    1103 Apr 19 12:02 my-key.pem
```

This `chmod` ("change file permissions") command sets the permissions to 400, which means read and write for the current user. Once you make this change, you'll be able to use `ssh` to connect to the server without it complaining about the permissions on your key.

Configuring SSH Hosts

It can be difficult to remember details about your virtual machines, such as the hostname, key location, and username. To make it easier and quicker to connect, you can create an entry in your *SSH config file* to store this information. This file is a dot file, a user-specific configuration file just like the ones discussed in Chapter 17, and is typically located at *~/.ssh/config*.

To create an entry for my virtual machine, I would add the following text to my *~/.ssh/config* file:

```
Host effective-shell-aws-linux
  HostName ec2-13-213-71-135.ap-southeast-1.compute.amazonaws.com
  User ec2-user
  IdentityFile "~/.ssh/effective-shell.pem"
```

The first part of this configuration is the host *alias*—that is, how you'll refer to the host when you want to connect to it. Use a short but descriptive name for maximum convenience (effective-shell-aws-linux, in my case). After the alias is a group of settings, each indented by a tab or two spaces (the indentation is not required but can help make the file more readable):

HostName The full address of the host

User The name of the user to connect as

IdentityFile The path to the private key file used to connect

Now if I want to connect to the virtual machine, I can simply run the following command:

```
ssh effective-shell-aws-linux
```

In fact, the ssh program supports shell completion, so I can just type ssh and a few letters of the hostname, followed by the TAB key, and the shell will suggest the hosts from my config:

```
ssh e<tab> # When I press Tab, the shell expands this to:
ssh effective-shell-aws-linux
```

Many other options are available for the SSH config file; you can run man ssh_config to see them all. You'll also see some other options in Chapter 24.

Running SSH Commands

You don't need to actually run a shell on a remote machine over SSH to execute commands. You can simply provide the commands that you want to run to the ssh program, and it will execute them on the server.

Here's an example:

```
$ ssh effective-shell-aws-linux 'curl effective.sh | ES_EXISTING_FOLDER_ACTION=o sh'
...
effective-shell: installed samples version 0.25.1 to '/home/ec2-user/effective-shell'
effective-shell: read 'effective shell' online at: effective-shell.com
```

You're downloading and running the *effective-shell* samples installer on the server. Now, normally when you install the samples, the installer will ask you whether to overwrite, delete, or keep the existing samples. This means that it will be requesting input from the terminal. But because the ssh program isn't actually attaching stdin to the remote machine, you use the ES_EXISTING_FOLDER_ACTION=o option instead to tell the installer to overwrite the samples.

If you want to be able to interact with the server by using your terminal to provide input, you can use the -t ("request TTY") parameter as follows:

```
$ ssh -t effective-shell-aws-linux 'curl effective.sh | sh'
...
effective-shell: downloaded samples, version 0.25.1
effective-shell: preparing to install the 'effective-shell.com' samples...
effective-shell: the '/home/ec2-user/effective-shell' folder already exists, would you like to:
effective-shell: [d]elete - remove the existing folder
effective-shell: [o]verwrite - extract over the existing folder
effective-shell: [q]uit
Your choice (d/o/q): d
```

In this example, my terminal is attached to the remote server via SSH, so I can use the keyboard to provide input to the installer script.

Handling Disconnections

If you are regularly using ssh to connect to remote machines, you'll soon encounter the pain of *disconnections*, or losing network connectivity. You might not even notice that you've been disconnected; more commonly, the ssh session simply freezes and stops responding to any input at all. Annoyingly, often the shell is so unresponsive that you can't even unfreeze it with CTRL-D or CTRL-C. In these cases, you can use the escape sequence ENTER ~ . to end the broken session.

In Chapter 24 we'll look at some ways to improve upon this technique, but for now, if you forget the "enter tilde dot" escape sequence, it's easiest to just close your terminal program.

When you disconnect from your SSH session, the commands you're running will also be terminated because your shell sends the "hang up" signal. Again, this can be frustrating if you want to keep a program running on the server. You'll learn how to work around this behavior as well in Chapter 24.

Transferring Files with scp

You can use the scp ("OpenSSH secure file copy") program as follows to copy files to and from any remote machine you have access to:

```
scp parameters source destination
```

Many of the parameters you might provide to scp are the same as those for the ssh command, such as -i for the identity file. The source and destination are normally a pair of designations: one local, one remote. However, you can also copy between two remote machines.

Here's an example of how an scp command might look:

```
scp -i ~/.ssh/my-project.pem ~/project/output.zip dwmkerr@myserver.com:~
```

- The -i flag specifies the path to a key.
- The source is a file called *output.zip* on the local machine.
- The destination is a server with the hostname myserver.com, connecting with a user named dwmkerr, and putting the file in the user's home folder.

The following scp example copies the *downloads/backup.zip* folder to the local *~/backups* folder:

```
scp -P 8022 effective-shell.com:~/downloads/backup.zip ~/backups
```

- No username or credentials are specified, so the current user's name is used (unless there's a matching entry in the ~/.ssh/config file), and any keys that are loaded in the SSH agent will be used to try to authenticate. The *SSH agent* is the key manager for SSH; it keeps keys and certificates in memory so that they can be reused without the key exchange having to be run for each message. The ssh program uses the SSH agent to get the keys required to exchange messages.
- The -P ("port number") flag specifies port 8022, rather than the default port, 22.

To see scp in action, you'll copy the dictionary lookup tool you created in Chapter 21 to your server. Then you'll run it, save some definitions, and copy them back to your local machine.

NOTE *If you haven't read Chapter 21, you can find the* lookup.py *file in* ~/effective-shell/ programs/lookup. *You'll need to install the book's sample files first by running the following command:*

```
$ curl effective.sh | sh
```

First, use scp to copy the lookup program to your remote machine:

```
$ cd ~/effective-shell/samples
$ scp ./programs/lookup/lookup.py effective-shell-aws-linux:~
lookup.py                    100% 4485      10.5KB/s    00:00
```

You've provided the path to the local file, the server you want to copy it to, and the file's location (which is the home directory).

Note that because you've created the alias *effective-shell-aws-linux* in your SSH config, you can use this alias for scp as well as ssh. Connect to the server now and run the script:

```
$ ssh effective-shell-aws-linux
Last login: Tue Apr  8 19:03:00 2022 from bb116-15-249-218.singnet.com.sg
```

```
            Amazon Linux 2 AMI

https://aws.amazon.com/amazon-linux-2/
[ec2-user@ip-172-31-23-196 ~]$ ./lookup.py cryptography
cryptography: The discipline concerned with communication security (e.g.,
confidentiality of messages, integrity of messages, sender authentication,
non-repudiation of messages, and many other related issues), regardless
of the used medium such as pencil and paper or computers.
```

Your lookup program has been copied to your server, and you've successfully run it to find a definition for the word *cryptography*.

Save this definition and close your connection to the server, then copy the definition back to your local machine:

```
[ec2-user@ip-172-31-23-196 ~]$ chmod +x ./lookup.py
[ec2-user@ip-172-31-23-196 ~]$ ./lookup.py cryptography > definition.txt
[ec2-user@ip-172-31-23-196 ~]$ exit
logout
Connection to ec2-13-213-71-135.ap-southeast-1.compute.amazonaws.com closed.

$ scp effective-shell-aws-linux:~/defintion.txt .
definition.txt                  100%  277      1.0KB/s   00:00

$ cat definition.txt
cryptography: The discipline concerned with communication security (e.g.,
confidentiality of messages, integrity of messages, sender authentication,
non-repudiation of messages, and many other related issues), regardless
of the used medium such as pencil and paper or computers.
```

Before running the script on the server, you use the chmod command to ensure the script can be executed. That's all there is to it! Copying files and folders to and from remote machines is remarkably easy to do with scp once you know the basics of how ssh works.

You can perform many other operations with scp; to learn more about the tool, run man scp.

Summary

In this chapter, we discussed the SSH protocol and how keys are used to protect connections to remote servers. You learned how to set up an AWS account, create a virtual machine with a given public key, connect to it with the ssh program, and configure SSH with an alias to make future connections faster. You also saw some of the challenges of network connectivity (Chapter 24 will show you some techniques to handle these) and learned how to copy files to and from remote machines.

Now that you can connect to remote servers, you need to know how to work within them. The next chapter will cover terminal editors, which allow you to rapidly work with text without leaving the shell, making them the perfect solution for remote machines or systems without a desktop environment.

23

THE POWER OF TERMINAL EDITORS

A *terminal editor* is a text editor that runs in the shell, optimized for a keyboard rather than a mouse. It is sometimes the only option for working on remote machines or systems without a desktop environment. But even when you have a desktop-based editor available, running a terminal editor from the shell can be more efficient for many text manipulation tasks.

Some of the most popular terminal editors are Vim, Emacs, and GNU nano. This chapter will focus on Vim, showing you a few features that will hopefully pique your interest in diving deeper into its capabilities.

Many users find terminal editors initially hard to use, and some editors—including Vim—have a reputation for being highly complex. So let's start by discussing why you'd want to use one at all.

Why Use a Terminal Editor?

Many technologists are familiar with desktop environment text editors, such as Visual Studio Code, Notepad++, and Sublime. Software engineers will likely be familiar with *integrated development environments (IDEs)* like Visual Studio and the JetBrains family of IDEs, which include dedicated environments for many languages, such as C# or Java.

With such a selection of powerful and user-friendly text-editing options available, why would you choose to use a terminal editor?

There are many reasons, but perhaps the most compelling is that you won't always have a desktop environment available. If you're working on a remote server with ssh as described in Chapter 22, there may not be a desktop environment running that can open a graphical tool. The easiest option available for you to edit text, code, or scripts in such an environment could be a terminal editor because the terminal is your main interface to the server. You also might not have easy access to a desktop environment if you're editing a file in a lightweight Linux environment such as a Docker container.

Here are some other good reasons to become familiar with terminal editors:

Minimal flow disruptions   If you're working in a shell already and need to edit text, being able to quickly do so without leaving the shell—and ideally without even having to touch the mouse—allows you to maintain your flow while you work.

Editing efficiency   Once you get over the initial learning curve, you can be *incredibly* efficient at editing text using editors such as Vim and Emacs. Vim in particular is designed to keep your fingers on the home row of the keyboard as much as possible so you can manipulate text very quickly.

Customization options   You can customize terminal editors to suit your working style and then manage those customizations through dot files that you share across environments, as described in Chapter 17.

Extendability to graphical editors and other tools   If you learn how to use Vim or Emacs and become adept at their idioms, you can install plug-ins in your graphical editors or IDEs that enable you to edit text with the same commands. There are even browser plug-ins that let you navigate web pages with Vim-style movement commands. This lets you bring your efficiency with keyboard interfaces to modern desktop editors.

All in all, it's extremely useful to get to grips with at least the basics of terminal editors. You'll be more efficient when working with remote machines and editing text from the shell, and you might even find that an editor like Vim replaces your other tools for many tasks.

Getting Started with Vim

Vim is an extremely popular editor that comes installed on most Linux distributions out of the box. But its style of editing, called *modal editing*, can be a bit confusing at first. In fact, I've chosen Vim because of its reputation as the most complex terminal text editor. However, you'll soon find that, with an hour or two of practice, it's quite straightforward to use Vim for simple tasks. Just a little knowledge can make you more effective, and the more time you invest in learning, the more efficient you'll become.

KEYBOARD SHORTCUTS AND CASE SENSITIVITY IN VIM

Vim relies heavily on case-sensitive keyboard shortcuts. To avoid confusion, this book uses the following shortcuts:

- **<C-u>**: Press the CTRL key at the same time as the lowercase u
- **<C-U>**: Press the CTRL key at the same time as an uppercase U (CTRL-SHIFT-c)

Vim commands are also case sensitive. For example, the sequence 2w has a different meaning than the sequence 2W. Be sure to use the correct case when following the examples in this chapter.

To open Vim, run the vi command:

```
$ vi

~
~
~
~
~
~                        VIM - Vi IMproved
~
~                         version 8.2.4314
~                       by Bram Moolenaar et al.
~                  Modified by <bugzilla@redhat.com>
~               Vim is open source and freely distributable
~
~                      Help poor children in Uganda!
~              type  :help iccf<Enter>        for information
~
~              type  :q<Enter>                to exit
~              type  :help<Enter>  or  <F1>   for on-line help
~              type  :help version8<Enter>    for version info
~
```

```
~
~
~
~
```

When Vim starts, it either displays the file that it has been asked to open or, if no file has been provided (as in this example), shows a welcome message. The working area that you will edit text in is called a *buffer*. Later, you will see how to commit your changes back to disk by saving this buffer to a file.

As a modal text editor, Vim runs in various modes, and the keyboard has different functions in each one. Vim starts in *normal mode* (sometimes called *command mode*). This means that you'll use the keyboard to enter commands, not text. To use the keyboard to input text as you would in a normal text editor, you need to use the i ("insert") command to enter *insert mode*:

```
i

```

The position of the cursor in the code block is indicated in gray. In the Vim samples, the exact keystrokes that you type are shown in bold on the first line, and the results that you'll see in Vim are shown on the following line(s). In insert mode, each character you type will be inserted at the cursor.

Now try entering some text:

```
Hello Vim!
```

When you enter insert mode, the status bar at the bottom of the screen shows you what mode Vim is in:

```
Hello Vim!
~
~
~
-- INSERT --                            1,11          All
```

Note that when Vim is in command mode, the status isn't shown; since it's the default, you can assume Vim is in that mode unless it tells you otherwise.

To return to command mode, you can press <C-c> or ESC. Remember that <C-c> means that you press the CTRL key and enter a lowercase c at the same time. In Vim, keys you press together like this are called *chords* and keys you press one after the other are called *sequences*.

Exit insert mode with the <C-c> chord. Notice that the -- INSERT -- text in the status bar is no longer shown, indicating that you're back in command mode.

In command mode, the keystrokes you enter are used to manipulate text or move around. To perform an administrative task, such as saving a file or calling another program, you need to change to *ex mode* (*ex* is short for "execute") with the *ex command*, which is a colon (:), like so:

```
:
:
```

Ex mode is a bit like insert mode but for writing commands. Let's use the q! ("quit without saving") command to close Vim. Enter the command now:

```
q!
:q!
```

Any keystrokes you enter in ex mode will display on the status line, showing the text for the command you're building. At this point, your terminal should look like this:

```
Hello Vim!
~
~
~
:q!
```

The status line is showing you that q! is your current command. Press ENTER to execute the command, and Vim will close.

You've now seen the basics of modal editing with Vim's command, insert, and ex modes. You've also learned how to close Vim, which is famously a task that Vim novices struggle with! Now you'll start building your own Vim cheatsheet to explore more of what it can do.

Building a Cheatsheet

Building a Vim cheatsheet is a great way to showcase what Vim can do while documenting your learning as you go along. You'll extend your personal cheatsheet over time with the commands that you find most useful.

Start by creating a folder to store the cheatsheet and initializing an empty Git repository to track changes to it:

```
$ mkdir ~/vim-cheatsheet
$ cd ~/vim-cheatsheet
$ git init -b main
Initialized empty Git repository in /home/dwmkerr/vim-cheatsheet/.git/
```

Here you've created a *vim-cheatsheet* folder, moved into it, and initialized an empty Git repository with a primary branch named main.

For more information on how Git works, see Chapter 18.

Creating a File

Now open Vim and tell it that you want to work on a file named *cheatsheet.md*:

```
$ vi cheatsheet.md


~

~
"cheatsheet.md" [New]                                        0,0-1          All
```

The text you're editing in Vim is called a *buffer*, which you can think of as a view on a file. When you open a file, you're loading the content into a buffer, which is what Vim shows. When you want to create a new file, you enter text in a new buffer and then save it when you're ready.

Vim shows you in the status line that you have a buffer named *cheatsheet .md* and that it is new—that is, you haven't yet saved it.

The file extension *md* is short for Markdown, a plaintext format that is great for documentation. You write text normally, but you can also use special characters to format that text, such as the hash mark (#) for headings and the hyphen (-) for bullets. Markdown is rendered in a very reader-friendly way when viewed in environments like GitHub.

Enter insert mode:

```
i

```

Create a title for your cheatsheet:

```
# Vim cheatsheet
# Vim cheatsheet
```

Then exit insert mode and enter command mode:

```
<C-c>
# Vim cheatsheet
```

Remember, you can also press ESC to return to command mode—just use whichever option feels most comfortable to you.

Now you'll use the w ("write") ex mode command to save the file. Enter :w and press ENTER. The Vim status line should confirm that it has written the buffer to disk:

```
# Vim cheatsheet
~
~
~
"cheatsheet.md" [New] 1L, 17B written                        1,16           All
```

Exit Vim by entering :q and then pressing ENTER. Now add this new cheatsheet file to your repository:

```
$ git add cheatsheet.md
```

Next, you'll tell your shell to use Vim as your text editor, since you'll be using Vim to work with Git for the rest of this chapter:

```
$ export EDITOR=vi
$ git commit



# Please enter the commit message for your changes. Lines starting
# with "#" will be ignored, and an empty message aborts the commit.
#
# Committer: dwmkerr
#
# On branch main
#
# Initial commit
#
# Changes to be committed:
#       new file:   cheatsheet.md
#
~
~
~
"~/vim-cheatsheet/.git/COMMIT_EDITMSG" 13L, 325B          1,0-1          All
```

When you're more familiar with Vim, using it to work with Git repositories and commands without leaving the shell will start to feel more natural and efficient.

Git has opened Vim to ask you to provide a commit message. Git has also provided some helpful information on the changes you're committing, such as that you have a new file called *cheatsheet.md* in the commit.

Now use Vim to enter a commit message. Start by entering insert mode:

```
i

```

Enter your commit message:

```
add the cheatsheet
add the cheatsheet
```

Then exit insert mode and enter command mode:

```
<C-c>
add the cheatsheet
```

Now type :wq to write and quit, and Git will use the message you've provided for the commit:

```
1 file changed, 1 insertion(+)
create mode 100644 cheatsheet.md
```

Congratulations! You've used Vim to create the initial cheatsheet file as well as to quickly set the Git commit message—all without leaving your shell!

Navigating Through Text

Vim commands that move the cursor are called *motions*, and understanding how they work is key to navigating Vim buffers efficiently. Table 23-1 lists what I think are the most essential motions. Remember that these motions are used in normal (command) mode, not insert or ex mode.

Table 23-1: Essential Vim Motions

Motion	Usage
gg	Go to the beginning of the buffer.
G	Go to the end of the buffer.
0	Go to the beginning of the line (note that this is a zero, not a capital letter O).
$	Go to the end of the line.
w	Go forward one word.
b	Go backward one word.
h	Go left.
j	Go down.
k	Go up.
l	Go right.
)	Go forward one sentence.
(	Go backward one sentence.

Let's see a few of these motions in action. Open your cheatsheet in Vim:

```
$ vi cheatsheet.md
```

To give yourself some text to play with, update the file so that it looks as follows:

```
# Vim cheatsheet

## Vim motions

Vim motions are commands used to move the cursor.
```

Make sure to use the <C-c> chord to exit insert mode and enter command mode before entering the following keystrokes.

Go to the beginning of the buffer:

```
gg
# Vim cheatsheet

## Vim motions
```

Go right:

```
l
# Vim cheatsheet

## Vim motions
```

Go left:

```
h
# Vim cheatsheet

## Vim motions
```

Go down:

```
j
# Vim cheatsheet

## Vim motions
```

Go up:

```
k
# Vim cheatsheet

## Vim motions
```

The hjkl motions—move left, down, up, and right, respectively—are all next to each other on the home row of the keyboard for the right hand. Although it takes a little getting used to, once you use the hjkl keys instead of the arrow keys to move around, you'll wonder how you lived without them. Being able to navigate without moving your right hand from the home row is a huge time-saver.

Try out some other motions, starting by going to the end of a line:

```
$
# Vim cheatsheet
```

Now go to the beginning of the line:

```
0
# Vim cheatsheet
```

Move forward by one word:

```
w
# Vim cheatsheet
```

Go backward by one word:

```
b
# Vim cheatsheet
```

In Vim, a *word* is a sequence of characters separated by whitespace or punctuation. For example, # Vim cheatsheet consists of three words: #, Vim, and cheatsheet.

Adding a Command Count

For many Vim commands, you can provide a count indicating how many times the command should be run. This makes motions far more flexible; instead of typing jjjjj to move down five lines, for example, you can just type 5j.

See how the cursor moves when you add counts to motion commands. Go to the beginning of a buffer like so:

```
gg
# Vim cheatsheet

## Vim motions
```

Go down three lines:

```
3j
# Vim cheatsheet

## Vim motions
```

Move forward three words:

```
3w
# Vim cheatsheet

## Vim motions
```

Now that you know how to move the cursor with motions, you can move to wherever you want to insert text. But, as you might have guessed, Vim has a way to streamline that task as well.

Inserting Text at Specific Positions

As you learned earlier, you can use the i command to enter insert mode to type text. However, Vim has a set of commands, listed in Table 23-2, that enter insert mode in specific positions—saving you from moving around unnecessarily.

Table 23-2: Essential "Enter Insert Mode" Commands

Command	Usage
i	Insert at cursor.
I	Insert before the first non-whitespace character in the current line.
a	Append text after the cursor.
A	Append text at the end of the current line.
o	Open a new line below the position.
O	Open a new line above the current line.

These commands allow you to quickly enter insert mode just where you like. To try them out, start by going to the beginning of the buffer:

```
gg
# Vim cheatsheet
```

Open a new line below the current line:

```
o
# Vim cheatsheet

```

Enter text, then enter command mode:

```
Hello<C-c>
# Vim cheatsheet
Hello
```

Enter insert mode before the first non-whitespace character in the line:

```
I
# Vim cheatsheet
Hello
```

Enter text, then enter command mode:

```
Welcome and <C-c>
# Vim cheatsheet
Welcome and Hello
```

Append text to the end of a line:

```
A
# Vim cheatsheet
Welcome and Hello
```

Enter text, then enter command mode:

```
Vim!<C-c>
# Vim cheatsheet
Welcome and Hello Vim!
```

Open a new line above the current line, then enter command mode:

```
O<C-c>
# Vim cheatsheet

Welcome and Hello Vim!
```

Using the `<C-c>` chord to quickly go back into command mode after inserting text should start to become habit as you use Vim. It's faster to enter small amounts of text and then go back to command mode to reposition the cursor than it is to enter lots of text and use the arrow keys to move around in insert mode.

Operating on a Range of Text

A Vim *operator* is any command that can be applied to a range of text. You can combine operators with counts and motions to rapidly manipulate a specific part of the buffer. Table 23-3 lists some particularly useful operators.

Table 23-3: Essential Vim Operators

Operator	Usage
c	Change the range—that is, delete the characters and move into insert mode at the beginning of the range.
d	Delete the range.
y	Yank the range—that is, copy it to a register (Vim's version of a clipboard) ready to paste later.
g~	Invert the range case (change uppercase characters to lowercase characters and vice versa).
gU	Make the range uppercase ("go upper").
gu	Make the range lowercase ("go lower").
!	Send the range through an external program.

You can use operators with a motion to alter a range of text. Try out these examples, starting by entering insert mode, typing some text, changing to command mode, and then moving to the beginning of the line:

```
iWelcome to Vim!<C-c>0
Welcome to Vim!
```

Move forward one word:

```
w
Welcome to Vim!
```

Change two words. Remember, in Vim, a word is a sequence of characters separated by whitespace or punctuation, so to Vim! is three words: to, Vim, and !:

```
c2w
Welcome !
```

Enter new text, then enter command mode:

```
the Terminal Editor<C-c>
Welcome the Terminal Editor!
```

Move to the beginning of the line, convert all characters to uppercase through to the end of the line (again, the first character is a zero, not a capital letter *O*):

```
0gU$
WELCOME THE TERMINAL EDITOR!
```

You're starting to get an idea of just how powerful modal editing is. It enables you to express complex changes to text, operate on ranges of text, and move in the buffer with just a few keystrokes.

You can also quickly apply these operators to the current line—just type them twice, as shown in Table 23-4.

Table 23-4: Operators That Act on the Current Line

Operator	Usage
cc	Change current line—that is, delete the line and move into insert mode at the beginning of the line.
dd	Delete the current line.
yy	Yank the current line.
g~~	Change the case for the current line.
gUU	Make the current line uppercase.
guu	Make the current line lowercase.

Searching for Text Patterns

Some of the most powerful motions are those that search for a specific character. With these *search motions*, you can quickly select a range of characters for an operator to perform on. Table 23-5 describes a few of the most essential search motions.

Table 23-5: Essential Search Motions

Motion	Usage
f*character*	Move forward to (onto) *character*.
F*character*	Move backward to (onto) *character*.
t*character*	Move forward to just before *character*.
T*character*	Move backward to just before *character*.

Now take a look at these motions in action by quickly moving around a little bit of Python code. Open a new line with **o**, then type a line of text, exit insert mode, and move to the beginning of the line:

```
def search_for_word(word):<C-c>0
def search_for_word(word):
```

Move forward onto (as follows:

```
f(
def search_for_word(word):
```

Move backward onto d twice:

```
2Fd
def search_for_word(word):
```

Move forward to just before the first underscore (_):

```
t_
def search_for_word(word):
```

Move backward to just before the f:

```
Tf
def search_for_word(word):
```

The difference between the f ("find") and t ("to") motions is that the former positions your cursor directly on the specified character, while the latter moves your cursor to right *before* that character. When you use Tf to move backward to before the f, your cursor ends up on the space between def and search because the space is what comes before the f when you're moving *backward* through the text.

As with any motion, you can add a count to indicate how many times you want the motion to run. You can also use the semicolon (;) to move to the next result and the comma (,) to move to the previous result.

Two other powerful motions you should know about are i ("inside") and a ("around"), which are useful when you want to change content within square brackets, parentheses, braces, and so on. If you use ca), you're saying "change *around* parentheses," which removes both the parentheses and the text between them and puts you into insert mode at the position they previously occupied. In comparison, ci{ says "change *inside* braces," removing the text between the braces but keeping the braces themselves.

Try this out, starting again by moving forward onto the first open parenthesis:

```
f(
def search_for_word(word):
```

Change the text *inside* parentheses, leaving the parentheses themselves:

```
ci)
def search_for_word():
```

Enter some text, then return to command mode:

```
word = "default"<C-c>
def search_for_word(word = "default"):
```

Change *around* quotes, deleting both the quotes themselves and the text they contain:

```
ca"
def search_for_word(word =):
```

Enter text, then return to command mode:

```
'sample'<C-c>
def search_for_word(word = 'sample'):
```

NOTE *When you use an open brace or parenthesis, Vim will add a space before and after the text you insert. When you use a closing brace or parenthesis, no additional spaces are added.*

You can also combine the a and i motions with operators. Move forward onto the first (again:

```
f(
def search_for_word(word = 'sample'):
```

Now convert all characters from the current position until the next closing parenthesis to uppercase:

```
gUi)
def search_for_word(WORD = 'SAMPLE'):
```

The i) motion specifies the range inside parentheses (from the first non-whitespace character to the closing parenthesis) for gU to transform, so after the operation, the cursor ends up on the first character of the upper-case text.

By now, you've seen how Vim motions can help you navigate through and work with text more easily. But they're not just useful in Vim; as you'll see next, they can also help you efficiently edit your shell commands.

Editing Commands

As another example of how you can use Vim in your day-to-day work, you'll enter a shell command that includes a mistake and use Vim to fix it.

First, make sure your shell's editor is set to Vim:

```
$ EDITOR=vi
```

NOTE *Chapter 15 describes how you can set your preferred editor in your shell configuration file so you don't have to type this command each time you open a new shell.*

Enter the following line of text in the shell (but don't press ENTER to execute it yet!):

```
$ git commit -m 'added more detail on motions'
```

This command will commit file changes—but you haven't added any changes yet. Rather than fixing the command by backspacing, adding the missing part, and then re-entering this text (which is time consuming), you'll open the current shell command line in Vim and fix it there.

Press CTRL-X, CTRL-E to tell the shell to open the current line in your configured text editor:

```
git commit -m 'added more detail on motions'
~
~
~
"/tmp/bash-fc-5094983766" 1L, 45B                    1,1          All
```

Now fix up the command with your new Vim skills. First, enter insert mode:

```
i
git commit -m 'added more detail on motions'
```

Add your text, then enter command mode:

```
git add . && <C-c>
git add . && git commit -m 'added more detail on motions'
```

Enter the wq ("write and quit") command:

```
:wq
```

Press ENTER to execute the command. Vim will close, and the shell then runs the command `git add .` to add changes, and `git commit` completes successfully.

Updating and Styling Your Vim Cheatsheet

At this stage, you can update your cheatsheet with any notes you find relevant. Here are the first few lines of mine:

```
# Vim cheatsheet

## Vim motions

Vim motions are commands used to move the cursor. Essential motions are:

* `hjkl` - move the cursor left/down/up/right
* `w` - forward one word
* `b` - back one word
* `(` - back one sentence
* `)` - forward one sentence
* `0` - beginning of line
* `$` - end of line
* `gg` - beginning of buffer
* `G` - end of buffer

Motions can take a `{count}` to indicate how many motions you want to make,
such as `3w` to move forward three words.
```

Three new Markdown syntax features are used here:

- The double hash marks (##) indicate a subheading.
- The asterisk (*) indicates an item in a bulleted list (as noted earlier, you can also use a hyphen for this).
- Any text within backticks (`) indicates code and should be rendered in monospaced type.

These simple formatting features will make your cheatsheet look professional when it is viewed on GitHub or in a suitable editor. Figure 23-1 shows how mine looks on GitHub.

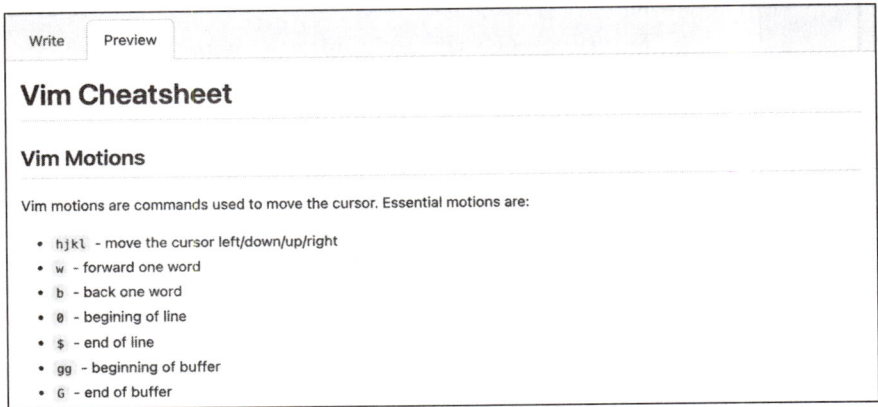

Figure 23-1: My Vim cheatsheet in GitHub

For more Markdown styling tips, see *https://www.markdownguide.org/basic-syntax/*.

Going Further with Vim

Vim is a huge topic, and we've barely scratched the surface, but I've tried to focus on the features that you can use most immediately. As you use Vim more, I suggest researching the following features in this order:

1. The dot command to repeat your last change
2. Visual mode to highlight text selections
3. Yank and paste and registers to extend basic clipboard behavior
4. Search and replace to make changes across your files more efficiently
5. The *~/.vimrc* file to customize Vim's behavior
6. Macros to automate complex sequences of commands

You can see how I manage my own Vim configuration at *https://github.com/dwmkerr/dotfiles*. I also recommend exploring the following resources to continue your Vim journey.

Vimtutor

Vim comes installed with the very useful `vimtutor` program. You can run this program to open Vim with a special file that describes Vim's functionality and shows examples so you can follow along and see features in action.

Use this program regularly while you're learning Vim to test your progress and refresh your skills!

Vimcasts

Drew Neil's excellent website Vimcasts (*http://vimcasts.org*) has some superb videos on how to use Vim, from the basics to some really advanced functionality.

Drew is an extremely skilled Vim user and does a great job of making a complex subject easy to follow.

Practical Vim and Modern Vim

If you're enjoying using Vim, Drew's books *Practical Vim*, 2nd edition (Pragmatic Bookshelf, 2015), and *Modern Vim* (Pragmatic Bookshelf, 2018) should be on your bookshelf! They are truly excellent and, just like Drew's Vimcasts, make a complex subject much more user-friendly.

Summary

This chapter introduced you to the basics of the Vim terminal editor: changing among the insert, command, and ex modes; working with motions and operators; and using Vim from within your shell. While terminal editors are sometimes the only choice when you don't have access to a desktop environment, they can also be the better choice, allowing you to handle many tasks without ever having to touch the mouse.

In the next and final chapter, we'll look at another powerful tool that will boost your productivity even more: the terminal multiplexer.

24

MASTERING THE MULTIPLEXER

A *terminal multiplexer* is a tool that lets you run multiple programs and shell sessions independently. You can switch between tasks, keep processes running in the background, and disconnect and reconnect without losing any settings or work in progress. These features are invaluable for multitasking and remote work. In this chapter, you'll learn how to use the popular terminal multiplexer tmux to handle everyday tasks and customize it to your needs.

Multiplexer sessions are containers that can hold multiple shell sessions and other programs, which persist independently of the terminal connection. You connect to your multiplexer sessions with your terminal using a shell, and when you exit your shell, the sessions continue running in the background. Users can switch between sessions, save them, resume them, and even invite others to join one to allow collaboration. Multiplexers also normally offer window management capabilities, allowing you to break your terminal into separate panes, tabs, or windows.

Figure 24-1 shows a multiplexer in action—the one I'm using as I write this chapter.

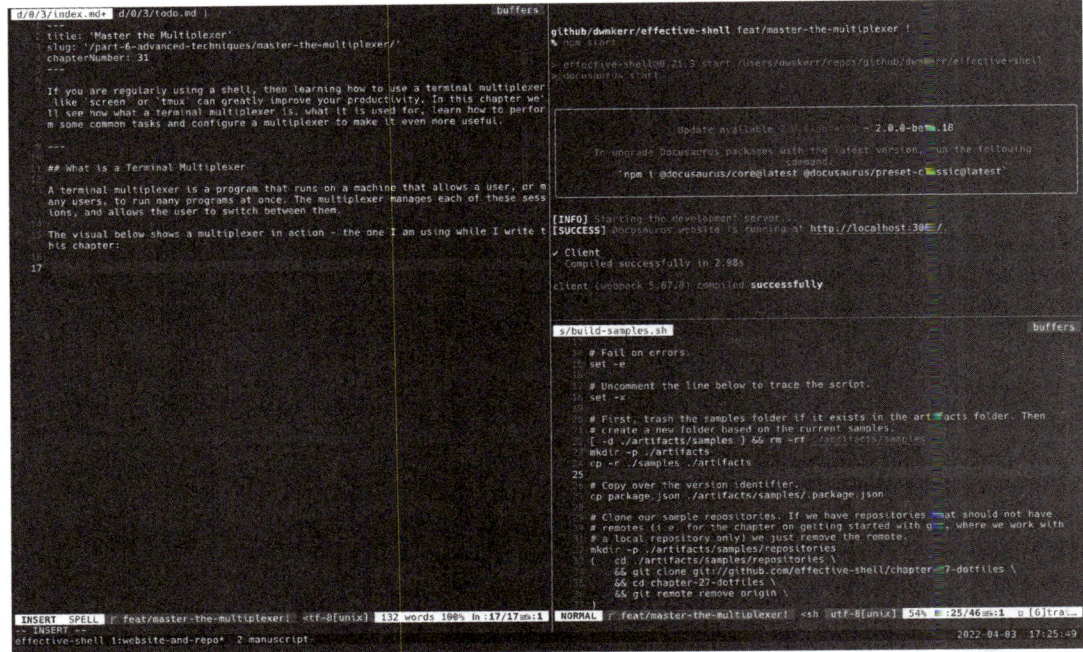

Figure 24-1: The tmux multiplexer I used while writing this book

I'm running the tmux multiplexer in my terminal. I've split the window into three panes: a large one on the left containing the text for the chapter, and two smaller ones on the right. The upper-right pane builds the *Effective Shell* website in real time while I am writing and checks for errors, and the lower-right pane contains a sample script I am working on.

When I want to switch between tasks, I don't need to start or stop any of the programs. Instead, I can just switch between the panes in my multiplexer.

At the bottom of the screen are two tabs: *website-and-repo*, which contains the website and the windows I'm currently working in, and *manuscript*, which has some windows for the book draft.

If I close my shell, the tmux server continues running the sessions, and I can reopen my terminal and resume. If I close my computer, when I restart, my multiplexer will restart these programs for me so I can pick up where I left off.

Benefits of Using a Multiplexer

While it's not essential to know how to use a multiplexer, it can certainly help you become a more effective shell user. Here are some of the key benefits:

Window management   As noted previously, multiplexers support multiple windows, tabs, and panes, allowing you to arrange your workspace exactly how you want it. You can also save your window configuration and use it later. You can even organize different windows into different sessions, which means you can switch between several running projects at once, each with a layout configured to your needs.

Session persistence   A multiplexer runs your programs independently from your terminal, so if your terminal crashes or freezes, your programs still run. You can run a multiplexer on a remote machine to manage your programs, and even if your connection to the machine is reset, the programs won't stop running. You can simply reconnect to the session later and pick up where you left off. Session persistence is incredibly useful—if you use the shell a lot, you'll wonder how you lived without it!

Configuration options   Multiplexers offer many configuration options to allow you to customize how you run and interface with your programs, allowing you to set up the ideal environment for maximum effectiveness.

Collaboration capabilities   A multiplexer is a *client/server* program. This means you as a user are a client and connect to a server that runs the multiplexer. But other users can connect as well, so you can easily collaborate with them to share your own work, connect to theirs, or work together on a shared remote machine.

We'll look at a few of the most immediately useful features of multiplexers in this chapter. Though it won't be a comprehensive discussion, it should be enough to help you decide whether to investigate further on your own and add a multiplexer to your toolkit.

Installing tmux

The two most popular multiplexers are probably GNU Screen and tmux. GNU Screen was created in the late 1980s and has been used widely ever since. It is preinstalled on many Linux systems.

A more modern multiplexer created in 2007, tmux has most of the features of GNU Screen, is also open source, and adds some very useful features to make it a little more user-friendly. However, tmux will not work with msys2 or Cygwin.

For the rest of this chapter, we'll look at tmux in detail. I've chosen tmux rather than Screen because I think its user-friendliness makes it a better option for multiplexer newcomers. Once you're comfortable with tmux, you might decide to switch to GNU Screen; if you do, it will be very familiar.

To check if tmux is already installed on your machine, run this command:

```
$ tmux -V
tmux 3.2a
```

If it isn't installed or you don't have version 3 or higher, you'll need to install the latest version of tmux with the package manager for your system. The package name on most distributions is just tmux. For example, on a Debian-based distribution, you would install tmux with the following command:

```
$ apt install -y tmux
```

On a Mac you would use:

```
$ brew install tmux
```

Once you've installed tmux, run it by entering the **tmux** command.

TMUX KEYBOARD SHORTCUTS

Like Vim, tmux relies heavily on case-sensitive keyboard shortcuts. For example, pressing CTRL and b (lowercase) is different from pressing CTRL-SHIFT-B (uppercase).

This book uses the standard tmux documentation format for shortcuts, where the caret (^) and prefix C are both equivalent to the CTRL key:

- **^b** or **C-b**: CTRL with lowercase b
- **^B** or **C-B**: CTRL with uppercase B

In tmux, most commands start with a sequence called the *prefix* (or *leader*) so that tmux's keyboard shortcuts will not clash with the shortcuts of any programs it is running. By default, the tmux prefix is ^b (CTRL-b).

For example, to send the command Z (an uppercase Z), you would use the sequence ^b Z or C-b Z (making sure to press SHIFT when entering the Z).

In this chapter, I'll consistently use the slightly more concise format ^b to describe keyboard shortcuts and sequences. Remember, always match the case shown in the examples.

Now let's explore some of the things you can do with the tmux program.

Window Management with tmux

We'll begin by looking at several techniques for working with windows in the multiplexer.

Creating and Moving Between Panes

A *split* separates your current window into panes that can each run their own program. You can create a vertical split by pressing ^b followed by the percent sign (%) or a horizontal split by pressing ^b followed by a double quote ("). Finally, to move between panes, press ^b followed by the appropriate arrow key.

Zooming Panes

You can zoom in on a pane so that it takes up the entire window by pressing ^b z. To zoom out of a pane, either move to another pane (even if it's hidden) or press ^b z again.

Creating and Moving Between Windows

To run a program in an entirely new window, use the ^b c command to create a window. To switch windows, press ^b w to choose from the list of available windows and sessions. This command is extremely useful if you have a lot of windows to move between.

Table 24-1 lists some other useful window management commands.

Table 24-1: Handy Commands for Working with Windows

Command	Description
^b n	Move to the next window.
^b p	Move to the previous window.
^b 0	Select the window numbered 0 (the window numbers are shown on the bottom left next to the window name).
^b &	Close the current window.
^b ,	Rename the current window.
^b w	Show the window navigator.

 Remember that tmux is case sensitive, so check your caps lock key when entering these commands.

The ^b , ("rename window") command is very useful if you have a lot of windows and want to give each one a descriptive name. As you'll see in the next section, tmux will remember these settings even if you detach (that is, disconnect) from a session and later reattach to it.

Session Management with tmux

Sessions in tmux are a collection of independently managed windows. They are great for creating lots of projects: each session can be a project with the appropriate windows and configuration for the work you're doing.

Starting a New Session

Close your existing tmux session so that you can start fresh:

```
$ exit
```

Now restart tmux, and name the session *effective-shell* using the s ("session") parameter as follows:

```
$ tmux new -s effective-shell
```

Now you'll create a new window and then create a new session:

```
# Create a new window.
^b c

# Enter tmux command mode.
^b :

# Create a second session.
new -s my-project

# Select from the list of sessions.
^b s
```

The ^b : command opens the tmux command pane, which is shown at the bottom of the screen and allows you to run a tmux command. When you open this pane, you no longer need to put tmux at the beginning of the command to create a new session, as you can see with the my-project session. The ^b s command opens the list of sessions. As you scan through the list using the arrow keys, tmux gives you a preview of each session.

Attaching and Detaching from Sessions

As noted earlier, one of the great things about sessions is that you can set them up, then detach from them to do other work. The sessions will keep running, and you can reattach to them later. This means you can close your terminal and reopen it and programs will still run.

If you're in the shell and want to open tmux and attach to the last session, run the following:

```
$ tmux attach
```

When you're in a tmux session, you can detach from it like so:

```
^bd
detach
```

Because tmux is *stateful* (has session persistence), if you close your terminal at this point, the tmux server saves your session information. Then when you reopen a terminal, you can reattach with the same command as before:

```
tmux attach
```

If you use tmux often, you might find you end up with lots of sessions. To delete a session, enter ^b s to show the session list, scroll to the session you want to delete, and press x. The tmux server will ask for confirmation before it closes the session.

Sessions are extremely powerful for organizing your work. Table 24-2 lists some other useful commands for working with them.

Table 24-2: Handy Commands for Working with Sessions

Command	Description
tmux attach	Attach to the last used session.
tmux new -s *name*	Start a new tmux session named *name*.
^b: new -s *another-name*	Enter command mode and start a session named *another-name*.
^b $	Rename the current session.
^b s	Show the session list. Close the selected session with x.
^b)	Move to the next session.
^b (	Move to the previous session.
^b w	Show all windows and sessions.

Now that you know how to manage multiple sessions and you understand the essential commands, you might want to fine-tune tmux to suit your preferences.

Configuring tmux

The out-of-the-box configuration for tmux is normally fine for everyday use. However, if you find yourself using tmux a lot, adding some customizations can make it work better for you.

The program's configuration pattern follows the very standard, Unix-style dot file structure. (If you're not familiar with dot files, see Chapter 17.) To begin configuring tmux, create a file named *.tmux.conf* in your home directory:

```
$ touch ~/.tmux.conf
```

Now open this file in your preferred editor so you can start adding some customizations. I'll walk you through the ones I find most useful.

Setting the Default Shell

First, you'll tell tmux to use your current shell program (for example, if you're using the Z shell, tmux will know to open windows with the Z shell):

```
# Set the default shell, and set the default command to use our shell (this
# means sourcing things properly, showing the correct PS1, and so on).
set -g default-shell $SHELL
set -g default-command $SHELL
```

With these settings, tmux will also source your shell dot files so that each window it opens has the same command prompt (set in the PS1 variable) and configuration as your standard shell.

Specifying the Working Directory

When you create a new window with ^b c, tmux will open it in the home directory by default. In general, I prefer to have the window open in my current working directory. Make this change as follows:

```
# Open new panes and splits in the same working directory.
bind c new-window -c "#pane_current_path"
```

This simple command saves you a step every time you open a new window.

Naming and Numbering Windows

By default, tmux tries to be smart and changes the name of each window to the program that window is currently running. I find it distracting to have window names change as I use them, so I disable this automatic renaming behavior. In general, I rename a window as soon as I've opened it and give it a descriptive name instead.

I also set tmux to number windows from 1 rather than 0, and to renumber them when I create or delete any windows so that the numbering remains sequential, without gaps. If you don't do this, you'll rapidly get into double-digit numbers, which are harder to select (you can only use ^b *window-number* to select windows 0 through 9).

Configure these settings like so:

```
# Set the name of the window initially, but then don't let tmux change it.
# The name can still be set at any time with: ^b ,
set-option -g allow-rename off

# Start windows and panes at 1.
set -g base-index 1
```

```
set -g pane-base-index 1

# When windows are added or removed, renumber them sequentially.
set -g renumber-windows on
```

Splitting Windows More Intuitively

I've always found ^b % and ^b " odd commands for splitting, and still to this day I regularly mix them up. Instead, I use ^b - to make a vertical split and ^b | to make a horizontal split. The direction of the hyphen or pipe is a much easier way to remember what kind of split I'll be making. Here's how to change this:

```
# Split panes using | and -
bind | split-window -h -c "#pane_current_path"
bind - split-window -v -c "#pane_current_path"
```

Sending Commands to Nested Sessions

I'm almost never not in a tmux session. This means that if I open a *nested session*—for example, by using ssh to connect to a virtual machine and running tmux there—I have trouble sending commands to the nested tmux. Using ^b c opens the new window on my machine, not in the nested session. By using bind-key b send-prefix, I can use ^b b to send a command to the nested session:

```
# Use ^b b to send the command to a nested session. This means if you are
# using tmux and then use ssh to connect to another machine that is also
# running tmux, you can run commands in this nested session using ^b b command.
bind-key b send-prefix
```

This might sound fiddly, but you'll get a sense of how useful it can be in "Collaboration with tmux" on page 372.

Enabling Mouse Support

If you have a mouse (which will normally be the case if you're working with your local machine), you can enable it for tmux so that you can drag panes to resize them, select panes and windows, and more.

If you want to really get into the mouseless flow, however, disable this option like so:

```
# Enable mouse mode (tmux 2.1 and above).
set -g mouse on
```

This configuration will force you to learn the commands!

Interfacing with Vim

I set a number of configuration options to help tmux interface more seamlessly with Vim, and I also use Vim directions rather than arrow keys to move around. This means I use ^b j to go to the pane below and ^b l to go to the pane to the right.

I've also configured a number of key bindings to make resizing panes more intuitive to Vim users, as well as to enable Vim-style text selection.

These more advanced options are of interest only to Vim users, however, so if you want to learn more, see my dot files project at *https://github .com/dwmkerr/dotfiles*.

Setting Advanced Configuration

We've really only touched on the most basic configuration options here, as you can customize tmux in almost any way imaginable. For example, you can change the visual style of the status bar, the colors, the information shown, and more. And there are plug-in managers for tmux to make it easier to install plug-ins for even more customizability.

These are more advanced configuration settings, however, so I recommend exploring them only after you're familiar with "vanilla" tmux. To see the available options, run man tmux or search for any of the excellent online guides on how to configure the program.

Collaboration with tmux

So far, you've run all of these sessions on your local machine. This is great for organizing your local work. But you can also run tmux on another machine or server, then connect to it from your machine like so:

```
ssh -t effective-shell-aws-linux tmux attach
```

The ssh program allows you to run a command on the server—in this case, the tmux attach command. If you ask ssh to run a command, by default it won't connect the input of your terminal to the server. The idea is that sometimes you're just using ssh to run one-off commands and don't need to stay connected. But for this command, you actually *want* to stay attached to the server, so you use the -t ("request TTY") flag to attach your terminal input to the SSH session.

You can set up your SSH config file to automatically attach to the tmux session. This is how I set up my *~/.ssh/config* file entry for the virtual machine created in Chapter 22:

```
Host effective-shell-aws-linux
    HostName ec2-13-213-71-135.ap-southeast-1.compute.amazonaws.com
    User ec2-user
    IdentityFile ~/.ssh/effective-shell
    RequestTTY yes              # Ensure that you attach your terminal input.
    RemoteCommand tmux attach # Attach to the tmux session.
```

With this configuration, when you use ssh to connect to the *effective -shell-aws-linux* box, you'll run the tmux attach command and attach your terminal. To connect to tmux on the server now, you only need to run the following:

```
ssh effective-shell-aws-linux
```

At this point, you're connected to the server and running tmux. You can run commands and background jobs, create windows, work with nested tmux sessions, and so on. Because all of these operations are running a tmux session, you can disconnect and resume later without losing any work.

A tmux Quick Guide

To quickly see all of the tmux commands, run the ^b ? command. The output of this command will look something like this (remember that tmux also uses C for CTRL):

```
C-b C-b      Send the prefix key
C-b C-o      Rotate through the panes
C-b C-z      Suspend the current client
C-b Space    Select next layout
C-b !        Break pane to a new window
C-b "        Split window vertically
C-b #        List all paste buffers
C-b $        Rename current session
C-b %        Split window horizontally
C-b &        Kill current window
C-b '        Prompt for window index to select
C-b (        Switch to previous client
C-b )        Switch to next client
C-b ,        Rename current window
C-b .        Move the current window
C-b /        Describe key binding
C-b 0        Select window 0
C-b 1        Select window 1
...
```

Table 24-3 offers a handy reference of common commands.

Table 24-3: tmux Command Quick Reference

Command	Description
Essentials	
tmux ls	List sessions.
tmux new [-s *name*]	Start a new tmux session (optionally named *name*).
tmux attach [-t *name*]	Attach to the last used session or the target session named *name*.

(continued)

Table 24-3: tmux Command Quick Reference *(continued)*

Command	Description
`tmux kill-session [-t name]`	Kill a session named *name*. If *name* is not specified, the current session is killed.
`tmux kill-session -a`	Kill all sessions except the current session.
`^b d`	Detach from current session.
`^b : new -s another-name`	Enter command mode, start the session named *another-name*.
`^b ?`	Show command help.
Session management	
`^b $`	Rename the current session.
`^b s`	Show the session list. Close sessions with x.
`^b )`	Move to the next session.
`^b (`	Move to the previous session.
`^b w`	Show all windows and all sessions.
Window management	
`^b n`	Move to the next window.
`^b p`	Move to the previous window.
`^b 0`	Select the window numbered 0 (use the number of any window from the status pane).
`^b &`	Close the current window.
`^b ,`	Rename the current window.
`^b w`	Show the window navigator.
`^b $`	Kill the current window.
Splits and panes	
`^b %`	Create a horizontal split.
`^b "`	Create a vertical split.
`^b <arrow>`	Move to the pane in the direction of the arrow key.
`^b z`	Zoom in to or out of a pane.
`^b !`	Convert pane to window.

Next Steps with tmux

As you start to use tmux more, you'll realize you can do some truly incredible things with a multiplexer. Selecting text from the shell without touching the mouse, seamlessly integrating tmux splits and Vim splits, sending commands to multiple machines at once, using plug-in managers to add advanced features—the list goes on.

The tmux program also lets you rapidly resize, swap, or reorder panes; break a pane into its own window or session; and more. These commands are probably the next ones to learn. If you've enabled mouse mode, you can also resize panes with the mouse if desired. In a similar way to how a modern integrated development environment allows you to customize your windows and layout to suit the work you're doing, tmux lets you customize, lay out, and manage almost any set of programs you might need.

I highly recommend using tmux as part of your standard workflow. Get familiar with the basic features shown in this chapter and then, as you start to encounter limitations and want to do more, explore some of the great books and blog posts out there that go into more advanced features. In particular, Brian Hogan's excellent book *tmux 3: Productive Mouse-Free Development* (Pragmatic Bookshelf, 2025) is suitable for anyone, from beginner to expert, and will help you take your tmux skills to the next level.

You can also see how I manage my own tmux configuration at *https://github.com/dwmkerr/dotfiles.*

Summary

This chapter introduced you to the tmux terminal multiplexer. You learned how to manage windows, panes, and sessions; how to configure tmux to suit your personal working style; and how to use tmux to manage sessions on remote machines and even collaborate in real time with other users.

At this point, you've learned the basics of the shell, optimized your setup for working with it, customized your shell configuration, and created several scripts and programs. You've also explored some really sophisticated topics like SSH, Vim, and terminal editors. You've truly become an effective shell user! As you use these techniques more and more, they'll become more natural, and you should find that you're able to work in the shell quickly, efficiently, and without disruptions to your flow.

There are many other topics to explore as you spend more time in the shell. The final part of this book looks at the future of the shell and generative AI. Check out *https://effective-shell.com* for even more topics and tutorials. Good luck with your journey!

AFTERWORD

GENERATIVE AI AND THE SHELL

Excitement and development around generative AI have increased enormously over the past few years. Many of us are finding that tools like ChatGPT can help us with tasks such as writing code, looking up how to execute certain operations, and tracking down the root causes of errors. Unfortunately, when you're working in the shell, accessing AI tools typically requires you to switch to a web browser, disrupting your flow. I found this annoying enough that I wrote a tool call Terminal AI that allows you to query ChatGPT directly from your shell and get results tailored to your environment.

In this afterword, I'll walk you through a few ways of using Terminal AI to maintain your workflow and effectiveness as a shell user. Given the pace at which generative AI is evolving, there will likely be many more options available to you by the time you're reading this.

Installing and Running the Terminal AI Tool

Before you can install Terminal AI, you'll need to install the npm ("Node Package Manager") program, which is part of the toolkit for the Node.js programming language. Follow the installation instructions for your operating system and hardware at *https://nodejs.org/en/download*. Once you've installed npm, install Terminal AI like so:

```
$ npm install -g @dwmkerr/terminal-ai
```

The -g ("global") flag tells npm to install Terminal AI globally so that you can call it from any location. Terminal AI installs a tool named ai, which you run as follows:

```
$ ai
Welcome to Terminal AI!

An API key must be configured so that Terminal AI can talk to ChatGPT.
Enter your key below, or for instructions check:
  https://github.com/dwmkerr/terminal-ai#api-key

? API Key:
```

You'll be prompted for an API key to talk to ChatGPT. For instructions on creating this key, search online for "ChatGPT API Key" or visit the Terminal AI project home page at *https://github.com/dwmkerr/terminal-ai*. Once you enter your key, you'll be able to use the tool.

Chatting with ChatGPT

Now you can run the ai command and start chatting with the tool. Here are some example queries:

```
$ ai
chat: What's my current shell and OS?
chatgpt: Your current shell is /bin/bash and your operating system is linux.

chat: Show 5 largest files in pwd recursively.
chatgpt: To display the 5 largest files in the current directory recursively,
you can use the following command:

find . -type f -exec du -h {} + | sort -rh | head -n 5

chat: Is it possible to print a colored message in a shell script?
chatgpt: Yes, you can print colored text in a shell script using ANSI
escape codes.

chat: Can you show me how to print "Hello" in red?
chatgpt: Here is an example of how you can print "Hello" in red using
```

ANSI escape codes in a Bash script:

```bash
#!/bin/bash

RED='\033[0;31m'
NC='\033[0m'

echo -e "${RED}Hello${NC}"
```

Save the script in a file, make it executable, and run it in your terminal to see the colored output.

When you've finished your conversation, press CTRL-C to quit.

Copying or Saving Results

You'll likely use Terminal AI to create code you wish to execute. The ai tool allows you to quicky copy the most recent answer to your clipboard or save it to a file. To see this in action, run a simple query to create a code snippet:

```
$ ai -- "code output only - python to create a folder if it doesn't exist"
import os

    folder_name = "example_folder"
    if not os.path.exists(folder_name):
        os.makedirs(folder_name)

(Reply below or press Enter for more options...)
chat: <Enter>
```

At the prompt, press ENTER instead of typing a reply. You'll see a menu that gives you the option to copy the code to the clipboard, save it to a file, execute it, or continue the chat:

```
? What next?:
> Reply
  Copy Response
  Save Response
  Execute Response
  Quit
```

Use the up and down arrows (or enter j and k if you remember your Vim shortcuts!) to select an option.

Executing AI-Generated Scripts

If you choose the Execute Response option from the ai menu, ai opens the response in your default editor so that you can review or change the generated code. Once you close your editor, you'll be asked to confirm whether you want to execute the script. Before doing so, check the script carefully to make sure it will do what you expect.

The following query, which writes a shell script to find the largest file in a folder, demonstrates this process:

```
$ ai -- "code: shell script for largest file in working directory, showing size"
chatgpt:

    #!/bin/bash

    # List files in current directory with sizes.
    ls -lh | awk '{print $9, $5}' | grep -v ^total | sort -k 2 -n | tail -n 1

✔ Verify your script - AI can make mistakes!
✔ Are you sure you want to execute this code? Yes
answer.txt 642B

? chat:
```

The code part of the command is a hint Terminal AI uses to tell ChatGPT to write only code, with no explanation. Pressing ENTER again at the chat prompt will show you the next set of available actions.

Redirecting Responses to a File

Like any good command line tool, ai allows you to redirect input and output to and from other programs. For example, you can repeat the previous query but send its results to a file like so:

```
$ ai -- "code: shell script for largest file in working directory, showing size" > find.sh
```

This command redirects the results to a new file called *find.sh*, which you could review and execute later.

The Shell of the Future

The possibilities are endless for using ChatGPT and other large language models (LLMs) in your day-to-day work. Given that LLMs are trained on public data (such as the full set of public repositories on GitHub and other locations), their answers to programming-related questions tend to be very reliable. That said, remember to check any AI-generated code before running it to avoid unexpected effects.

I wrote the Terminal AI tool for fun to show you how easily you can integrate ChatGPT into a shell-oriented workflow, and I'm adding new features to it regularly. A host of other tools, code editors like Cursor (*https://cursor.com*), and various platforms are currently building on AI technology as well. I encourage you to explore as many as you can to become an even more effective shell user.

A

SETUP

If you're new to the shell, this appendix will walk you through how to access the shell on your machine, configure your system, and install some software to set up a simple and standardized shell environment.

You can skip this appendix if you are already comfortable running a shell in a terminal program and have a recent version of bash or a bash-like shell installed.

Accessing the Shell

The name of the shell program you'll use and the way you access it will differ depending on your operating system.

Microsoft Windows

A number of shell programs are available for Windows. You'll be using Command Prompt, the basic shell program that comes preinstalled in Windows.

To open Command Prompt, click the Windows icon to open the Start menu and type **command prompt** in the search box.

When Command Prompt opens, type **whoami** and press ENTER. You should see the username of the logged-in user, as shown on the second line here:

```
C:\Users\dave>whoami
davekerr9d36\dave
```

That's all there is to it! You've still got some configuration to do to make Command Prompt behave more like a Linux shell, which this book uses as the standard, but you'll learn about that in the next section.

macOS

If you're using a Mac, you'll use the Terminal program to open your shell. Press ⌘-spacebar and then type **terminal**.

When Terminal opens, type **whoami** and then press RETURN. You should see the username of the logged-in user, as shown on the second line here:

```
% whoami
dwmkerr
```

That's it! In the next section, you'll make some minor configuration changes to keep things consistent with the examples in the book.

Linux

If you're using a Linux or Unix system, I'll assume that you're familiar enough with it to open a shell. Your specific shell (known as a *terminal* in Linux, not to be confused with the Terminal program in macOS) should not affect how you use this book, but note that most of the book's examples use bash version 5.

Configuring the Shell

Shells can vary enormously between different systems. In general, Linux systems tend to use bash and require little configuration. macOS is based on BSD Unix and differs under the hood from most Linux systems. Windows is completely unrelated to either Linux or Unix and operates in a fundamentally different way from both of them.

In this book, I assume that you are using a "Linux-like" system—that is, one that operates like a modern Linux distribution. This is a deliberate choice. Once you're comfortable using a Linux-like shell, you can generally apply the techniques shown here to macOS with no difficulties. For Windows, the techniques are not necessarily transferable immediately, but they're still valuable to know. Windows is increasingly making its own shell environment more Linux-like with the Windows Subsystem for Linux (WSL). However, WSL does require some setup, which I'll describe shortly.

This section will ensure that you're running a Linux-like setup, preferably with the latest version of the popular bash program. If you are familiar with bash but prefer to use another shell, that's fine—most of the book will work with any modern shell. However, if you have no preference, I recommend following the guidelines given here.

Microsoft Windows

Because Windows isn't anything like Linux under the hood, it takes a few steps to get a shell working. You have three options.

Option 1: Install Linux Tools

Installing Linux tools is probably the easiest option and the one I would recommend for most users. You'll be able to run a Linux-like shell when you choose to, but it won't interfere with your day-to-day computer usage.

To get a Linux-esque experience on a Windows machine, you'll install Cygwin. Cygwin provides a large set of programs that are designed to work on Windows and are generally available on Linux systems.

Go to *https://www.cygwin.com* to download the Cygwin installer. Start the installation. When prompted to choose a download source, make sure **Install from Internet** (the default) is selected, as shown in Figure A-1, and then click **Next**.

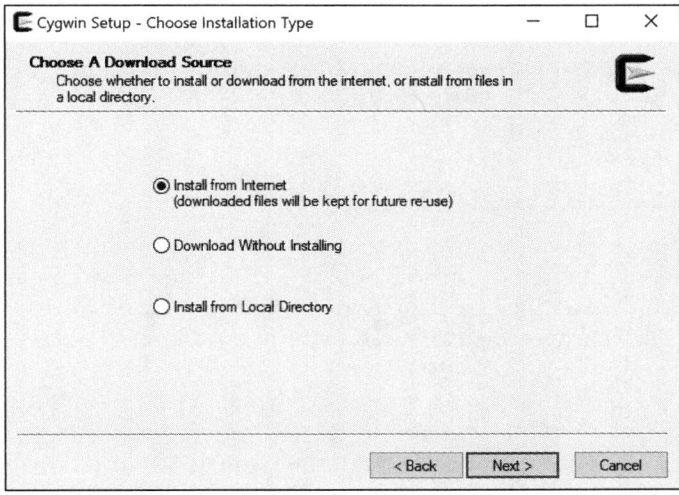

Figure A-1: Installing Cygwin from the internet

In the Select Root Install Directory dialog, leave the default location selected and select **All Users** (see Figure A-2). Click **Next**.

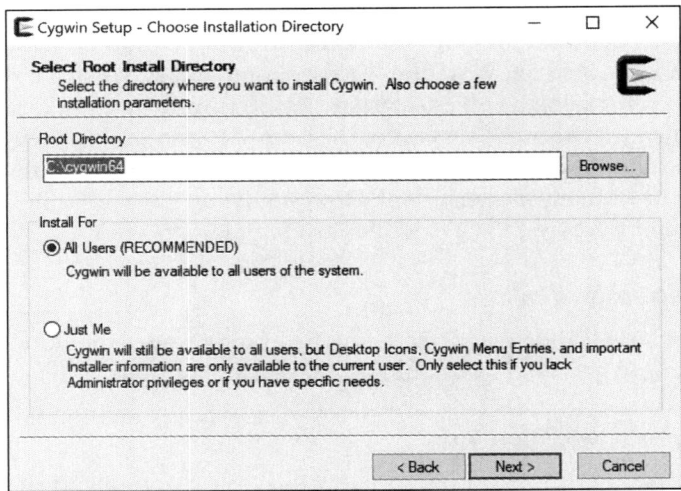

Figure A-2: Choosing where and for whom to install Cygwin

In the next dialog, Cygwin will ask you where to install downloaded packages, whether a proxy is needed, and what download sites to use. Leave these options at their default settings unless you know what you're doing and why you'd need to change them.

Once Cygwin has downloaded the list of available packages, it will ask which packages you want to install. Choose the default option **All**, and click **Next**.

When Cygwin has finished installing, you'll have a link to open Cygwin available on the desktop and the Start menu. You can click this link to start using bash. Or, if you prefer, you can open Command Prompt as described in "Accessing the Shell" on page 381 and type the command bash --norc to start a bash session.

Option 2: Run a Virtual Machine

Using a virtual machine is the best option if you want to practice with the shell but keep it completely separate from your main computer and files. Virtual machines are a great way to create a Linux *sandbox*, an isolated environment where you can safely experiment without affecting the rest of your system.

There are many ways to run a virtual machine on Windows. For this example, you'll use a free Oracle tool called VirtualBox to host a virtual machine on which you'll install the popular Ubuntu distribution of Linux.

First, go to *https://ubuntu.com/download/desktop* and start downloading the latest version of Ubuntu's Desktop Edition (which at the time of writing is version 22.04.4). The file is quite large, so the download might take a while. In the meantime, you can install VirtualBox.

Go to *https://www.virtualbox.org/wiki/Downloads* and download the VirtualBox installer for "Windows hosts." Run it and click **Next** from the first screen to start the installation setup.

First, you'll be asked to configure the installation options. The defaults, shown in Figure A-3, should be fine for most users. Click **Next**.

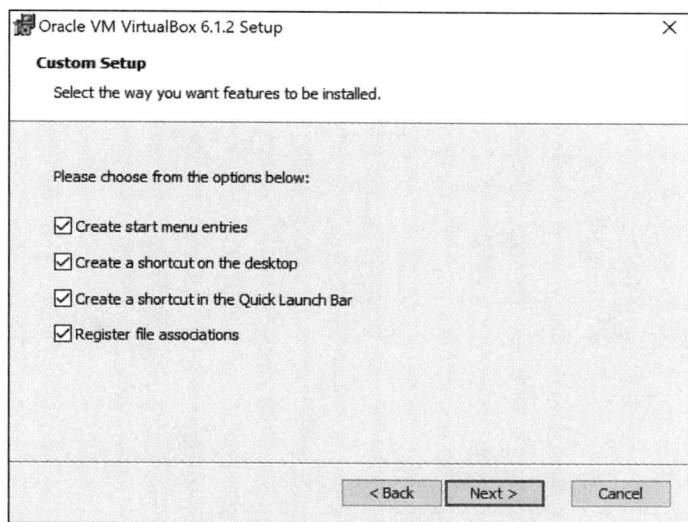

Figure A-3: Setting up the VirtualBox features

The installation might take a few minutes. You should see a progress bar indicating the status. When the installation is complete, click **Next**.

Open VirtualBox and choose **New** to create a new virtual machine. For Name, enter **Ubuntu**, and for ISO Image, select the Ubuntu image you downloaded. Check the **Skip Unattended Installation** box, as shown in Figure A-4, and then click **Next**.

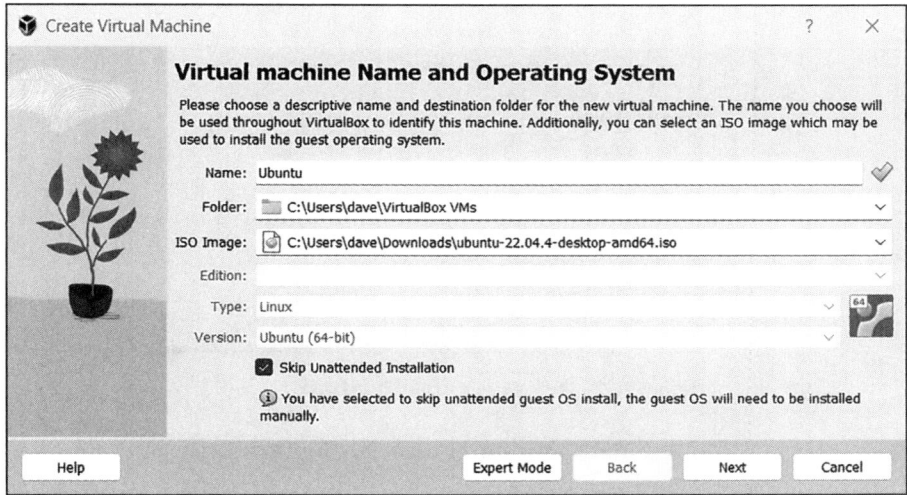

Figure A-4: Setting up your new virtual machine

The Hardware screen allows you to set the memory and the number of processors for the machine. Leave these options at their default settings, shown in Figure A-5, and click **Next**.

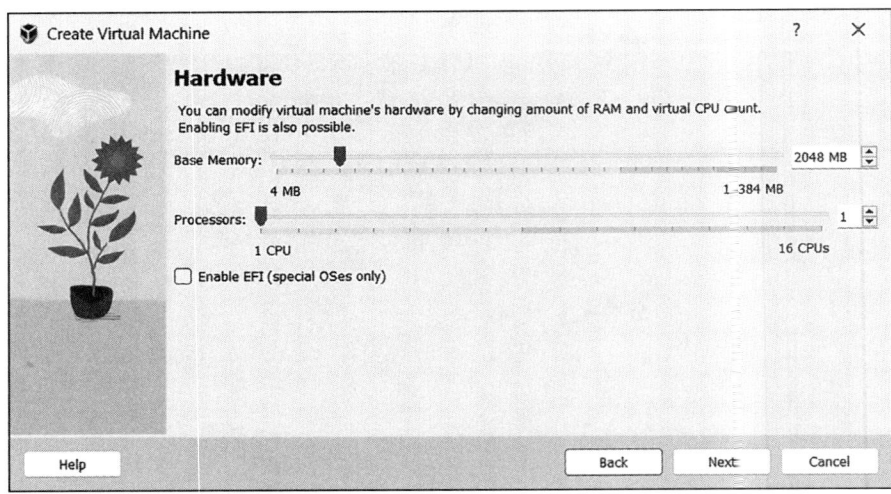

Figure A-5: New virtual machine hardware options

You'll be prompted to set up a virtual hard disk. I recommend the default options for most users (see Figure A-6). Click **Next**.

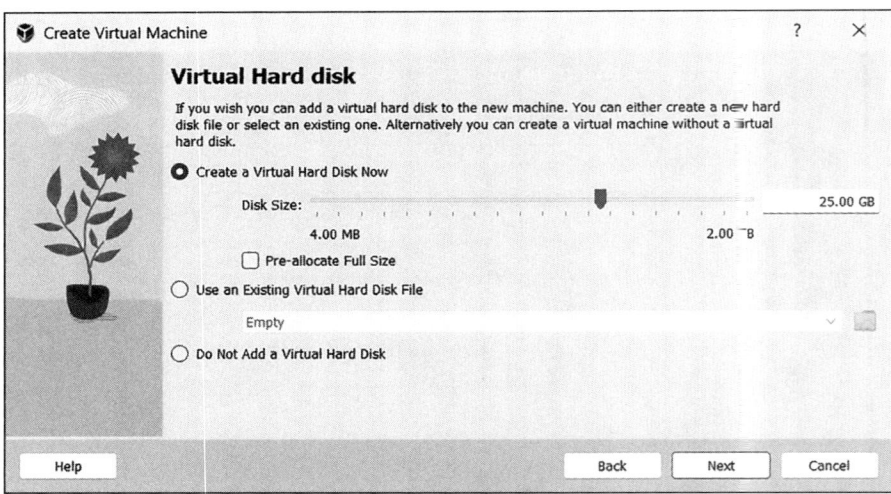

Figure A-6: Setting up a virtual hard disk

Finally, you should see the Summary screen shown in Figure A-7. Click **Finish**.

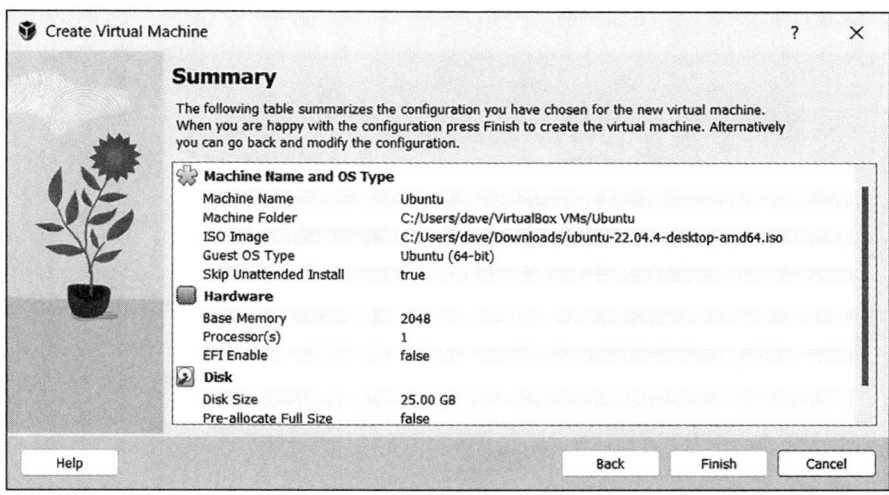

Figure A-7: The Summary screen for your virtual machine

After a few minutes, you should see your new virtual machine in the main VirtualBox window. Select the machine and click the **Start** button (the green arrow). It may take a few minutes for the first startup to complete. You'll be presented with a black-and-white screen with some options, but you can safely ignore this, and the Ubuntu installer will automatically run after a couple of minutes.

NOTE *If this step fails, you may need to go to **Turn Windows Features On or Off** in the control panel and disable the Hyper-V and Windows Sandbox features.*

When the Ubuntu installer starts up, choose **Install Ubuntu**, as shown in Figure A-8.

Figure A-8: The Ubuntu installer main page

The next series of screens allow you to configure language preferences, which components are installed, and more. You can leave these options at their default settings. In the Installation Type dialog, shown in Figure A-9, choose **Erase Disk and Install Ubuntu**. This won't remove any of the data on your Windows machine; it will just ensure that you have a clean installation on your virtual machine. Click **Install Now**.

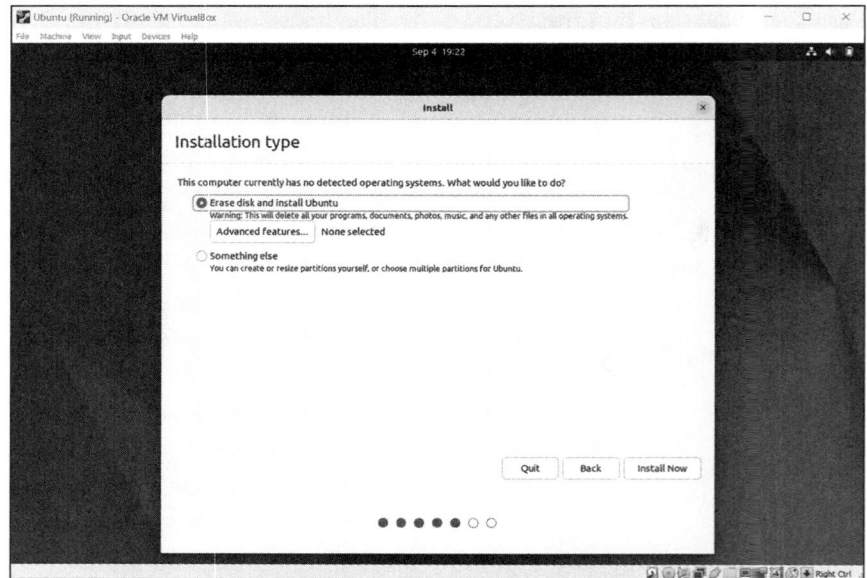

Figure A-9: Choosing the installation type

When you see a pop-up message reading "Write the changes to disk," choose **Continue**.

The final step, shown in Figure A-10, is to choose a name for the computer, a username, and a password. You can use any values you like here, but make sure to record your username and password as you'll need them to log in later on. Click **Continue** to start the installation.

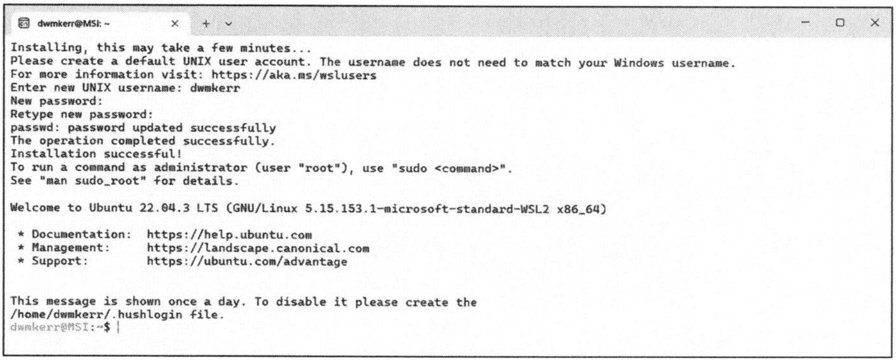

Figure A-10: Setting your Ubuntu login credentials

The installation might take a little while. When it is complete, you'll need to restart. If you get the error "Please remove installation medium," power off the machine and restart it. After that, you should be able to log in to the machine with the credentials you specified earlier.

Once you've logged in, click the applications icon on the bottom left of the screen. Type `terminal` in the search box to find and then launch the Terminal application.

You are now running bash in the Terminal program. You can run the `whoami` command to show the current user or `bash --version` to see the version of bash that's installed.

Congratulations! You now have a virtual machine running Ubuntu and bash, and you're ready to start experimenting with the shell.

Option 3: Set Up the Windows Subsystem for Linux

WSL is a set of features that allows users to install a Linux distribution on their Windows machine. This is a great way to use bash without having to set up a virtual machine. And it's the best option for power users or experts who want to use the latest WSL features and build their skills with the platform as soon as possible.

First, go to **Start ▸ Command Prompt ▸ Run as Administrator**. At the command prompt, enter the following:

```
$ wsl --install
```

You'll be asked to enter your password. For any pop-ups that appear asking for permissions, click **Yes**.

Next, open the Microsoft Store and type `Ubuntu` in the search box. Click **Get** to install the Ubuntu app. Once it is installed, choose **Open** from the Microsoft Store page or search for **Ubuntu** in the Start menu to open it. The app will take a few minutes to initialize. If you get an error message, restart Windows. To complete the setup, enter a username and password when prompted.

Now you should have a running Ubuntu environment on your machine, as shown in Figure A-11.

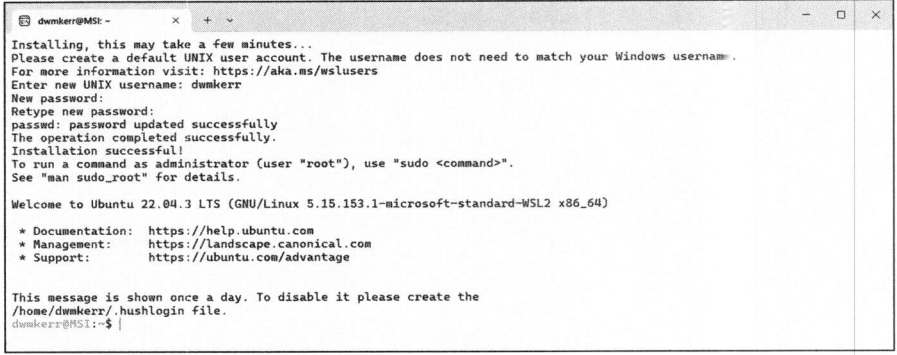

Figure A-11: Completing the setup

You're done! Now you can open the Ubuntu app at any time to use Ubuntu on Windows, with bash as the interface.

macOS

If you're a Mac user, you can probably run the standard Terminal program and follow the material in this book without making any changes. However, the version of bash that comes installed by default on macOS is version 3.2.*x*, which is out of date, so I strongly suggest that you upgrade it. Not only that, but as of macOS Catalina, the default shell is the Z shell. While the Z shell should work fine for all of this book's examples, you might want to switch to bash to be on the safe side (you can always change it back later).

To install the right software, you'll use Homebrew, which is free and open source. Homebrew is a *package manager*, a tool used to install software on your computer from the shell. It's kind of like the App Store but for shell users.

First, go to *https://brew.sh* and follow the instructions to install Homebrew (see Figure A-12).

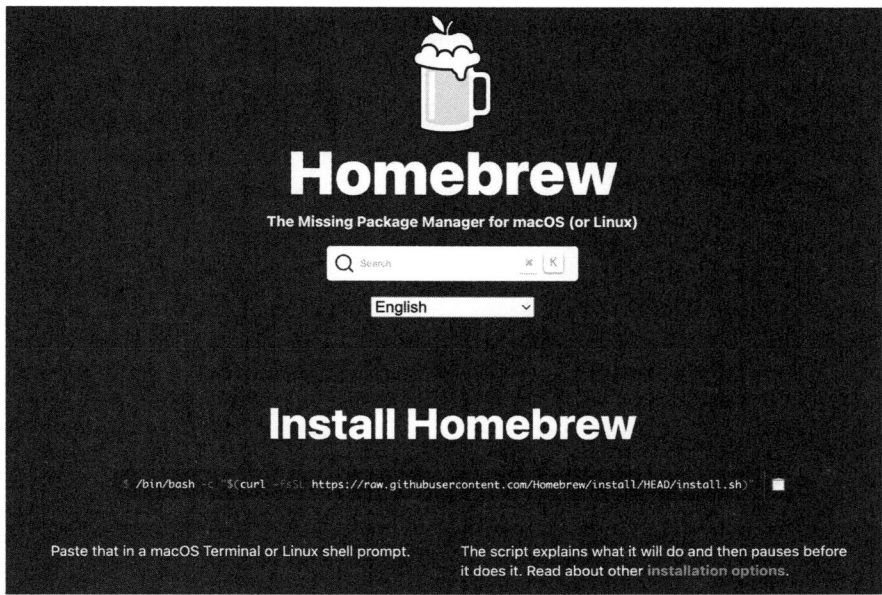

Figure A-12: The Homebrew installation instructions on its home page

In most cases, this will require opening the Terminal program and running a snippet like this:

```
% /bin/bash -c "$(curl -fsSL https://raw.githubusercontent.com/Homebrew/
install/HEAD/install.sh)"
```

NOTE *The exact code might have changed since the time of this writing, so check the website for the latest instructions. Be sure to use double quotes; otherwise, this command won't work properly.*

Once Homebrew is installed, install bash by running the following command in the shell:

```
% brew install bash
```

The brew command uses the newly installed Homebrew tool to install the bash program.

Next, you need to update your Terminal preferences to use the version of bash you've just installed, rather than the default. Open the Terminal program, go to **Terminal ▸ Settings ▸ General**, and set the shell location to */usr/local/bin/bash* (see Figure A-13).

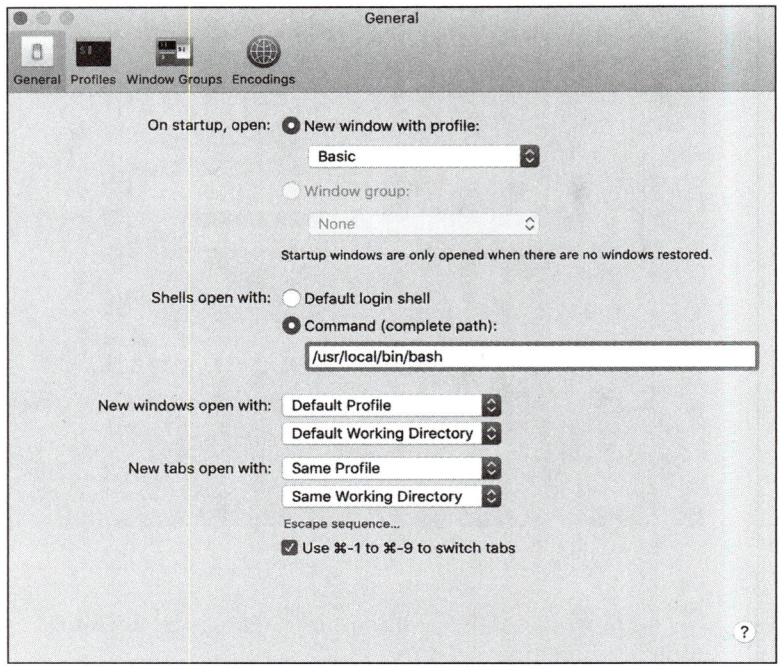

Figure A-13: Updating your Terminal settings to use the newly updated version of bash

Once you've made this change, open a new Terminal window and run `echo $BASH_VERSION` to confirm that it's running the latest version of bash, which should be version 5 or greater.

There's a more sophisticated way to change your system's default shell: with the special `chsh` ("change shell") command. Chapter 15 goes over this approach.

Linux

If you're running Linux, I assume you can open a terminal and set up the appropriate shell. You'll be able to follow along with the content in this book with any recent bash-like shell.

B

SHELL BASICS

Performing basic operations in the shell—such as navigating your filesystem, managing files and folders, copying and pasting text, and getting help—can be a bit daunting at first. This appendix is a quick-start guide to build your confidence with these tasks.

You can skip this appendix if you're comfortable running a shell, if you know what bash is, and if you can run basic commands like ls and cd.

Navigating Your Filesystem

Switching from a graphical user interface (GUI) to the shell can take some getting used to. We'll start by taking a look at how to navigate your filesystem and get information on files and folders using the shell.

This section will introduce the pwd, ls, pushd, popd, and cd commands, as well as the related concepts of directories, stacks, and paths. To follow

along, make sure you've downloaded and installed the *Effective Shell* samples
and tools by running this command:

```
$ curl effective.sh | sh
```

Note that the exact output you see will differ slightly from mine to
reflect your user and system information.

Identifying the Working Directory

When you open a folder in a GUI, you can see its contents and interact with
them (for example, by copying or moving files). In the shell, the same prin-
ciple applies: you're always working in a specific folder or directory. This is
the *working directory*, and any command you type will run here unless you
specify otherwise.

To find out your current working directory, use the pwd ("print working
directory") command:

```
$ pwd
/home/dwmkerr
```

Your output may be formatted slightly differently depending on your
operating system.

Listing the Contents of the Working Directory

In a GUI environment like the folder system on Windows and macOS, files
and folders in the current directory are normally represented as icons. In
the shell, you don't have this graphical view, so instead you use the ls ("list
directory contents") command to see the files and folders in your working
directory:

```
$ ls
Desktop     Downloads        fontconfig  Pictures  Templates
Documents   effective-shell  Music       Public    Videos
```

Again, you'll see different files and folders specific to your system.

Commands like ls and pwd can be combined with options that modify
how they work. For example, using the -l ("long") option with ls lists the
directory's contents with some extra detail:

```
$ ls -l
total 40
drwxr-xr-x  2 dwmkerr dwmkerr 4096 Apr  2 19:18 Desktop
drwxr-xr-x  2 dwmkerr dwmkerr 4096 Apr  2 19:18 Documents
drwxr-xr-x  2 dwmkerr dwmkerr 4096 Apr  2 19:18 Downloads
drwxr-xr-x 13 dwmkerr dwmkerr 4096 Apr  3 18:02 effective-shell
drwxr-xr-x  2 dwmkerr dwmkerr 4096 Apr  3 14:07 fontconfig
...
```

Adding the -l option indicates that you want more information than just the filenames and folder names, such as who owns the file or folder and when it was last modified. Many GUIs have a similar option.

Changing the Directory

To move to a new directory in the shell, you run the cd ("change directory") command. Here I move to my *pictures* folder within the *effective-shell* folder:

```
$ cd effective-shell/pictures
```

My working directory is now */home/dwmkerr/effective-shell/pictures*, which I can confirm by running pwd again:

```
$ pwd
/home/dwmkerr/effective-shell/pictures
```

Another common operation is to show *all* of the files in a directory, including any hidden files. In Linux systems, any file that starts with a dot is considered a hidden file and normally isn't shown when you list the contents of a folder or view the folder in a GUI.

To list all of the files in a folder, including hidden files, you use the ls command with both the -l option and the -a ("all") option. Here I list all of the files in my *pictures* folder:

```
$ ls -al
total 2364
drwxr-xr-x  2 dwmkerr dwmkerr    4096 Apr  3 16:43 .
drwxr-xr-x 12 dwmkerr dwmkerr    4096 Apr  3 18:42 ..
-rw-r--r--  1 dwmkerr dwmkerr 1899165 Apr  3 16:43 laos-gch.JPG
-rw-r--r--  1 dwmkerr dwmkerr  504568 Apr  3 16:43 nepal-mardi-himal.jpeg
-rw-r--r--  1 dwmkerr dwmkerr      61 Apr  3 16:43 .notes
```

The -a option tells the `ls` command *not* to hide files that start with a dot. As you can see, my *pictures* folder contains a hidden *.notes* file, as well as two special folders that I'll describe in "Navigating with the Dot and Double-Dot Folders" on page 397.

You might notice a pattern here: shell commands are typically very short, making them easier to enter quickly, and they're often made up of the first letters of the description of their purpose.

OPTIONS, PARAMETERS, FLAGS, AND ARGUMENTS

You've seen two options so far: the -1 and -a options for the `ls` command. Options are sometimes referred to as *flags*, *parameters*, or *arguments*. In most cases—and in this book—the terms are used interchangeably, although *flag* generally means a simple option you can switch on or off. Don't worry too much about which word is used; they all just refer to ways you can modify a command's default behavior.

Returning to the Home Directory

The *home directory* is a special folder where a user can keep their personal files, apart from the system files or files shared by all users.

In most systems, every user has their own home directory, and the contents of this directory are accessible only to that user. Generally, you can't see the contents of another user's home directory (unless you're a system administrator who updates the security settings to allow this, which would be very unlikely in practice). When you open a shell, it starts in the home directory by default. In most of the examples you've seen so far, my working directory has been my home directory, */home/dwmkerr*.

You'll likely use your home directory a lot since that's where most of your personal files will be. You can always move back to your home directory, no matter where you are, by running the `cd` command without any parameters. There's also a special shorthand you can use for it the tilde (~). For example, I could shorten the command

```
cd /home/dwmkerr/effective-shell
```

to this:

```
cd ~/effective-shell
```

As you can imagine, using the tilde shortcut can save you a lot of keystrokes over time.

Now that you can move around to different folders, let's talk a bit about how paths work.

Using Absolute and Relative Paths

A *path* is the location of a file or folder within the filesystem structure. There are two types of paths: absolute and relative.

An *absolute path* gives the exact location of a file—for example, */home/ dwmkerr/effective-shell*. Absolute paths always start with a slash. The first slash represents the *root* of the filesystem, or the single folder that every other folder lives in. If you come from a Windows background, you might be used to *drives*, such as *c:/* or *d:/*, instead of roots. On Linux, all files and folders live within one single root folder.

A *relative path* is expressed in relation to your current working directory, rather than the root, and does not start with a slash. For example, the relative path of a file in the */home/dwmkerr/effective-shell/pictures* folder would be *effective-shell/pictures/laos-gch.jpg*.

If I wanted to move into my *pictures* folder from a working directory other than my home directory, I would use an absolute path:

```
$ cd /home/dwmkerr/effective-shell/pictures
```

If I were already in my home directory (*/home/dwmkerr*), I could use a relative path instead:

```
$ cd effective-shell/pictures
```

As a rule of thumb, use relative paths to save yourself some typing when you want to move to a location within the current working directory. Use absolute paths when you need to move to somewhere completely outside your current working directory.

Moving Around Efficiently

You can use a few tricks to speed up your navigation and quickly move to particular directories.

Navigating with the Dot and Double-Dot Folders

When you combine the ls command with the -a and -1 flags to list *all* the contents of a folder in detail, you'll see two extra entries in the output: . (a single dot) and .. (two dots). These are two special folders that are added by the system but are typically hidden. Let's see how they work.

First, I'll list all of the files in my *effective-shell* folder in detail:

```
$ ls -al ~/effective-shell
total 52
drwxr-xr-x 12 dwmkerr dwmkerr 4096 Apr  3 19:54 .
drwxr-xr-x 18 dwmkerr dwmkerr 4096 Apr  3 19:54 ..
drwxr-xr-x  2 dwmkerr dwmkerr 4096 Apr  3 19:00 data
drwxr-xr-x  2 dwmkerr dwmkerr 4096 Apr  3 19:00 docs
drwxr-xr-x  3 dwmkerr dwmkerr 4096 Apr  3 19:00 logs
...
```

Displaying the output in a detailed list reveals the dot and double-dot folders. The dot folder represents the current folder, so in this case it's essentially an alias for the *effective-shell* folder. The dot folder can be useful because sometimes you'll want a quick way to say, "Right here—the folder I'm in right now!" in a command. For example, to copy the *effective-shell* folder to the *backups* folder, I can do the following:

```
$ cp -r . ~/backups
```

The `cp` command is the copy command. The `-r` ("recursive") option tells the shell to copy *recursively*, meaning it will copy the given folder and all of its contents. I'll discuss the `cp` command in more detail in "Copying a File" on page 404 and the box "Copy and Move Tips" on page 406. But one thing to note for now is that copying requires you to specify both the source folder and the destination folder. In this case, instead of typing out the full path of the source folder, I've used `.` to say "copy the current folder to ~/*backups*."

The double-dot folder is a shortcut to the folder just above the current folder in the file hierarchy, known as the *parent* folder. You'll use this shortcut frequently. For example, to quickly jump to the parent of the current working directory, you can type the following:

```
$ cd ..
```

This command tells the `cd` command to move "up" to the parent folder.

The double-dot folder can also be helpful to specify paths outside of your current working directory. Say I'm currently in the */home/dave/Downloads* folder. I can use this shortened command to move to the */home/dave/effective -shell* folder:

```
$ cd ../effective-shell
```

This is like saying, "Go up one level to the */home/dave* folder, then move into the *effective-shell* folder."

Because every folder has a dot and a double-dot folder, you can chain these commands together. For example, if I were in the */home/dwmkerr/ effective-shell/pictures* folder, I could move to */home* like so:

```
$ cd ../../..
```

This tells the shell to move up three folders from the current working directory.

Going Back to the Previous Directory

The `cd` command has a special option that lets you quickly go back to the previous working directory:

```
$ cd -
```

Running this command again would return you to the working directory where you started.

NOTE *You can also move to the last directory, second-to-last directory, and third-to-last directory with the commands* `cd -1`, `cd -2`, *and* `cd -3` *(and so on), respectively.*

The `cd -` command only really works to toggle between the directory you were in last and the one you're in now. If you need to go back and forth multiple times between folders or through a history of directories, using `pushd` and `popd` is a better option.

Pushing and Popping the Working Directory

You can quickly move from one location to another and back again with the `pushd` and `popd` commands. The `pushd` ("push directory") command moves you to a new folder but keeps a record of your current working directory. This way, you can easily move back afterward, using the `popd` ("pop directory") command. Let's look at this in practice.

Say I'm in my *pictures* folder and I want to quickly check my *Downloads* folder:

```
❶ $ pwd
  /home/dwmkerr/effective-shell/pictures
❷ $ pushd ~/Downloads
  $ pwd
  /home/dwmkerr/Downloads
❸ $ ls
  New-Wallpaper.jpeg
  effective-shell.zip
❹ $ popd
  $ pwd
  /home/dwmkerr/effective-shell/pictures
```

Let's break this down. First, I show my current working directory with the `pwd` command ❶. Then I "push" the *Downloads* folder ❷ and show my working directory again to verify that I'm now working in *Downloads*. I use `ls` to check which files are in this folder ❸. Finally, I "pop" back to where I started, *pictures*, and use the `pwd` command once again to confirm the move ❹.

You might be familiar with the concepts of pushing and popping if you've ever studied computing or programming, but if not, you're probably wondering where these terms come from. They have to do with the *directory stack*, the structure the shell uses to keep track of your current working directory. You can picture the directory stack as a stack of plates in a cafeteria. You can easily put plates on top of that stack but not in the middle or at the bottom. When you remove plates, you start by removing the top plate, then the next, and so on.

Take a look at Figure B-1, which illustrates the directory stack for the previous example.

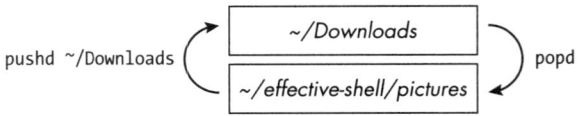

Figure B-1: The pushd and popd directory stack

When I used the pushd command, the shell recorded my current working directory (*/home/dwmkerr/effective-shell/pictures*) and then "pushed" the new location (the *Downloads* folder) to the top of the stack. Then, when I used the popd command, the shell "popped" *Downloads* off the top and moved to the location beneath it in the stack, the *pictures* folder. The item at the top of the stack is always your current working directory.

You can also run pushd without providing any parameters to *swap* the top two items on the stack. This is a handy trick to quickly switch between two directories you're working in regularly.

Now that you've seen some ways to move around your system more efficiently, let's take a look at how you can manage your files and folders.

Managing Your Files and Folders

In this section, you'll learn how to manipulate files and folders in the shell as you would in a GUI. Once you can organize your files, you'll be well on your way to using the shell more effectively for day-to-day tasks. Here you'll learn to download, unzip, copy, move, rename, and delete files.

Downloading a File

First, you'll download a playground area you can work in to avoid messing with your own personal files as you practice. I've created an *Effective Shell* playground folder and made it available as a ZIP file at *https://effective-shell.com/downloads/effective-shell.zip*. You could open a browser, download the file, unzip it, and start from there, but since this appendix is all about how to handle everyday tasks in your shell, you'll do it from the command line instead:

```
$ cd
$ wget https://effective-shell.com/downloads/effective-shell.zip

--2025-01-18 16:45:37-- https://effective-shell.com/downloads/effective-shell.zip
Resolving effective-shell.com (effective-shell.com)... 185.199.110.153, 185.199.111.153,
185.199.108.153, ...
Connecting to effective-shell.com (effective-shell.com)|185.199.110.153|:443... connected.
HTTP request sent, awaiting response... 200 OK
Length: 4881890 (4.7M) [application/zip]
Saving to: 'effective-shell.zip'

effective-shell.zip
100%[===============================================================================================>]
4.66M  1.70MB/s  in 2.7s

2025-01-18 16:45:42 (1.70 MB/s) - 'effective-shell.zip' saved [4881890/4881890]
```

First, using the `cd` command with no parameters moves you to your home directory. Then, the `wget` ("web get") command downloads the playground content at the given web address to your working directory. It also shows a progress indicator, which is especially useful if you're downloading a large file.

COMMAND NOT FOUND ERRORS

Not every command is available out of the box on every system. If you get a command not found error for wget or any other command covered in this section, install it for your particular system like so (if you're using the Windows Subsystem for Linux, follow the instructions for the flavor of Linux you have installed):

Debian, Ubuntu, Mint

```
sudo apt install update
sudo apt install -y command
```

RHEL, Fedora, CentOS

```
sudo yum install command
```

SuSE, OpenSusE

```
sudo zipper install command
```

Arch/MSYS2

```
sudo pacman -S command
```

macOS

```
brew install command
```

Cygwin

```
setup-x86_64.exe -q -P command
```

Be sure to replace *command* with the missing one when you run this in your shell. If your distribution isn't listed here, check its documentation for instructions on installing packages.

To specify a particular folder in which to download a file, use `wget` with the `-O` ("output file") parameter followed by the destination path:

```
$ wget https://effective-shell.com/downloads/effective-shell.zip -O ~/effective-shell.zip
```

To check that the file has downloaded, use the `ls` command with the tilde shortcut and the asterisk (*) wildcard character to see all the ZIP files in your home directory:

```
$ ls ~/*.zip
/home/dwmkerr/effective-shell.zip
```

Congratulations! You've successfully downloaded the ZIP file to your home directory.

NOTE *You'll learn more about wildcard characters in "Working with Wildcards" on page 409.*

Unzipping a File

You know this download is a ZIP file because it ends in *.zip*, but say the extension was missing. To learn more about a file, you can use the `file` ("determine file type") command with the file location like so:

```
$ file ~/effective-shell.zip
/home/dwmkerr/effective-shell.zip: Zip archive data, at least v1.0 to extract
```

The output of the `file` command will vary based on the type of file. This output tells you that the file is a *ZIP archive* (a collection of files and folders bundled together into one file for easier sharing) that has been compressed with version 1 of the ZIP format. To extract the files and folders this archive contains, you'll need to *unzip* it.

First, use `cd ~` to navigate to the directory the file is in, which should be the home directory. Then unzip the playground folder with the `unzip` ("unzip archive") command:

```
$ unzip effective-shell.zip

Archive:   /home/dwmkerr/effective-shell.zip
   creating: effective-shell /
   creating: effective-shell /data/
  inflating: effective-shell /data/top100.csv
...
```

Running `unzip` prints the name of each file and folder as it unzips. To check that the folder has been unzipped, use `ls` to list the contents of the current working directory:

```
$ ls
...
effective-shell.zip
effective-shell
...
```

You should see a folder named *effective-shell* in the list, as well as the *effective-shell.zip* file you downloaded. This confirms that you've successfully unzipped the playground file and now have a folder named *effective-shell* containing its contents. You no longer need the ZIP file, so read on to learn how to delete it.

Deleting a File

Now that you've extracted the contents of the ZIP file you downloaded, delete it with the rm ("remove") command as follows:

```
$ rm ~/effective-shell.zip
```

If you were to list the contents of the working directory now, you'd no longer see the ZIP file.

WARNING *Be very careful with the rm command. Unlike in a GUI environment, deleted files aren't moved into a recycle bin where you could still retrieve them if you needed to; they're gone forever. In Chapter 15, you'll see some ways to customize this behavior, but as a rule of thumb, only use the rm command to remove files you want to delete for good.*

By default, the rm command deletes only files, so it will fail if you try to delete a folder:

```
$ rm ~/effective-shell
rm: /home/dwmkerr/effective-shell: is a directory
```

You'll see how to delete a folder shortly.

You can use the -i ("interactive") flag with the rm command to delete *interactively*, meaning you'll be shown a prompt for each file in the target directory and offered the option to delete it or not:

```
$ rm -i ./effective-shell/data/*
rm: remove regular file 'effective-shell/data/top100.csv'?
```

Notice the use of the wildcard * to find all the file types in the *data* folder (see "Working with Wildcards" on page 409 for more on this character). When the shell asks you to confirm that you want to delete a file, enter y to delete it or n to keep it.

Viewing a Directory Tree

The useful command tree allows you to see a treelike view of a directory and its contents, similar to a GUI representation of a filesystem.

NOTE *The tree command is not installed on all systems by default, so if you get a command not found error message when you try to run it, follow the installation instructions in the "Command Not Found Errors" box on page 401.*

Let's take a look at the playground folder:

```
$ tree ~/effective-shell

/home/dwmkerr/effective-shell
├── data
│   └── top100.csv
├── logs
│   ├── apm-logs
│   │   ├── apm00.logs
│   │   ├── apm01.logs
├── pictures
│   ├── laos-gch.JPG
│   └── nepal-mardi-himal.jpeg
├── programs
│   └── web-server
│       └── web-server.js
├── quotes
│   ├── iain-banks.txt
│   └── ursula-le-guin.txt
...

11 directories, 18 files
```

I've abbreviated this output for readability, so on your system you'll likely see a lot more files and folders.

If you want more information about a particular file, you can use the file command, as mentioned earlier.

Copying a File

I talked briefly about the cp command in "Navigating with the Dot and Double-Dot Folders" on page 397. The cp command takes the form

```
cp source destination
```

where *source* is the name of the file you want to copy and *destination* is the new location and name for the file.

Now you'll try it out to make a copy of one of the files in the *pictures* folder. First, move to the *pictures* folder and then list its contents:

```
$ cd ~/effective-shell/pictures
$ ls
laos-gch.JPG            nepal-mardi-himal.jpeg
```

Then, use cp as follows to make a copy of the *loas-gch.JPG* photo:

```
$ cp laos-gch.JPG laos-gch-copy.JPG
```

You can confirm that you've made a copy by listing the contents of the current working directory:

```
$ ls
laos-gch-copy.JPG
laos-gch.JPG
nepal-mardi-himal.jpeg
```

You can use relative or absolute paths for the source and destination files.

Renaming and Moving Files

The mv ("move") command renames or moves files, and like cp it follows the form *source destination*. To rename your newly copied image file with the extension *.jpeg*, run the following:

```
$ mv laos-gch-copy.JPG laos-gch-copy.jpeg
```

Then run ls again to see the results:

```
$ ls
laos-gch-copy.jpeg
laos-gch.JPG
nepal-mardi-himal.jpeg
```

As you can see, your copied file has been renamed, or "moved" into the same folder under a new name. You can also use mv to move a file to another folder and change its name in one step. Move your copied image file to the *tmp* folder and change its name again like so:

```
$ mv laos-gch-copy.jpeg /tmp/climbing-photo-backup.jpeg
```

You've moved the *loas-gch-copy.jpeg* file from *pictures* to *tmp* and renamed it to *climbing-photo-backup.jpeg* in one operation.

COPY AND MOVE TIPS

You'll see the copy and move commands a lot throughout the book, so let's go over a few tips to make working with them easier.

First, remember that the cp and mv commands both have the basic structure *source destination*. When you're copying or moving (renaming) a file inside the working directory, you don't need to provide a destination folder path:

```
cp file1 file2
mv file1 filenew
```

The first command makes a copy of *file1* in the working directory and names it *file2*. The second command renames *file1* to *filenew* in the working directory.

If you're copying or moving a file to a different folder, you don't need to provide the new filename unless you *want* to rename the file; you can just provide the destination folder path:

```
cp filenew ~/backups
mv file3 ~/backups
```

The first command copies *filenew* from the working directory to the *backups* folder in your home directory. The second command moves *file3* from the working directory to the *backups* folder in your home directory. In both cases, the filename doesn't change because you haven't specified a new one.

When copying a folder, you must add the -r flag to copy the folder and all of its contents; otherwise, only the folder itself would be copied. Here's an example:

```
cp -r ~/backups ~/backups.old
```

This makes a copy of the *backups* folder, including all of its contents, in your home directory and names it *backups.old*.

The mv command doesn't require the -r flag:

```
mv somefolder newfolder
```

This command renames the *somefolder* folder to *newfolder* in the working directory; none of the folder's contents are lost.

Finally, remember that you can mix and match relative and absolute paths:

```
cp -r /home/dwmkerr/backups ./backups
mv scripts/test-script.sh /tmp
```

In the first example, I'm copying the *backups* folder from my home directory to my current working directory. The source path (the first parameter) is an absolute path, as indicated by the opening slash, and the destination path (the second parameter) is a relative path that explicitly uses the dot folder.

In the second example, I'm moving a file from the *scripts* folder in my current working directory to the system's *tmp* folder. The first path is relative; the second is absolute.

In general, when using these commands, use the form you find easiest to type and understand.

Creating a Folder

The `mkdir` ("make directory") command creates a new folder. Move back into the *~/effective-shell* folder and run `mkdir` to create a new folder called *photos* as follows:

```
$ cd ~/effective-shell
$ mkdir photos
```

Then run tree like so to see the results:

```
$ tree -L 1
.
├── data
├── logs
├── pictures
├── photos
├── programs
├── quotes
├── scripts
├── text
└── websites

9 directories, 0 files
```

The `-L` ("level") parameter specifies how many levels of folders you want to see. By setting the level to 1, you're indicating that you want to see only the immediate children (subfolders) of the *effective-shell* folder. You can also see that you've successfully created the new *photos* folder. Running `ls -l` would show you that the new *photos* folder has a more recent date than the others.

Now you'll organize your photos by year and topic. Say you want to create a *2019* subfolder containing an *outdoors* subfolder, which in turn contains a *climbing* subfolder, so that you have the folder structure *photos/2019/outdoors/climbing*. In most GUIs, you'd have to create each subfolder one at a time. In the shell, however, you can create nested folders with a single command:

```
$ mkdir -p photos/2019/outdoors/climbing
$ tree photos
photos
└── 2019
    └── outdoors
        └── climbing

directories, 0 files
```

The -p flag means "create intermediate directories," but it's easier to remember as "-p for *parent*": you're creating the *climbing* folder and its parent folders as well.

You're starting to see how working in a shell can be more efficient than using your GUI. Now create another set of directories for 2020 climbing photos:

```
$ mkdir -p photos/2020/outdoors/climbing
$ tree photos
photos
├── 2019
│   └── outdoors
│       └── climbing
└── 2020
    └── outdoors
        └── climbing

6 directories, 0 files
```

Notice that mkdir did not delete or replace the *photos* directory. If you provide the -p flag, mkdir will check whether the parent directories already exist and create them only if need be. If you don't include the -p flag, but the parent directory already exists, the shell assumes you're making a mistake and shows an error.

Creating a File

The purpose of the touch ("create files and set access times") command is twofold: it's used to create a new file without any content and to update an existing file's *timestamp*, a record of the last time someone opened or changed ("touched") the file. Here's how it works:

```
$ touch ~/my-notes.txt
```

This command creates a new, empty file in the home directory called *my-notes.txt*. If a file by that name had already existed, touch would simply have updated its "last access" and "last modified" times to the current time. You can see the last modified time by running ls -l:

```
$ ls -l ~
...
-rw-r--r--  1 dwmkerr  staff  1899165 Aug  21 22:20 my-notes.txt
...
```

The last modified time—which, in this case, is the same as the file creation time—is 11:20 PM on August 21.

Using touch is just one way to create a file in the shell; you'll see many
others throughout the book.

Working with Wildcards

A *wildcard* is a special symbol that represents more than one character.
The most common wildcard is the asterisk, which represents any sequence
of characters. You've seen it already, such as in "Downloading a File" on
page 400, where you used ls ~/*.zip to find files that end in *.zip* in your
home directory. Now you'll use it to copy all the files from the *pictures*
folder into the *photos/2019/outdoors/climbing* folder:

```
$ cp pictures/* photos/2019/outdoors/climbing/

$ tree photos
photos
├── 2019
│   └── outdoors
│       └── climbing
│           ├── laos-gch-copy.jpeg
│           ├── laos-gch.JPG
│           └── nepal-mardi-himal.jpeg
└── 2020
    └── outdoors
        └── climbing

6 directories, 3 files
```

Here the * represents everything and anything, so everything from
pictures is copied. You can also use wildcards to filter on file type, as you did
with *.zip earlier, or to filter on filename, such as l* for any files starting with
l (which would match *laos-gch-copy.jpeg* and *laos-gch.JPG* but not *nepal-mardi
-himal.jpeg*, which contains two *l*s but doesn't *start* with one). You'll learn
about other wildcards throughout the book.

Deleting a Folder

The rmdir ("remove directory") command deletes folders. Now that you have
your more organized *photos/2019/outdoors/climbing* folder, you can delete the
pictures folder:

```
$ rmdir pictures
rmdir: pictures: Directory not empty
```

As you can see, rmdir will fail if the directory isn't empty to prevent you from unintentionally deleting any files or folders it contains. To remedy this, use a wildcard to delete all the files in the *pictures* folder, then delete the folder itself:

```
$ rm pictures/*
$ rmdir pictures
```

The *pictures* folder has now been deleted. You can also delete the folder and its contents with one single command by using the -r parameter:

```
$ rm -r pictures
```

You can use whichever method you prefer. Most people use rm -r as it will delete the folder whether it's empty or not, but I suggest you use rmdir to be certain you don't delete files unintentionally—it gives you a bit of a safety net and reminds you to check the files inside first!

One final folder trick: if you decide you don't want the *2020/outdoors/ climbing* directory, you can use rmdir -p to remove the empty folder and any empty parents:

```
$ rmdir -p photos/2020/outdoors/climbing
rmdir: photos: Directory not empty

$ tree photos
photos
└── 2019
    └── outdoors
        └── climbing
            ├── laos-gch-copy.jpeg
            ├── laos-gch.JPG
            └── nepal-mardi-himal.jpeg

3 directories, 3 files
```

This command deleted *2020/outdoors/climbing* but stopped at the *photos* folder because that folder still contains *2019* and its subfolders.

Showing Text Content

The cat ("concatenate") command writes out the contents of one or many text files. This is a handy way to see the text in a file without leaving the shell. For example, the *effective-shell* playground's *quotes* folder contains two *.txt* files:

```
$ ls quotes
iain-banks.txt        ursula-le-guin.txt
```

Using cat, write out the contents of the *ursula-le-guin.txt* file to the screen like so:

```
$ cat quotes/ursula-le-guin.txt
"What sane person could live in this world and not be crazy?"
- Ursula K. Le Guin
```

You can give the cat command many files, and it will write them all out. To write out all the text from all the *quotes* files, use the * wildcard:

```
$ cat quotes/*
"The trouble with writing fiction is that it has to make sense, whereas real life doesn't."
- Iain M. Banks
"What sane person could live in this world and not be crazy?"
- Ursula K. Le Guin
```

You can also use the cat command to join, or *concatenate*, the contents of many files together:

```
$ cat quotes/* > quotes/all-quotes.txt
```

This command moves the content of all the *quotes* files into a single *all-quotes.txt* file. You can check the folder's contents with tree quotes or ls quotes.

The > is a *redirection operator* that tells the shell to write to a file instead of to the screen. If the file you're moving the content to doesn't exist, the shell will create it for you. Redirection is a big theme in Part I, and you'll be seeing a lot more of the cat command there as well.

Zipping a File

Earlier you used the unzip command to extract the zipped playground file you downloaded. You've made a lot of changes to the playground folder since then, so you'll finish off this section by using the zip command to zip up the whole folder:

```
$ zip -r new-playground.zip .
```

The -r flag tells zip to zip the folder you specify and all of its contents. As its first parameter, the zip command takes the name and location of the file you want to create—in this example, *new-playground.zip*. Then you pass the files or folders you want to zip. Here, the dot folder specifies that you want to zip the current folder, so make sure you're in the top-level *effective-shell* folder before you execute the command.

You can also give zip more than one file or folder. To zip both the *quotes* and the *photos* folders, run this command:

```
$ zip -r images-and-words.zip photos quotes
```

The more you use zip and the other commands I've described here, the more familiar the parameters will become. But if you get stuck, help is readily available. See "Getting Help" on page 415.

The Clipboard

Different shell environments and operating systems manage the clipboard in different ways. Being able to quickly copy and paste to and from the shell is essential to using it effectively. This section will explain how the clipboard works on different systems and how to create your own clipboard commands that will work across systems.

Mastering Clipboard Essentials

You're probably familiar with the common keyboard shortcuts to copy and paste content to and from the clipboard: CTRL-C and CTRL-V on Linux and Windows, and ⌘-C and ⌘-V on macOS. However, these commands don't work the same way in every shell. For example, here I've tried to use CTRL-V a few times to paste into a terminal on Ubuntu:

```
$ ^V^V^V
```

Instead of pasting the contents of the clipboard into the shell, this key combination has written the characters ^V to the terminal. Why is this?

One reason is historical (the shell has been around for a long time, so you'll see this answer a lot). Using CTRL in a shell sends a *signal*—a special command the shell uses to control programs. Specifically, by using CTRL you're signaling your intention to perform an action rather than enter text with your next keystroke. Most modern operating systems have adopted this convention. For example, CTRL-S is used almost universally as a shortcut for the save command.

Modern shells tend to follow the conventions established by earlier shells to ensure a consistent experience for users. Both CTRL-C and CTRL-V have long had specific meanings in the shell that predate the current copy and paste shortcuts. Using CTRL-C cancels a running program by telling the shell to send an *interrupt signal* to the program, which terminates it. You'll see signals again and again throughout the book.

What about CTRL-V? This is the fancy-sounding *verbatim insert* command. It tells the shell to write out the subsequent keystroke directly to the screen rather than interpreting it as a CTRL command. By using CTRL-V, you can write out special characters like the escape key, left or right keys, and even the CTRL-V combination itself as in the previous example.

If you type CTRL-V twice, the shell writes out the text ^V. The caret or hat symbol (^) represents CTRL. The first CTRL-V tells the shell to write out the following command, so the second CTRL-V is written out *verbatim*, meaning the text representation of the command is displayed.

You can try writing out some different sequences. You'll see various odd-looking symbols for special keys like the ALT key.

Because the shell is already using the keyboard combinations you'd normally use for clipboard commands, you'll need alternatives for those functions. Follow the instructions I've provided next for your particular platform.

Windows

If you're using Command Prompt, then the usual shortcuts will work fine. However, if you are using Windows Subsystem for Linux (WSL) and bash, you will need to tweak the configuration.

To set up an alternative, go to **Properties ▸ Options**, select **Use Ctrl+Shift+C/V as Copy/Paste**, and click **OK**. You can now use CTRL-SHIFT-C for copy and CTRL-SHIFT-V for paste. To select text, hold down the right mouse button and drag over it.

Linux

On most Linux systems, you'll be using GNOME Terminal or KDE's Konsole, which means that you can use CTRL-SHIFT-C for copy and CTRL-SHIFT-V for paste. To select text, hold down the right mouse button and drag over it, or right-click the text.

macOS

Mac users can just use ⌘-C for copy and ⌘ -V for paste. The shell doesn't recognize the special Mac command character ⌘, so these shortcuts don't clash with any existing ones. To select text, hold down the left mouse button and drag over it.

Creating Custom Clipboard Commands

Copying and pasting text to and from the clipboard is useful, but you can do a lot more. With a couple of basic commands, you can hugely expand your capabilities and make everyday tasks far easier to accomplish. However, there's one small hurdle to clear first: the clipboard is accessed in different ways on Windows, Linux, and macOS. In other words, there's no standard tool you can use across all three platforms to manage the clipboard.

To address this problem, I'll walk Windows and Linux users through creating two clipboard commands that will work across platforms: pbcopy and pbpaste. If you're a Mac user, you don't need to do anything; pbcopy and pbpaste are built in to macOS.

Windows

Assuming you're using WSL, you'll need to run the following two commands:

```
$ alias pbcopy="clip.exe"
$ alias pbpaste="powershell.exe -command Get-Clipboard | tr -d '\r' | head -n -1"
```

Don't worry for now about how these commands work; by the time you've gone through the book, they should make perfect sense.

Linux

On Linux, first you'll install the `xclip` program and then set up the `pbcopy` and `pbpaste` commands to use it:

```
$ sudo apt install -y xclip
$ alias pbcopy="xclip -selection c"
$ alias pbpaste="xclip -selection c -o"
```

If you're already confident with how `xclip` works and want to use it directly, there's no need to run these commands.

For both Windows and Linux, you've used the `alias` command to create `pbcopy` and `pbpaste`. In bash (and most shells), an *alias* is a shortcut for a longer command.

NOTE   *You'll need to repeat these instructions every time you close and reopen your terminal. Chapter 15 explains how to make permanent customizations to your shell so that you don't have to repeat this setup.*

Copying and Pasting with pbcopy and pbpaste

Now you can use the `pbcopy` and `pbpaste` commands to access the clipboard from the shell.

The *~/effective-shell* folder contains a text file with the names of some characters from the TV show *The Simpsons*. Open *simpsons-characters.txt* in your text editor and copy the following text from it:

```
Kirk Van Houten
Timothy Lovejoy
Artie Ziff
```

Then paste it into the shell as follows:

```
$ pbpaste
Kirk Van Houten
Timothy Lovejoy
Artie Ziff
```

Rather than copying the text by opening your text editor (which breaks you out of your shell flow), you could use the cat command to write the entire contents of the *simpsons-characters.txt* file to the screen and then manually select the text and copy it. However, this approach is fiddly and wouldn't be convenient if the file was large and you had to scroll to find text.

Instead, you'll use a *pipeline* to pass the output of the cat command into the pbcopy command:

```
$ cat ~/effective-shell/text/simpsons-characters.txt | pbcopy
```

Now try pasting—you should see the contents of the file.

The | symbol is the *pipe* operator, which is used to "chain" commands together in a *pipeline*. Here, the pipe tells the shell to take the output from the command on the left and send it straight to the input of the program on the right. Pipelines are covered in detail in Chapter 2, and you'll see them in use throughout the book.

Getting Help

Being able to access help quickly, without jumping to a browser and disrupting your flow, is one of the most crucial things you can do to become an effective shell user. A wealth of information is available directly in the shell, only a few keystrokes away.

This section will introduce you to the man ("manual") command, the standard help system available on all Unix-like systems. You'll also learn about a useful tool you can install called tldr, which might be more helpful for day-to-day use. Finally, we'll take a look at the *cht.sh* site for those circumstances when you do need to access a browser for help.

Using the Manual

The man command can help you with tools, commands, and concepts. Most tools you encounter in the shell have manual pages (*man pages* for short) available.

The most basic way to get help with a command is by entering the command name as the first parameter of man:

```
$ man cp
```

```
CP(1)                     BSD General Commands Manual                     CP(1)

NAME
     cp -- copy files

SYNOPSIS
     cp [-R [-H | -L | -P]] [-fi | -n] [-apvX] source_file target_file
     cp [-R [-H | -L | -P]] [-fi | -n] [-apvX] source_file ...
        target_directory

DESCRIPTION
     In the first synopsis form, the cp utility copies the contents of the
     source_file to the target_file. In the second synopsis form, the
     contents of each named source_file is copied to the destination
     target_directory. The names of the files themselves are not changed. If
     cp detects an attempt to copy a file to itself, the copy will fail.

...
```

This opens the man page for the cp command, detailing all of its command line options and specifics on how to use it. This information can be rather lengthy, but fortunately the shell includes a feature to help you navigate it.

QUICKLY CHECKING PARAMETERS

If you just need to check what parameters are available for a command, you can often skip the man page. Simply enter the name of the command followed by a hyphen (-) and then press TAB. Try it out by entering **mkdir** - and then pressing TAB. You should see the following output:

```
-m  -- set permission mode
-p  -- make parent directories as needed
-v  -- print message for each created directory
```

This convenient shortcut gives you only the information you need and thus can be much easier to navigate than a man page.

The Pager

The shell uses a tool called a *pager* that allows you to use the arrow keys to scroll through content that doesn't easily fit on a screen, such as man pages. In other words, the pager provides the keyboard interface to look through the file.

On most systems, this pager is the less program. These are the most common commands for navigating through files with less:

d Scroll down half a page.

u Scroll up half a page.

j/k Scroll down or up a line. You can also use the arrow keys for this.

q Quit.

/searchterm Search for the text specified after the forward slash.

n When searching, find the next occurrence.

N When searching, find the previous occurrence.

Alternative pagers are available (on many Unix-like systems, you'll have less, more, and most), but in general, less will provide what you need.

Builtins

Sometimes you will look up a command in the manual and get the "built-ins" page:

```
$ man cd
BUILTIN(1)              BSD General Commands Manual              BUILTIN(1)

NAME
     builtin, !, %, ., :, @, {, }, alias, alloc, bg, bind, bindkey, break,
     breaksw, builtins, case, cd, chdir, command, complete, continue,

...
```

This happens when the command you are looking up—cd, in this case—is a built-in shell command rather than a program with a man page. Most shells still offer a way to get help with such commands. For example, bash has the help command:

```
$ help cd
cd: cd [-L|[-P [-e]] [-@]] [dir]
    Change the shell working directory.

    Change the current directory to DIR. The default DIR is the value of the
    HOME shell variable.

...
```

NOTE *The Z shell doesn't have an equivalent of the* help *command for builtins. Instead, it has a set of man pages. To get help on builtins, use* man zshbuiltins. *Type* man zsh *and press* TAB *to see a list of suggested topics.*

This is all I'll say about help for now, but you'll see it used where appropriate throughout the book.

Manual Sections

In man pages, you'll often see tools listed with numbers after them. Take a look at man less as an example:

```
$ man less
LESS(1)                                                          LESS(1)



NAME
        less - opposite of more
...
```

The number after less is the manual's *section*, which is used to categorize certain help topics. On most Unix-like systems, you can find the section definitions in the manual documentation by running man man. Here's a snippet of what you might see:

```
- **Section 1 - Executable programs or shell commands
- **Section 2 - System calls (functions provided by the kernel)
- **Section 3 - Library calls (functions within program libraries)
- **Section 4 - Special files (usually found in `/dev`)
- **Section 5 - File formats and conventions (e.g. `/etc/passwd`)
Section 6 - Games
Section 7 - Miscellaneous (including macro packages and conventions), e.g. `man(7)`,`groff(7)`
Section 8 - System administration commands (usually only for root)
Section 9 - Kernel routines (Non standard)
```

You can specify which section of the manual to search (for example, if there's an entry in multiple sections) by running the following:

```
$ man sectionnumber searchterm
```

To get more information about a section itself, open its intro page like so:

```
$ man 1 intro
INTRO(1)                    BSD General Commands Manual                    INTRO(1)

NAME
     intro -- introduction to general commands (tools and utilities)

DESCRIPTION
     Section one of the manual contains most of the commands which comprise...
```

In general, you won't need to worry about the section specifics unless you're looking for a tool that has an entry in more than one section or you need to look up the section number that appeared in online or offline documentation for the tool.

Man Page Titles and Summaries

You can search man page titles and summaries like so:

```
$ man -k cpu
cpuwalk.d(1m)                 - Measure which CPUs a process runs on. Uses DTrace
dispqlen.d(1m)                - dispatcher queue length by CPU. Uses DTrace
gasm(n), grammar::me::cpu::gasm(n) - ME assembler
```

You can also use the apropos or whatis commands to search through the manuals. However, for simplicity's sake, just remember man -k!

Summarizing Output with tldr

Say you want to compress some files. You know you can do this with the zip command, but you've forgotten the syntax, so you run man zip as follows:

```
$ man zip
ZIP(1L)                                                                  ZIP(1L)

NAME
      zip - package and compress (archive) files

SYNOPSIS
      zip [-aABcdDeEfFghjklLmoqrRSTuvVwXyz!@$] [--longoption ...] [-b path] [-n suffixes]
      [-t date] [-tt date] [zipfile [file ...]] [-xi list]
```

```
zipcloak (see separate man page)

zipnote (see separate man page)

zipsplit (see separate man page)

Note: Command line processing in zip has been changed to support long options and
handle all options and arguments more consistently. Some old command lines that
depend on command line inconsistencies may no longer work.
```

DESCRIPTION

```
zip is a compression and file packaging utility for Unix, VMS, MSDOS, OS/2, Windows
9x/NT/XP, Minix, Atari, Macintosh, Amiga, and Acorn RISC OS.  It is analogous to a
combination of the Unix commands tar(1) and compress(1) and is compatible with PKZIP
(Phil Katz's ZIP for MSDOS systems).

A companion program (unzip(1L)) unpacks zip archives. The zip and unzip(1L) programs
can work with archives produced by PKZIP (supporting most PKZIP features up to PKZIP
version 4.6), and PKZIP and PKUNZIP can work with archives produced by zip (with some
exceptions, notably streamed archives, but recent changes in the zip file standard
may facilitate better compatibility). zip version 3.0 is compatible with PKZIP 2.04
```

Wow, that's a lot of detail—and this is just the first page of about 30!
Now compare that to this output from the tldr (short for "too long,
didn't read") tool:

```
$ tldr zip
zip

Package and compress (archive) files into a Zip archive.
See also: `unzip`.
More information: <https://manned.org/zip>.

- Add files/directories to a specific archive ([r]ecursively):
    zip -r path/to/compressed.zip path/to/file_or_directory1 path/to/file_or_directory2 ...

- Remove files/directories from a specific archive ([d]elete):
    zip -d path/to/compressed.zip path/to/file_or_directory1 path/to/file_or_directory2 ...
```

The first example is exactly what you're looking for. More information
is shown later on, and for some more complex details, you might have to go
to the manual, but this is great for the basics.

The tldr tool is available on most package managers, including Homebrew
and Apt. It's open source and community maintained. You can find instructions for installing it at *https://tldr.sh*.

Accessing Online Cheat Sheets

One final resource well worth sharing is cheat.sh (*https://www.cheat.sh*), a fantastic online collection of "cheatsheets" covering tools, programming languages, and more. But its real beauty lies in how it integrates into the shell. To see what I mean, run the following command:

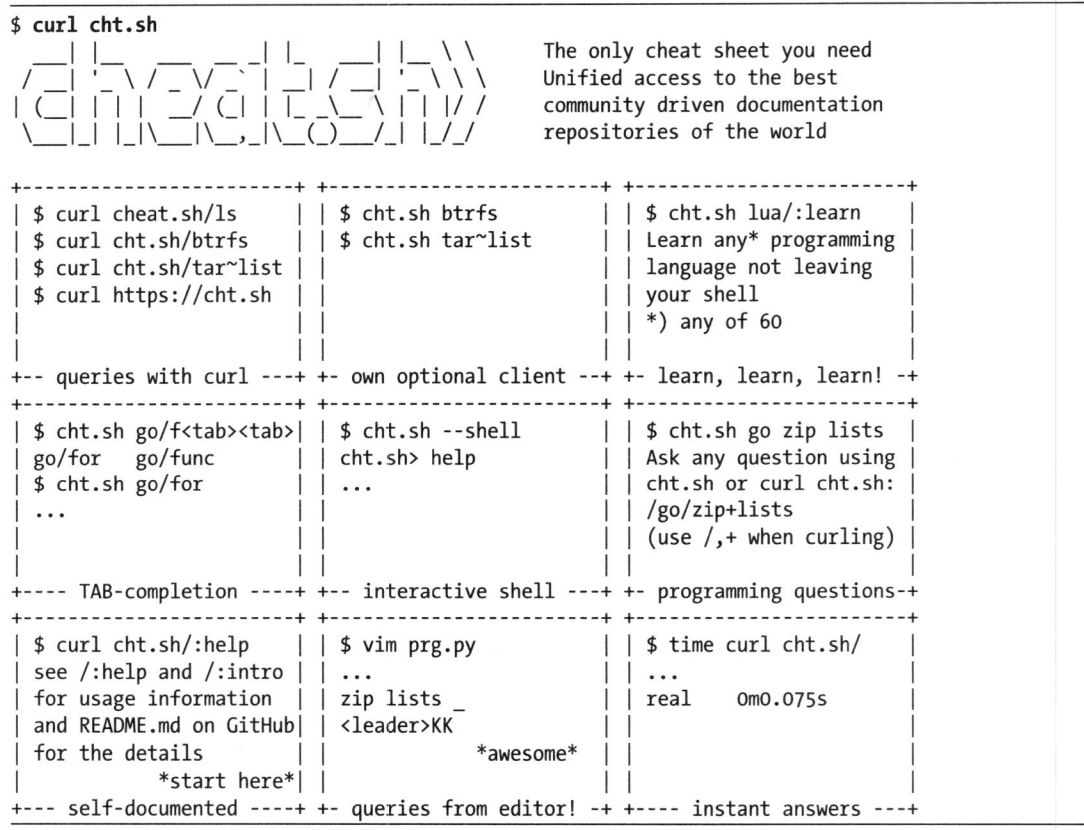

```
$ curl cht.sh
   __| |_  ___ __ _| |_   ___| |_\ \
  / _| ' \/ -_) _` |  _| / _| ' \ \ \
 | (__| || | _/\__,_| __| __\_\ | | |/ /
  \___|_||_\___|,_|\_(_)__/_| |_|/_/

The only cheat sheet you need
Unified access to the best
community driven documentation
repositories of the world
```

```
+-----------------------+  +-----------------------+  +-----------------------+
| $ curl cheat.sh/ls    |  | $ cht.sh btrfs        |  | $ cht.sh lua/:learn   |
| $ curl cht.sh/btrfs   |  | $ cht.sh tar~list     |  | Learn any* programming|
| $ curl cht.sh/tar~list|  |                       |  | language not leaving  |
| $ curl https://cht.sh |  |                       |  | your shell            |
|                       |  |                       |  | *) any of 60          |
|                       |  |                       |  |                       |
+-- queries with curl ---+ +- own optional client --+ +- learn, learn, learn! -+
+-----------------------+  +-----------------------+  +-----------------------+
| $ cht.sh go/f<tab><tab|  | $ cht.sh --shell      |  | $ cht.sh go zip lists |
| go/for   go/func      |  | cht.sh> help          |  | Ask any question using|
| $ cht.sh go/for       |  | ...                   |  | cht.sh or curl cht.sh:|
| ...                   |  |                       |  | /go/zip+lists         |
|                       |  |                       |  | (use /,+ when curling)|
|                       |  |                       |  |                       |
+---- TAB-completion ----+ +--- interactive shell ---+ +- programming questions-+
+-----------------------+  +-----------------------+  +-----------------------+
| $ curl cht.sh/:help   |  | $ vim prg.py          |  | $ time curl cht.sh/   |
| see /:help and /:intro|  | ...                   |  | ...                   |
| for usage information |  | zip lists _           |  | real    0m0.075s      |
| and README.md on GitHub| | <leader>KK           |  |                       |
| for the details       |  |           *awesome*   |  |                       |
|           *start here*|  |                       |  |                       |
+--- self-documented ----+ +- queries from editor! -+ +---- instant answers ---+
```

The curl command, which you'll see again and again, is a tool for downloading content from the web. If you load cheat.sh (or its shortened version, cht.sh) from the shell, you get a text version of the website. You can then look at all sorts of content by following the guide shown.

The cheat.sh website aggregates many data sources—including tldr. This means you can get information on tools without even having to install them locally.

Now *that* can be a real time saver!

INDEX

Symbols

& (ampersand), 24

&& (and) operator, 145

* (asterisk)
  parameter variable, 178
  regex quantifier, 51
  wildcard character, 16, 34, 49, 124, 264, 304, 359, 402

@ (at sign), 49, 51–52
  parameter variable, 178, 179

\ (backslash), 37, 55, 88, 112, 264
  looping through lines in a file, 167
  starting continuation using, 229

` (backtick), 306, 359

{} (braces), 104, 105
  in variable syntax, 127
  in xargs examples and man pages, 105

^ (caret or circumflex), 55, 90, 93, 366, 412

: (colon), 106, 347

, (comma), 74, 356

- (dash or hyphen), 53, 217, 348, 416

$ (dollar sign), 122, 133, 222
  end-of-line anchor, 55, 298
  parameter expansion, 298, 299–300
  in regular expressions, 89

. (dot) character, 4, 49

./ (dot-slash), 25

" (double quotes), 125, 126

>> (double right angle brackets), 22, 26

;; (double semicolon), 148

! (exclamation mark), 10

/ (forward slash), 78, 87, 264, 304

(hash mark), 29, 87, 111, 348
  in command prompt, 222
  parameter variable, 178

(hash marks, double), 359

|| (or) operator, 145, 150, 152, 167, 190

% (percent sign), 6, 367

. (period), 304

| (pipe) operator, 415

+ (plus sign), 51, 73, 88, 135, 192, 229

? (question mark), 57, 126
  searching for files or folders using, 35
  as wildcard, 310

> (redirect symbol), 24, 25, 27

> (right angle bracket), 113, 229

; (semicolon), 39, 145–146, 152, 308, 356

#! (shebang), 116–117
  configuring options in, 203
  to locate python3 program, 324
  omitting, 202

' (single quote), 124–125, 126

[] (square brackets), 75
  in command prompt, 225
  in conditional expressions, 150

~ (tilde), 88, 125–126, 272, 298, 299, 396

A

absolute paths, 397

ack tool, 70

actions in find expressions, 38

addresses in sed functions, 87

ag tool, 70

ai command, 378–379

AI-generated scripts, 379–380

alias command, 414

aliases, 209, 414
  with different users, 216
  saving time with, 209–210

all parameters array ($a), 196

alternate value in parameter expansion, 301

Amazon Web Services, 328
  creating virtual machine on, 331–335
  credit card use for paid services from, 330
  setting up account, 329–330

ampersand (&), 24

anchors in regexes, 55–56

AND expressions, 36

and (&&) operator, 145

angle bracket (>), 113, 229

ANSI C quoting, 124–125

ANSI escape sequences, 197, 199,
    225, 227

ANSI formatting sequences, 226

anti-patterns for shell scripts,
    201–203
  configuring options in
      shebangs, 203
  omitting shebangs, 202
  using complex logic, 203

appending
  to files, 22, 26
  text with sed, 89–90

append redirection operator (>>),
    22, 26

Applied Cryptography (Schneier), 328

apropos command, 418

Apt package manager, 419

argparse Python module, 321

arguments, use of term, 396

arithmetic expansion, 126, 136,
    298, 306

arithmetic operations, 135–137

arrays
  associative, 130
  expanding, 303
  finding length of, 303
  looping through with for loop, 157
  overview, 128–129
  sparse, 129
  using operators in parameter
      variables, 179

ASCII EOT (end of transmission)
    character, 201

asterisk (*)
  parameter variable, 178
  regex quantifier, 51
  wildcard character, 16, 34, 49, 124,
      264, 304, 359, 402

atomic groups, 59

awk standard output applications as
    alternative to sed, 97

AWS. *See* Amazon Web Services

B

backslash (\), 37, 55, 88, 112, 264
  looping through lines in a file, 167
  starting continuation using, 229

backtick (`), 306, 359

backtracking, 58, 59

basename command, 192

BASH_ENV variable, 216, 218

-bash parameter, 217

BASH_REMATCH array, 151

basics of shell, 393–420
  clipboard, 412–415
  getting help, 415–420
    accessing online cheat sheets, 420
    summarizing output with tldr,
        418–419
    using manual, 415–418
  managing files and folders, 400–412
    copying files, 404–405
    creating files, 408–409
    creating folders, 407–408
    deleting files, 403
    deleting folders, 409–410
    downloading files, 400–402
    renaming and moving files,
        405–407
    showing text content, 410–411
    unzipping files, 402–403
    viewing directory tree, 404
    working with wildcards, 409
    zipping files, 411
  navigating filesystem, 393–400
    changing directory, 395–396
    going back to previous directory,
        398–399
    identifying working directory, 394
    listing contents of working
        directory, 394–395
    navigating with dot and double-
        dot folders, 397–398
    pushing and popping working
        directory, 399–400
    returning to home directory, 396
    using absolute and relative
        paths, 397

bin directory for custom commands,
    210–211

bindkey command, 10

bind -p command, 10
brace expansion, 100, 126, 159,
    164–165, 298–299
braces ({}), 104, 105
    in variable syntax, 127
    in xargs examples and man pages, 105
branches in Git, 250, 257–262
    creating, 257–260
    diverged, 261–262
    merges
        fast-forward, 260
        recursive, 261–262
    resolving conflicts between, 263–267
break statements, 169–170
brew command, 391
BSD Unix, 382
bugs, GitHub repository for
    reporting, xxx
builtins, 416–417

C

C (programming language), 315
capture groups, 56–57, 94, 150
caret or circumflex (^), 55, 90, 93,
    366, 412
case-insensitive searches
    with find, 36
    with grep, 66
case sensitivity in Vim, 346
case statement, 148–149, 196, 199
cat (concatenate) command, 17, 410,
    411, 414
catastrophic backtracking, 58
cd command, 211, 398, 401
CDPATH settings, 244
Chacon, Scott, 292
chaining commands, 151–152
character classes, 75
characters
    counting number of, 19
    lowercase, translating to uppercase, 23
    sequences of, creating, 298–299
character sets and metacharacters,
    52–57
    adding special characters, 53–54
    negating characters, 54–55
    specifying ranges, 52–53
ChatGPT, 378–379, 380

cheat sheets
    accessing online, 420
    Vim example, 347, 359–360
chmod command, 42, 115, 119, 337, 341
chords in Vim, 346
chroot command, 240
chsh command, 219, 391
clearing screen, 9
Click Python package, 325
clipboard, 412–415
    content as standard input, 20
    copying and pasting with pbcopy and
        pbpaste, 414–415
    creating custom commands, 413–414
    essentials, 412–413
collaboration techniques, 286–288
    forking, 286–287
    making pull requests, 287–288
    using multiplexer, 365
    using tmux, 372–373
colon (:), 106, 347
color
    adding to command prompt,
        225–228
    adding to text displayed in shell,
        197–199
comma (,), 74, 356
command history
    searching through, 6–7
    viewing, shortcut for, 9–10
command line, 3–11
    editing in place, 7–9
    navigation techniques, 4–6
    searching through command history,
        6–7
    shortcuts, 9–10
command mode in Vim, 346
"command not found" error
    message, 401
command prompt, 221–235
    adding color and text formatting to,
        225–228
    adding data to, 228–229
    shell prompt variables, 229–231
    showing Git information in, 290–291
    structure of, 222–225
    writing shell script to customize,
        231–235

commands. *See also* command prompt;
    common command functions; xargs
    command
  building, 99–106
    handling whitespace, special
      characters, and tracing,
      101–102
    organizing parameters, 103–105
    xargs, 100–103
  built-in shell commands, 416–417
  chaining, 151–152
  connecting. *See* pipelines
  custom, 413–414
  determining whether available, 200
  differentiating filepaths from, 25
  executing on search results, 39–40
  format of in this book, xxix–xxx
  Git
    quick reference, 272–273
    recap, 293–294
  in history file, rerunning, 10
  output
    in functions, 182–183
    storing in variables, 127–128
  running, 105–106
    SSH, 338
    in subshells, 201
    too many on startup, 214
  searching for using grep, 63
  searching through command history,
    6–7
  sending to nested sessions, tmux
    configuration, 371
  in shell scripts, 112–115
  shell startup, 210–214
  using Vim, 352, 358–359
command substitution, 126, 298,
    305–306
comments
  adding to shell scripts, 111
  stripping with sed, 89
committing changes in Git, 254–257
  commit messages, conventions for, 257
  commit signing, 292
common command, 119, 146, 147, 195
  enhancing with variables, 137–138
  extending to handle different shells,
    152–154

simplifying with functions, 187–188
  updating to loop through results,
    171–172
compact loops, creating, 170–171
complex logic, problems requiring, 314
concatenating
  contents of files, 411
  strings, 136
conditional expressions, 149–151
conditional logic, 141–154
  case statement, 148–149
  chaining commands, 151–152
  combining statements on single line,
    145–146
  conditional expressions, 149–151
  elif clause, 146–147
  else clause, 146
  extending common command to
    handle different shells, 152–154
  if statements, 142
  test command, 143–145
configuration files. *See* dot files
configuring shell
  changing shell, 219–220
  interactive shells, 207–214
    common startup file
      customizations, 209–214
    default shell startup file, 208–209
  in Linux, 392
  login shells, 216–217
  in macOS, 390–392
  in Microsoft Windows 383–392
    installing Linux tools, 383–384
    running virtual machine, 384–389
    Windows Subsystem for Linux,
      389–390
  non-interactive shells, 214–216
conflicts in Git, resolving, 264–267
connecting commands. *See* pipelines
content, adding to file, 22
continuation character, 112
continuations, 229
continue statements, 169–170
copying
  files, 404–405
  with pbcopy, 414–415
counting words lines, characters, and
  bytes, 19

count variable, 176
cp command, 86, 87, 88, 89, 157, 398, 404, 406, 415
cryptography, 340
C-style loops, iterating with, 163–164
CTRL-C, handling, 325
curl command, 320, 321, 420
cursor, maneuvering, 4–6
Cursor tool website, 380
cut command, 75
cutting text, 75–78
Cygwin, 383–384

D

dash (-), 53, 217, 348, 416
date command, 306
debian_chroot variable, 240
debugging with trace option, 191–192
declare command, 130, 192
default shell
    dot file, 238–240
    setting in tmux, 370
    startup file, 208–209
-delete action, 39
deleting
    files, 403
    folders, 409–410
    interactively, 403
dictionary lookup tool
    improving, 325
    installing, 324
    writing in Python, 316–323
        defining basic structure, 317–319
        downloading definition, 319–321
        formatting output, 321–323
directories
    changing, 395–396
    directory stack, 399
    directory tree, viewing, 404
    home directory, returning to, 396
    previous directory, going back to, 398–399
    working directory
        identifying, 394
        listing contents of, 394–395
        pushing and popping, 399–400
disconnections in SSH, 339

diverged branches, handling in Git, 261–262
do keyword, 169
dollar sign ($), 122, 133, 222
    end-of-line anchor, 55, 298
    parameter expansion, 298, 299–300
    in regular expressions, 89
dot (.) character, 4, 49
dot files, 237–248
    custom, creating, 241–244
        cleaning up variables and configuring keyboard shortcuts, 243
        creating folder for, 241
        creating *shell.sh*, 241
        setting preferred editor, 242–243
        setting shell history options, 244
        working with folders, 243–244
    default shell dot file, 238–240
    defined, 238
    installation script, 247–248
    location of, 238, 245
    sharing on GitHub, 285–286
    sourcing from folder, 245–247
    testing, 244–245
dot folder, 33
    navigating with, 397–398
dot notation to source scripts, 117
dot-slash (./), 25
double-dot folders, navigating with, 397–398
double quotes ("), 125, 126
double right angle brackets (>>), 22, 26
double semicolon (;;), 148
downloading files, 400–402
duplicates, removing, 17, 79–80
dynamic scoping, 175

E

echo command, 22, 90, 103, 134, 137, 142, 166, 192, 214, 216, 219
editing in place, 7–9, 96–97
editors, setting in dot file, 242–243
EDITOR variable, 9, 212, 242
elif clause, 146–147
else clause, 146
Emacs, 344
empty folders, finding and removing, 43

end of transmission (EOT), 14

engines, regex, 50–52

env (set or print environment and
    execute command) command, 116,
    117, 122

environment variables
    configuring, 212
    scope of, 122–123
    shell variables as, 123–124

envsubst (substitute environment
    variables) command, 96

errors, 183, 325
    in functions, 185–187
    logging, 25
    in parameter expansion, 301
    redirecting to null, 25–26
    standard, 23–26
    suppressing display of, 26

escape character, 125

escape sequences
    coloring text displayed in shell using,
        197–199
    customizing command prompt,
        223–225

escaping
    regex characters, 55
    special characters, 37

events, trapping, 193–195

exclamation mark (!), 10

ex command in Vim, 347

-exec action, 39, 42

executable scripts, making non-
    executable, 42

exit command, 168, 184, 336

exit on failure, ensuring, 190

expansion operations, 297–311. *See also*
    parameter expansion
    arithmetic expansion, 306
    brace expansion, 298–299
    command substitution, 305–306
    pathname expansion, 309–310
    tilde expansion, 299
    word splitting, 306–309

export keyword, 123, 124

expressions
    in case statements, 148
    grouping parts of, 36–37
    in sed, 85

extended regular expressions, 50

extracting
    information with sed, 91
    text, first and last part of file, 71–73

F

failure, ensuring exit on, 190

fast-forward merges in Git, 260

fetching changes in GitHub, 281–284

file command, 402

file descriptor, 16

filepaths, differentiating from
    commands, 25

files. *See also* finding files and folders;
    streams
    adding content to, 22
    appending to, 22, 26
    with changed permissions, finding, 42
    configuration files, sourcing
        additional, 212–213
    copying, 404–405
    creating, 348–350, 408–409
    deleting, 403
    downloading, 400–402
    extracting text from, 71–73
    looping through with for loop,
        160–161
    moving, 405–407
    redirecting to, 22, 25, 380
    renaming, 405–407
    in repositories, 267–270
    running operations on set of,
        160–161
    sample, xxx
    searching through, 67–68
    showing text content, 410–411
    startup files
        customizing, 209–214
        default, 208–209
        loading, 216–219
    template, creating with sed, 96
    transferring with scp, 339–341
    unzipping, 402–403
    using as input, 19–20
    writing to, 25
    zipping, 411

filesystem, navigating, 393–400
    changing directory, 395–396
    with dot and double-dot folders,
        397–398

going back to previous directory, 398–399
identifying working directory, 394
listing contents of working directory, 394–395
pushing and popping working directory, 399–400
returning to home directory, 396
using absolute and relative paths, 397
filtering
search results using grep, 68–69
standard input, 21
find command, 39, 306
extra options, 41–43
searching by file or folder name, 34–35
searching by path, 35
searching for only files or folders, 33
searching with, 31–32
finding files and folders, 31–43
acting on search results, 38–40
excluding search results with NOT operator, 38
grouping parts of expression, 36–37
handling symbolic links, 40–41
large files, 41
recently modified files, 42
running case-insensitive searches, 36
specifying multiple search options, 35–36
flags, use of term, 396
folders. *See also* finding files and folders
copying text from to another location, 104–105
dot files
configuring options for working with folders, 243–244
creating folders for, 241
empty, finding and removing, 43
looping through with for loop, 160–161
managing in shell, 400–412
creating, 407–408
deleting, 409–410
viewing directory tree, 404
working with wildcards, 409
navigating with dot and double-dot folders, 397–398
running operations on set of, 160–161
searching for, 33–35

forking in Git, 286–287, 293
for loop, 156–164
iterating with C-style loops, 163–164
looping over sequences, 164–165
looping through arrays, 157
looping through files and folders, 160–161
looping through find command results, 162–163
splitting loop input into words, 157–160
wildcards in, 157, 160–161
for statement, 170
forward slash (/), 78, 87, 264, 304
function keyword, 174
functions, 173–188. *See also* commands
adding to startup file of interactive shells, 210
checking for existing, 192–193
creating, 174–176
error handling, 185–187
making more flexible, 177
to open pull request, 288–289
passing parameters to, 177–180
return values, 180–184
simplifying common command with, 187–188
unneeded, cleaning up, 193

G

getopts command, 195, 196
Git, 249–273
adding and resetting changes to index, 251–254
branches, 257–262
creating, 257–260
diverged, 261–262
performing fast-forward merges, 260
performing recursive merges, 261–262
commands, 272–273, 294, 297
git add, 252, 256, 273, 294
git branch, 257, 273
git checkout, 251, 257, 258, 259, 269, 270, 294
git clean, 292
git clone, 294
git commit, 255, 256, 261, 268, 273, 294
git diff, 292

Git (continued)
   commands (continued)
      git fetch, 280, 281, 283–284, 294
      git init, 67, 251, 273, 294
      git log, 262, 273
      git merge, 260, 294
      git mv, 270
      git pull, 280, 284, 294
      git push, 280–281, 289, 294
      git remote, 280–281
      git reset, 253, 269, 273, 294
      git rev-list, 291
      git rm, 268, 273
      git status, 251, 255, 257–258,
         268, 273, 292
   committing changes, 254–257
   creating repositories, 250–251
   definition of, 250
   log, 262–264
   managing files in repositories, 267–270
   remote repositories, 275–294
      collaborating on, 286–288
      key concepts and commands,
         293–294
      sharing dot files, 285–286
      showing Git information in
         command prompt, 290–291
      writing shell function to open pull
         request, 288–289
   resolving conflicts, 264–267
   restoring working tree, 270–272
   workflows in, 267
  GitHub, 276–285
   changes
      fetching, 281–284
      pulling, 284–285
      pushing, 280–281
   creating repositories, 276–280
   forking with, 286–287
   making pull requests, 287–288
   Vim cheatsheet in, 360
  globally scoped variables, 175
  globs, 149, 161
  GNOME Terminal, 413
  GNU Screen multiplexer, 365
  Go programming language, 314
  Graham-Cumming, John, 58
  graphical user interface (GUI), xxiv,
      393–395

greedy regexes, 57, 58
grep command, 61–70
  advanced features, 65–69
    combining with other
      commands, 69
    filtering and piping of commands,
      68–69
    getting additional context for
      search results, 66–67
    making search case-insensitive, 66
    searching through multiple files,
      67–68
  alternatives to, 69–70
  definition, 62–63
  origin of name, 62
  pipelines and, 69
  recursive searching using, 68
  searching through text, 63–64
  using with regular expressions,
    64–65
GUI (graphical user interface), xxiv,
    393–395

H

hash mark (#), 29, 87, 111, 348
  in command prompt, 222
  parameter variable, 178
head command, 21, 73
help, getting, 415–420
  accessing online cheat sheets, 420
  summarizing output with tldr,
    418–419
  using manual, 415–418
--help option, 323
highlighting of syntax, 197–199
HISTFILE variable, 10, 62, 64, 154
history
  rerunning commands in, 10
  searching using grep, 63
  setting options in dot files, 244
  using with shell scripts, 112–113
history command, 64
Hogan, Brian, 375
Homebrew, 390–391, 419
home directory, returning to, 396
HOME variable, 122, 299
host alias, 337
HostName setting, 337
hosts, SSH configuring, 337–338

hunks, interactive staging for, 292
hyphen. *See* dash

I

`IdentityFile` setting, 337
IDEs (integrated development
    environments), 344
`if` command, 146
`if...else` statement, 193
IFS (internal field separator) variable,
    162, 163, 307, 308
`if` statement, 142, 146, 148–149, 154,
    184, 187
index
    in Git, 251–254, 293
    retrieving element after defining
        array, 128
indirection, 132, 192
infinite loop, 168
input, standard, 18–21
    clipboard content as, 20
    files as, 19–20
    filtering as, 21
    output from shell code as, 19
input, user
    hiding, 134
    limiting, 134–135
    prompting for, 133–134
    reading, 132–133
        into custom variable, 133
input-process-output (IPO) pattern,
    14–16
insert mode in Vim, 346
installed programs, checking for, 200
integrated development environments
    (IDEs), 344
interactive shells, 207–214, 218
    default shell startup file, 208–209
    distinction between login shells
        and, 217
    startup file customizations,
        209–214
        adding functions, 210
        configuring environment
            variables, 212
        creating local *bin* directory for
            custom commands, 210–211
        pitfalls, 213–214
        shell options, 211–212

shell startup commands, 213
sourcing additional configuration
    files, 212–213
using aliases, 209–210
interactive staging (Git), 292
interrupt signal, 412
IPO (input-process-output) pattern,
    14–16
iterate expression (i), 164

J

jail, 240
Java, 315
JavaScript, 314

K

keyboard
    input from, 16
    shortcuts
        configuring in dot files, 243
        in Vim, 346
keys, 130
    creating pair, 328–329
    dealing with permission errors,
        336–337
key-value format, 92
Konsole, 413

L

large files, finding, 41
large language models (LLMs), 380
lazy regexes, 57
`less` program, 21–22, 80, 122, 416
`let` keyword, 136
level of indirection, 192
lexical scoping variables, 175
line mode editors, 242
lines
    combining statements on single,
        145–146
    counting number of, 19
    deleting, 5–6
    input, customizing processing of in
        `xargs`, 102–103
    looping through in files, 166–167
    moving to beginning or end of, 4
    removing parts of with `sed`, 88
    replacing text on with `sed`, 86–87
    of text, removing duplicate, 79–80

Linux
  clipboard essentials, 413
  creating custom commands, 414
  shell
    accessing, 382
    configuring, 392
LLMs (large language models), 380
ln (create link) command, 119
local keyword, 175, 176
locally scoped variables, 175
log, Git, 262–264
logging errors, 25
logic, conditional. *See* conditional logic
login shells, 216–217
lookaround, 58
lookbehind, 58
lookup command, 325
loops, 155–172
  adding to common command, 171–172
  compact, creating, 170–171
  continue and break statements, 169–170
  for, 156–164
    iterating with C-style loops, 163–164
    looping over sequences, 164–165
    looping through arrays, 157
    looping through files and folders, 160–161
    looping through find command results, 162–163
    splitting loop input into words, 157–160
  while, 165–169
lowercase
  converting parameter value to, 305
  searching files regardless of case using grep, 66
  transforming variable value to, 132
  translating to uppercase, 23
lowercase function, 181–182
lower character class, 75
ls command, 157, 228, 394, 397, 402

M

macOS
  accessing shell, 382
  appearance of shell in, xxiv
  clipboard essentials, 413
  configuring shell, 390–392

main branch, 257–264, 266, 281, 285, 291
man command, 64, 415
manual pages (man pages), 325, 415–418
  builtins, 416–417
  man page titles and summaries, 418
  pager, 416
  sections, 417–418
Markdown styling tips website, 360
menu, showing in bash, 200–201
merges (Git)
  fast-forward, 260
  recursive, 261–262
metacharacters. *See* character sets and metacharacters
Microsoft Windows
  accessing shell, 381–382
  appearance of shell in, xxiv
  clipboard essentials, 413
  configuring shell, 383–392
    installing Linux tools, 383–384
    running virtual machine, 384–389
    setting up Windows Subsystem for Linux, 389–390
  creating custom commands, 413
mkdir command, 7, 23–25, 407–408
modal editing, 345
Modern Vim (Neil), 361
modified files, finding, 42
motions in Vim, 350, 356–357
mouse support, enabling in tmux, 371
multiplexer, 363–375. *See also* tmux
  benefits of, 365
  session management, 368–369
  window management, 367
mv command, 157, 406

N

nano editor, 242
navigation techniques using cursor, 4–6
  deleting lines, 5–6
  deleting words, 5
  moving back or forward one word, 4–6
  moving to beginning or end of line, 4
  undoing changes, 6
Neil, Drew, 361

nested sessions, sending commands to
    in tmux, 371
nesting of if statements, 154
network connectivity, losing, 339
newlines
    character for, 74
    when looping through lines in a
        file, 167
    word splitting and, 162
Node.js, 97, 314
non-interactive shells, 214–216
normal mode in Vim, 346
NOT operator, to exclude search
    results, 38
npm (Node Package Manager)
    program, 378
null, redirecting errors to, 25–26
nullglob command, 161
numbers, sequences of, 298–299

O

offset, specifying in parameter
    expansion, 302
Oh-My-Zsh project, 233–234
-ok action, 40
OpenSSH, 328
operating system, checking,
    199–100
operations
    running on set of files or folders,
        160–161
    in Vim, 354–355
operators in test command, 143–144
options
    common shell options, 212
    use of term, 396
option strings, 195
or (||) operator, 145, 150, 152,
    167, 190
OR expressions, 36
output
    avoiding printing during shell
        startup, 213
    of commands
        in functions, 182–183
        storing in variables, 127–128
    printing during shell startup, 213
    from shell code as input, 19

standard
    appending to files, 22
    displaying onscreen, 21–22
    redirecting standard error to,
        24–25
    redirecting to files, 22
    writing results of function to,
        181–182
storing, 22
summarizing with tldr, 418–419

P

package manager, 390
pager
    paging through text, 80–81
    scrolling through man pages, 416
PAGER variable, 122, 212
Panes (Tmux), 367
parameter expansion, 299–300
    arrays, expanding, 303
    converting to lowercase or
        uppercase, 305
    default values, 300–301
    displaying error if value is null or
        unset, 301
    finding length of parameter or
        array, 303
    patterns, removing/replacing, 304
    specifying offset and length, 302
    using alternate value, 301
    using parameter indirection, 305
    variable names, expanding,
        302–303
parameters
    available, checking for, 416
    for commands, organizing with
        xargs, 103–105
    expanding, 130–132
    of find command, 38
    passing to functions, 177–180
    passing to scripts, 184
    processing complex script, 195–196
    term usage, 396
    variables of, common, 177–178
parentheses
    in command prompt, 225
    grouping parts of expression using,
        36–37

passwords, using SSH keys instead of, 279

pasting with `pbpaste`, 414–415

patch staging (Git), 292

pathname expansion, 126, 160, 298

paths

  absolute and relative, 397

  pathname expansion, 309–310

  searching by, 35

  in search results, printing, 39

PATH variable, 106, 116, 119, 210, 216, 217, 218, 308

patterns

  in parameter expansion, 304–305

  supplying, 34

pbcopy command, 413, 414–415

pbpaste command, 413, 414–415

PEM (Privacy Enhanced Mail), 328

percent sign (%), 6, 367

period (.), 304

Perl, 315

permissions, changed, 42

pipefail option, 190

pipelines, 13–31

  commands in, 113–115

  composing for `grep` commands, 68–69

  example of, 17–18

  exiting script when commands fail, 190

  filtering input, 21

  `grep` command and, 69

  input-process-output (IPO) pattern, 14–16

  redirection with both stdout and stderr, 26–27

  in standard error applications, 23–26

  in standard input applications, 18–21

  in standard output applications, 21–22

  T-pipe, 27–28

  and Unix philosophy, 28–29

  using with copying and pasting, 414–415

placeholders in `xargs` examples and man pages, 105

playground folder, 400

plus sign (+), 51, 73, 88, 135, 192, 229

popd command, 399–400

portability across systems, 314

Practical Vim (Neil), 361

prepending text with `sed`, 90–91

`-print` (print to stdout) action, 102

`-print` action, 39

`-print0` action, 102

printf command, 197, 204

printing output during shell startup, avoiding, 213

Privacy Enhanced Mail (PEM), 328

profile loading, differences in depending on operating systems, 218

Pro Git (Chacon, Straub), 292

programming languages

  alternatives to `sed`, 97

  choosing, 314–315

programs

  connecting. *See* pipelines

  installed, checking for, 200

prompting for input, 133–134

prompt string, customizing, 223

prompt variables, 229–231

  PROMPT_COMMAND, 229, 231

  PROMPT_DIRTRIM, 229, 230–231

  PS1, 222–225, 227–229, 232, 233–234, 240

  PS2, 229–230

  PS3, 229, 230

  PS4, 229, 230

pstree command, 118

pulling changes from GitHub, 284–285

  making pull requests, 287–288

  writing shell function to open pull requests, 288–289

pushing

  changes to GitHub, 280–281

  working directory, 398–400

pwd (print working directory) command, 394

Python, 97, 314, 315

  dictionary lookup tool in

    improving, 325

    installing, 324

    writing, 316–323

Q

q! (quit without saving) command, 347

quantifiers in regex, 51–52

question mark (?), 57, 126
    searching for files or folders
        using, 35
    as wildcard, 310
quotes in variable syntax, 124–126

R

randomart, 329
RANDOM variable, 166
rc (run commands), 208
read command, 131, 133, 134, 135, 167
rebasing (Git), 292
recursive merges (Git), 261–262
redirecting
    with both stdout and stderr, 26–27
    in standard error applications, 24–26
    standard output to file, 22
    symbol (>), 24, 25, 27
redirection operator, 411
regexes (regular expressions), 47–59
    advanced concepts, 57–59
    to avoid backtracking, 59
    basic, 65
    breaking up into smaller parts, 56
    building, 48–57, 93
        anchors, 55–56
        capture groups, 56–57
        character sets and metacharacters,
          52–57
        lazy and greedy expressions, 57
        quantifiers, 51–52
        regex engines, 50–52
    complexity of, 48
    conditional expressions and, 150–151
    continuing until finds no further
        matches, 57
    edge cases and, 51
    for email validation, 48–49
    engines, 50–52
    escaping characters in, 55
    extended, 65
    identifying greedy matches, 58
    matching patterns of text at certain
        points on a line, 55–56
    online, 93
    overview, 48–52
    Regular Expressions 101 website,
        49–50, 51, 58, 59

stopping search as soon as finds
    match, 57
testing, 49–50
using grep with, 64–65
using in different languages, 59
using with sed, 85–94
relative paths, using, 397
remotes, Git, 276
REPLY variable, 133
repositories, Git, 293
    creating, 250–251, 276–280
    managing files, 267–270
        deleting, 267–268
        restoring and renaming,
          268–270
requests module, 321
resources, online, xxx
restructuring text with sed, 92–95
return values of functions, 180–184
    avoiding pitfalls with command
        output, 182–183
    returning status codes, 183–184
    writing to standard output,
        181–182
rev (reverse) command, 78
reversing text, 78
rev tool, 315
right angle bracket (>), 113, 229
ripgrep tool, 70
rm command, 40, 100, 101, 103, 190,
    209, 403
rmdir command, 85–88, 409–410
root of filesystem, 397
Ruby, 314
Rust, 315

S

sample files, xxx
sandbox, Linux, 384
Schneier, Bruce, 328
scp program, transferring files with,
    339–341
screen, clearing, 9
scripting alternatives, 313–325
    characteristics of shell-friendly tools,
        315–316
    choosing programming language,
        314–315

scripting alternatives *(continued)*
  dictionary lookup tool, writing in
      Python, 316–323
    defining basic structure, 317–319
    downloading definition, 319–321
    formatting output, 321–323
  whether to use, 314
scripts, xxiv, 109–120
  AI-generated, executing, 379–380
  behavior of, 214–216
  benefits of, 110–115
  creating, 110–118
    adding and formatting
        commands, 112–113
    adding code comments, 111
    making shell scripts executable, 115
    pipelining commands, 113–115
    sourcing shell scripts, 117–118
    specifying program to run script,
        116–117
  customizing command prompt,
      231–235
  executable scripts, 42
  for installing dot files, 247–248
  installing locally, 118–119
  patterns for, 189–204
    adding syntax highlighting,
        197–199
    anti-patterns, 201–203
    checking for existing variables or
        functions, 192–193
    checking for installed
        programs, 200
    checking operating system, 199–100
    debugging with trace option,
        191–192
    ensuring exit on failure, 190
    processing complex parameters,
        195–196
    running commands in
        subshells, 201
    showing menu, 200–201
    trapping signals and events,
        193–195
    unsetting values, 193
  tidying up, 302–303
  using history file with, 112–113
search expression, 33

searching
  through command history, 6–7
  with find command
    case-insensitive, 36
    by file or folder name, 34–35
    introduction to, 31–32
    for only files or folders, 33
    by path, 35
  with grep
    case-insensitive, 66
    through multiple files, 67–68
    through text, 63–64
  by path, 35
  specifying multiple options, 35–36
search motions in Vim, 355–356
search results
  acting on, 38–40
  excluding with NOT operator, 38
  getting additional context with grep,
      66–67
Secure Hash Algorithm (SHA),
    262–263, 270
secure shell. *See* SSH
sed command, 19, 83–98, 114, 134,
    315, 316
  advanced applications
    creating template files, 96
    editing in place, 96–97
    restructuring text, 92–95
  alternatives to, 97
  text manipulation with, 83–98
  transformations with
    appending text, 89–90
    applying multiple expressions,
        85–88
    extracting information, 91
    prepending text, 90–91
    replacing text, 84–85
    stripping comments, 89
  using addresses in sed functions, 87
  using regexes with, 85–94
select command, 200, 229
semicolon (;), 39, 145–146, 152, 308, 356
sequences
  looping over, 164–165
  of numbers or characters, creating,
      298–299
  in Vim, 346

session management with tmux, 365, 368–369

set (set option) command, 186

SHA (Secure Hash Algorithm), 262–263, 270

sh command, 114, 123

shebang (#!), 116–117
 configuring options in, 203
 to locate python3 program, 324
 omitting, 202

shell. *See also* basics of shell; configuring shell
 accessing, 381–382
 configuration cheat sheet, 218
 future of, 380
 idioms, handling errors using, 316
 overview, xxiv–xxv
 reasons for using, xxiv

shell-friendly tools, characteristics of, 315–316

shell options ($-) parameter, 242

SHELL variable, 122, 154, 219, 336

shifting parameters, 179–180

shopt command, 161, 209

shortcuts. *See also* symbolic links (symlinks)
 clear screen, 9
 for maneuvering cursor, 4–6
 show all, 10
 transpose text, 10
 view command history, 9–10

signals, trapping, 193–195

single quote ('), 124–125, 126

sleep command, 225

sort command, 17, 28, 79, 113, 114

sorting text, 79–80

sourcing shell scripts, 117–118

spaces. *See* whitespace

sparse arrays, 129

special characters
 escaping, 37
 handling in xargs, 101–102

splitting
 loop input into words, 157–160
 streams, 27–28
 text into words, 126, 159–160, 298, 306–309
 in txux, 367

square brackets ([ ]), 75
 in command prompt, 225
 in conditional expressions, 150

squashing (Git), 292

SSH, 327–341
 configuring hosts, 337–338
 connecting to virtual machine, 335–336
 creating a key pair, 328–329
 creating virtual machine on AWS, 331–335
 definition of, 327–328
 handling disconnections, 339
 key permission errors, dealing with, 336–337
 keys, 279
 running commands, 338
 setting up AWS account, 329–330
 transferring files with scp, 339–341

ssh-keygen OpenSSH authentication key utility, 328

ssh program, 336, 338, 339, 372

standard error, 23–26
 appending to file, 26
 redirecting, 24–26
 writing to file, 25

standard input, 18–21
 clipboard content, 20
 files, 19–20
 filtering input, 21
 output from shell code as, 19
 reading from, 315

standard output, 21–22
 appending to file, 22
 displaying onscreen, 21–22
 redirecting standard error to, 24–25
 redirecting to file, 22
 writing to, 315

startup commands, 213–214

startup files
 for default shell, 208–209
 interactive shells, 209–214
 adding functions, 210
 configuring environment variables, 212
 creating local bin directory for custom commands, 210–211
 pitfalls to avoid, 213–214
 setting shell options, 211–212

startup files *(continued)*
    interactive shells *(continued)*
        setting shell startup commands, 213
        sourcing additional configuration
           files, 212–213
        using aliases, 209–210
    loading for login shell, 217–219
    loading with BASH_ENV, non-
        interactive shells, 216
statements, combining on single line,
    145–146
status codes, returning in functions,
    183–184
stderr stream
    input-process-output (IPO) pattern,
        15–16
    and stdout, redirection with both,
        26–27
stdin stream, 15–16
stdout stream
    input-process-output (IPO) pattern,
        15–16
    and stderr, redirection with both,
        26–27
storing output, 22
Storti, Brian, 27
Straub, Ben, 292
stream redirection operator, 20
streams
    input-process-output (IPO) pattern, 15
    splitting in two, 27–28
stripping comments with sed, 89
subject line of commit messages, 257
subshells, 123, 201
substring, returning, 131
sudo (run command as superuser)
    command, 119
summaries of man pages, 418
symbolic links (symlinks), 40–41, 119
syntax
    highlighting, adding, 197–199
    of variables, 124–127
        using braces, 127
        using quotes, 124–126

T

tabs, word splitting and, 162
tags, 292

tail command, 72–73, 113, 154
template files, creating with sed, 96
Terminal AI, 377–380
    chatting with ChatGPT, 378–379
    copying or saving results, 379
    executing AI-generated scripts,
        379–380
    installing and running, 378
    redirecting responses to files, 380
    shell of future, 380
terminal editors, 343–361. *See also* Vim
    adding command count, 352
    editing commands, 358–359
    inserting text at specific positions,
        352–354
    navigating through text, 350–352
    operating on range of text, 354–355
    reasons to use, 344
    searching for text patterns, 355–358
test command, 143–145, 161
    advantages of conditional
        expressions over, 150
    checking multiple conditions
        simultaneously, 145
    operators for expressions and files,
        143–144
text
    appending with sed, 89–90
    displayed in shell, coloring, 197–199
    formatting, adding to command
        prompt, 225–228
    inserting at specific positions using
        Vim, 352–354
    navigating through using Vim,
        350–352
    operating on range of using Vim,
        354–355
    patterns, searching for using Vim,
        355–358
    prepending with sed, 90–91
    replacing with sed, 84–85
        on specific lines, 86–87
    restructuring with sed, 92–95
    searching through using grep, 63–64
    showing content of files, 410–411
    splitting into words, 298
    transposing shortcut, 10
text editor. *See* terminal editors

text manipulation, 71–81. *See also* sed command
  cutting text, 75–78
  extracting first and last part of file, 71–73
  paging through text, 8–81
  replacing text, 74–75
  reversing text, 78
  with sed, 83–98
  sorting text and removing duplicate lines, 79–80
tilde (~), 88, 125–126, 272, 298, 299, 396
tldr tool, 62, 415, 418–419
tmux
  collaboration with, 372–373
  commands in, 373–374
  configuring, 369–372
  installing, 365–366
  keyboard shortcuts, 366
  quick guide, 373–374
  session management with, 368–369
  session persistence, 365
  window management with, 367
tmux 3: Productive Mouse-Free Development (Hogan), 375
Torvalds, Linus, 250
touch command, 408
T-pipe, 27–28
tput command, 199
trace option, debugging with, 191–192
tracing, handling in xargs, 101–102
transposing text, shortcuts for, 10
trap command, 193
trapping signals and events, 193–195
tr command, 23–25, 74, 181
tree, working, 270–272
tree command, 258–259, 407
Typer package, 325

U

Ubuntu's Desktop Edition, 384
uname command, 199
undoing changes, 6
uniq (omit duplicate lines) command, 17, 27–28, 79, 113
unset command, 193
unsetting values, 193
until loop, 168–169

unzip command, 402, 411
unzipping files, 402–403
uppercase
  converting parameter value to, 305
  searching files regardless of case, 66
  transforming variable value to, 132
  translating lowercase characters to, 23
upper character class, 75
urllib library, 321
user input. *See* input, user
User setting, 337
USER variable, 122

V

values variable, 179
variables, 121–139
  checking for existing, 192–193
  cleaning up in dot files, 243
  common operations, 127–137
    arrays, 128–129
    associative arrays, 130
    expanding shell parameters, 130–132
    performing arithmetic operations, 135–137
    storing command's output in variables, 127–128
    user input, reading and storing in variables, 132–135
  common parameter values, 177–178
  configuring environment variables, 212
  enhancing common command with variables, 137–138
  environment variables, 123–124
  expanding names of, 302–303
  in functions, 174–175
  indirection, 132
  returning default value of, 131
  returning length of, 130–131
  scope of
    environment vs. shell variables, 122–123
    in functions, 175–176
  syntax, 124–127
  transforming value of to uppercase/ lowercase, 132
  unneeded, cleaning up, 193

verbatim insert command, 412

version control system. *See* Git

Vim, 345–350, 360–361

  adding command count, 352

  buffers, 346, 348

  case sensitivity in, 345

  configuring tmux to interface with, 372

  editing commands, 358–359

  "enter insert mode" commands, 353

  keyboard shortcuts in, 345

  motions in, 350, 356–357

  operators in, 354–355

  text

    inserting at specific positions, 352–354

    navigating through, 350–352

    operating on range of, 354–355

    searching for patterns in, 355–358

  updating and styling cheat sheet, 359–360

  Vimcasts website, 361

  vimtutor program, 361

VirtualBox, 384–385

virtual machine

  creating on AWS, 331–335

  shutting down, 335

  using SSH to connect to, 335–336

VISUAL variable, 242

W

website-and-repo tab of tmux multiplexer, 364

wget command, 190, 401–402

whatis command, 418

while loop, 165–169, 195

  looping forever, 168

  looping through lines in files, 166–167

  until loop, 168–169

while statement, 170

whitespace

  handling in xargs, 101–102

  when looping through lines in a file, 167

  word splitting and, 162

whoami command, 389

wildcards, 409

  character (*), 16, 34, 49, 124, 264, 304, 359, 402

  in for loops, 157, 160–161

  in pathnames, expanding, 298

  searching for files or folders using, 34

windows

  creating and moving between, 367

  managing using multiplexer, 365

  naming and numbering, 370–371

  splitting, 371

  zooming panes, 367

Windows, Microsoft. *See* Microsoft Windows

Windows Subsystem for Linux (WSL), 383, 389–390, 413

words

  counting number of, 9

  deleting, 5

  moving back or forward one word, 4–6

  splitting text into, 126, 159–160, 298, 306–309

  in Vim, 352

working directory

  identifying, 394

  listing contents of, 394–395

  pushing and popping, 399–400

  specifying in tmux configuration, 370

working tree in Git, 251, 270–272, 293

wq (write and quit) command, 359

WSL (Windows Subsystem for Linux), 383, 389–390, 413

X

xargs command

  braces used as placeholders, 105

  handling whitespace, special characters, and tracing, 101–102

  input lines, 102–103

  organizing parameters for commands, 103–105

  overview, 99–101

  running commands, 105–106

xclip command, 20

Z

ZIP file
  containing files found, 42
  unzipping, 402
  zipping, 411
Z shell, 233–234, 390
zsh_regex variable, 150

Effective Shell is set in New Baskerville, Futura, Dogma, and TheSansMono Condensed.

RESOURCES

Visit *https://nostarch.com/effective-shell* for errata and more information.

More no-nonsense books from **NO STARCH PRESS**

**THE LINUX COMMAND LINE,
2ND EDITION**

A Complete Introduction
BY WILLIAM SHOTTS
504 PP., $39.95
ISBN 978-1-59327-952-3

**HOW LINUX WORKS,
3RD EDITION**

What Every Superuser Should Know
BY BRIAN WARD
464 PP., $49.99
ISBN 978-1-7185-0040-2

DEVOPS FOR THE DESPERATE

A Hands-On Survival Guide
BY BRADLEY SMITH
176 PP., $29.99
ISBN 978-1-7185-0248-2

POWERSHELL® FOR SYSADMINS

Workflow Automation Made Easy
BY ADAM BERTRAM
320 PP., $39.99
ISBN 978-1-59327-918-9

**AUTOMATE THE BORING STUFF
WITH PYTHON, 3RD EDITION**

**Practical Programming for Total
Beginners**
BY AL SWEIGART
672 PP., $59.99
ISBN 978-1-7185-0340-3

THE BOOK OF BATCH SCRIPTING

**From Fundamentals to Advanced
Automation**
BY JACK MCLARNEY
488 PP., $59.99
ISBN 978-1-7185-0342-7

PHONE:
800.420.7240 OR
415.863.9900

EMAIL:
SALES@NOSTARCH.COM
WEB:
WWW.NOSTARCH.COM